Investment Theory and Risk Management

Founded in 1807, John Wiley & Sons is the oldest independent publishing company in the United States. With offices in North America, Europe, Australia, and Asia, Wiley is globally committed to developing and marketing print and electronic products and services for our customers' professional and personal knowledge and understanding.

The Wiley Finance series contains books written specifically for finance and investment professionals as well as sophisticated individual investors and their financial advisors. Book topics range from portfolio management to e-commerce, risk management, financial engineering, valuation, and financial instrument analysis, as well as much more.

For a list of available titles, please visit our website at www.WileyFinance.com.

Investment Theory and Risk Management

STEVEN P. PETERSON

WILEY

John Wiley & Sons, Inc.

Published by John Wiley & Sons, Inc., Hoboken, New Jersey.
Published simultaneously in Canada.

For general information on our other products and services or for technical support, please contact our Customer Care Department within the United States at (800) 762-2974, outside the United States at (317) 572-3993 or fax (317) 572-4002.

Wiley also publishes its books in a variety of electronic formats. Some content that appears in print may not be available in electronic books. For more information about Wiley products, visit our website at www.wiley.com.

Library of Congress Cataloging-in-Publication Data:

Peterson, Steven P.
    Investment theory and risk management + website/Steven P. Peterson.
        p. cm.—(Wiley finance series)
    Includes index.
    ISBN 978-1-118-12959-3 (cloth); ISBN 978-1-118-22496-0 (ebk);
    ISBN 978-1-118-23841-7 (ebk); ISBN 978-1-118-26304-4 (ebk)
    1. Investment analysis.   2. Portfolio management.   3. Risk management.
    I. Title.
    HG4529.P478 2012
    332.601—dc23   2011050888

Printed in the United States of America

10 9 8 7 6 5 4 3 2 1

To my Father

Contents

Preface

A successful fund manager and former academic once told me that business school research is focused too much on topics that get professors published and promoted and too little on explaining how markets actually work. This was not an entirely facetious remark. He was referring to what he perceived to be a fundamental disconnect between the objectives of mainstream business school curricula and those of investment professionals. As both an academic and an investment professional, I not only echo that sentiment but I also see the gap widening. This book attempts to bridge that gap.

My experience over the past thirty years confirms a continuing trend in core business school curriculums away from rigorous analytics. It should come as no surprise, therefore, to see practitioners discount the value of strong analytic skills in their decision-making processes. Indeed, my conversations with practitioners reveal a heavy bias to their instincts as investment managers and a tone that challenges me to prove to them that there is somehow a cost associated with not understanding the details of various concepts such as mean variance optimization, the decomposition of risk, derivatives, and so forth. They simply point to their portfolio outperformance relative to their benchmarks as evidence suggesting that these skills are at best superfluous. I might note here as well that most of the professionals around today learned to manage assets during the long-running bull market that began in the early 1980s—a period of time when it was arguably difficult not to have made money. I don't think it was a coincidence that business schools began to deemphasize scientific rigor at about the same time.

The past 30 years have also coincided with a second "industrial revolution" made possible in part by unprecedented gains in computer processing power. Improvements in information technology followed which revolutionized both the quantity and quality of information available which, in turn, gave rise to an array of new securities and trading innovations, strategies, tactics, and portfolio design and ushered in a new era of market globalization. It is interesting that the skills that complemented the new technology (mathematics, statistics, and programming for instance) were being deemphasized at about the time they should have been leveraged upon. Anyone with a Bloomberg terminal and a spreadsheet was thought to have the requisite skill set to handle any empirical questions that may have arisen while those individuals who actually understood the math were thought to possess purely gratuitous skill sets. This mindset should have changed as the credit crisis unfolded but, ironically, a large part of the burden of blame for the crisis was heaped on the technology itself and not the fact that the users of that technology were grossly underprepared to wield it responsibly.

The simple facts are that technology and the credit crisis together have accelerated the pace of globalization. In turn, the global economic environment will continue to challenge the status quo while markets will become even more competitive, more volatile, and inherently more risky. These developments would seem to suggest that both business school curricula and investment managers embrace opportunities to attain skills that will make them more effective competitors in this global environment.

Investment managers are sometimes fond of saying that they rely on their "gut" instincts, that they understand implicitly the tenets of modern portfolio theory and that investment management is more an art than a science, begging the question of why we bother with the science—a logic that would apply equally well, I suppose, to children petitioning to skip their music lessons. The truth is, however, other things constant; we'd all prefer to be better at the science. The problem is that the level of rigor is often far beyond our abilities either because we had little formal training initially or that the outcome of that training has long since lapsed into disuse. The objective of this book is to help the reader fill the gaps in that knowledge in a step-wise fashion that emphasizes the underlying theoretical principles in an environment rich with direct applications using market data.

My approach is to write in a conversational tone, introducing a problem in financial economics and then following by developing the intuition behind the theory. I try to get the reader to think of the problem in a way that compels the construction of the model used to solve it in a way that makes the solution method seem natural. I try not to skip any steps in the mathematical derivations and provide chapter appendices when I think further discussion may distract the reader from the point at hand. All through the book, emphasis is on practical applications. To that end, most chapters have a companion set of spreadsheets that contain the data and applications. These too are completely solved, step by step. All data used in the text appear in the chapter spreadsheets. All tables and figures included in the text also appear in the chapter spreadsheets. The reader can therefore replicate all the results that appear in the text. Since the spreadsheets are all linked to the data I provide, then swapping new data will update the existing links including all tables and graphs.

I have always felt that most students understand complex subjects more clearly through applications. Using real data enhances the relevance of an application. Providing the ability to update data on open source spreadsheets enables the student to continue to learn in a hands-on fashion long after closing this book. My experience with this format has been very well received in the classroom and typically students find ways to integrate what they learn in these applications into their everyday work on the job.

The coverage in this book is somewhat broader than what is found in standard texts. I include, for instance, an early chapter devoted to equity pricing models and how pricing is approached by practitioners along with some caveats associated with these models. I also develop optimization and statistical concepts more rigorously than what is usually found in investments textbooks and I spend a lot more time on portfolio optimization and construction and risk management. There are chapters on topics that I think practitioners are increasingly interested in such as anomalies, active management, Monte Carlo techniques, factor models, systemic risk, hedging, private equity, and structured finance (collateralized debt obligations). Derivatives have also become more important to portfolio managers. I acknowledge that there are some excellent texts that cover derivative securities and therefore devote only three chapters to futures, forwards, swaps, and options and refer the reader to sources cited in the end of chapter references for deeper study. These three chapters are followed by a chapter devoted to hedging portfolio risk using derivatives and finally by the chapter on structured credit. The options treatment benefits greatly from the spreadsheets and these provide another valuable tool that students can take away for future use.

This book is targeted to graduate students in finance and economics, CFAs, and experienced portfolio managers. Although I try to derive my results from first principles, the material in this book is not a substitute for courses in calculus and statistics. As such, students with some formal training in these two areas will benefit greatly. Upper level undergraduates will also find many chapters and applications easily accessible, especially Chapters 1–8, 11, 15, and 19. The usual disclaimer applies as I take full responsibility for all errors and omissions.

STEVE PETERSON
Richmond, Virginia

Acknowledgments

This book is a synthesis of my many years of teaching across a broad spectrum of courses. Still, all books are collaborative efforts and I am indebted to my many graduate students who helped shape the way I think about the subject material covered herein. In particular, I have benefited from many discussions with the investment team at the Virginia Retirement System, most notably J.T. Grier, Ross Kasarda, Justin White, David Waltenbaugh, Matt Lacy, Alex Muniz, and Charles Grant as well as Rodney Sullivan at the CFA Institute. I would also like to thank my former colleagues in the economics department at Virginia Commonwealth University who, through my roughly 20-year tenure there, helped forge the foundations of both my teaching and research methodology. This book would never have made it past the manuscript stage without the production team at Wiley and I owe a special thanks to my editors Bill Falloon and Meg Freeborn. Finally, I thank my wife, Joyce, and daughter, Catherine, for their patient indulgence of my many evenings and weekends spent writing and working through problems.

CHAPTER 1

Discount Rates and Returns

The most powerful force in the universe is compound interest.
—Albert Einstein

ESTIMATING RETURNS

The total return on an investment in any security is the percentage change in the value of the asset including dividends over a specific interval of time. Assuming asset value is captured in the market price P and dividends by d, then the one period *total return*, r_1, is equal to $100 * \frac{(P_1 + d_1 - P_0)}{P_0}$ percent, in which the subscripts index time. For simplicity, we will ignore dividends, which gives us the price return, which, in decimal form, is equal to $r_1 = \frac{(P_1 - P_0)}{P_0} = \left(\frac{P_1}{P_0}\right) - 1$. Thus, $1 + r_1 = \left(\frac{P_1}{P_0}\right)$ is the *gross return* (the return *plus* the initial one-dollar outlay in the security) on the investment for one period, and r_1 is the *net return*; it is the return on a \$1 investment. We can geometrically link returns to get the time equivalent of a longer-term investment. For example, suppose that the period under study is one month and that $1 + r_1 = \left(\frac{P_1}{P_0}\right)$ is therefore the one-month return. We can annualize this return by assuming the investment returns this amount in each month. Compounding this for one year is a product yielding the amount:

$$r_A = (1 + r_1)^{12} - 1$$

Here, r_1 is the monthly return, while r_A is the annualized equivalent. On the other hand, we may observe a time series of past monthly returns (called *trailing returns*), which we geometrically link to estimate an annualized figure, that is, the previous 12 monthly returns generate an annual return given by:

$$1 + r_A = (1 + r_1)(1 + r_2)(1 + r_3) \cdots (1 + r_{11})(1 + r_{12})$$

We can similarly link quarterly returns to estimate an annual equivalent, for example, $1 + r_A = (1 + r_1)(1 + r_2)(1 + r_3)(1 + r_4)$, and we can do the same for weekly, daily, or any frequency for that matter, to achieve a lower frequency equivalent return. Focusing once again on monthly gross returns, annualization is a compounded return that is the product of monthly relative prices, each measuring price appreciation from the previous month, that is, by generalizing from the fact that if $1 + r_1 = \left(\frac{P_1}{P_0}\right)$, then the following must also be true:

$$1 + r_A = \left(\frac{P_1}{P_0}\right)\left(\frac{P_2}{P_1}\right)\left(\frac{P_3}{P_2}\right) \cdots \left(\frac{P_{11}}{P_{10}}\right)\left(\frac{P_{12}}{P_{11}}\right)$$

Upon canceling, this reduces to the following, which is consistent with our definition of gross return given earlier.

$$1 + r_A = \frac{P_{12}}{P_0}$$

This suggests that we can calculate the gross return over any period by taking the ratio of the market values and ignoring all intermediate market values. Similarly, we can solve for any intervening periodic average return by using the power rule; in this case, if the annual return is $1 + r_A$, then the *geometric average* monthly return r_M must be

$$(1 + r_A)^{\frac{1}{12}} = (1 + r_M)$$

For example, the average monthly return necessary to compound to a 15 percent annual return must be approximately 1.17 percent per month:

$$(1.15)^{\frac{1}{12}} = (1.011715)$$

EXAMPLE 1.1

Quarterly returns to the Russell 3000 Domestic Equity Index for the years 2005 to 2007 are given in Table 1.1.

TABLE 1.1 Russell 3000 Dom Eq Index

Date	Return (%)
2005Q1	−2.20
2005Q2	2.24
2005Q3	4.01
2005Q4	2.04
2006Q1	5.31
2006Q2	−1.98
2006Q3	4.64
2006Q4	7.12
2007Q1	1.28
2007Q2	5.77
2007Q3	1.55
2007Q4	−3.34

a. Geometrically link these quarterly returns to generate annual returns.
b. Calculate the return for the three-year period.
c. What is the *arithmetic average* annual return for these three years?
d. What is the *arithmetic average* quarterly return over this three-year period?

SOLUTIONS

(Refer to Table 1.2)

a. Annual Return (Column E) $= \prod_{n=0}^{n+3} (Column\ C) - 1$
b. The return for the three-year period $= \prod [Column\ C] - 1 = 0.29 = 29\%$; annualized, this is $\prod [Column\ C]^{\frac{1}{3}} - 1 = 1.088896 - 1 = 8.9\%$ geometric average.
c. The arithmetic average annual return $= AVG(Column\ E) = 9.0\%$.
d. The arithmetic average quarterly return $= AVG[Column\ B] = 2.2\%$.

(continued)

(continued)

TABLE 1.2 Geometric Returns

Quarter	Return (%)	Return/ 100 + 1	Geometric Mean	Annualized Return (%)
(A)	(B)	(C)	(D)	(E)
2005Q1	−2.20	0.98		
2005Q2	2.24	1.02		
2005Q3	4.01	1.04		
2005Q4	2.04	1.02	1.06	6.10
2006Q1	5.31	1.05		
2006Q2	−1.98	0.98		
2006Q3	4.64	1.05		
2006Q4	7.12	1.07	1.16	15.70
2007Q1	1.28	1.01		
2007Q2	5.77	1.06		
2007Q3	1.55	1.02		
2007Q4	−3.34	0.97	1.05	5.10

 Go to the companion website for more details.

GEOMETRIC AND ARITHMETIC AVERAGES

If things weren't already complicated enough, we now see that there are two distinct averages—geometric as well as arithmetic. It is important to understand the difference. If you want to know what an asset actually returned, then geometrically link the N gross returns over the relevant time. And, upon doing that, if you then want to know what the average return (geometric) was for each period in the return series, then take the Nth root and subtract one. Using a trailing series of the past 12 monthly returns as an example, we get:

$$1 + r_A = (1 + r_1)(1 + r_2)(1 + r_3) \cdots (1 + r_{11})(1 + r_{12})$$

The annual return is r_A. The *geometric average* of the monthly returns is

$$(1 + r_A)^{\frac{1}{12}} = [(1 + r_1)(1 + r_2)(1 + r_3) \cdots (1 + r_{11})(1 + r_{12})]^{\frac{1}{12}}$$

Clearly, this is different from the *arithmetic average*:

$$\bar{r} = \frac{r_1 + r_2 + r_3 + \cdots + r_{12}}{12}$$

The difference is not subtle. For example, suppose we observe a sequence of four returns {0.9, 0.1, –0.9, 0.2}. The arithmetic average is 0.075 (7.5 percent), while the geometric average is –29 percent! Why the large discrepancy? If you had a dollar invested over these four periods, the return you would have received would have been affected to a greater degree (in a negative way) by the third period's negative 90 percent return, that is, you would have lost 90 percent of your accumulated investment by the end of the third period and then earned a 20 percent return on whatever was left for the final period. The arithmetic average, however, places equal weight on all returns and, therefore, the impact of the large negative return is diluted by $1/N$. As the sample size increases, the impact of a single bad return declines asymptotically and it does not matter if that single bad return occurred early or late in the sample. In reality, that is not how money is earned and that is why we use geometric averages. In this example, the investment indeed earned an average –29 percent return in each period. Had you invested a dollar at the beginning of the first period, that dollar would have shrunk to about $0.25 in four periods. This is certainly not an amount implied by the arithmetic mean.

We will not prove the following formally, but it is intuitive that, in general, as the variance in the individual periodic returns declines, so does the difference between the arithmetic and geometric means. In the limit, if the four returns in our example were identical, then the arithmetic and geometric means would also be identical. Otherwise, it can be shown that the arithmetic mean is always greater than the geometric mean because the arithmetic mean ignores the correlations across returns over time. The takeaway is that these two measures tend to diverge in value as volatility in returns rises.

CAVEATS TO RETURN EXTRAPOLATION

Practitioners prefer to compare annualized returns and therefore extrapolate higher frequency returns (daily, monthly, and quarterly) to annual frequency. This practice, though common, can be misleading and it is important to know why. Consider the set of monthly returns to the S&P 500 index given in Table 1.3. The returns are for the year 2006.

TABLE 1.3 Monthly S&P 500 Returns

Month	Monthly Return	Gross Monthly Return	Quarterly Return
(A)	(B)	(C = B + 1)	(D)
Jan-06	0.0132	1.0132	
Feb-06	−0.0016	0.9984	
Mar-06	0.0134	1.0134	1.0251
Apr-06	0.0065	1.0065	
May-06	−0.0093	0.9907	
Jun-06	−0.0286	0.9714	0.9686
Jul-06	0.0056	1.0056	
Aug-06	0.0214	1.0214	
Sep-06	0.0238	1.0238	1.0515
Oct-06	0.0346	1.0346	
Nov-06	0.0185	1.0185	
Dec-06	0.0200	1.0200	1.0749

We can geometrically link these monthly returns to get an annualized return, which is computed by taking the product of the gross monthly returns in column C and subtracting one, yielding 12.23 percent. This is the return that you would have received had you held the index for those 12 months. The table also geometrically links monthly returns to estimate quarterly returns, which are given in column D of the table. These quarterly returns are then geometrically linked by taking their product (and subtracting one) to get an annual return, also equal to 12.23 percent.

Now imagine that it is April 1, 2006, and having just observed the March return, we estimate the first-quarter return for 2006 at 2.51 percent. Your supervisor wants to know what this is on an annualized basis. In response, you compute $(1 + r_{Q1})^4 - 1$, which upon substitution, computes to $(1.0251)^4 - 1 = 10.42$ percent. What you have done is extrapolate a higher frequency return (quarterly) to a lower frequency estimate (annual). The implicit assumption in extrapolation is that the return observed for the period just realized (first quarter 2006) will hold for the remaining three quarters. (This is what is referred to as a *naïve forecast*). In general, this will not be the case and the extrapolated return will therefore most likely contain errors. In the example given, you can readily see the error embodied in each of these quarterly extrapolations by comparing them to the true observed annual return in column C.

It is also important to realize that extrapolation generates more measurement error the greater the difference in the frequencies we extrapolate between. For example, if we extrapolate the monthly returns, that is,

$(1 + r_M)^{12} - 1$, then clearly, a single extraordinary monthly return will translate into an even more extraordinary annual return. Practitioners seem to know this and that is why higher frequency returns (weekly or daily) are generally never annualized. Returns are random. Extrapolation is not. The greater the difference between the frequencies we extrapolate between, the less we believe in randomness and the more we believe that the current observation portends all future observations. We are all most certainly aware of this problem but, nevertheless, we continue to extrapolate. It is important to remind ourselves and our colleagues of the weaknesses in these numbers.

DISCOUNTING PRESENT VALUES OF CASH FLOW STREAMS

As individual consumers, we are always trying to maximize our intertemporal utilities by trading off future and present consumption. That is, we will consume a dollar's worth of goods today if we feel that the satisfaction we receive from doing so exceeds the satisfaction we'd get had we saved that dollar and consumed it somewhere in the future. The decision to consume intertemporally therefore depends on our abilities to compare wealth today with future wealth, which is what we mean when we talk about the *time value of money*. A dollar cash amount invested in the future will be worth $C = (1 + r)$ after, say, one year. Therefore, the present value P of a cash flow C to be received one period from now is the future C discounted at rate r:

$$P = \frac{C}{(1+r)}$$

Alternatively, investing P for one period at rate r will generate value equal to $P(1 + r) = C$. The present value of a cash flow received two time periods from now is therefore:

$$P = \frac{C}{(1+r)^2}$$

If the cash flow is received more than once (say, three periods), then it has present value:

$$P = \frac{C}{(1+r)} + \frac{C}{(1+r)^2} + \frac{C}{(1+r)^3}$$

An example of discrete discounting is *net present value* (NPV), which is present value minus the initial outlay. The NPV function in Excel is: = NPV(rate, cash flow 1, cash flow 2, . . .). Suppose, for instance, that you were to undertake an investment that requires an initial cash outlay of $100 but will return dividends over the next two years in the amount of $100 per year with certainty. Suppose the opportunity cost of capital is 10 percent (this is the return you could have received had you invested your $100 in the market instead). Then the net present value is:

$$NPV = -100 + \frac{100}{1.1} + \frac{100}{(1.1)^2} = -100 + 90.91 + 82.64 = \$73.55$$

What exactly is the *discount rate?* It is the rate at which we are willing to trade present for future consumption. For example, suppose you are waiting to receive $C = \$100$ one year from now. Rather than wait, you agree to receive a smaller amount $P = \$90$ now. The smaller amount is consistent with consumers' preference for present versus future consumption; it suggests we are impatient, that we discount future gains (for a whole host of reasons) or more specifically, that we have our own set of time preferences that determine our individual decisions to consume our wealth intertemporally. We examine derivation of the discount rate in more rigorous detail in Chapter 4. The implication in this example is that the interest rate that is consistent with your time preferences is 11 percent and that your discount rate is $^1/_{1.11} = 0.9$, which is your willingness to trade the future $100 for current consumption worth $90. That is, you discount the future at 10 percent. The converse argument is that you would be willing to give up $90 today only if you knew you'd receive in exchange an amount of $100 one year from now.

Discount rates and market returns are obviously linked. Returns are determined by changes in the market prices of assets that more fundamentally reflect market participants' utility preferences that manifest themselves through the interaction of supply and demand. In this sense, returns can be thought of as an aggregate of all of our revealed preferences, that is, our attitudes regarding present over future consumption. We discount cash flows using observed market rates and we use different market rates to discount different types of cash flows, for example, risk-free Treasury rates to discount riskless bond coupons and more risky equity returns to discount private equity cash flows. For now, we will abstract from these details and study only the process of discounting. Generalizing the cash flow discounting problem, then, to t periods, we get a sum of periodic discounted cash flows:

$$P = \sum \left[\frac{C_t}{(1+r)^t} \right]$$

Note how we index C by time. Suppose, now, that the rate r is *compounded discretely* m times per year (that is, you receive a fraction $\frac{r}{m}$ percent, m times each year). Instead of t periods, we now have $m * t$ periods to discount, each at $\frac{r}{m}$ percent. Thus,

$$P = \sum \left[\frac{C_t}{\left(1 + \frac{r}{m}\right)^{mt}} \right]$$

The quantity $\left(1 + \frac{r}{m}\right)^m$ has a limit as m goes to infinity, that is, as interest is paid continuously. This limit is very important. It is

$$e^r = \lim_{m \to \infty} \left(1 + \frac{r}{m}\right)^m$$

More fundamentally, recall that

$$e = \lim_{m \to \infty} \left(1 + \frac{1}{m}\right)^m$$

Therefore,

$$e^{-rt} = \lim_{m \to \infty} \frac{1}{\left(1 + \frac{r}{m}\right)^{mt}}$$

Continuous compounding is therefore the limit of discrete compounding. For example, semiannual compounding (that is, interest paid twice each year) is

$$\left(1 + \frac{r}{2}\right)^2 = \left(1 + \frac{r}{2}\right)\left(1 + \frac{r}{2}\right)$$

Compounding interest quarterly over the year,

$$\left(1 + \frac{r}{4}\right)^4 = \left(1 + \frac{r}{4}\right)\left(1 + \frac{r}{4}\right)\left(1 + \frac{r}{4}\right)\left(1 + \frac{r}{4}\right)$$

Finally, paying interest monthly over the year is equal to the already familiar geometric return, or annual equivalent, equal to $\left(1 + \frac{r}{12}\right)^{12}$.

Taking the compounding frequency to the limit results in continuous compounding, e^r. This means that an amount C received at the end of time t with continuous compounding has a present value:

$$P = Ce^{-rt}$$

The discount rate in this case is e^{-rt}. Let me digress a bit on this concept. Assume I have capital to be invested right now in the amount P_0, and at the end of one period, it grows to P_1. Thus, $P_1 = P_0 e^{rt}$. Taking natural logs and noting that $t = 1$ for this example gives us the following:

$$\ln(P_1) = \ln(P_0) + r$$

Equivalently,

$$\ln\left(\frac{P_1}{P_0}\right) = r$$

where r in this case is the rate of return on the investment. It also determines the discount rate in the sense that it represents the opportunity cost of investment, that is, r is what I give up if I choose to consume P_0 today. Had I invested (saved) it, it would have grown to P_1 in one period.

In general then, an equivalent amount C earns the following over time t with continuous compounding:

$$C = Pe^{rt}$$

Thus, the process of evaluating future obligations as a present value problem is referred to as *discounting*. The present value of the future monetary amount (C) to be received is less than the face value of that amount because the future is discounted, reflecting, among other things, time preferences (a dollar today is worth more to me than a dollar to be received sometime in the future).

I define the k-period discount rate in discrete time as

$$d_k = \left(1 + \frac{r}{m}\right)^{-mk}$$

In continuous time, we have

$$d_k = e^{-rk}$$

It should be obvious that future value is the inverse function of present value. For example, let $(C_1, C_2, \ldots C_n)$ refer to a cash flow stream. Assume each cash flow is received at the beginning of the period and that the interest rate is constant at r. Then the *future value* (FV) is the sum of the compounded cash flow values:

$$FV = C_1(1 + r)^n + C_2(1 + r)^{n-1} + \cdots + C_n$$

Likewise, it should be clear that FV has present value P equal to $\frac{FV}{(1+r)^n}$, that is,

$$P = C_1 + \frac{C_2}{1+r} + \cdots + \frac{C_n}{(1+r)^n}$$

And, therefore, with compounding m times per period:

$$P = \sum_{k=0}^{n} \left[\frac{C_k}{\left(1 + \dfrac{r}{m}\right)^{mk}} \right]$$

This relationship can be written more compactly with continuous compounding:

$$P = \sum C_k e^{-rk}$$

Although we develop this concept more fully in Chapter 2, this is our first pricing model. It is a simple discounted cash flow model with certain (riskless) cash flows.

INTERNAL RATE OF RETURN AND YIELD TO MATURITY

We now assume that the discount rate is endogenous, in which case we solve for the rate that equates two sets of cash flows. Suppose you make an investment in a business equal to P_0 dollars. This investment is expected to yield a stream of cash flows for n periods equal to $C_1, C_2, \ldots C_n$. The internal rate of return (IRR) is the discount rate, which makes the two streams, the outflow P_0 and the present value of the inflows $C_1, C_2, \ldots C_n$, equivalent. That is, the IRR is the value of r that discounts the following set of cash flows to the initial outlay P_0:

$$P_0 = \frac{C_1}{(1+r)} + \frac{C_2}{(1+r)^2} + \cdots + \frac{C_n}{(1+r)^n}$$

Since P_0 is an outlay, hence, a negative cash flow, then the preceding equation is the same as:

$$0 = -P_0 + \frac{C_1}{(1+r)} + \frac{C_2}{(1+r)^2} + \cdots + \frac{C_n}{(1+r)^n}$$

Notice that this is a net present value, too, but with the important exception that the discount rate is exogenous in NPV problems. The internal rate of return, on the other hand, is the solution objective. The internal rate of return gets its name from understanding that it is the interest rate implied by the internal cash flow stream to the firm. In a sense, it is the firm's required rate of return necessary to achieve a breakeven level on its investments. It is therefore not a market rate. Firms use the IRR most often to compare alternative investments.

In general, the IRR is difficult to solve because it doesn't have an analytic solution; rather, one must resort to iterative techniques to arrive at a solution. Most software packages' solvers use some form of Newton's method to solve for the IRR (see the IRR and XIRR functions in Microsoft Excel).

EXAMPLE 1.2

Let's put numbers in Example 1.1. Assume the initial outlay is $100 and we expect to receive cash flows in years 1 to 4 equal to ($50, $0, $100, $100). Then the IRR is the rate that solves:

$$0 = -100 + \frac{50}{(1+r)} + \frac{0}{(1+r)^2} + \frac{100}{(1+r)^3} + \frac{100}{(1+r)^4}$$

This is equal to:

$$0 = -100 + 50C + 100C^3 + 100C^4$$

where $C = \frac{1}{(1+r)}$. This is a polynomial of order four. The solution is $r = $ IRR $ = 39$ percent, whose details can be found on the chapter spreadsheet.

What does this mean? Well, suppose again that this is your firm. Then this rate discounts your cash flows to a present value equal to your outlay of $100. This is a pretty good rate of return if all other investments generate cash flows with IRRs less than 39 percent. Thinking differently, if your firm requires an annual rate of return over four years on their cash flows equal to 39 percent, then a $100 investment with the stated cash flows will meet that requirement.

EXAMPLE 1.3

Suppose the required return is 39 percent on a $100, four-year invest-
ment with expected cash flows in each of the four years given by
($0, $0, $100, $150). What is the estimated IRR (r in the denominator
of the following equation) and will this investment be undertaken?

$$0 = -100 + \frac{0}{(1+r)} + \frac{0}{(1+r)^2} + \frac{100}{(1+r)^3} + \frac{150}{(1+r)^4}$$

Example 1.3 Table

Initial Outlay	−100
Year 1 Cash Flow	0
Year 2 Cash Flow	0
Year 3 Cash Flow	100
Year 4 Cash Flow	150
Required Rate of Return (RRR)	**39%**
Internal Rate of Return	**29%**
RRR = IRR	**FALSE**
Check the IRR Calculation	
Initial Outlay	−100
$C =$	0
$C^2 =$	0
$C^3 =$	46.289
$C^4 =$	53.711
SUM =	0

In this example, the IRR = 29 percent, which is below the required return of 39 percent. Therefore, the investment should not be
undertaken.

Now let's briefly jump ahead and look at the similarity between
the IRR and what bond analysts call the *yield to maturity*. Suppose
you lend $100 for a period of five years. The borrower promises to
pay you $25 in each of those five years to expunge his debt. What is
the rate of return that equates the present value of the creditor's payments to the loan amount? We set this up as:

$$100 = \frac{25}{(1+r)} + \frac{25}{(1+r)^2} + \frac{25}{(1+r)^3} + \frac{25}{(1+r)^4} + \frac{25}{(1+r)^5}$$

(continued)

> (*continued*)
>
> The IRR that solves this problem is 8 percent. As a lender, you therefore receive an 8 percent annual return on your investment—in this case, a loan. This is essentially a bond, and in the world of bonds, the 8 percent is the yield to maturity. The yield to maturity is a return that is equal to an IRR. Thus, bond yields are IRRs.
>
> **Go to the companion website for more details.**

REAL AND NOMINAL RETURNS

Inflation erodes the real returns on cash flows. For example, if the inflation rate is 4 percent, then a nominal cash flow of $1 has a real inflation-adjusted value of $\frac{\$1.00}{\$1.04} = \$0.96$. Using our discounting rules already developed, we can generalize that a nominal *gross* return $(1 + r)$ has an equivalent real *gross* return of:

$$1 + r_0 = \frac{1+r}{1+f}$$

where f is the inflation rate (in our example, 4 percent) and r_0 is the real *net* return.

Note that if the inflation rate is $f = 0$, then the nominal return is identical to the real return. Also, note that we can simplify this equation for the real gross return to get at the net return as follows:

$$r_0 = \frac{(r-f)}{(1+f)}$$

The important point is that inflation affects the relevant discount rate that one uses to value a cash flow stream. We return to this topic when we look at Treasury Inflation Protected Securities, or TIPS, in the next chapter.

SUMMARY

Returns measure growth rates in asset value over time. They are the observed reward to postponing present for future consumption. Returns may be measured discretely over any frequency such as daily, monthly, or quarterly and higher frequency returns can be converted into lower frequencies—annualizing monthly returns is one such case. The notion of compounding is linked to how often interest is paid; thus, annual returns can represent a single yearly payment, or higher frequency returns can be geometrically linked, or compounded, to form annualized equivalents. In the limit, continuously compounded returns represent the continuous payment of interest. In sum, we can work with returns over any interval and extrapolate those returns to either any longer interval of time or average them to any subinterval of time. An example of extrapolation is annualizing discrete monthly returns, and an example of averaging is finding the geometric average monthly return from an annual return. Caveats relate to the implicit assumption that observed returns will hold into the future.

Discounting links cash flows over time. The discounted present value of a cash flow to be received in the future is the result of finding the amount of cash in present dollars that, when invested at the discount rate, will grow to an amount stipulated by the future cash flow. Discount rates are intimately linked to returns; in the simplest case, the discount rate is the reciprocal of the gross return and the discount rate may be applied discretely or continuously. The role that discount rates play in the trade-off of present over future consumption is a topic that I develop more fully in Chapter 4.

The internal rate of return is an application of discounting in cash management and the yield-to-maturity on a coupon-paying bond is itself an internal rate of return. We can thus link the subject of Chapter 2 on bond pricing to the discount function developed in this chapter. In fact, almost all asset-pricing models will rely on some form of discounting since they all involve the valuation of cash flows that occur over time.

Finally, we recognize the impact that inflation has on the value of cash flows, which requires us to distinguish between inflation adjusted (real) returns and nominal returns and model them accordingly.

CHAPTER 2

Fixed Income Securities

What's past is prologue.

—William Shakespeare, *The Tempest*

A *security* is a financial asset that yields a measurable payoff, which may be state dependent (for example, it pays $1 if it rains and zero otherwise). The return to the security is the percentage change in the security's value over some well-defined period of time. That return is fixed if payoffs do not vary over the life of the asset. Bonds are securities paying fixed payoffs (coupons). U.S. Treasuries are the least risky bonds because they have the smallest relative likelihood of defaulting on their payoffs. Corporate and municipal bonds are generally riskier because they do not have the power of the federal government (the taxpayer) to guarantee that bondholders will receive the promised payoffs. Bond market participants will therefore pay close attention to bond rating agencies like Standard & Poor's, Moody's, and Fitch when pricing the present value of future coupon streams. Credit risk is covered in more detail in Chapter 11.

In general, a bond is a loan; the holder of the bond is a creditor and the original seller of the bond is the borrower. In the case of government bonds, creditors have a claim on taxpayers (unless the government defaults on its debt). In the case of the corporate bond, the bondholder (creditor) has a claim to the assets of the firm and their claims generally are senior to shareholders (holders of equity, or stock). Thus, there are risks that cash flows like coupons or principal will not be paid and, as a result, bondholders may seek to insure their claims by holding credit default swaps. Credit default swaps are similar to insurance policies. Buying and selling credit default swaps is commonly referred to as buying and selling protection. If the borrower defaults, then the creditor collects on the credit default swap, which allows them to partially or fully hedge their loss. The CDS market is large

17

and generally unregulated, which was partly responsible for the collapse of credit markets in 2008 (for example, the insurance giant AIG defaulted on billions of dollars in CDS contracts that they underwrote for bondholders).

We can categorize fixed income securities into the following categories:

- Savings deposits (demand deposits, time deposits, and CDs), which earn a fixed interest payment.
- Money market instruments, which are short-term securities of maturity less than a year. These include commercial paper (unsecured corporate borrowing) and to a lesser extent, bankers' acceptances as well as Euro-dollars (dollar-denominated deposits in European banks).
- U.S. government securities, which we discuss further on.
- Mortgages, which are a fixed income security to the lender—the monthly mortgage payment performs in much the same way as a coupon payment.
- Other miscellaneous bonds such as municipals and corporate bonds.
- Annuities (*consols* in Great Britain), which pay a perpetual (infinite) coupon.

We will learn how to price these securities.

Let's concentrate first on U.S. government securities, which are issued through the U.S. Treasury to finance government expenditures (for example, if Congress appropriates $100 billion in expenditures in a fiscal year, but collects only $50 billion in tax revenues, then they must borrow $50 billion. They do this through their agent, the U.S. Treasury). Treasuries (U.S. government securities), come in two basic types: those that mature in one year or less and pay only the face value (but no coupon), and those that mature in more than one year that pay face value at maturity in addition to periodic coupon payments. The former are referred to as Treasury bills while the latter are either Treasury notes (10 years maturity or less) or Treasury bonds. Only bills pay no coupons. These are therefore referred to as *zero coupon bonds,* or, for short, just *zeros.* They are sold at discount (through Treasury auctions) and perhaps later through secondary bond markets. Let's do these first, since they are easiest.

First, a word on notation: Let P be the price, C the cash flow to the holder, and r, the interest rate—the bond's yield to maturity. Consider then the simple case in which the government desires to borrow $100 for one year. That is, suppose the Treasury prints up a bond certificate with a face value of $100 to be paid to the holder in one year at maturity. This is the principal. Suppose that the outcome of a sealed bid auction is that someone will agree to purchase this paper for $90 now and in one year, will redeem it for its face value at maturity ($100).

Then that person has bought this zero at *discount* for 90 and earns:

$$1 + r = \frac{C}{P} = \frac{100}{90} = 1.11; \; r = 11\%$$

Thus, the return on this bond, if held to maturity, is 11 percent. This is also called the *yield* on the bond. If the market price were $95 instead, then this would generate a yield of about 5.26 percent. Notice that the bond's price and return are inversely related. This means that, in general, if the Treasury borrows more, the supply of bonds rises, driving down their market prices, which increases their yields.

Looked at differently,

$$P = \frac{C}{(1 + r)} = \frac{100}{1.11} = 90$$

Here, we see that the market price of the bond is the discounted present value of C; P represents the price bid to receive $100 one year from now. In equilibrium, market forces price this bond at $90 because the investor could alternatively have lent out her $90 at a rate of 11 percent, earning $100 in one year on an investment of equivalent risk. So, a willingness to buy this bond for more than $90 is irrational because the investor is earning a relatively lower rate of return.

COUPON-BEARING BONDS

Think now of a coupon-bearing instrument like a Treasury bond that matures in, say, n years. For example, assume that you are considering a bond that matures in n years with yield r, face value M, and certain (that is, riskless) *annual coupon* payments equal to C. You want to find the value (the fundamental price) of this stream of cash flows accruing over an n-year period. By lending P, you will receive the stream of cash flows: $C_1, C_2, \ldots, C_n, M$. You wish to value this stream. To do so, you need to discount this stream at a rate that makes the price paid for the bond, P, just equal to the present value of this stream of cash flows. That is, r, which is the *bond yield*, or *yield to maturity*, solves

$$P = \frac{C_1}{(1 + r)} + \frac{C_2}{(1 + r)^2} + \cdots + \frac{C_n}{(1 + r)^n} + \frac{M}{(1 + r)^n}$$

Since this is a constant coupon, then $C_1 = C_2 = \cdots = C_n = C$ and so $P = \frac{C}{(1+r)} + \frac{C}{(1+r)^2} + \cdots + \frac{C}{(1+r)^n} + \frac{M}{(1+r)^n}$, or more compactly as

$$P = \sum_{k=1}^{n} \frac{C}{(1+r)^k} + \frac{M}{(1+r)^n}$$

Solving for the bond's yield is an iterative procedure that uses some variation of Newton's method. Note: $r(t+1) = r_t - f/df$. Here, the function f is the discounted stream P and the derivative is with respect to r. The *par yield* solves $100 = \frac{C_1}{(1+r)} + \frac{C_2}{(1+r)^2} + \cdots + \frac{C_n}{(1+r)^n} + \frac{M}{(1+r)^n}$ for known $C_1, C_2, \ldots, C_n, M$.

EXAMPLE 2.1

Calculate P for a 10-year bond paying annual coupons of $10 with face value equal to $1,000 and yield to maturity of 5 percent. The solution is outlined in Table 2.1. The present value is the sum of the discounted cash flows and is equal to about $691. Therefore, if our time preferences are consistent with this discount rate and the cash flows are risk free, then this is the fair market value of the bond. Stated differently, if there was a transaction in the bond market for this bond at $691, then someone had preferences that reflected this particular set of discount rates given by $d(0, i) = 1/(1+r)^i$ for $i = 1, \ldots, 10$.

TABLE 2.1   Price Calculation for Coupon Bond

Year	Discount	Cash Flow	Present Value
1	0.9524	10	9.524
2	0.9070	10	9.070
3	0.8638	10	8.638
4	0.8227	10	8.227
5	0.7835	10	7.835
6	0.7462	10	7.462
7	0.7107	10	7.107
8	0.6768	10	6.768
9	0.6446	10	6.446
10	0.6139	1010	620.052
Price			691.131

A bond has a given price P along with C and M. Therefore r is the yield that equates this cash flow stream to its present value P (just like an internal rate of return).

Now, suppose the coupon is paid semiannually as is the convention. How does this change our thinking? First of all, it means that instead of n cash flows, the holder of the bond will receive $2n$ coupons plus the face value. Each coupon will be paid after six months, so the semiannual rate of return is one-half of r. Using the 10-year bond example, this translates into the following present valuation scheme:

$$P = \frac{\frac{C}{2}}{\left(1 + \frac{r}{2}\right)} + \frac{\frac{C}{2}}{\left(1 + \frac{r}{2}\right)^2} + \cdots + \frac{\frac{C}{2}}{\left(1 + \frac{r}{2}\right)^{2n}} + \frac{M}{\left(1 + \frac{r}{2}\right)^{2n}}$$

The first two terms on the right-hand side correspond to the first year's discounted cash flows. So, for a 10-year bond, there are 20 such semiannual flows and a single terminal flow M equal to the face value of the bond.

In all the examples given here, the term r is constant and is referred to as the yield to maturity on the bond. It is the rate that equates the present value of the cash flow stream to its price P. In this way, it behaves like an internal rate of return.

 Go to the companion website for more details.

INFINITE CASH FLOW STREAMS (PERPETUITIES)

Defined benefit pensions are *perpetuities;* they are like a bond with a coupon paid indefinitely (until death). A perpetuity's cash flows have to be discounted at r into the infinite future. Assuming annual payments, this is represented by:

$$P = \sum_{k=1}^{\infty} \frac{C}{(1 + r)^k}$$

$$P = \frac{C}{(1 + r)} + \frac{C}{(1 + r)^2} + \cdots + \frac{C}{(1 + r)^n} + \cdots$$

Solving this power series yields

$$P = \frac{C}{r}$$

See Appendix 2.1 for the complete derivation. Therefore, a bond paying a $10 coupon in perpetuity with interest rate of 10 percent is worth $100. We sometimes see this written in yield form as $r = \frac{C}{P}$. *Yield* is a very general concept in finance and one you should familiarize yourself with. For example, if a commercial property lease generates $1 million in revenues every year and you can buy this property for $20 million, then you buy the right to receive these cash flows, which have a yield of 5 percent. You can compare this yield to other asset class yields of comparable risk.

GENERAL PRICING FORMULAS FOR FINITE CASH FLOW STREAMS

Again, assume the bond pays a coupon C for a definite period, n, as in:

$$P = \frac{C}{(1+r)} + \frac{C}{(1+r)^2} + \frac{C}{(1+r)^n} + \frac{M}{(1+r)^n}$$

Solving this finite power series yields

$$P = \frac{C}{r}\left[1 - \frac{1}{(1+r)^n}\right] + \frac{M}{(1+r)^n}$$

See Appendix 2.1 for the complete derivation. Suppose C stands for any payment (like a payment on an *installment loan*). It has no terminal face value, so we set M to zero. Then if P represents the loan amount, C (the payment) can be solved for as:

$$C = \frac{Pr(1+r)^n}{(1+r)^n - 1}$$

This is an *amortization* formula that gives the pay down on a loan over time n at interest rate r for n periods with principal P. It is of interest to amortize a loan into interest and principal payments.

EXAMPLE 2.2

This example calculates the amortization schedule for each year in a 10-year loan with annual payments on a principal of $1,000 and interest rate equal to 10 percent.

This example clearly separates the *principal and interest payments* on the loan—the total payments equal $1,627.45, of which

TABLE 2.2 Amortization of a 10-Year Loan

Year	Beginning Balance	Interest on Balance	Payment	Forward Balance
1	1,000.00	100.00	162.75	937.25
2	937.25	93.73	162.75	868.23
3	868.23	86.82	162.75	792.31
4	792.31	79.23	162.75	708.80
5	708.80	70.88	162.75	616.93
6	616.93	61.69	162.75	515.88
7	515.88	51.59	162.75	404.72
8	404.72	40.47	162.75	282.45
9	282.45	28.25	162.75	147.95
10	147.95	14.80	162.75	0.00

$1,000 is on the original principal, while $627.45 goes to interest. Extending this example, suppose that you are interested in buying a home with price P and mortgage rate r that will be financed over a 30-year period with monthly *mortgage* payments each equal to C. Then the price of the home must equal the sum of its discounted stream of monthly mortgage payments:

$$P = \frac{C}{\left(1 + \frac{r}{12}\right)} + \frac{C}{\left(1 + \frac{r}{12}\right)^2} + \cdots + \frac{C}{\left(1 + \frac{r}{12}\right)^{360}}$$

Solving this series (just like we did earlier) results in the following relationship between the price of the home and the monthly mortgage payment:

$$P = \frac{C}{\left(\frac{r}{m}\right)}\left[1 - \frac{1}{\left(1 + \frac{r}{m}\right)^{n(m)}}\right]$$

where $m = 12$ and therefore $n(m) = 12 * 30 = 360$. More importantly, the amortization formula is equal to:

$$C = \frac{\frac{rP}{12}\left(1 + \frac{r}{12}\right)^{12n}}{\left(1 + \frac{r}{12}\right)^{12n} - 1}$$

This amortization formula is useful for computing the monthly payment for any n period loan with interest rate r and financing period n.

 Go to the companion website for more details.

EXAMPLE 2.3

This example calculates the amortization schedule for each month in a 30-year mortgage with monthly payments on a principal of $200,000 and interest rate equal to 5 percent. Note that almost half of the cost of this loan is in the form of interest payments. This is the power of compound interest.

TABLE 2.3 Monthly Amortization Schedule for a 30-Year Mortgage

		Monthly Amortization Schedule		
Month	Beginning Balance	Interest on Balance	Payment	Forward Balance
1	200,000.00	833.33	1,073.64	199,759.69
2	199,759.69	832.33	1,073.64	199,518.38
3	199,518.38	831.33	1,073.64	199,276.06
4	199,276.06	830.32	1,073.64	199,032.74
5	199,032.74	829.30	1,073.64	198,788.40
...	...	...	...	...
356	5,301.76	22.09	1,073.64	4,250.21
357	4,250.21	17.71	1,073.64	3,194.27
358	3,194.27	13.31	1,073.64	2,133.94
359	2,133.94	8.89	1,073.64	1,069.19
360	1,069.19	4.45	1,073.64	0.00
Total		186,511.57	386,511.57	

 Go to the companion website for more details.

INTEREST RATE RISK

Consider again the bond pricing formula for an n period coupon-paying bond (assume only one coupon payment per year for mathematical simplicity).

$$P = \frac{C_1}{(1+r)} + \frac{C_2}{(1+r)^2} + \frac{C_n}{(1+r)^n} + \frac{M}{(1+r)^n}$$

Clearly for fixed C, then r, the yield to maturity, equates the present value of this stream to the price P. Note that for fixed C, changes in the price of the bond (through supply and demand shifts in the bond market) will reflect changes in r. The relative attractiveness of bonds in investors' portfolios makes bond prices variable and, therefore, bond yields variable as well. Fiscal policy that requires deficit financing, for example, will increase the supply of bonds that the Treasury auctions and these actions, in general, will cause bond prices to fluctuate. Similarly, monetary policy executed by central banks in the form of money supply growth (Fed easing) will have implications for interest rates (and therefore discount rates). Together, market forces, policy induced or not, will cause bond yields to move around over time, which will produce compensating variations in bond prices. Investors who hold bonds in their portfolios will therefore see the value of their bond holdings, and therefore the return on bonds in their portfolios, respond to these factors. Bonds are therefore risky even if their cash flows are not. This is what we refer to as *interest rate risk*, also known as *capital risk*. It is not a risk if you hold the bond to maturity. In that case, your risk is the yield available when you reinvest coupons and face value. On the other hand, if you are holding a portfolio of bonds, then interest rate risk is very real because the value of the portfolio varies with interest rate volatility when the portfolio is periodically marked to market. Thus, if the portfolio is held as collateral, for example, and interest rates are rising, then the value of the collateral is declining—your counterparty in this case may require you to post more collateral.

The yield on bonds and the return on bonds are often misunderstood. The *bond return* is identical to its yield if held to maturity (with coupons reinvested at the original yield to maturity). For example, if you purchase a bond at price P, you do so because you feel that P fairly represents the discounted present value of the promised future coupon stream (plus ending face value). If you hold the bond to maturity, then the yield to maturity is identical to the return.

For example, consider the value of an n-period bond:

$$P = \frac{C_1}{(1+r)} + \frac{C_2}{(1+r)^2} + \cdots + \frac{C_n}{(1+r)^n} + \frac{M}{(1+r)^n}$$

The price P represents the discounted present value of cash flows that are paid at various times into the future. To convert to a future value, multiply both sides by $(1+r)^n$:

$$P(1+r)^n = C(1+r)^{n-1} + C(1+r)^{n-2} + \cdots + C + M$$

The left hand side is the future value of investing P today for n periods earning a return r in each period compounded over time. $C(1+r)^{n-1}$ earns interest for $n - 1$ periods, $C(1 + r)^{n-2}$ for $n - 2$ periods, and so on while the terminal cash flows C and M earn no interest. Thus, we see that the yield to maturity (the IRR) assumes all cash flows are reinvested for the remaining time at the internal rate of return, r. Therefore, the return to the bond if held to maturity is the difference $P(1 + r)^n - P$. The *periodic* return is therefore r, which is also the yield to maturity.

Many times, however, the bond is not held to maturity. For example, the bond may be sold to provide liquidity against an unexpected liability. At the time of sale, the bond's price is determined through the interaction of market supply and demand. The return on the bond is now related to the percentage change in the price of the bond from the original date of purchase, which is no longer required to be equal to the original yield. Therefore, bond yields and bond returns can be quite different. The risk is that the bond's return will be lower than its yield if the investor is forced to liquidate before maturity.

Suppose that C is a given percent of M, the face value. For example, suppose the coupon payment is 10 percent of the face value $M = \$100$. Then the bond is a 10 percent coupon bond. If the price P is \$100 and the yield to maturity is also 10 percent, then this is called a *par bond*. Prove this to yourselves using the Price-Yield-Relation worksheet. A bond that sells at discount (premium) sells for less (more) than \$100. As you can see from this worksheet, when $r > 10$ percent, the bond sells for less than 100 percent, and when $r < 10$ percent, it sells for a premium (over 100 percent of \$100). *In general, when the coupon yield exceeds (is less than) the yield to maturity, the bond is selling at a premium (discount).*

More precisely, the yield to maturity is a by-product of the market price P. That is, bond market participants interact to set price, which, in turn, implies a yield to maturity and not the other way around. Thus, the bond selling at a premium (discount) determines that the yield to maturity is less than (greater than) the coupon yield.

A central question for the bond portfolio manager is, "How sensitive is P to small changes in interest rates?" Specifically, we are referring to the yield to maturity when we speak of interest rates but, in general, all rates are related, as we shall see. The intuition here is that bond market participants determine bond prices depending on their individual preferences, which include their perceptions of the opportunity cost of their capital. Thus, the yield to maturity is a discounting rate that must be consistent, on average, with discounting rates on other investments of similar duration and risk.

The answer to this central question depends a lot on how long the bondholder will have her capital at risk, that is, the maturity of the bond or, more specifically, its *duration*. Bonds with longer maturities require waiting longer to receive the cash flows in the form of coupons. Duration is therefore a temporal measure and the longer the duration, the longer we wait for the future to unfold, and therefore the longer we wait for the possibility for bad things to happen that may affect prices and interest rates. Therefore, bonds with longer maturities are those that are less likely to be held by a single investor from date of issue to maturity. Thus, bonds with longer maturities, all other things constant, have longer durations than those of shorter maturity and, hence, longer duration means greater capital risk. This risk is a function of the time to maturity and the interest rate (the yield to maturity).

To see this, consider the several examples in the companion website's Chapter 2 Examples.xlsx (Duration Tab). Take a 10-year, a 20-year, and a 30-year 10 percent bond with $M = \$100$. Put the yield r at 10 percent initially to see that each bond has $P = \$100$ (that is, they are all par bonds). Now, change r to 11 percent and then to 9 percent and compare the changes in P across maturities. You should get results consistent with those in the following table.

Clearly, the prices of bonds with longer maturities, or durations as we shall see further on, are more sensitive to interest rate changes. Duration will therefore become a natural measure of interest rate risk. We derive and analyze the properties of bond duration shortly. Before we do that, however, let's explore some more of the intuition behind the example given in Table 2.4.

Duration measures the sensitivity of the bond's price to changes in yield, that is, duration is a slope, or derivative, dP/dr. But, as we can see from this example, the change in bond price for a given change in its yield to maturity is nonlinear—a 1 percent change in yield has different implications for changes in price and depends on the duration itself. This suggests that there is some curvature in the relation between dP and dr. This

TABLE 2.4 Price-Yield Relationship

	9% Yield	10% Yield	11% Yield
Face	$100	$100	$100
Rate	9%	10%	11%
Coupon %	10%	10%	10%
N (years)	10	10	10
# of coupons per year	2	2	2
Price$_{10}$	$106.50	$100.00	$94.02
Price$_{20}$	$109.20	$100.00	$91.98
Price$_{30}$	$110.32	$100.00	$91.28

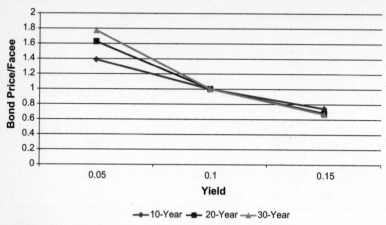

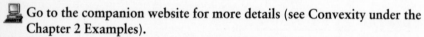

FIGURE 2.1 Convexity

curvature is called the bond's *convexity* and is captured through the second derivative, d^2P/dr^2. Convexity measures the curvature in the price/yield trade-off. Using the three bonds in the duration worksheet, I plot several price-yield points on a graph with price as a percentage of face value on the vertical axis and yield to maturity on the horizontal axis.

Go to the companion website for more details (see Convexity under the Chapter 2 Examples).

Notice that for each maturity, the relationship is convex to the origin and the *convexity* increases with maturity. What does this mean to investors? To begin with, the pricing model is highly nonlinear in the discount factor (recall, that it is a power series to the order $2n$). Duration, as we illustrate further on, is a first-order approximation to risk (it is the change in price given a one unit change in yield). A first-order approximation is like a tangent line to a curve; the slope of the tangent line approximates the trade-off between price and yield as long as we don't move very far away from the point of tangency (this is the common point above at yield = 0.10). As we move away from the tangency point, duration will not do a very good job accounting for the trade-off (in this case, the risk) because it is linear and can't capture the convexity in the bond pricing relationship. That is why we specifically look at convexity; it is the second-order approximation to risk. Longer duration bonds have higher order discount rates—their pricing formulas are higher-order polynomials—and therefore more risk and more convexity. That is why the curves associated with longer maturity bonds are more convex. They are riskier. To see more clearly the differences in risk across maturities, look at Table 2.5, in which we pick two maturities and,

TABLE 2.5 Price-Yield Response

Yield	$Price_{10}$	$Price_{20}$	$Price_{30}$	$\Delta Price_{10}$	$\Delta Price_{10}$	$\Delta Price_{10}$
0.15	74.51	68.51	67.10			
0.14	78.81	73.34	71.92	4.30	4.82	4.82
0.13	83.47	78.78	77.45	4.66	5.45	5.53
0.12	88.53	84.95	83.84	5.06	6.17	6.39
0.11	94.02	91.98	91.28	5.49	7.02	7.44
0.1	100.00	100.00	100.00	5.98	8.02	8.72
0.09	106.50	109.20	110.32	6.50	9.20	10.32
0.08	113.59	119.79	122.62	7.09	10.59	12.30
0.07	121.32	132.03	137.42	7.73	12.24	14.79
0.06	129.75	146.23	155.35	8.44	14.20	17.93

beginning with the point at which these two convex curves intersect for their par valuations, change the yield up or down and compare the relative changes in the implied bond prices. It should be clear that the change in the price is relatively higher for a given yield change when the bond has higher maturity.

ANALYSIS OF DURATION

The previous discussion describes the intuition that the duration on a bond is a measure of this interest rate sensitivity. I develop this relationship more rigorously in this section and end it with a rule of thumb based on *modified duration,* which is used by bond managers to assess interest rate risk on their portfolios. Duration is actually a weighted average of the cash flow delivery dates. To see this, consider again the standard present valuation of a cash flow stream on an n period coupon-bearing bond. We are interested in the interest rate sensitivity of the bond's price. This sensitivity is what we call the bond's *delta,* or $\Delta P / \Delta r$. To see this, take the derivative with respect to the interest rate. (The derivative is a simple application of the exponent rule). Note that $dP/d(1+r) = dP/dr$.

$$\frac{dP}{d(1+r)} = -\frac{C}{(1+r)^2} - \frac{2C}{(1+r)^3} - \frac{3C}{(1+r)^4} - \cdots - \frac{nC}{(1+r)^{n+1}} - \frac{nM}{(1+r)^{n+1}}$$

$$\frac{dP}{d(1+r)} = \frac{-1}{(1+r)} \left[\frac{C}{(1+r)^1} + \frac{2C}{(1+r)^2} + \frac{3C}{(1+r)^3} + \cdots + \frac{nC}{(1+r)^n} + \frac{nM}{(1+r)^n} \right]$$

Now consider the terms $\frac{C}{(1+r)^2}, \frac{C}{(1+r)^3}, \ldots$ and recognize that these are weights $w_1, w_2, \ldots$ on the timing of the cash flows. Rewriting the equality, we get:

$$\frac{dP}{d(1+r)} * (1+r) = -w_1(1) - w_2(2) - w_3(3) - \ldots - w_n(n)$$

The right-hand side is a weighted average of the times $t = 1, 2, \ldots, n$ with the weights being the discounted cash flows.

If we then divide $\frac{dP}{d(1+r)} * (1+r)$ by the price of the bond P, we get the familiar form of an *elasticity*; in this case, $\frac{dP}{P}$ divided by $\frac{dr}{r}$. This quotient is called *Macaulay duration*. It is an elasticity, but the best way to think of duration is that it is the weighted average of times until delivery of cash flows. Collecting terms, Macaulay duration is written as:

$$\left[\frac{dP}{dr}\right]\frac{(1+r)}{P} = \sum_{t=1}^{n} -P^{-1}\left[\frac{tc_t}{(1+r)^t}\right]$$

Go to the companion website for more details (see the Duration spreadsheet).

This is a complicated formula. You will find the Duration.xlsx spreadsheet much more intuitive since it breaks this computation down into separable and additive parts.

Now, to get back to the issue of sensitivity of the bond's price to changes in yield, understand that Macaulay duration D can be written as:

$$D = \left(\frac{dP}{P}\right)\left(\frac{(1+r)}{dr}\right)$$

which, upon multiplying both sides by P and dividing by $(1+r)$, gets us:

$$P\left(\frac{D}{(1+r)}\right) = \frac{dP}{dr}$$

The term $D/(1+r)$ is *modified duration* and it measures the rate sensitivity of the bond's price. Given a bond's modified duration, we can then approximate its instantaneous risk $\frac{dP}{dr}$ by substituting in the current bond price P and its yield r.

EXAMPLE 2.5

The data for a 10-year bond that pays a 10 percent coupon and has a 5 percent yield is available on the companion website. This bond is priced at \$138.97 (confirm this for yourselves) and has Macaulay duration of 7.11. The modified duration is $\frac{D}{(1+r)} = 6.77$ and therefore, the price sensitivity dP. For a 1 percent change in yield, $dr = 0.01$ is equal to $138.97 * 6.77 * 0.01 = \$9.41$.

 Go to the companion website for more details.

EXAMPLE 2.6

In 2009, the central bank targeted effective rates at close to zero. A bond manager estimates his portfolio as having duration 5. If the central bank were to tighten interest rates by 100 bps (1 percent), then his portfolio would lose approximately 5 percent of its value, that is,

$$\frac{dP}{P} = \left(\frac{D}{(1+r)}\right)(dr) \sim 5.$$

INTEREST RATE RISK DYNAMICS

As a final application, think of an investor who purchases a bond with no intention to hold it to maturity. Then the investor is exposed to risk because the price of the bond may fall and the yield will rise between the time of purchase and the time of sale. The question is how much will the price change by? Duration will not help here because the bond is not held to maturity; rather it is liquidated at some intermediate point $t < n$. To understand the risk, consider a \$1 par bond (that is, $M = \$1$, and $c\% = r\%$ and thus, $c = r$).

$$P = \frac{c}{(1+r_0)} + \frac{c}{(1+r_0)^2} + \cdots + \frac{c}{(1+r_0)^n} + \frac{M}{(1+r_0)^n}$$

Clearly, $P = \$1$. Now, consider what happens if r_0 is allowed to change to, say, r_1, instantaneously.

$$P = \frac{c}{(1 + r_1)} + \frac{c}{(1 + r_1)^2} + \cdots + \frac{c}{(1 + r_1)^n} + \frac{M}{(1 + r_1)^n}$$

which, upon solving for P, gives us:

$$P - P(1 + r_1) = -c + \frac{c}{(1 + r_1)^n} + \frac{M}{(1 + r_1)^n} - \frac{M}{(1 + r_1)^{n-1}}$$

Collecting terms and simplifying,

$$P = \frac{c}{r_1}\left[1 - \frac{1}{(1 + r_1)^n}\right] + \frac{1}{(1 + r_1)^n}$$

We began with $P = \$1$ (the par bond) and end up with a situation in which c and r_1 are no longer equal. Since $c = r_0$ originally at par, then

$$P = \frac{r_0}{r_1}\left[1 - \frac{1}{(1 + r_1)^n}\right] + \frac{1}{(1 + r_1)^n}$$

and the change in price must be this quantity minus $P = \$1$, or

$$\Delta P = \frac{r_0}{r_1}\left[1 - \frac{1}{(1 + r_1)^n}\right] + \left[\frac{1}{(1 + r_1)^n}\right] - 1$$

Now, to complicate things, let's generalize this so that r changes to r_k at time $t = k$ (k periods from now). That is, r_0 has changed to r_k over a period of time equal to k periods. Then the n period bond is now a $n - k$ period bond. If this is the case, then the change in the price of the bond is, in general:

$$\Delta P = \frac{r_0}{r_k}\left[1 - \frac{1}{(1 + r_k)^{n-k}}\right] + \left[\frac{1}{(1 + r_k)^{n-k}}\right] - 1$$

Go to the companion website for more details (see Interest Rate Risk under Chapter 2 Examples).

IMMUNIZATION AND DURATION

Here, I use two cases to show how duration can be used to immunize a portfolio from changes in interest rates. The first case is simple: consider an employer with a single pensioner who is to retire in 10 years and to whom is promised $1 million at that time—in this case, a single balloon payment. (See Luenberger, Example 3.10). The employer wishes to invest an amount of money now to pay this obligation 10 years hence. This is, in fact, a simple example of *liability-driven investment* that is popular in corporate defined benefit pension plan management. If there were a 10-year zero coupon bond, the problem would be solved immediately because the zero would have duration matching the duration of the obligation—just calculate the amount of the zero necessary to produce $1 million in 10 years. Suppose, however, there are no zeros available. Instead, suppose the choice is among three coupon bonds: a 30-year, a 20-year, and a 10-year bond. As we shall see, the employer need consider purchasing only two bonds.

 Go to the companion website for more details (see Duration for specifics on each bond).

Intuitively, the portfolio of bonds should be selected such that the present value of the portfolio is exactly equal to the present value of the $1 million obligation and, secondly, that the duration of the portfolio is as close as possible to the duration of the obligation. Thus, the portfolio must offset both the value and the timing of the obligation. There are two necessary conditions here that we can use to solve for the required proportions of each bond in the portfolio that will serve to discharge the obligation when the time comes. And, as we shall see as well, the value of the portfolio will move in tandem with the value of the obligation in the event that interest rates (that is, the discount rate) change over the 10-year period in question. Thus, this portfolio's value is immunized against unexpected changes in interest rates; as such, one need hold only the original shares of the bonds in this portfolio.

Denote the investments in the two bonds as P_1 and P_2 and their respective durations as D_1 and D_2. Then, formally, we require the two conditions:

1. $P_1 + P_2 = PV$, which says that the present value of the obligation must equal the portfolio value of the two coupon bonds. Moreover, we require
2. $D_1 P_1 + D_2 P_2 = 10PV$. This means that the duration-weighted sum of the bond prices must equal the duration-weighted present value of the obligation.

Assume all are par bonds and that the annual interest rate is 9 percent. Then the durations are 10.78, 9.61, and 6.8 years for the 30-year, 20-year, and 10-year bonds, respectively. Since the duration of the obligation is 10 years, then no single bond will suffice. However, a linear combination of bonds will work as long as this portfolio includes the 30-year bond; that is, there is some weighted average of the 30- and 20-year bonds or the 30- and 10-year bonds that have a duration of 10 years.

Since bonds pay semiannual coupons, then interest is compounded semiannually. We will use this formulation in computing the present values of all assets and liabilities. For example, the PV of the obligation is $\frac{\$1\text{million}}{1.045^{20}} = \$414,642.86$, since the yield is assumed to be 9 percent. D_1 and D_2 are known as well. Therefore, we have two equations in two unknowns, P_1 and P_2. Solving these will generate the total investment X Corporation needs to make in each bond.

Solution

Find the solution to this system of equations (*Note:* Because of the rounding of the duration estimates, the calculations may not be exact):

$$P_1 + P_2 = PV$$

$$D_1 P_1 + D_2 P_2 = 10PV$$

First, solve the first equation for P_1:

$$P_1 = PV - P_2$$

Second, substitute the solution for P_1 into the other equation and solve for P_2:

$$D_1(PV - P_2) + D_2 P_2 = 10PV$$

$$P_2 = \frac{10PV - D_1(PV - P_2)}{D_2} = \frac{PV(10 - D_1)}{-D_1 + D_2}$$

Third, substitute P_2 back into the first equation in order to get P_1 in terms of PV and durations:

$$P_1 = PV - P_2 = PV - \frac{PV(10 - D_1)}{-D_1 + D_2}$$

Combination 1: 30-Year and 20-Year

$$P_1 = PV - \frac{PV(10 - D_1)}{-D_1 + D_2} = 414,642.86 - \frac{\$414,642.86(10 - 10.7834)}{-10.7834 + 9.6148} \approx 136,674.02$$

$$P_2 = \frac{PV(10 - D_1)}{-D_1 + D_2} = \frac{\$414,642.86(10 - 10.7834)}{-10.7834 + 96148} \approx 277,968.84$$

Combination 2: 30-Year and 10-Year

$$P_1 = PV - \frac{PV(10 - D_1)}{-D_1 + D_2} = 414,642.86 - \frac{\$414,642.86(10 - 10.7834)}{-10.7834 + 6.7966} \approx 333,168.02$$

$$P_2 = \frac{PV(10 - D_1)}{-D_1 + D_2} = \frac{\$414,642.86(10 - 10.7834)}{-10.7834 + 6.7966} \approx 81,474.84$$

Dividing these values by the computed bond prices gives the numbers of units needed in each bond. Notice that $P_1 + P_2 = \$414,642.86$ by definition.

This is an example of a flat yield curve, or as we will understand in the next chapter, a flat term structure in which all maturities have the same yield. If the yield changes from 9 percent, then D_1, D_2, P_1, P_2, and P will change as well, but their changes will be offsetting so that the portfolio value matches that of the obligation. Therefore, the parameters of the model have changed. But the original number of bonds purchased for the portfolio remains the same. This means that the value of the portfolio has changed as shown in Table 2.6. As you can see, if yields fall to 8 percent, then bond prices P_1 and P_2 have risen, PV has risen, but $P_1 + P_2$ is still

TABLE 2.6 Immunizing against Interest Rate Movements

	8% Yield	9% Yield	10% Yield
Obligation	$1,000,000	$1,000,000	$1,000,000
Rate	8%	9%	10%
N (years)	10	10	10
# of coupons per year	2	2	2
PV of Obligation	$456,387	$414,643	$376,889
Price$_{10}$	106.8	100	93.77
Price$_{20}$	111.31	100	90.54
Price$_{30}$	109.9	100	91.54
Duration$_{10}$	6.9103	6.7966	6.6816
Duration$_{20}$	10.0623	9.6148	9.1793
Duration$_{30}$	11.5695	10.7834	10.0565
Combination 1: 30-Year & 20-Year			
P_1	−18,848.62	136,674.02	352,610.68
P_2	475,235.57	277,968.84	24,278.80
Combination 2: 30-Year & 10-Year			
P_1	302,645.45	333,168.02	370,578.89
P_2	153,741.50	81,474.84	6,310.59

essentially the same as *PV*. Note that immunization requires shorting the 30-year bond when yields fall to 8 percent. This is because the duration on the 20-year bond is now 10.06 which, by itself, almost exactly matches the duration on the liability. Thus, the second, longer-duration 30-year bond is not needed and is therefore sold short to provide funds to purchase more of the 20-year bond.

Immunization also holds in the opposite direction for small increases in rates to, say, 10 percent. Therefore, the value of the portfolio relative to the obligation is immunized from interest rate changes and the employer has constructed a dynamic hedge against interest rate risk, ensuring that the obligation can be met with no further investment.

APPLICATIONS—LIABILITY DISCOUNTING AND CASH MATCHING

EXAMPLE 2.7

Extending the concept of this example, suppose a pension plan has liabilities that are expected to grow over time and wants to invest in bonds to provide the necessary cash flows against these future obligations. Suppose it does so at a time when yields are near historic lows. What, specifically, should the bond portfolio manager be concerned about with respect to interest rate risk beyond duration? (Hint: think convexity.)

EXAMPLE 2.8

When regulation Q was lifted, savings & loans (S&Ls) suddenly found themselves competing with commercial banks for savings deposits. S&Ls' balance sheets were dominated by long-term mortgage loans. Detail the changing landscape for S&L risk as a result of this deregulation. (Hint: the duration of liabilities and assets diverged.)

EXAMPLE 2.9

Cash matching: let's add some realism to the pension problem. Suppose, as given, there are 10 bonds, ranging in maturity from a one-year zero to a six-year bond.

 Go to the companion website for more details (see Pension under Chapter 2 Examples).

The coupons and cash flows are given in the following table.

Example 2.9 Table A

					Bonds							
Year	1	2	3	4	5	6	7	8	9	10	Reqd	Actual
1	10	7	8	6	7	5	10	8	7	100	100	
2	10	7	8	6	7	5	10	8	107	0	200	
3	10	7	8	6	7	5	110	108	0	0	800	
4	,10	7	8	6	7	105	0	0	0	0	100	
5	10	7	8	106	107	0	0	0	0	0	800	
6	110	107	108	0	0	0	0	0	0	0	1200	
p	109	94.8	99.5	93.1	97.2	92.9	110	104	102	95.2		
x												

The market prices of the bonds are given in the second-to-last row. The pension has estimated its retirement obligations for the next six years, which are given in the next-to-last column (Req'd). We wish to invest in a portfolio of bonds whose cash flows will be sufficient to honor these obligations. Letting the last row, x, denote the quantity of each bond and the last column (Actual) denote the realized cash flow in dollars for each year, we wish to invest an amount, px, that is just enough to cover the obligations. That is, we want a solution to the problem:

$$\min \sum_{j=1}^{6} p_j x_j \quad \text{subject to}$$

$$\sum_{j=1}^{6} c_{ij} x_j \geq y_i; \ i = 1, \ldots, 6$$

$$x_j \geq 0; \ j = 1, \ldots, 6$$

Here, c_{ij} refers to the coupon in year i on bond j.

(continued)

(continued)

This is a *linear programming* problem that we solve in the *Pension* tab of Chapter 2 Examples.xlsx, using Excel's Solver (click on Excel's Data tab at the top of the sheet). Cell L9 is the sum of our expenditure, which we want to minimize, and we are searching for a combination of bonds (x), zero amounts or better (first constraint), whose total value in each year is sufficient to cover the necessary obligation (second constraint). The problem is set up in the spreadsheet as this:

Example 2.9 Table B

	Bonds											
Year	1	2	3	4	5	6	7	8	9	10	Reqd	Actual
1	10	7	8	6	7	5	10	8	7	100	100	
2	10	7	8	6	7	5	10	8	107	0	200	
3	10	7	8	6	7	5	110	108	0	0	800	
4	10	7	8	6	7	105	0	0	0	0	100	
5	10	7	8	106	107	0	0	0	0	0	800	
6	110	107	108	0	0	0	0	0	0	0	1200	
p	109	94.8	99.5	93.1	97.2	92.9	110	104	102	95.2		
x	0.0	11.2	0.0	6.8	0.0	0.0	0.0	6.3	0.0	0.0		

The Solver Parameters window used to solve this problem looks like this:

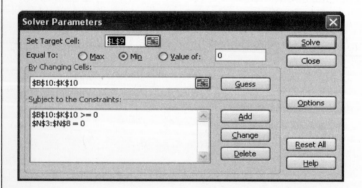

Solving this problem gives us the solution:

Example 2.9 Table C

						Bonds						
Year	1	2	3	4	5	6	7	8	9	10	Reqd	Actual	Difference
1	10	7	8	6	7	5	10	8	7	100	100	172	−72
2	10	7	8	6	7	5	10	8	107	0	200	200	0
3	10	7	8	6	7	5	110	108	0	0	800	800	0
4	10	7	8	6	7	105	0	0	0	0	100	119	−19
5	10	7	8	106	107	0	0	0	0	0	800	800	0
6	110	107	108	0	0	0	0	0	0	0	1200	1200	0
p	109	94.8	99.5	93.1	97.2	92.9	110	104	102	95.2	2381.1388		
x	0.0	11.2	0.0	6.8	0.0	0.0	0.0	6.3	0.3	0.0			

Notice that in some cases, the actual cash flow exceeds the required cash flow, suggesting that this particular set of bonds will not match our objective perfectly and that we have therefore overallocated to this portfolio. Nevertheless, we have satisfied our obligation.

PENSION LOGIC

Here is a practical savings problem that involves compounding. Suppose you are 25 years old and earn a salary set at the beginning of the year to Y. Your plan for retirement is to save a fraction, d, of each year's salary. This savings, dY will earn interest each year equal to r. Also, your salary is expected to grow at rate g annually. Derive an expression for the cumulative savings if you work N years.

It makes sense to break this problem into parts. The first year's savings is dY dollars, and this earns interest, compounded annually, for N years. Therefore at the end of N years, you should have $dY(1 + r)^N$. At the beginning of the second year, your salary has grown to $Y(1 + g)$ and you save the same fraction of this salary, which earns interest for $N - 1$ years (and so on). Thus, this part grows to $dY(1 + g)(1 + r)^{N-1}$. Let's now extend this logic. The total S of all your savings over the N years until retirement will be equal to the sum:

$$S = dY(1 + r)^N + dY(1 + g)(1 + r)^{N-1}$$
$$+ \cdots + dY(1 + g)^{N-1}(1 + r)^{N-(N-1)} + dY(1 + g)^N$$

We solve this like any other geometric series (see the appendix to this chapter). In this case, we multiply both sides of this relation by

$\frac{(1+r)}{(1+g)}$ yielding:

$$S\left(\frac{1+r}{1+g}\right) = dY\left[\frac{(1+r)^{N+1}}{(1+g)}\right] + dY(1+r)^N + \cdots + dY(1+g)^{N-2}(1+r)^2$$
$$+ dY(1+g)^{N-1}(1+r)$$

Now, subtract this equation from the first equation, and because the bulk of these two equations cancel, we get:

$$S - S\left(\frac{1+r}{1+g}\right) = -dY\left[\frac{(1+r)^{N+1}}{(1+g)}\right] + dY(1+g)^N$$

$$S = \frac{dY\left[(1+g)^{N+1} - (1+r)^{N+1}\right]}{(g-r)}$$

The chapter spreadsheet contains an example (labeled DC, for defined contributions) which states that for a 30-year career with a starting salary of \$31,000, growth rate of 4 percent, rate of return of 7 percent, and an annual contribution rate of 15.2 percent, you would have saved a total of \$749,519 for retirement.

Let's shift the problem a bit and consider the idea of income replacement. Now, you contemplate retirement thinking you will require an annuity of \$A per year to begin with but which will have to grow by π percent to keep your purchasing power constant (COLA adjustment). Mortality tables indicate that you should expect to live T years in retirement. You think you will need a nest egg equal to \$R to draw from and that any savings that remain each year are invested at r percent. How much should R be?

Assume that both interest and annual annuity withdrawal occur at the end of each year. The following schedule shows that at the end of year one, your savings have grown to $(1+r)R$ and that you withdraw your first

TABLE 2.7 Pension Logic

Time	Net Savings
0	R
1	$(1+r)R - (1+\pi)A$
2	$(1+r)[(1+r)R - (1+\pi)A] - (1+\pi)A$
3	$(1+r)[(1+r)^2R - (1+r)(1+\pi)A - (1+\pi)^2A] - (1+\pi)^3A$
4	$(1+r)^4R - (1+r)^3(1-\pi)A - (1+r)^2(1+\pi)^2A - (1+r)(1+\pi)^3A - (1+\pi)^4A$

payment equal to $(1 + \pi)A$. The entries in the table show the balance to your savings.

Generalizing to time T, we see that the compounded value of the nest egg R must be sufficient to cover the sum of all the annuity payments.

$$(1 + r)^T R - A \sum_{t=0}^{T} (1 + \pi)^{T-t}(1 + r)^t \geq 0$$

The ratio R/A is the multiple required in savings over the annual annuity. Given the expected time in retirement (T), the return on savings (r), and the expected COLA (π), then one can solve for the required nest egg (given an annual annuity target).

$$\frac{R}{A} \geq \frac{\sum_{t=0}^{T} (1 + \pi)^{T-t}(1 + r)^t}{(1 + r)^T}$$

While this equation is solvable using a spreadsheet, it is tedious. Let's simplify the math by assuming continuous compounding. This will give us an equivalent expression in continuous time that we can integrate easily:

$$\sum_{t=0}^{T} (1 + \pi)^{T-t}(1 + r)^t \approx \int_{0}^{T} \left[e^{\pi(T-t)} e^{rt} \right] dt = \int_{0}^{T} e^{\pi(T-t)+rt} dt$$

Solving the integral yields the solution:

$$= \left(\frac{1}{r - \pi} \right) e^{\pi T + (r-\pi)t} \Big|_{0}^{T}$$

Therefore R/A must equal this expression:

$$= \left(\frac{1}{r - \pi} \right) \left[e^{rT} - e^{\pi T} \right]$$

If, for example, savings earn 5 percent and the COLA is 2.5 percent and he wishes to receive the annuity for $T = 25$ years, then the multiple would be equal to:

$$\frac{R}{A} = \frac{\left(\frac{1}{r - \pi} \right) \left[e^{rT} - e^{\pi T} \right]}{e^{rT}}$$

$$\frac{R}{A} = 18.6$$

The chapter spreadsheet contains an example illustrating this problem (labeled DB, for defined benefit). If you require $50,000 per year to begin retirement and expect to earn 7 percent on any balance to your retirement fund and expect 2.5 percent inflation (COLA adjustment), then with 25 years of expected longevity in retirement, you would have required a nest egg of $750,386.

Workers often contemplate how much they'd need to retire. Given the rates suggested here and the 25-year life expectancy after retirement, an individual who needs to replace 50 percent of an ending salary equal to $150,000, will require A = $75,000 to start with. With these assumptions, savings, R, will need to be $1.4 million. If, at retirement, all savings are invested in Treasury bonds yielding 4 percent, then savings will have to increase to approximately $1.56 million. This solution requires that $r > \pi$.

Let's compare this to an annuity. Suppose for simplicity that there is no inflation and therefore $\pi = 0$ and bonds yield 4 percent. (You can substitute these numbers into the pension logic spreadsheet for details.) In this case, with 25 years' life expectancy, the nest egg required is $1,185,226. Consider, instead, an annuity that the retiree could purchase that pays $75,000 in perpetuity. This would hedge longevity risk (living past his 25-year postretirement life expectancy). We priced this annuity earlier; it is $P = c/r$, where c now = $75,000. The annuity costs $1,875,000.

Many public and private pension plans are defined benefits (DB), in which employees receive credit for service equal to some fixed percentage of their salary for every year of service. Suppose that service credit is 2 percent. Thus, after N years of service, the liability to the state pension plan is $N*2$ percent times some average of ending salary. Therefore, an individual who works 30 years and ends with an average ending salary of $125,000 will be entitled to $75,000 until death (there are survivorship options that we will ignore for simplicity). This amount is also typically adjusted for an annual COLA.

What is interesting here is that the DB has a market value to the employee of $1,875,000; it is the amount of his savings that would equal his defined benefit.

RISKY COUPONS

In general, all cash flows are risky. Although U.S. Treasury securities are secured by the government's power to tax, that does not make them riskless. Nevertheless, we typically refer to a U.S. Treasury rate as the riskless rate and will continue to do so, as is the convention. Corporate bonds, on the other hand, carry no such guarantees and, to a lesser extent, neither do state nor municipal bonds. As such, these bonds are priced taking into account the perceived likelihood that the issuer may default on its obligation to make payments to creditors. We are now faced with the challenge of pricing bonds that are subject to *credit risk*.

Here is the intuition on how these bonds are priced: Assume that at each coupon date there is a small likelihood δ that the firm will default and the coupon (plus any subsequent coupons) will not be paid. Assume as well that the likelihood of default in any given period does not depend on the likelihood of default in any other period (default events are independent). Then, for an n-period bond, we can write the expected price as a discounted present value of expected coupons, that is, as:

$$P = \frac{(1-\delta)C}{(1+r)} + \frac{(1-\delta)^2 C}{(1+r)^2} + \cdots + \frac{(1-\delta)^n C}{(1+r)^n} + \frac{(1-\delta)^n M}{(1+r)^n}$$

Thus, $(1-\delta)$ is the likelihood that the coupon will be paid in period one, $(1-\delta)^2$ is the likelihood that the coupon is paid in periods one *and* two and finally, $(1-\delta)^n$ is the likelihood that the coupon is paid in period n and all previous periods. We can solve this power series using the techniques outlined previously to get:

$$P = \frac{(1-\delta)C}{(\delta+r)}\left[1 - \frac{(1-\delta)^n}{(1+r)^n}\right] + \frac{M(1-\delta)^n}{(\delta+r)(1+r)^{n-1}}\frac{(r+\delta)}{(1+r)}$$

Compare this to our earlier solution:

$$P = \frac{C}{r}\left[1 - \frac{1}{(1+r)^n}\right] + \frac{M}{(1+r)^n}$$

Admittedly, allowing for default makes pricing more complicated. Upon examination, it is easy to see, though, that setting the default likelihood to zero makes this equal to the standard pricing formula for an *n*-period bond with riskless coupons. In general, however, if default probabilities are nonzero, then the bond's value clearly declines with δ. In fact, as long as the default probability is greater than zero, then the price with risk is strictly less than the price of riskless bonds. Bondholders therefore pay a discount for risk bonds (alternatively, they pay a premium for riskless bonds).

INFLATION RISK AND TIPS

TIPS, which stands for Treasury Inflation Protected Securities, offer insurance against inflation risk. Inflation reduces the *real* return from

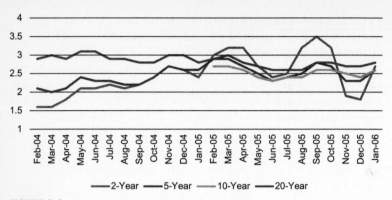

FIGURE 2.2 Breakeven Rate: Nominal over TIPS

nominal coupon payments, that is, the purchasing power of this stream of cash flows. TIPS compensate the bondholder by adjusting the coupon for realized inflation. In principle, the spread between nominal Treasuries and TIPS should provide a noisy gauge of market inflation expectations. The noise reflects a liquidity premium as well as an unexpected inflation premium. TIPS investors require the liquidity premium because the TIPS market is relatively small compared to the conventional Treasury market. The unexpected inflation premium arises because TIPS yields are adjusted using *actual* inflation while conventional Treasury yields reflect *expected* inflation. The spread in nominal Treasuries over TIPS is therefore a rough forecast of inflation expectations. Figure 2.2 (see TIPS in Chapter 2 Examples.xlsx) shows nominal Treasury yields over TIPS for the period February 2004 to January 2006.

These spreads represent bond market participants' inflation *expectations* for different horizons (they understate inflation expectations because TIPS also carry a liquidity premium). For example, in 2004, these expectations were converging over horizons 2 to 20 years to about 2.7 percent (see the table in the TIPS spreadsheet for specific values) at the end of 2004 with long-term expected inflation (embedded in 20-year TIPS) still close to 3 percent and short-term expected inflation as embodied by the two-year TIPS around 2.5 percent. There were two distinct jumps in the two-year TIPS in 2005 coinciding with the Fed's response to its own perceptions of inflationary pressures and its tightening of short-term yields.

A BOND PORTFOLIO STRATEGY (OPTIONAL)

Bond managers typically make yield curve bets based on their perceptions of general movements in the yield curve over the portfolio-holding period (Peterson and Gardiner 2006). Portfolios are typically formed on the basis of these expectations and rebalanced monthly to reflect both changes in realized yields as well as expectations revisions.

At the beginning of each quarter, we construct a bond portfolio (the active portfolio) consisting of 2-year, 5-year, 10-year, and 30-year Treasury securities reflecting a yield curve bet based on current one-step ahead forecasts at each of these four points on the yield curve. The so-called benchmark portfolio is also constructed from the same four Treasury securities. Our desire is that the active portfolio adds value over the benchmark portfolio (see Chapter 10 on active management for a deeper explanation). Our strategy is this: if the current quarter yield is forecasted to fall (rise) relative to the last observed yield for a specific on-the-run (OTR) security, then the portfolio takes a long (short) position in that bond.

Each bond's weight in the portfolio is a function of relative yield curve duration (using the beginning of month [BOM] durations) and BOM market value of the OTR bonds. Appropriate OTR securities for each month were obtained through Lehman Brothers along with relevant information for each security, such as month-end price, yield, modified duration, and total return. Citigroup provided the 30-day Treasury bill return (to proxy the return on cash) and the amount outstanding for each security for each month that was pulled from the Bureau of Public Debt website.

Both the active portfolio and the benchmark portfolio were rebalanced in subsequent months of each quarter. This particular benchmark eliminates the performance impact due to risk factors other than interest rate risk (for example, credit or prepayment risk). The portfolio holds the benchmark securities plus a long or short cash position as needed to maintain proper interest rate exposure. There are no transactions costs. The performance measure is the monthly gross return of the portfolio over the benchmark (we call this the active return, or alpha).

A typical portfolio evaluation example is presented below in Table 2.8 for the first quarter 1988. The top of the table lists the latest observed yields (end of month yields for December 1987) and the analyst's initial forecasts for the upcoming quarter. Our fictional client calculates the forecasted change in the yield and makes a tenth of a year duration bet, that is, takes a long or short position of duration 0.1 for each security in the portfolio

TABLE 2.8 Portfolio Construction Example

Initial Data

Maturity	Current Yield*	Forecast	Difference	Bet (DC)		
					Analyst:	XX
					Quarter:	1988Q1
2-year	7.78	7.6	-0.18	0.1		
5-year	8.41	8.2	-0.21	0.1		
10-year	8.86	8.6	-0.26	0.1		
30-year	8.98	8.7	-0.28	0.1		

*31 Dec 87

	Benchmark			Performance			Portfolio		Value		
JAN	BOM MV	BOM Dur	Yield	MV_wt	DC	Return	req'd DC	MV	MV_wt	Return	Alpha
Cash	$0.00	0.00	0.45	0.00	0.00	0.45	0.00	-$3,694.13	-0.10	0.45	
2-year	$9,304.98	1.81	7.25	0.26	0.47	1.56	0.57	$11,271.57	0.32	1.56	
5-year	$7,682.83	4.15	7.78	0.22	0.90	3.24	1.00	$8,539.64	0.24	3.24	
10-year	$9,359.57	6.70	8.27	0.26	1.77	4.59	1.87	$9,889.83	0.28	4.59	
30-year	$9,198.28	10.44	8.44	0.26	2.70	6.40	2.80	$9,538.75	0.27	6.40	
	$35,545.67			1.00	5.84	3.97	6.24	$35,545.67	1.00	4.22	0.25
FEB											
Cash	$0.00	0.00	0.45	0.00	0.00	0.45	0.00	-$3,837.23	-0.10	0.45	
2-year	$9,409.23	1.81	7.12	0.25	0.46	0.72	0.56	$11,449.29	0.31	0.72	
5-year	$7,926.14	4.09	7.69	0.21	0.88	1.01	0.98	$8,829.44	0.24	1.01	
10-year	$9,789.15	6.69	8.21	0.27	1.77	1.04	1.87	$10,340.67	0.28	1.04	
30-year	$9,787.19	10.78	8.36	0.27	2.86	1.53	2.96	$10,129.54	0.27	1.53	
	$36,911.71			1.00	5.97	1.08	6.37	$36,911.71	1.00	1.13	0.05

MAR

	MV	Dur						MV	DC	DC
Cash	$0.00	0.00	0.42	0.00	0.00	0.42	0.00	–$3,708.07	–0.10	0.42
2-year	$8,839.74	1.82	7.37	0.25	0.45	0.19	0.55	$10,820.71	0.30	0.19
5-year	$7,694.87	4.17	8.05	0.21	0.89	–0.98	0.99	$8,557.71	0.24	–0.98
10-year	$9,890.88	6.62	8.56	0.28	1.82	–1.93	1.92	$10,434.48	0.29	–1.93
30-year	$9,539.76	11.22	8.78	0.27	2.97	–3.74	3.07	$9,860.43	0.27	–3.74
	$35,965.26			1.00	6.13	–1.69	6.53	$35,965.26	–0.12	–1.80

BOM: Beginning of month
Dur: Duration
MV: Market value
DC: Duration contribution

47

relative to the benchmark. From the BOM market values, he then calculates the market value weights (MV_wt). The benchmark return for January 1988 is simply the sum of the market value weighted end-of-month observed returns (for example, $3.97 = 0.26 * 1.56 + 0.22 * 3.24 + 0.26 * 4.59 + 0.26 * 6.40$).

The individual duration contributions (DC) required to place the desired bet at each point on the yield curve are also calculated from the market value weights as DC = (MV_wt) × BOM duration). The *portfolio* return for January 1988 is based on the *required* duration contribution, which is the observed duration contribution (DC), plus the duration contribution bet (0.1). The portfolio holdings consist of the BOM market value ($35,546) allocated across securities with weights given by the relative required DC, that is, the required DC divided by the BOM duration. For example, the portfolio invests $11,272 = (0.57/1.81) * $35,546 in the two-year note to increase the duration contribution from 0.47 to 0.57 to reflect a long duration bet on this point on the yield curve (the analyst in this case forecasted the yield to fall). The short cash position is required because the portfolio is overexposed relative to the benchmark due to the expected decline in the yield curve. The new market value weights reflect the increase in the required duration contribution and, using these, the month's return to the portfolio (4.22 percent) can be compared to the benchmark return (3.97 percent) to arrive at the alpha (0.25 percent).

SUMMARY

Valuation of fixed income securities is basically an exercise in finding the discounted present value of their cash flows. This process involves solving finite and infinite (in the case of annuities) geometric series. Understanding this methodology provides a powerful tool in determining value not only for bonds but for virtually any kind of installment loan including mortgages. That methodology leads us immediately to amortization, which, in turn, is linked to the relationship between price and interest and the time horizon. For bonds, these concepts help us motivate the notion of duration and convexity, which help us understand interest rate risk in the pricing model. We then develop ways to immunize, or hedge, interest rate risk—hedging is a topic we return to many times in succeeding chapters. Applications are extended to cover a diversity of topics, including cash matching of pension assets and liabilities for hedging purposes, the impact of risky coupons (not all bonds are riskless Treasuries), general cash flow analysis (pension logic) and finally, a first look at a portfolio strategy that invests in bonds.

APPENDIX 2.1: SOLVING INFINITE AND FINITE POWER SERIES

Infinite Series

$$P = \frac{C}{(1+r)} + \frac{C}{(1+r)^2} + \cdots + \frac{C}{(1+r)^n} + \cdots \qquad \text{Eq. A.1}$$

Multiply both sides of Eq. A.1 by $(1+r)$:

$$P(1+r) = C + \frac{C}{(1+r)} + \cdots + \frac{C}{(1+r)^n} + \cdots \qquad \text{Eq. A.2}$$

Subtract Eq. A.2 from Eq. A.1:

$$P - P(1+r) = \frac{C}{(1+r)} + \cdots + \frac{C}{(1+r)^n} + \cdots - C - \frac{C}{(1+r)} - \frac{C}{(1+r)^2}$$
$$- \cdots - \frac{C}{(1+r)^n} - \cdots$$

Collect terms and simplify:

$$P - P(1+r) = -C$$
$$-Pr = -C$$
$$P = \frac{C}{r}$$

Finite Series

$$P = \frac{C}{(1+r)} + \frac{C}{(1+r)^2} + \frac{C}{(1+r)^n} + \frac{M}{(1+r)^n} \qquad \text{Eq. A.3}$$

Multiply both sides of Eq. A.3 by $(1+r)$:

$$P + Pr = C + \frac{C}{(1+r)} + \frac{C}{(1+r)^{n-1}} + \frac{M}{(1+r)^{n-1}} \qquad \text{Eq. A.4}$$

Subtract Eq. A.4 from Eq. A.3 and solve for P to get:

$$P - P(1 + r) = -c + \frac{c}{(1 + r)^n} + \frac{M}{(1 + r)^n} - \frac{M}{(1 + r)^{n-1}}$$

$$P = \frac{-c}{-r} + \frac{c}{-r(1 + r)^n} + \frac{M}{-r(1 + r)^n} - \frac{M}{-r(1 + r)^{n-1}}$$

$$P = \frac{c}{r}\left[1 - \frac{1}{(1 + r)^n}\right] + \frac{M}{-r}\left[\frac{1}{(1 + r)^n} - \frac{1}{(1 + r)^{n-1}}\right]$$

$$P = \frac{c}{r}\left[1 - \frac{1}{(1 + r)^n}\right] + \frac{M}{r}\left[\frac{r}{(1 + r)^n}\right]$$

$$P = \frac{c}{r}\left[1 - \frac{1}{(1 + r)^n}\right] + \frac{M}{(1 + r)^n}$$

REFERENCE

Peterson, Steven, and Bryan Gardiner. 2006. *The value of yield curve forecasts.* Virginia Retirement System, Working Paper.

CHAPTER 3

Term Structure

What wise men do in the beginning, fools do in the end.
— Warren Buffett

DISCOUNTING USING SPOT RATES

There are plenty of excellent treatments of the term structure. I therefore keep this chapter short and to the point. The *yield curve* is a plot of Treasury spot rates. The *spot rate* is the current market interest rate for a given term (for example, the yield on the one-year Treasury bill). For example, lending $1 at 10 percent for a single year means that the one-year spot rate is 0.10. If you were to lend the $1 for a period of two years at 10 percent annually, then the two-year spot rate is also 0.10. So, for the one-year spot, s_1, and a $1 investment, the factor by which that investment will grow is $(1 + s_1)$. For the same $1, over two years, that investment will grow to $(1 + s_2)^2 = (1 + s_2)(1 + s_2)$, or 100^*s_2 percent in each of two years. In general, then, $1 will grow at $(1 + s_t)^t$ for a period of t years at an annual rate equal to s_t. If the rate is compounded m times per year, then this changes to: $\left(1 + \frac{s_t}{m}\right)^{mt}$. And, if the rate is compounded continuously, then as we have shown before, $\lim\left(1 + \frac{s_t}{m}\right)^{mt} = e^{s_t * t}$, where the second time term (t) denotes the span of years. Discounting is just the inverse operation. For example, a cash flow of $1 that is to be realized in t years has value $\frac{1}{(1+s_t)^t}$ at the present time. If interest is compounded m times per year, then the discount factor $d(t)$ becomes $\frac{1}{\left(1+\frac{s_t}{m}\right)^{mt}}$, and if continuously compounded, $d(t) = e^{-rt}$. Moreover, if we knew the term structure of spot rates, then a cash flow stream through time of $\{c_0, c_1, c_2, \ldots, c_n\}$ to be received in periods $t = 1, \ldots, n$ has present value $PV = (d_0 * c_0) + (d_1 * c_1) + \ldots + (d_n * c_n)$, where the d_i are the aforementioned discount factors. Notice that this formulation is different from that for valuing bond-paying coupons $\{c_0, \ldots, c_n\}$. The difference is that in the bond valuation case, we determined the internal rate of return (the yield to maturity), which was a single discount factor; it was a geometric mean (see Chapter 1). In reality, if one knew the spot rates for differing time periods, then one could discount a stream of cash flows using the proper discount factors and not a single factor like the yield to maturity. Keep in mind, however, that the purpose of calculating yield to maturity on a bond was to find a unique rate of return that equated the present value of a cash flow stream to its market price.

EXAMPLE 3.1

As an example, suppose the interest rate is constant at 4 percent, implying that the yield curve is flat. When applied to a 10-year stream of net cash flows, each of which is $2 million, the estimated present value is $PV = \sum \frac{2M}{(1.04)^t}$ for $t = 1, \ldots, 10$. The discount factors $d(t)$ are $\frac{1}{(1.04)^t}$ here. This method would certainly give misleading results if the yield curve were not flat. The point here is that we always seek the proper discount factor; rarely is it constant over time, and any example that assumes so is going to produce some model error as a result. That's why you should recompute this PV using the proper set of discount rates. Suppose the proper set of discount rates $(Disc_S)$ were based on the following term structure of interest rates $(Yield_S)$ (from Chapter 3 Examples.xlsx).

TABLE 3.1 Fixed versus Floating Discount Factors

Time	Yield$_C$	Yield$_S$	Discount$_C$	Discount$_S$	Flows	Present Value$_C$	Present Value$_S$
1	0.0400	0.0309	0.9615	0.9700	2,000,000	1,923,076.92	1,940,052.38
2	0.0400	0.0345	0.9246	0.9344	2,000,000	1,849,112.43	1,868,826.59
3	0.0400	0.0362	0.8890	0.8988	2,000,000	1,777,992.72	1,797,625.55
4	0.0400	0.0374	0.8548	0.8634	2,000,000	1,709,608.38	1,726,811.85
5	0.0400	0.0386	0.8219	0.8275	2,000,000	1,643,854.21	1,654,963.44
6	0.0400	0.0397	0.7903	0.7919	2,000,000	1,580,629.05	1,583,824.47
7	0.0400	0.0407	0.7599	0.7563	2,000,000	1,519,835.63	1,512,694.10
8	0.0400	0.0414	0.7307	0.7231	2,000,000	1,461,380.41	1,446,107.63
9	0.0400	0.0420	0.7026	0.6903	2,000,000	1,405,173.47	1,380,687.81
10	0.0400	0.0427	0.6756	0.6583	2,000,000	1,351,128.34	1,316,546.67
Total						16,221,791.56	16,228,140.51

Thus, while the *PV* was $16,221,791.56 using a constant 4 percent discount rate, it is now $16,228,140.51. In general, we would prefer to use discount rates that more precisely match the market's time preferences, which would suggest working with the term structure of interest rates and their implied forward rates.

 Go to the companion website for more details.

FORWARD RATES

Forward rates are interest rates for money *to be* borrowed between *any two dates in the future,* but determined *today.* For example, I don't know what the one-year spot rate will be next year. I do know, however, what the one-year spot rate is today. I also know the two-year spot rate today. So, I could do one of two things:

1. I could lend $1 today for a period of two years at the two-year spot rate, earning $(1 + s_2)^2$.
2. I could lend $1 today for one year, earning $(1 + s_1)$ and then roll this amount over at the spot rate that materializes one year from now (whatever that is).

The one-year spot rate, one year hence, is unobserved. Let's denote this *forward* rate by f. Then it must be true that the following relation holds:

$$(1 + s_1)(1 + f) = (1 + s_2)^2$$

The rate f is referred to as the one-year *forward* rate. The presence of s_1 and s_2 *imply* a forward rate in this case. It is:

$$f = \frac{(1 + s_2)^2}{1 + s_1} - 1$$

For example, if $s_1 = 5.571$ and $s_2 = 6.088$, then $f = 6.6$ percent $f = 6.6\%$. That is,

$$(1.05571)(1.066) = (1.6088)^2$$

which means that the one year forward implied by s_1 and s_2 must equal 6.6 percent for us to be indifferent between a two-year loan at s_2 and two consecutive one-year loans at s_1 and f (assuming no transactions costs).

In sum, the forward rate structure is implied by the existing term structure of spot rates. Let's elaborate some on this concept. The notation f_{ij} is the forward rate between times t_i and t_j. So f_{12} is the forward rate between periods one and two; it is the forward one-year spot rate in the second year; f_{13} is the *two-year* forward implied to hold between the first and third year's known spot rates; f_{23} is the *one-year* forward in the third year; and so on. Generally then, we have:

$$\left(1 + s_j\right)^j = \left(1 + s_i\right)^i \left(1 + f_{ij}\right)^{j-i}$$

EXAMPLE 3.2

Let j, $i = 10,1$ respectively with spot rates 8 percent and 3 percent. Then f_{ij} is the nine-year forward rate—it is the annual rate over the nine-year period in question that is implied by the term structure to hold between years 1 and 10. Mathematically:

$$f_{ij} = \left[\frac{\left(1 + s_j\right)^j}{\left(1 + s_i\right)^i}\right]^{\frac{1}{j-i}} - 1$$

$$f_{1,10} = \left[\frac{(1 + 0.08)^{10}}{(1 + 0.03)^1}\right]^{\frac{1}{10-1}} - 1 = 0.086$$

With continuous compounding, the math is easier. We've already established that

$$\left(1 + s_i\right)^i = e^{s_i * t_i}$$

where we assume that s_i is the spot rate over t_i years. Therefore the forward/spot relationship given by:

$$\left(1 + s_j\right)^j = \left(1 + s_i\right)^i \left(1 + f_{ij}\right)^{j-i}$$

is now equivalent to:

$$e^{s_j * t_j} = \left(e^{s_i * t_i}\right)\left(e^{f\left(t_j - t_i\right)}\right)$$

Taking natural logarithms of both sides:

$$\left(s_j\right)\left(t_j\right) = \left(s_i\right)\left(t_i\right) + f\left(t_j - t_i\right)$$

$$f = \frac{(s_j)(t_j) - (s_i)(t_i)}{t_j - t_i}$$

Here t_j and t_i are integers. For example, with $t_j = 10$ and $t_i = 1$, then the nine-year forward rate (to appear as implied one year from now) is the difference between the 10 times the current 10-year and 1-year continuous spot rates divided by the integer nine.

EXAMPLE 3.3

Compute the forward curve using the following table of spot rates:

Example 3.3 Table A

Year	1	2	3	4	5	6	7
Spot	5.571	6.088	6.555	6.978	7.361	7.707	8.02
Forward	6.605	7.047	7.447	7.809	8.134	8.428	

Why do you think that these forward rates are plausible forecasts of future rates? The answer is that the forward rates are consistent with the current spot rate structure, and unless spot rates change over time, then these forwards will have to hold. Let's now fill out a matrix for all the possible forward rates implied by this term structure.

Example 3.3 Table B

Year	1	2	3	4	5	6	7
Spot	5.571	6.088	6.555	6.978	7.361	7.707	8.02
Forward	6.605	7.047	7.447	7.809	8.134	8.428	
	7.489	7.868	8.210	8.517	8.793		
	8.247	8.570	8.859	9.119			
	8.893	9.165	9.409				
	9.437	9.668					
	9.898						

Interpreting, 6.605 is the one-year forward rate (the rate to hold for one year beginning one year from now), 7.047 is the two-year forward (again, one year from now), and so on. The third row shows the

(continued)

(continued)
implied forward rates, consistent with the current term structure, that will hold two periods from now, the fourth row shows forward rates implied to hold three periods from now, and so on.

 Go to the companion website for more details (see **Forward Rates** under Chapter 3 Examples).

NPV REVISITED

EXAMPLE 3.4

Using the term structure given earlier, consider a net present value problem with initial outlay equal to $400 and with expected payout of $100 for each of the next five years (payable at the end of each year). What is the net present value of this project?

There are two equivalent ways of solving this problem. We first present the most direct method—and one that will be most intuitively appealing given what we know at this point about the term structure. We have five future cash flows and an initial (period 0) outlay. We want to discount the five future cash flows to the present. To that end, we compute the five discount rates using the spot curve.

Example 3.4 Table A

Year	1	2	3	4	5
Spot	5.571	6.088	6.555	6.978	7.361
Discount	0.947	0.889	0.827	0.764	0.701

Then we present value the cash flows and sum them:

Example 3.4 Table B

Period	0	1	2	3	4	5
Cash Flow	−400	100	100	100	100	100
Discount	1	0.947	0.889	0.827	0.764	0.701
PV	−400	94.72	88.85	82.66	76.35	70.11

The net present value of this investment is therefore $12.70.

SHORT RATES

Another way of approaching this problem involves working with the term structure's short rates. Short rates are one period implied forward rates, and because they will become so important later in asset valuation problems, we develop them now. The short rates are given in the first column of our forward rate analysis—this column is highlighted in Table 3.2 and italicized.

To reiterate, 6.605 percent is the one period rate implied by the current spot curve to hold one year from now. Likewise, 7.489 percent is the one period rate implied two years from now and so on. Geometrically linking these short rates will reproduce the original spot curve. For example: $[(1.0571)(1.06605)]^{0.5} - 1 = 0.06088$. These are useful for discounting single-period cash flows. For the current problem under consideration, we are expecting five years of cash flows, each in the amount of $100. The present value of the last $100 received in the last year is therefore $100. The present value of the project at the end of the fourth year is the discounted PV of this amount plus the $100 received in year four. The PV of the project at the end of the third year is the discounted value of this new amount plus, again, the $100 cash flow in period three. This is called a *running present value* and it is a convenient way to present value cash flows on the run. The problem is set up in Table 3.3:

TABLE 3.2 Estimating Short Rates

Year	1	2	3	4	5	6	7
Spot	5.571	6.088	6.555	6.978	7.361	7.707	8.02
Forward	*6.605*	7.047	7.447	7.809	8.134	8.428	
	7.489	7.868	8.210	8.517	8.793		
	8.247	8.570	8.859	9.119			
	8.893	9.165	9.409				
	9.437	9.668					
	9.898						

TABLE 3.3 Running PV

Period	0	1	2	3	4	5
Cash flow	−400	100	100	100	100	100
Discount	0.947	0.938	0.930	0.924	0.918	1
Run PV	12.74	435.73	357.90	277.22	191.83	100

The discount rates are the reciprocals of the short rates, that is, $0.947 = 1/(1.05571)$ and $0.918 = 1/(1.08893)$. These two solutions are equivalent (up to a rounding error).

Thus, we see that the current Treasury spot curve implied a term structure of forward rates, which become the discount factors that we use to solve present value problems. The short rates become important because any set of short rates can be used to build the entire term structure. Thus, all one needs are the short rates to solve any term structure problem. With running PV methods, we can present value projects and securities on the run using only short rates. The intuition is this—the standard present value method uses the discount factors d_i from the spot structure as we did in our first solution, that is:

$$PV(0) = c_0 + d_1 c_1 + d_2 c_2 + \cdots + d_n c_n$$

We can rewrite this basic discounting relation however as:

$$PV(0) = c_0 + d_1 \left(c_1 + \frac{d_2}{d_1} c_2 + \cdots + \frac{d_n}{d_1} c_n \right)$$

In the limit, any problem can be written as:

$$PV(t) = c_t + d_{t,t+1} PV(t + 1)$$

We therefore work backward to get the solution using the one period short rates $d_{t,t+1}$.

Finally, we show the entire short rate structure implied by the Treasury yield curve as of January 6, 2010. The spot rates for years 4, 6, 8, and 9 are interpolated since there are no Treasuries issued for these maturities.

The short rate structure is given in Table 3.5.

Each row in this table can be used to present value future cash flows beginning in the current year (row 1), beginning one year from now (row 2), and so on.

THE BOOTSTRAP METHOD

It is convenient to be able to determine a set of discount rates for zero coupon bonds from current coupon bonds. Recall, for example, the immunization problem of the previous chapter for which the liability had duration 10 years but there were no matching zero coupon bonds available to hold

TABLE 3.4 The Treasury Curve on January 6, 2010

Maturity	1	2	3	4	5	6	7	8	9	10	20	30
Spot Rate	0.004	0.010	0.016	0.021	0.026	0.030	0.033	0.035	0.037	0.039	0.046	0.047
Forward Implied	0.016	0.022	0.027	0.032	0.035	0.038	0.039	0.041	0.042	0.049	0.048	
	0.028	0.032	0.037	0.039	0.042	0.043	0.044	0.046	0.052	0.050		
	0.036	0.041	0.043	0.046	0.046	0.047	0.048	0.055	0.053			
	0.046	0.047	0.049	0.049	0.049	0.050	0.058	0.055				
	0.047	0.051	0.050	0.050	0.051	0.060	0.056					
	0.054	0.051	0.051	0.052	0.062	0.058						
	0.048	0.050	0.051	0.065	0.058							
	0.051	0.053	0.070	0.061								
	0.055	0.080	0.064									
	0.104	0.069										
	0.033											

TABLE 3.5 Implied Short Rates on January 6, 2010

Short Rates (Single Period)											
0.004	0.016	0.028	0.036	0.046	0.047	0.054	0.048	0.051	0.055	0.104	0.033
0.016	0.028	0.036	0.046	0.047	0.054	0.048	0.051	0.055	0.104	0.033	
0.028	0.036	0.046	0.047	0.054	0.048	0.051	0.055	0.104	0.033		
0.036	0.046	0.047	0.054	0.048	0.051	0.055	0.104	0.033			
0.046	0.047	0.054	0.048	0.051	0.055	0.104	0.033				
0.047	0.054	0.048	0.051	0.055	0.104	0.033					
0.054	0.048	0.051	0.055	0.104	0.033						
0.048	0.051	0.055	0.104	0.033							
0.051	0.055	0.104	0.033								
0.055	0.104	0.033									
0.104	0.033										
0.033											

against that liability. Bootstrapping is a method that extracts discount rates for zero coupon bonds using observed prices on existing coupon bonds. I will demonstrate the method and follow it with an application.

Assume all bonds have a face value M of $100. The following table lists some hypothetical bond information on maturity, coupon, and price.

Bootstrap Table A

M	Maturity (Years)	Annual Coupon	Market Price
$100	0.25	0	98.5
$100	0.5	0	97
$100	1	0	93
$100	1.5	$4	94
$100	2	$8	98

We will use continuous discounting, which means that the continuously discounted rate r_c is determined as before, that is, as

$$e^{r_c} = \lim_{m \to \infty} \left(1 + \frac{r}{m}\right)^m$$

Taking natural logarithms extracts the continuously compounded rate of return, viz.,

$$r_c = m \ln\left(1 + \frac{r}{m}\right)$$

The first bond is a 90-day maturity zero coupon bond that returns $1.5 on the $98.5 price for a discrete annual return of $4*\$1.5/\$98.5 = 6.09$ percent. Converting to continuous time, this rate is $4*\ln(1 + .0609/4) = 6.04$ percent. We do likewise for the six-month and the one-year bonds, which have discrete annual returns of 6.19 percent and 7.53 percent, respectively. Their continuously compounded analogs are 6.14 percent and 7.46 percent, respectively. The 1.5-year bond pays a $2 semiannual coupon and has market price equal to $94.

$$2\,e^{-0.0614/2} + 2e^{-0.0746} + 102e^{-r_c*1.5} = 94$$

This is easy to solve and gives $r_c = 8.19$ percent, which is the yield on a 1.5-year zero bond. Likewise, for the two-year bond paying a semiannual coupon of $4 with market price $98, we solve

$$4e^{-0.0614/2} + 4e^{-0.0746} + 4e^{-0.0819*1.5}104e^{-r_c*2} = 98$$

This returns a two-year zero yield, equal to 9 percent.

Bootstrap Table B

M	Maturity (Years)	Annual Coupon	Market Price	Annual Return	Continuous Return
$100	0.25	0	98.5	0.0609	0.0605
$100	0.5	0	97	0.0619	0.0614
$100	1	0	93	0.0753	0.0746
$100	1.5	$4	94		0.0819
$100	2	$8	98		0.0900

The last column in the table shows the continuous zero coupon yield. Using this method we can bootstrap an entire set of zero coupon yields across the term structure.

A *yield curve play* is a strategy that tries to exploit the forward rate structure. If, for example, we believe that short rates will remain low and the term structure is rising, then we could conceivably borrow by paying lower short yields and investing long, rolling over our short-term loans over time. Using the preceding table and forecasting that rates on 90-day bonds will stay near 6 percent, then we borrow at this rate and invest in two-year bonds yielding 9 percent. Every quarter, we could roll over our loans, effectively refinancing at the new 90-day yield. As long as short rates stay low, this is a good bet. But, as we saw in the previous chapter, this play does not come without its risk—the Fed could raise rates, for example, which would not only increase the cost of short-term borrowing but also depress the value of the bonds we invested in (as their yields begin to rise). The classic case of the yield curve play going wrong is Orange County, California in the mid-1990s.

DURATION REDUX

In the previous chapter, we worked exclusively with a flat term structure, in which interest centered on the sensitivity of bond prices to a change in yield, dP/dr. The assumption of a flat term structure is very restrictive. What happens when we relax this constraint? In a world in which spot rates differ across maturities, interest rate risk and duration are no longer tied to a single yield but to the entire term structure; more specifically, to movements in the term structure. That is, we now wish to evaluate $dP/d(r_i + \Delta)$, where the r_i are the spot rates that vary across maturities and Δ is a constant that shifts the term structure up or down in a parallel fashion. *Parallel shifts* are also restrictive but a necessary simplification—since we cannot control for spot rates varying independently by random amounts we instead study parallel shifts $\{s_1 + \Delta, s_2 + \Delta, \ldots, s_n + \Delta\}$.

With continuous compounding, the bond price formula from the previous chapter becomes:

$$P = \sum_{i=0}^{n} c_{ti} e^{-s_i t_i}$$

If the cash flows are constant across time, then $c_{ti} = c_i$. As before, duration is the weighted sum of the elapsed times to wait for cash flows divided by the bond price, that is,

$$D_{FW} = \frac{1}{P} \sum_{i=0}^{n} c_{ti} e^{-s_{ti} t_i} \, t_i$$

We call this the *Fisher-Weil duration*. If we shift the term structure by Δ, then the price of the asset changes accordingly:

$$P(\Delta) = \sum_{i=0}^{n} c_{ti} e^{-(s_i + \Delta) t_i}$$

We seek the delta of the asset given by the derivative evaluated at $\Delta = 0$:

$$\frac{dP}{d\Delta_{\Delta=0}} = - \sum_{i=0}^{n} c_{ti} e^{-s_i t_i} \, t_i$$

This is not only convenient, it is also essentially the primary result we derived in the previous chapter, $\frac{dP}{d\Delta} \frac{1}{P} = -D_{FW}$.

Let's expand our thinking to pricing general cash flow streams that include everything from bonds to mortgages to installment loans. Since many of these loans pay interest periodically, then their valuations will be sensitive to changes in rates as well as their periodicity (compounding). As an example, consider a typical installment loan that makes payments m times per year. We therefore have the familiar pricing model given by:

$$P(\Delta) = \sum_{i=0}^{n} c_i \left(1 + \frac{s_i + \Delta}{m}\right)^{-i}$$

Interest rate risk is therefore:

$$\frac{dP}{d\Delta_{\Delta=0}} = \sum_{i=0}^{n} -\frac{i}{m} c_i \left(1 + \frac{s_i}{m}\right)^{-(i+1)}$$

We can derive the quasi-modified duration measure by dividing both sides by P:

$$D_Q = -\frac{dP}{d\Delta_{\Delta=0}}\frac{1}{P} = \frac{1}{\sum_{n}^{i=0} c_i \left(1 + \frac{s_i}{m}\right)^{-i}} \sum_{i=0}^{n} -\frac{i}{m} c_i \left(1 + \frac{s_i}{m}\right)^{-(i+1)}$$

This is rather cumbersome but not difficult to code onto a spreadsheet, as we can see in Example 3.5.

EXAMPLE 3.5   Immunization

Let's consider an immunization problem similar to the one we studied in the last chapter except that now we have a $1 million obligation in five years and two bonds available to invest in today that, hopefully, would be able to generate cash flows sufficient to pay the obligation in exactly five years' time. Here, however, we relax the flat yield curve restriction. Suppose instead that the yield curve is upward sloping as shown in the second column and that bond A is a 10-year bond that pays a 10 percent coupon and bond B is a 7-year bond that pays a 5 percent coupon. We will assume that coupons are paid annually.

Example 3.5 Table

Year	Spot	Discount	Bond A	PV_A	PV'_A	Bond B	PV_B	PV'_B
1	5.571	0.947	10	9.47	8.97	15	14.21	13.46
2	6.088	0.889	10	8.89	16.75	15	13.33	25.13
3	6.555	0.827	10	8.27	23.27	15	12.40	34.91
4	6.978	0.764	10	7.64	28.55	15	11.45	42.82
5	7.361	0.701	10	7.01	32.65	15	10.52	48.98
6	7.707	0.641	10	6.41	35.68	15	9.61	53.52

7	8.02	0.583	10	5.83	37.76	115	67.01	434.27
8	8.37	0.526	10	5.26	38.81			
9	8.6	0.476	10	4.76	39.44			
10	9	0.422	110	46.47	426.29			
Sums				109.98	688.17		138.53	653.09
D_Q					6.26			4.71

Go to the companion website for more details.

The quasi-modified duration is given in the last row: 6.26 years and 4.71 years for bonds A and B, respectively. Our obligation has present value equal to $1M * 0.701 = $701,079.49. As before, we want a portfolio of the two bonds such that the present value of the portfolio's cash flows is equal to the present value of the liability. Also, the sum of the duration-weighted present values will equal the duration-weighted present value of the liability. Once again, therefore, we require the two conditions:

$$PV_A * x_A + PV_B * x_B = PV_{liability}$$

$$D_A PV_A * x_A + D_B PV_B * x_B = PV_{liabilitiy} * D_{liability}$$

Setting up the algebra, we wish to solve the following system of two equations:

$$\$109.98 * x_A + \$138.53 * x_B = \$701,079.49$$
$$\$688.17 * x_A + \$653.09 * x_B = \$3,505,397.43$$

We can solve this by elimination as we did in Chapter 2 or by using matrix algebra, which I illustrate here because it is so much more practical, especially for larger problems involving more unknowns. First, write the problem algebraically in matrix form as follows:

$$\begin{bmatrix} 109.98 & 138.53 \\ 688.17 & 653.09 \end{bmatrix} \begin{bmatrix} x_A \\ x_B \end{bmatrix} = \begin{bmatrix} 701,079.49 \\ 3,505,397.43 \end{bmatrix}.$$

Call this system $Ax = b$, where A is 4×4 and x and b are the two 2×1 column vectors. (The appendix to Chapter 6 contains a review of matrix algebra). We want the solution $x = A^{-1}b$ which, consulting the worksheet examples for this chapter (Example 3.5) yields $x_A = 1,180, x_B = 4,124$.

The value of this portfolio is exactly $701,079.49. Note that bond B is over-weighted because its duration is close to the duration of the liability.

What happens if there is a parallel shift in the yield curve? Column K on the worksheet represents a 1 percent upward shift in the yield curve. Copying and pasting this vector over the old spot rates in column B (copy/paste special/values) indicates that the present value of the obligation is now equal to $669,321.81, which is exactly offset by the value of the portfolio which, again, contains a short position in bond A. Note as well that the duration on both bonds have declined because of the heavier discounting associated with the higher yield curve.

SUMMARY

We expand the concept of the last chapter's single discount rate to include the term structure of interest rates. The term structure then motivates the concept of the forward curve and the implications of using the forward curve and its derivatives (for example, short rates) to discount cash flows that will materialize at some future point in time. Recognizing that discount rates are now time dependent random variables, we revisit the NPV methodology as well as running PV and bootstrapping.

We then extend the immunization analysis from Chapter 2 to accommodate variable term structures, specifically, non–flat term structures that experience parallel shifts. This analysis requires modifying the concept of Macaulay duration to a variable yield curve. The analog to Macaulay is Fisher-Weil duration and the duration we use in immunization is the discrete compounding analog of Fisher-Weil given by quasi-modified duration. The analysis of immunization under parallel shifts in yield curves is a very important tool in fixed income risk management for all financial institutions having long exposure to the bond market. The tools learned in this chapter apply directly to derivative pricing models, real and financial options, and structured credit models covered in Chapters 14, 15, and 18.

CHAPTER 4

Equity

The truth is rarely pure and never simple.

—Oscar Wilde

Shareholders have an equity interest, that is, direct ownership, in the companies whose shares they hold. Share value is determined by the firm's earnings potential, its prospects for paying future dividends, and investors' subjective valuation of future payoffs. Dividends are paid out of earnings and earnings are related to sales, which, themselves, turn on consumer demand, itself a function of income, relative prices, and sentiment. In this complex environment, reported earnings, especially at the company level, can be quite volatile. Efforts by the firm's managers to smooth the market's assessment of share value during periods of fluctuating earnings is clearly a challenging task in a volatile market, especially during crises such as the credit market collapse of 2008.

While the fates of shareholders are tied inexorably to the anthropology of market dynamics, holders of investment grade bonds are optimistic about their prospects of receiving scheduled coupons. Thus, while bondholders forfeit prospects of bigger gains by not buying shares, they can enjoy the greater certainty of a more modest, yet stable, stream of cash flows. Bondholders are the firm's creditors; they will get paid their promised coupons unless the firm defaults, in which case bondholders will get to divide the remaining value while shareholders go home empty-handed. I discuss the nature of the firm's capital structure as it relates to options theory in Chapter 16. Thus, other things constant, bondholders face relatively less risk. They occupy a higher place in the capital structure than do shareholders, which means that shareholders suffer losses before bondholders. For example, coupons are paid out of available earnings even when things go bad, and dividends may suffer if the firm has no alternative way of paying share-holders. Thus, shareholder expectations are adversely affected in down markets and the return to equity is generally thought to require a premium over bonds so as to induce investors to hold shares, which are inherently riskier than bonds. The excess return to equity over bonds is therefore referred to as the equity risk premium.

THE DETERMINATION OF STOCK PRICES

A simple, intuitive model of stock prices posits that the expected value of the current share price is the discounted present value of tomorrow's expected share price plus any expected dividend payout (cash flows), that is,

$$p_t^e = \frac{1}{(1+r)} p_{t+1}^e + \frac{1}{(1+r)} d_{t+1}^e$$

This equation is the basis of the *dividend discount model* and has a forward solution by successive substitution, that is, substituting in for p_{t+i}^e for $i = 1, \ldots, \infty$. For example, we first substitute the following for p_{t+1}^e on the right-hand side ($i = 1$):

$$p_{t+1}^e = \frac{1}{(1+r)} p_{t+i+1}^e + \frac{1}{(1+r)} d_{t+i+1}^e$$

This yields the following:

$$p_t^e = \left(\frac{1}{1+r}\right)^2 p_{t+2}^e + \left(\frac{1}{1+r}\right)^2 d_{t+2}^e + \left(\frac{1}{1+r}\right) d_{t+1}^e$$

In the limit, successive substitution generates the following forward solution:

$$p_t^e = \sum_{i=0}^{\infty} \left(\frac{1}{1+r}\right)^i \left(\frac{d_{t+1+i}^e}{1+r}\right)$$

We assume that the terminal value (as t approaches ∞) is equal to zero, that is:

$$\lim_{t \to \infty} \left(\frac{1}{1+r}\right)^t \left(\frac{d_\infty^e}{1+r}\right) = 0$$

If we assume that the expected dividend is constant, it is now easy to show from what we know about power functions, namely that:

$$\sum_{i=0}^{\infty} \left(\frac{1}{1+r}\right)^i = \left(\frac{1+r}{r}\right)$$

Thus, our expression for price is equivalent to:

$$p_t^e = \left(\frac{1+r}{r}\right)\left(\frac{\overline{d}}{1+r}\right) = \frac{\overline{d}}{r}$$

The constant dividend assumption is probably too restrictive but it does serve to make clear that the price of equity is the solution to a simple dividend discounting process. The constant dividend and infinite life of the firm together imply that price is like an annuity, that is, a constant dividend payment in perpetuity. Rearranging terms, we can see that r acts like the capitalization rate (or cap rate); it is the yield on the asset:

$$r = \frac{\overline{d}}{p_t^e}$$

To put this in perspective, take the March 2009 S&P 500 level, once again, of 757 but with the long run average p/e ratio equal to 16 and assume a dividend payout ratio of 0.4. The dividend is 0.4 times earnings. The p/d ratio is therefore 37.5, implying a cap rate equal to 2.67 percent, which was very close to the 2.82 percent yield on the 10-year Treasury at the time. Annual earnings were very depressed, however. If these earnings were to rebound to their pre-crisis levels, say, $80, then the cap rate of 2.67 percent would indicate an index level equal to $\frac{4*\$80}{.0267} = \$1198$, a level the S&P 500 did finally reach by November of 2010. The index achieved that level, however, through exceptional earnings growth over that one-and-a-half year period, in which annual real earnings rose from $7.2 to $77.1! This growth was due in large part to massive monetary and fiscal stimulus coupled with cost-cutting efficiency at the corporate level (including rising unemployment) and historically low capital costs. One important point to be made here is that despite the cap rate of 2.67 percent, this index managed to grow, not by 2.67 percent annually, but by 36 percent annually, all due to abnormal earnings growth as the economic recovery began in earnest in the summer of 2009.

The dividend discount model follows from the efficient markets hypothesis (EMH)—the notion that prices reflect firm fundamentals. The world of the EMH is dominated by rational agents, whose subjective models describing how markets work coincide with the objective, or true, market dynamic. These agents therefore have rational expectations derived from complete information sets, which effectively eliminate any chance that prices could systematically deviate from fundamentals. Consistent with the EMH, therefore, is the premise that prices are somehow right, suggesting that when they deviate from fundamentals, rational agents will exploit arbitrage opportunities that force prices back to fundamentals.

Shiller (1981) showed that actual stock prices are too volatile for the dividend discount model (he substitutes the average historical dividend and uses an average discount rate on equity). In reality, investors probably do not use an average of historical dividend; rather, they more likely try to estimate future dividends, in which case the model would predict more volatile prices consistent with Barsky and DeLong (1993).

In any case, this pricing model is a function of our notion of expected dividends $\bar{d}$ and the interest rate, r. While this may appear to be a simple pricing model, understand that the determination of both future expected dividends and the discount rate are econometrically challenging pursuits. Moreover, while the theoretical price depends on both an econometric model of future expected dividends and a theoretical interest rate, the observed price is the market's notion of present value and, clearly, these two numbers can be quite different. Thus, as we see further on, though models may be intuitively appealing, they often produce forecasts that are wildly inconsistent with actual outcomes. We will return to the topic of modeling error later.

DISCOUNT RATES REDUX

Recall from Chapter 1 the discussion of the role of the discount rate in computing present value. There, we stated that this is the rate at which we are willing to trade present for future consumption. This is the role that the term r in the dividend discount model implicitly plays. Specifically, the one period discount rate is $\frac{1}{(1+r)}$, where r is the relevant interest rate. The discount rate tells us how valuable a dollar one period into the future is to us today. If $r = 10$ percent, then that dollar feels like about $0.92 today. If $r = 5$ percent, it feels a little more like $0.95 today. As interest rates fall, the present value of a dollar to be received one year out means more to us. Stated differently, as r falls, we need less tomorrow to compensate us for giving up a dollar today. That is, as r falls to zero, the opportunity cost of consuming a dollar today is zero; there is no foregone payoff by failing to save for the future. In the limit, r equal to zero means we are indifferent between a dollar today and a dollar in the future; the discount rate in this case is one. Therefore, high discount rates follow from lower interest rates. In general, high discount rates are consistent with the idea that the market doesn't value the future as much and this preference shows in the form of low market rates (usually consistent with lots of liquidity, that is, money supply). So, r is a market rate but how is it arrived at? The simple answer is through the interaction of demand and supply in the money markets. But there is a deeper meaning underlying the determination of the discount rate that is meaningful to our development of all our pricing models. It has to do with intertemporal choice. Here is how that works.

Think of the phrase "trading present for future consumption" and consider a two-period model (the present and the future) for a consumer who wants to maximize his utility in both periods. Assume he has a utility function U with diminishing marginal utility ($U' > 0$, $U'' < 0$). Denote periodic consumption by C_t (present) and C_{t+1} (future). Like all of us, this individual has a budget constraint, that is, his current period income, Y_t, must cover current period consumption C_t, and if there's anything left over, it goes to savings S_t. Thus, the present period constraint is $Y_t = C_t + S_t$. In the future period, if he has savings, they have grown to $(1 + r)S_t$. He also has future income, Y_{t+1}, so that the future budget constraint must be $(1 + r)S_t + Y_{t+1} = C_{t+1}$. That is, what he gets to consume in the future will depend on future income and what he did not consume in the present. Likewise, we can say that the present value of lifetime consumption must equal his lifetime, or permanent, income:

$$\overline{Y} = C_t + C_{t+1}/(1 + r)$$

Now, we can write his general lifetime utility as the sum of present and future utility:

$$U(C_t, C_{t+1}) = u(C_t) + \beta u(C_{t+1})$$

Here, the parameter β is the agent's subjective time preference, that is, his rate of impatience (which is unobserved—more on that later). It represents his preference for present over future consumption; the higher this value, the less he values future consumption. The consumer's objective is to maximize this utility subject to his budget constraint. That is:

$$\text{Max } U(C_t, C_{t+1}) = u(C_t) + \beta u(C_{t+1})$$

$$\text{subject to } C_t + C_{t+1}/(1 + r) - \overline{Y} = 0$$

The standard way to solve this constrained optimization problem is through the method of Lagrange. Form the Lagrangian L with budget constraint using the Lagrange multiplier λ as follows to maximize the budget-constrained lifetime utility given by:

$$L(C_t, C_{t+1}, \lambda) = u(C_t) + \beta u(C_{t+1}) - \lambda[C_t + C_{t+1}/(1+r) - Y]$$

By taking partial derivatives with respect to present and future consumption (and the constraint λ), we get three first-order conditions:

$$\frac{\partial L(C_t, C_{t+1}, \lambda)}{\partial C_t} = u'(C_t) - \lambda = 0$$

$$\frac{\partial L(C_t, C_{t+1}, \lambda)}{\partial C_{t+1}} = \beta u'(C_{t+1}) - \frac{\lambda}{(1+r)} = 0$$

$$\frac{\partial L(C_t, C_{t+1}, \lambda)}{\partial \lambda} = C_t + \frac{C_{t+1}}{(1+r)} - \overline{Y} = 0$$

We can solve the first equation for λ and substitute this into the second equation (thus eliminating λ) to get the Euler equation:

$$u'(C_t) = (1+r)\beta u'(C_{t+1})$$

The Euler equation says that, when utility is *at an optimum*, the value the consumer places on small changes in consumption (either now or in the future) must be the same. Rearranging terms

$$\frac{\beta u'(C_{t+1})}{u'(C_t)} = \frac{1}{1+r}$$

This result is important to understand. *The discount rate is determined by the ratio of future to present marginal utility of consumption.* Observed market interest rates are therefore the outcome of the average of agents' behaviors as they go about the business of optimizing lifetime consumption. For given β, falling market rates (higher discount rates) indicate an increase in the marginal utility of future consumption relative to present consumption and vice versa. During recessions, for example, falling interest rates are reminiscent of households anticipating lower future consumption and, hence, the marginal utility of future consumption rises relative to current and past consumption. In the aftermath of the 2008–2009 credit crisis, household saving rose significantly and current consumption was curtailed in an effort to provide for future consumption. The discount rate therefore signals households' degree of impatience; higher discount rates (lower interest rates and time value of money) imply more patience and vice versa. High interest rates, on the other hand, push the discount rate down, indicating that the marginal utility of future consumption is low relative to the marginal utility of current consumption. This would suggest that consumers require greater compensation in the form of higher interest rates to induce them to forgo current consumption. John Cochrane (2001) presents a well-written and more rigorous treatment of this problem.

PRICE AND DIVIDEND MULTIPLES

Price to earnings (p/e) and its reciprocal (e/p) along with the dividend yield (d/p), where p is share price and e and d are earnings per share and dividend per share, are common multiples scrutinized by equity analysts and, as we shall see, have many applications. The concept of *value stocks,* for example, are stocks with low p/e ratios. The value is in the belief that the price is too low for the stated earnings per share and will therefore mean-revert earning the holder a greater return. *Growth stocks,* on the other hand, are stocks in companies whose earnings have shown high growth in the past and are expected to grow at above-average rates going forward. Growth companies are therefore those believed most capable of expanding earnings and revenue.

The growth and value concepts have spawned an industry in what is called *style analysis*—small versus big capitalization stocks and value versus growth. The original research was presented in a series of seminal papers by Kenneth French and Eugene Fama, who suggested the existence of certain style factors to supplement the single market index in the capital asset pricing model (CAPM). We will derive the CAPM in the next chapter. The point made here is that fundamental factors on market capitalization (size), and multiples describing book value to market value and earnings to price (value and growth) are instrumental in price determination. Figure 4.1, for example, is from French's website and describes how the universe of stocks can be divided on the basis of these factors.

High book-to-market value of equity (BE/ME) firms are those that the market currently undervalues, like a stock with a low p/e ratio. These are considered to be value bets. Conversely, low book-to-market value of equity is associated with growth stocks. Size is dimensioned on market value of

	←———————Median ME ———————→			
70th BE/ME percentile	small value		big value	
	small neutral		big neutral	
30th BE/ME percentile	small growth		big growth	

FIGURE 4.1   Fama-French Style Analysis

equity, or what we call *capitalization.* For example, big stocks are those firms with above median capitalizations. Fama and French subtracted the returns of stocks in the bottom tier (thirtieth percentile) from those in the top tier (seventieth percentile) to construct a value factor (they call it HML—high minus low) and as well as a size factor (they call it SMB; small minus big) to supplement the single factor (the broad market return on the S&P 500) in the CAPM. We analyze the three-factor model and factor models, in general, in more detail in later chapters.

See Kenneth French's website for information and data on these fundamental attributes:

 http://mba.tuck.dartmouth.edu/pages/faculty/ken.french/index.html

EXTRAPOLATING MULTIPLES TO FORECAST RETURNS

There are less rigorous methods for predicting the direction of stock prices. Look, for example, at the price level of an equity index like the Standard & Poor's 500. At the depths of the recent market decline in March of 2009, Robert Shiller estimated the p/e ratio for the S&P 500 at about 13.3. The price of the index was measured relative to the trailing 10-year average of the index's quarterly earnings.

See Shiller's site for details.

 http://www.econ.yale.edu/~shiller/data.htm

Looking back historically, every time the p/e was in this range, the subsequent average 10-year return to the S&P 500 was approximately 8.5 percent since 1926 and 10.5 percent since World War II. At the time this chapter was written, the S&P was trading at about 12× earnings. Historically, when the p/e multiple is within 11× and 13×, subsequent 10-year returns have been 11.8 percent since 1871. These numbers are not meant to be precise, but rather, to illustrate how one could extrapolate from the historical record to forecast forward returns. Thus, one could appeal to the historical record and forecast equity returns moving up into this range over the next decade. While convenient, we must keep in mind that these are long-run return forecasts grounded completely in the belief that history repeats itself, that is, that the market mean-reverts to its historical average performance level. The implication here is that fundamentals in the future will behave much as they have historically.

Looked at differently, if the historic average p/e is 16 and we believe that the stock market is mean-reverting, then for any current level of earnings, we can extrapolate the change in the price of the index required to get us back to the long-term average. To illustrate, the S&P 500 fell to a closing low of 757 at the end of March 2009. For argument's sake, suppose that the analyst consensus forecast for forward earnings was $70 per share over the next year. If we believe in mean reversion (strictly speaking, mean reversion is a trend stationary process whereby the trend is a constant growth rate), then a multiple of 16 would imply that the index level would rise to 16*$70, or 1120, to support the consensus earnings forecast. The S&P was trading a little above 1100 by year's end. The growth in the index value exceeded 65 percent over this period.

The foremost problem with extrapolation of multiples—or any trend reversion model for that matter—is timing, or rather, the lack thereof. These models provide no guidance as to when the predicted reversion will occur. It could occur in the next month or the next decade. Another weakness is that the multiple itself has two random components and no descriptive model governing the dynamics of either. In the case of the p/e, it is price and earnings, neither one of which has a forward model going forward. Hence, mean reversion, as it were, is not just a function of one or the other but both components of the multiple. Does the p/e multiple revert due to changes in price (reflecting fundamentals or merely noise) or changes in expected earnings (reflecting economic fundamentals)? We don't know. Moreover, particularly stressful periods may reflect structural changes to economic fundamentals, which will manifest in prices and cash flows, and these may suggest that multiples are quite independent of what's really going on in the economy. Yet, multiples are quiet on these developments in the sense that they do not inform us about the structure of their respective markets.

PITFALLS OF TREND ANALYSIS

Anchoring on linear time trends as a basis to support returns forecasts also appeal to mean reversion logic. This is illustrated in Figure 4.2.

Superimposed on the (log) price history of the index are two trend lines—trend growth from January 1871 to December 2009, which is 4.27

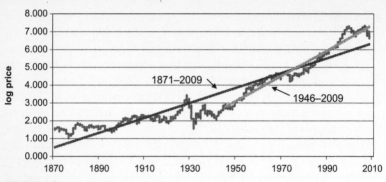

FIGURE 4.2   S&P 500 Trend Growth

percent annual growth and annual trend growth after World War II (January 1946 to December 2009) at 7.35 percent. These are monthly index values. Trend growth is estimated by regressing ln(Price) $= \alpha + \beta$ time and computing annual growth in percent using $100*((1 + \beta)12 - 1)$. These are clearly distinct trend estimates, and the conclusions drawn from mean reversion arguments are naturally going to be sensitive to which trend one is referring to. To see how sensitive trend estimates are, consider that the annual trend growth in the S&P was 1.88 percent from 1871 to 1928, 5.86 percent from 1929 to 1989, 6.81 percent from 1929 to 2009 and, as mentioned before, 7.35 percent from 1946 to 2009. This is a rather wide range and, depending on which trend line we use, mean reversion from any given spot index level may be up or down!

For example, historically, when the level of the S&P 500 was as far below the post–World War II trend as it was on, say, April 30, 2009, the subsequent average 10-year return was 13.44 percent. Many market analysts pointed to this statistical artifact to support claims that the index could look forward to a rebound to 7.35 percent growth over the next decade. This is interesting; the index was indeed below trend (note the vertical distance between the index and the post-1946 trend line in Figure 4.2) but it was not below trend associated with the entire history of the S&P. The trend based on the longer series suggests that the S&P is still *above* trend, not below it, and therefore suggests mean reversion in the opposite direction to a long-run growth rate of 4.27 percent. Strictly speaking, both claims are wrong because there is no single deterministic trend. Instead, it makes more sense (and this is supported by careful statistical analysis) that trend growth in the S&P is variable in the short run and in the long run, tied to fundamentals that determine economic growth.

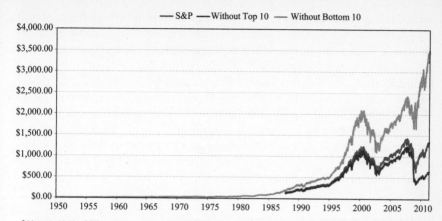

$1 invested in the S&P in 1950 would be worth $1,326 today. If you missed the10 best days, that dollar is worth $639.
If you missed the 10 worst days, you would have $,3457 today.

FIGURE 4.3 S&P 500 Total Returns Since 1950

I would like to drive home this point by demonstrating how sensitive trends can be to the presence of a few outliers. Figure 4.3 shows the sensitivity of total returns to the S&P 500 from 1950 to the present when 10 observations are removed from 15,444 observed daily returns. Perhaps this graph is a better example of how risky markets are, but it serves to also indicate how sensitive trends are to a few extreme returns. The middle line shows that a dollar invested in the index on January 3, 1950, would have grown to $1,356 by April 11, 2011. Had we been able to avoid the 10 worst days in the market, our investment would have grown to $3,457. Had we not been in the market on the 10 best days, our investment would have grown to only $639. These 10 days represent 0.065 of 1 percent of the returns, yet the entire investment turns on these events. It is interesting to note as well that 8 of the 10 best days occurred during the recent credit crisis as did half of the worst days. As suggested before, this may say more about risk than anything else—in particular, risks that have extremely low likelihood but very big impact, a topic we return to when we study systemic risk in Chapter 13. But it also serves to make clear the risks of extrapolating historical trends—a single extreme event can easily obviate any trend and the decisions predicated on that trend.

Clearly, the shortcomings with extrapolative models are that they rely on the historical record repeating and that they do not require any structural understanding of how fundamentals (for example, earnings and dividends) are related to returns. Yet their popularity among analysts hasn't suffered. In part, that is because extrapolation from perceived linear trends is easier than constructing complex equilibrium models describing market dynamics. Trend extrapolation is a good example of the *representative heuristic,* that is, when the index level has been high for some time (like since World War II), then agents believe that current high observed returns are normal, and deviations from trend will therefore mean-revert to this notion of normality (Tversky and Kahneman 1974). The mistake agents make in this case is that they base their choices on how well they resemble available data (for example, recent trends) instead of a more comprehensive analysis that combines theory and broader data selection optimally. I have more to say about behavioral finance in Chapter 8.

THE GORDON GROWTH MODEL

Let's return to the fundamental pricing model. The dividend discount model derived earlier is closely related to the *Gordon Growth model.* The latter also assumes that the market is infinitely lived and pays a periodic dividend (d), but which grows at a rate (g) over time. The current price of the index (p) is therefore the present value of the cash flow stream (we will derive our results without time subscripts):

$$p = \frac{(1+g)d}{(1+r)} + \frac{(1+g)^2 d}{(1+r)^2} + \frac{(1+g)^3 d}{(1+r)^3} + \cdots$$

Solving this power series yields the following for which price is essentially the capitalized value of the expected dividend payout in the next period:

$$p = \frac{(1+g)d}{r-g}$$

If we assumed zero growth, then the Gordon Growth is identical to the dividend discount model derived at the beginning of this chapter. If dividends are expected to grow at a rate g, then for a given level, p, we can solve for the return on equity, r, as:

$$r = \frac{(1+g)d}{p} + g$$

For example, assume that the growth rate of *nominal* earnings is 5 percent and the dividend payout is .40. Also assume that the current price level on the S&P is 900 and that the current p/e multiple is 13.3. Then the *p/d* multiple is $p/(.4e) = 13.3/.4 = 33.25$ and the Gordon Growth model forecasts a return, $r = 1.05/33.25 + .05 = .0816$. or 8 percent. If the yield on the 10-year Treasury is 4 percent, then the implied equity risk premium is 4 percent. Again, this is meant to be purely illustrative. For example, had we used an earnings growth of 7 percent, our forecasted return would be above 10 percent.

If we assume a constant dividend payout ratio, we can then convert the model to study the relationship between the p/e ratio and returns over time. Setting $d = y^d e$, where y^d is the dividend payout ratio (0.4 in the preceding example):

$$p = \frac{y^d(1+g)e}{(1+r)} + \frac{y^d(1+g)^2 e}{(1+r)^2} + \frac{y^d(1+g)^3 e}{(1+r)^3} + \cdots \qquad (4.1)$$

It's easy to see that dividing both sides by earnings transforms the pricing model into a p/e model. We return to this relationship later.

Equation (4.1) is, in fact, a perpetuity (consol). We observe the price (p) and wish to solve for the return (the yield), which in this case is an internal rate of return (IRR). Let's fix a 10-year forecast horizon that implies the following (with $n = 10$):

$$p = \frac{y^d(1+g)e}{(1+r)} + \frac{y^d(1+g)^2 e}{(1+r)^2} + \cdots + \frac{y^d(1+g)^n e}{(1+r)^3} + p_n \qquad (4.2)$$

Dividends ($y^d e$) are assumed to grow at rate g annually for n years, and the return r discounts these cash flows to equal the current price of the index. This is still a perpetuity because the terminal condition p_n is the discounted present value of all cash flows realized after the nth year. It is written as:

$$p_n = \frac{y^d(1+g)^{n+1} e}{(1+r)^{n+1}} + \frac{y^d(1+g)^{n+2} e}{(1+r)^{n+2}} + \frac{y^d(1+g)^{n+3} e}{(1+r)^{n+3}} + \cdots \qquad (4.3)$$

We can still solve equation 4.3 as a closed form. Doing so, we get:

$$p_n = \frac{\left[y^d(1+g)^n e\right](1+g)}{(r-g)(1+r)^n} \qquad (4.4)$$

This says that the residual value of the asset after n years is the capitalized value (where the cap rate is $r - g$) of the earnings at that time (which is given in the numerator). Plugging this into equation 4.2 will give us a closed form that we can solve in a spreadsheet.

This model discounts 10 years of expected cash flows but imposes a price correction factor that uses the condition that the terminal price p_n be equal to the long-term average p/e multiple times earnings.

Thus, there are two parts to this model—the first part is the sum of the n cash flows that span the forecast horizon and the second part is the price correction embedded in the terminal value, which in this case is imposed to be consistent with a long-term p/e multiple. We can see therefore that this model is also mean reverting because it imposes the constraint that market price at the end of n years reverts back to the price implied by a long-term p/e multiple.

Using this model, we estimate a set of forward returns for a 10-year period over a range of starting prices and p/e ratios. These are presented in Table 4.1. The top row is the current price of the index. The remaining rows are forward returns conditional on each starting index value with price correction given by final p/e shown in the last column on the right. These calculations assume current annual earnings of $100 with dividend payout equal to 40 percent and nominal annual dividend growth of 4 percent. Historically, average nominal dividend growth has been 4 percent and the Shiller p/e using 10-year trailing average earnings is about 15. Dividend payout in 2009 was 43 percent. For example, if the current value of the index is $1,200, and the terminal p/e is set at 15, then the forward expected return is 8.8 percent.

These estimates are quite sensitive to both starting price and ending value (p/e × earnings). It is tempting to apply a model like this to day-to-day

TABLE 4.1 Forward Returns Conditional on Ending P/E and Current Price

800	850	900	950	1000	1050	1100	1150	1200	1250	1300
0.169	0.161	0.153	0.146	0.139	0.133	0.127	0.121	0.116	0.111	0.106
0.164	0.155	0.148	0.141	0.134	0.128	0.122	0.116	0.111	0.106	0.101
0.158	0.150	0.142	0.135	0.129	0.122	0.116	0.111	0.105	0.100	0.095
0.152	0.144	0.137	0.130	0.123	0.117	0.111	0.105	0.100	0.095	0.090
0.146	0.138	0.131	0.124	0.117	0.111	0.105	0.099	0.094	0.089	0.084
0.140	0.132	0.124	0.117	0.111	0.104	0.099	0.093	0.088	0.083	0.078
0.133	0.125	0.118	0.111	0.104	0.098	0.092	0.086	0.081	0.076	0.071
0.126	0.118	0.111	0.104	0.097	0.091	0.085	0.079	0.074	0.069	0.064
0.119	0.111	0.103	0.096	0.090	0.083	0.078	0.072	0.067	0.062	0.057
0.111	0.103	0.095	0.088	0.082	0.075	0.070	0.064	0.059	0.054	0.049
0.102	0.094	0.087	0.080	0.073	0.067	0.061	0.056	0.050	0.045	0.041

movements in the index which, during turbulent times, can give off highly volatile point estimates as shown within the table. One should be cautioned: The purpose of the model is to forecast returns over the long run; price corrections may take a lot less time to revert. Nevertheless, the model will conclude that the impact on returns is averaged over a much longer time when in fact it may not be. The point is that we use a model like this to arrive at an estimate of the long-run mean return and not periodic point estimates, which are highly variable.

The forward return we solve for holds for the 10-year horizon. But, what does this return imply for the horizon beyond the tenth year? These results are provided in the shaded column. To see how these numbers are estimated, recall that the p/e ratio *at year n* is defined by equation 4.4 as:

$$\frac{p_n}{(1+g)^n e} = m = \frac{y^d(1+g)}{(1+r)^n(r-g)}$$

The first term is the p/e at time n. This is set to some integer, say, $m = 15$, that imposes the terminal value of the index. The question of interest now is what the multiple m implies about the return that is *required* from year 10 onward that is consistent with the return solved for the first 10 years. For example, we just showed in the preceding example that the average forward return (the IRR, if you will) for the first 10 years is 8.8 percent. But, the forward return for years 11 onward is different. Plugging our numbers into the previous equation describing the terminal p/e, it must satisfy the following:

$$15 = \frac{0.4(1.04)}{(1+r)^{10}(r-0.04)}$$

The return that satisfies this relation is 5.6 percent. Thus, we have implicitly constrained the return for the future beginning after the tenth year. Implicitly, this return, too, is part of our forecast indicating that there are two forward returns that equate discounted cash flows to current price—one for the first 10 years and one thereafter.

To see this implication more clearly, Table 4.2 presents the unconstrained forward return, that is, the very-long-term return with no price correction imposed; it is the solution to equation (4.1).

Since there is no terminal condition, meaning no price correction, then we get a single solution—not to 10 years but for all years. This indicates that the forward expected return on the index priced currently at \$1,200 is 7.5 percent. There is no assumption about future index levels. Thus, Table 4.1 presents two separate forward returns; in this case,

TABLE 4.2   Forward Returns with No Price Correction

800	850	900	950	1000	1050	1100	1150	1200	1250	1300
0.092	0.089	0.086	0.084	0.082	0.080	0.078	0.076	0.075	0.073	0.072

when the index value is currently $1,200 (which is about 12× earnings) and we require a future p/e ratio to rise to 15, then we require 8.8 percent growth in the first 10 years, followed by 5.6 percent growth thereafter. Alternatively, we could require 7.5 percent growth with no price correction imposed.

Here is a better example. Suppose the index falls to 800, which is consistent with a multiple of 8×. Table 4.1 shows, for all cases, the forward return on the index will have to be at least 10.2 percent if the multiple is to be anywhere above 10×. So, most of the forward-looking return is front loaded while the return after the tenth year is somewhat less at 9.2 percent. Experimenting with the length of the horizon shows that making n small forces the price correction into the first n years with the slack occurring thereafter. The point here is to recognize that results presented in Table 4.1 are sensitive to *n* but the results in Table 4.2 are not.

SOURCES OF RETURN

Building Blocks

Roger Ibbotson has proposed several building blocks methods that decompose observed stock market returns (for a summary, see Ibbotson 2001). These models begin with an identity and then decompose this relationship into equivalent measures. The basic identity states that nominal stock returns are the product of inflation, the real risk-free rate (on long-term Treasuries) and the equity risk premium:

$$r_t = (1 + infl_t)(1 + rrf_t)(1 + rp_t) - 1$$

In the analysis that follows, we will assume that inflation is measured as the year-over-year percentage change in the consumer price index and that the risk-free rate is the nominal yield on the 10-year Treasury. The equity risk premium is defined as follows:

$$rp_t = \frac{(1 + r_t)}{(1 + rf_t)} - 1 = \frac{(r_t - rf_t)}{(1 + rf_t)}$$

and where the real risk-free rate is defined by:

$$rrf_t = \frac{(1 + rf_t)}{(1 + infl_t)} - 1 = \frac{(rf_t - infl_t)}{(1 + infl_t)}$$

Substituting rp_t and rrf_t into the first equation establishes the identity.

Using Shiller's annual data spanning 1871 to 2009, I estimate the average long-term return on the 10-year nominal Treasury to be 4.66 percent and a 2.26 percent average inflation rate. The average real return to the S&P 500 over this period was 8.0 percent. Therefore, the nominal stock return is approximated by $(1.08)*(1.0226) - 1 = 0.104$, or 10.4 percent. Using the formula for rp_t, I then solve for a 5.5 percent annual equity risk premium. This model says that the observed long-run average nominal return to stocks can be decomposed into a 2.26 percent inflation rate, a 2.35 percent real yield on the 10-year Treasury, and a 5.5 percent risk premium. Some analysts stop here; if they have views on forward inflation, real bond yields, and the risk premium, they can use these to get a rough estimate of the forward return on equity.

Earnings Model

Ibottson and Chen break the equity return into real capital gains (*rcg*) and income (*inc*), rewriting the first identity as follows:

$$r_t = [(1 + infl_t)(1 + rcg_t) - 1] + inc_t + Rinv_t$$

The last term is reinvested income (Ibottson assigns this a value of 0.2 percent) whereas income itself is assumed to come in the form of dividends. We therefore use the real dividend yield in place of *inc*. The real capital gain can be written in terms of p/e growth and earnings growth as follows:

$$rcg_t = \frac{p_t}{p_{t-1}} - 1$$

This definition can be expanded upon by substituting earnings:

$$rcg_t = \frac{p_t/e_t}{p_{t-1}/e_{t-1}} x \frac{e_t}{e_{t-1}} - 1 = \left(1 + g_{pe_t}\right)\left(1 + g_{reps_t}\right) - 1$$

Therefore, real capital gains are the product of growth rates in the price-to-earnings ratio and real earnings per share. Substituting this into the identity gives us the following expression:

$$r_t = \left[(1 + infl_t)\left(1 + g_{pe_t}\right)\left(1 + g_{reps_t}\right) - 1\right] + inc_t + Rinv_t$$

We could evaluate this expression a couple of ways: If we simply substitute for annual p/e and real earnings growth plus the real dividend yield along with the reinvestment rate on income of 0.2 percent, we find from Shiller's data that p/e growth is 4.03 percent over this period while real earnings growth was 4.61 percent and the growth in real dividend yield has been 1.87 percent. Together, these imply a nominal return to equity equal to 13.3 percent annually. Shiller smoothes the p/e ratio by dividing the current index price by a 10-year moving average of trailing earnings. The growth rate of this series is 1.75 percent. Substituting this for the 4.03 percent produces a nominal equity return of 10.9 percent. This is slightly higher than the 10.4 percent measure derived from the building blocks model.

Let's assume for the moment that *Rinv* is fixed at 0.2 percent. Then, again, given our views on inflation and the growth rates of p/e, real earnings, and real dividends, we could come up with an equity return forecast.

Forecasting Earnings

Let me propose a simple structural model to forecast earnings. Using the Shiller data, suppose we estimated a vector autoregression (VAR) with a single lag selecting the variables used in the earnings model, that is, inflation and growth in both Shiller's 10-year smoothed earnings and smoothed p/e along with the growth rate in the real dividend yield. We forecast out 10 years (VARs are by definition mean-reverting). These forecasted paths represent the model's long-run forecasted conditional means for the variables. This model and method (VAR) is conceptual and intended to illustrate how analysts might use more disciplined approaches to pricing that are based on our understanding of the structural economy and how earnings behave, conditional on that structure. It is therefore not a normative model of earnings.

The average growth rates for this 10-year forward window are 1.92 percent for real dividends, 3.2 percent for the smoothed p/e multiple, 0.2 percent for real smoothed earnings, and 2.34 percent for inflation. Geometrically linking these growth rates and adding in 0.2 percent reinvestment of income produces an expected nominal equity return equal to 7.88 percent. This forecast is illustrated in the following building blocks diagram.

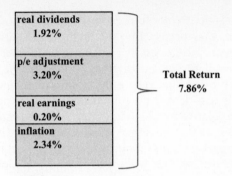

FIGURE 4.4 Building Blocks

We could substitute inflation expectations using TIPS or CPI swap spreads. The squishy component in the forecast is the price adjustment variable (p/e). It should be clear that while building blocks help isolate attention to the components of returns, it does not provide the forecast; rather, forecasts are generally extrapolated from history (a very tenuous process as discussed earlier in the section on trend analysis) or from forward markets such as the TIPS or CPI spreads, forward p/e ratios, and so forth. The advantage of the VAR approach is that its structural form gives us the ability to produce confidence intervals for forecasts, analyze how forecasts respond to unanticipated shocks (impulse responses), and conduct sensitivity analysis.

SUMMARY

The foundation of equity pricing is also a discounted cash flow model. Unlike bonds, however, equity cash flows have inherent uncertainty (these are not contractual cash flows as are coupons) and the discount rate is not an internal rate of return. Instead, the discount rate is the rate that satisfies the Euler relation between the marginal utilities of present and future consumption. Thus, we extend the development of the discount rate developed through the first three chapters to a fundamental model that motivates the discount rate as the solution to optimizing utility in an intertemporal consumption problem.

The Euler relation is a subtle reminder of the role of behavioral economics in pricing models. We therefore lay some groundwork anticipating departures from rationality, which we develop more fully in Chapter 8 on anomalies. We also introduce some simple models of trend extrapolation and its weaknesses, perhaps signaling that simple extrapolative heuristics may suggest that agents are not fully rational and that, possibly, departures from fundamentals may persist. But, the major contribution is once again the notion that agents price assets by evaluating the sum of their discounted expected cash flows. The dividend discount model and the Gordon Growth model are important developments in the evolution of equity pricing models. These models are driven by fundamentals—earnings and discount rates—while extrapolative trend models appeal not to fundamentals, but to univariate models based on historical trend analysis that implicitly rely on rather restrictive assumptions about what the true equilibrium return should be. I argue instead that while extrapolative models may be useful gauges of performance, they do not rely on fundamentals and are therefore not informative. I then introduce a structural model of earnings that is tied to macroeconomic factors that helps explain how earnings respond to changes in the underlying economy. This was a VAR regression model that also has the property of mean reversion and could be useful as a long-run forecasting model.

It should be obvious that these models together produce a wide range of return forecasts. None of them forecasted the exceptional earnings growth that the economy experienced in 2009 and that is stark evidence on the state of the art in equity return forecasting.

REFERENCES

Barsky, Robert B., and J. Bradford DeLong. 1993. Why does the stock market fluctuate? *Quarterly Journal of Economics* 108.

Cochrane, John. 2001. *Asset pricing*. Princeton, NJ: Princeton University Press.

Ibbotson, Roger G., and Peng Chen. 2001. The supply of stock market returns. Yale International Center for Finance, Yale School of Management.

Shiller, Robert. 1981. Do stock prices move too much to be justified by subsequent changes in dividends? *American Economic Review* 71.

Tversky, Amos, and Daniel Kahneman. 1974. Judgement under uncertainty: Heuristics and biases. *Science* 185.

CHAPTER 5

Portfolio Construction

Good management is better than good income.

—Portuguese proverb

A portfolio consists of a collection of assets. The portfolio itself is an asset, too, since it is a collection of assets. The return to the portfolio is a weighted average of the returns to the underlying assets. For example, consider a portfolio of two assets, X and Y. Suppose that the amounts invested in X and Y are $1,000 and $500, respectively. Then X comprises $\frac{\$1,000}{\$1,500} = \frac{2}{3}$ of the value of the portfolio and Y comprises $\frac{1}{3}$ of the portfolio's value. The weights, w_i, are therefore $\frac{2}{3}$ and $\frac{1}{3}$. Note that the weights sum to unity. If the returns to X and Y are known and denoted at r_x and r_y, then the return to the portfolio is $r = \frac{2r_x}{3} + \frac{r_y}{3}$.

STOCHASTIC RETURNS AND RISK

Now allow for risk and uncertainty (strictly speaking, these are different concepts—see the discussion in Chapter 11). We could think of returns as being random, or stochastic, but it is more intuitively appealing to model returns as being state dependent. For example, suppose the dollar payoff to asset j, X_j, depends on which state of nature is observed. Assume there are six such states and the payoff will be one of the following $\{4, -1, 2, 1, 3, 0\}$, all with likelihood $\frac{1}{6}$. Clearly, the payoff (and return) to X_j is random with uniform distribution in this case. We are interested in estimating the expected payoff, which, to us, is the mean value of X_j across all states. In general, the expected value $E(X_j)$ is a weighted average of the possible outcomes. Formally, this is $E(X) = \sum f(x_j) * X_i$; where X_i is a state value and $f(x_i)$ denotes the probability of that state being realized; here, $f(X_i) = \frac{1}{6}$ for all i outcomes.

That is:

$$E(X) = \sum f(x_i) * X_i = \frac{1}{6}(4 - 1 + 2 + 1 + 3 + 0) = \frac{3}{2}$$

So, the expected payoff is 1.5. This statistic conveys a notion of average value across all states. That is, if we were to keep track of our payoffs over time, averaging them as we go along, that average would approach 1.5 by the central limit theorem.

Because the realized payoff is not known with certainty, an investment in X is risky. Although the expected payoff is constant at $\frac{3}{2}$, the observed payoff will vary, being as high as 4 and as low as –1. Translating payoffs into returns is simple—if we have an initial investment $\$X0 = $ say, \$1, then the return is the percentage change in value upon realizing the payoff, for example, if $X_i = 2$, then the return is 100 percent.

Risk is captured in the variability of payoffs. See Appendix 5.1 for a review of statistics. Variance is defined as:

$$Var(X) = E(X - \mu)^2 = E\left(X - \frac{3}{2}\right)^2$$

This is also a weighted sum—in this case, a weighted sum of squared deviations from the mean:

$$E\left(X - \frac{3}{2}\right)^2 = \sum f(x_i) * \left(X_i - \frac{3}{2}\right)^2 = \frac{1}{6} * (16 + 1 + 4 + 1 + 9) - \left(\frac{3}{2}\right)^2 = 2.92$$

The square root of 2.92 is 1.71, which is the standard deviation—what financial analysts refer to as *volatility*. We can summarize our stochastic world of payoffs as having an expected payoff of 1.5 and a standard deviation of 1.71 around this mean. Payoffs, and therefore, returns, have a central tendency (the mean) and dispersion (the volatility) that captures our notion of risk. Risk increases with volatility.

Let's expand this thinking to two assets, X and Y, but with their returns state dependent. A portfolio of X and Y will have variance that is the sum of the variance of X and the variance of Y *plus* two times their covariance. To illustrate, consider Figure 5.1, which depicts returns for assets X and Y in three possible states. State probabilities are given in the interior of the table and correspond to the likelihood of joint returns (for example, the probability that X returns 10 *and* Y returns 8.5 occurs 26 percent of the time). The probability that X's outcome is 10 is called the marginal probability for X and is 0.3, or 30 percent. Similar thinking holds for Y. For example, the marginal probability for Y returning 8.5 is 0.36 and so on. Thus, the marginal probability of $Y = 8.5$ is the likelihood that Y will have this outcome regardless of what outcome X has jointly; it is $P(Y = 8.5|X = 10 \text{ or } X = 5 \text{ or } X = -5) = 0.36$. The | operator denotes a conditional probability.

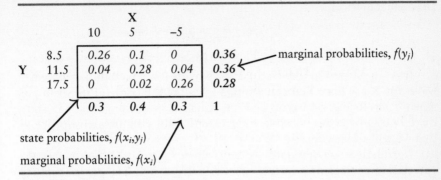

FIGURE 5.1 State Contingent Claims

Let's estimate the following statistics (see also Chapter 5 Examples. xlsx):

$$E(X) = 0.3(10) + 0.4(5) + 0.3(-5) = 3 + 2 - 1.5 = 3.5$$

$$\text{Var}(X) = 0.3(10 - 3.5)^2 + 0.4(5 - 3.5)^2 + 0.3(-5 - 3.5)^2 = 35.25$$

$$\sigma(X) = \sqrt{35.25} = 5.94$$

The reader should confirm the statistics $E(Y) = 12.1$, $\text{Var}(Y) = 12.96$, $\sigma(Y) = 3.6$.

We also note that X and Y are obviously not independent—independence would imply their joint probabilities to be zero. That means the covariation between these two random variables is nonzero. We denote this covariance by $\text{Cov}(X,Y)$ and define it as:

$$\text{Cov}(X, Y) = E[(X_i - E(X))(Y_i - E(Y))] = E\left[(X_i - \mu_x)\left(Y_i - \mu_y\right)\right]$$

Again, this is an expected value and it is therefore a weighted sum of the products. This expression can be simplified since (see Appendix 5.1):

$$E(X_i - E(X))(Y_i - E(Y)) = E(XY) - \mu_x \mu_y$$

and where $E(X) = \mu_x$ and $E(Y) = \mu_y$.

Therefore, $\text{Cov}(X, Y) = E(XY) - \mu_x \mu_y$ and $E(XY) = \sum\sum f(x,y)* (X_i Y_i)$.

Referring to Figure 5.1 again, we see that this is a double summation because we must sum over X (or Y) first, and then the other term Y (or X).

Doing that gives us

$$\text{Cov}(X, Y) = -18.6$$

It is a negative number because the payoffs for Y tend to be high when those for X are low. You can see this from the tabled data; for example, when Y has its highest payoff at 17.5, X has its lowest payoff at –5. Thus, these two payoffs are negatively correlated. That's an attractive property that we will address shortly.

Correlation is a standardized covariance. Standardization places the correlation coefficient ρ in the interval, $-1 \le \rho \le 1$. The correlation coefficient itself is just the covariance between X and Y divided by the product of their standard deviations. Thus,

$$\rho = \frac{\text{Cov}(X, Y)}{\sigma_x \sigma_y}$$

You should confirm for the data in the preceding table that $\rho = -0.87$.

To make the intuition a little easier, recall that any random variable's covariance with itself is the same as its variance, that is, $\text{Cov}(X, X) = E(X^2) - \mu_x^2$. Covariance is critical to understanding and managing portfolio risk and forms the basis of asset allocation and risk diversification, as we shall see shortly.

Suppose we form a portfolio on X and Y in which X has weight w and Y has weight $(1 - w)$ so that the portfolio is fully invested, that is, the weights sum to one. Then the return to this portfolio, r, is:

$$r = wr_x + (1 - w)r_y$$

The expected return on the portfolio is therefore:

$$E(r) = wE(r_x) + (1 - w)E(r_y) = w * 3.5 + (1 - w) * 12.1$$

The expected portfolio return therefore depends on what proportion of each asset is held in the portfolio. The risk on the portfolio will depend on the individual risks to assets X and Y as well as the degree to which the returns on these two assets covary. The variance of the portfolio return is defined as:

$$\sigma^2 = E(r - E(r))^2 = E[w(r_x - E(r_x)) + (1 - w)(r_y - E(r_y))]^2$$

Expanding the square and taking expectations yields:

$$\sigma^2 = w^2 E(r_x - E(r_x))^2 + (1 - w)^2 E(r_y - E(r_y))^2 + 2w(1 - w) \\ * E(r_x - E(r_x))(r_y - E(r_y))$$

More simply,

$$\sigma^2 = w^2 \sigma_x^2 + (1 - w)^2 \sigma_y^2 + 2w(1 - w)\sigma_{xy}$$

Here, σ_{xy} is the covariance. Since returns are expressed in percent and variance in percent squared, taking the square root converts risk back to percent; hence, we typically refer to the risk on the portfolio as its percent volatility, or standard deviation, σ.

We will find it useful later to use the definition of the correlation and write the portfolio variance as follows:

$$\sigma^2 = w^2 \sigma_x^2 + (1 - w)^2 \sigma_y^2 + 2w(1 - w)\rho\sigma_x\sigma_y$$

Notice that as the correlation between the two asset returns moves from $+1$ towards -1, portfolio risk declines.

Let's generalize to N assets in a portfolio again, each of which has random return r_i. Suppose we know the individual expected returns on the assets in the portfolio as $E(r_i)$ for $i = 1, \ldots, n$. The return on the portfolio is: $r = w_1 r_1 + w_2 r_2 + \cdots + w_n r_n$ and has expected return (mean) equal to:

$$E(r) = w_1 E(r_1) + w_2 E(r_2) + \cdots + w_n E(r_n)$$

The expected return on the portfolio is the weighted sum of the expected returns on the individual assets in the portfolio.

The variance of the portfolio is therefore defined as:

$$\sigma^2 = E\left[\left(\sum_{i=1}^{n} w_i(r_i - \bar{r}_i)\right)\left(\sum_{j=1}^{n} w_j(r_j - \bar{r}_j)\right)\right]$$

Notice that this is a quadratic form (it involves a sum of squares). The weights w_i take the place of the probability weights $f(x_i)$ in our state contingent claims example while the $\bar{r}_j$ replace the means μ_x and so forth. When $j = i$, we are then looking at the variance. Otherwise, we are estimating the covariances between returns on different assets.

An equivalent expression is:

$$\sigma^2 = E\left[\sum_{i,j=1}^{n} w_i w_j (r_i - \bar{r}_i)(r_j - \bar{r}_j)\right]$$

which, after passing the expectations operator past the sum of the product of the weights (these are constants, remember, and the expectation of a constant times a random variable is the constant times the expectation of the random variable). Therefore, the expectations of the product of the deviations of the returns from their means are the covariances (variances if $i = j$), which is:

$$\sigma^2 = \sum_{i,j=1}^{n} w_i w_j \sigma_{ij}$$

Note that $\sigma_{ij} = \sigma_i^2$; for $i = j$.

DIVERSIFICATION

We showed that the variance and covariances of returns to a portfolio is given by

$$\sigma^2 = E\left[\sum_{i,j=1}^{n} w_i w_j (r_i - \bar{r}_i)(r_j - \bar{r}_j)\right]$$

I want to get at the intuition behind asset diversification, the idea of not putting all your eggs in one basket, as they say. The intuition is that diversification spreads risk. Let's show this intuition. We can illuminate this concept more easily if we look at a portfolio in which the assets have identical weights—an equally weighted portfolio of N assets with each $w_i = w_j = \frac{1}{N}$. With no loss in generality, also assume their expected returns are all the same. Then the variance-covariance for this portfolio can be written as:

$$\sigma^2 = \frac{1}{N^2} E\left[\left(\sum_{i=1}^{n}(r_i - \bar{r})\sum_{j=1}^{n}(r_j - \bar{r})\right)\right]$$

The bracketed terms are just the cross-products of all the returns with themselves and the other assets' returns. The expectation operator takes the sum of these squares and divides by the number of terms (we'll get to this later but for now understand that if there are N assets, then there are N^2 cross-products in total). We can parse this out into the variances and covariances as follows:

$$\sigma^2 = \frac{1}{N^2} \sum_{i,j=1}^{n} \sigma_{ij} = \frac{1}{N^2} \left[\sum_{i=j} \sigma_{ij} + \sum_{i \neq j} \sigma_{ij} \right]$$

The first term in the square brackets is the sum of the individual asset variances. This second term is the sum of the covariances among assets. The total sum is the risk on the portfolio. Clearly, it is larger if there is positive covariance between the returns. If, on the other hand, the covariances are zero, meaning the returns are independent, then portfolio variance (volatility) is just a function of the individual variances that each asset contributes to the portfolio. If the covariances are negative, on sum, then the overall risk (variance) on the portfolio can be reduced even further. Separately, we state without proof that under fairly general circumstances, as the number of assets in the portfolio increases, the variance of the portfolio falls (this result depends on the denominator N^2 increasing at a faster rate than the sum of covariances). The point we make here is showing how diversification of assets in the portfolio affects the risk on the portfolio. Since covariances are generally weaker than variances, then N^2 increases faster than the sum of the covariances and variances demonstrating that diversification (rising N) can help reduce portfolio risk. How large does N have to be to capitalize on the risk reduction benefits of diversification? The answer depends on the pool of assets we are selecting from; if the pool consists of similar assets (say, investment grade bonds), then N may have to be quite large. On the other hand, N may be as small as 15 or 20 stocks randomly chosen across the Russell 3000 index. It depends on how heterogeneous the population of assets one is selecting from.

THE EFFICIENT FRONTIER

Now, let's return to our two-asset portfolio. Let's call the expected return to X, r_1, and the expected return to Y, r_2. Let's also refer to the risks on the returns to X and Y as their standard deviations σ_1 and σ_2 with covariance σ_{12}. Suppose that the proportion of the portfolio held in asset Y is a fraction, w, and for X, this fraction is $(1 - w)$. Then, the return to the portfolio is:

$$r = (1 - w)r_1 + (w)r_2$$

The variance of these returns is

$$\sigma^2 = (1 - w)^2\sigma_1^2 + w^2\sigma_2^2 + 2w(1 - w)\sigma_{12}$$

The standard deviation is the square root of this expression. Recall that the definition of the correlation coefficient ρ between the returns on X and Y requires ρ to be a number in absolute value between 0 and 1 and that by definition, $\rho = \frac{\text{cov}(r_1, r_2)}{\sigma_1\sigma_2} = \frac{\sigma_{12}}{\sigma_1\sigma_2}$. We can use this result to rewrite the variance formula then as a function of the correlation coefficient:

$$\sigma^2 = (1 - w)^2\sigma_1^2 + w^2\sigma_2^2 + 2w(1 - w)\sigma_1\sigma_2\rho$$

We will use this result to derive the *efficient frontier,* which is a set of portfolios (of X and Y) that yield the greatest return per unit of risk. Its shape will depend on the returns correlation. First, note we have two equations of interest: one is the return to the portfolio and the other is the standard deviation on the portfolio (the risk). To begin, think of a quadrant in risk-return space and begin by setting $\rho = 1$, indicating the two returns are perfectly correlated (for example, they are in effect the same asset in this case). Call this *Case I.* We now have the two equations:

$$r = (1 - w)r_1 + (w)r_2$$

$$\sigma^2 = (1 - w)^2\sigma_1^2 + w^2\sigma_2^2 + 2w(1 - w)\sigma_1\sigma_2 = [(1 - w)\sigma_1 + w\sigma_2]^2$$

Since we want to work in r,σ space, taking the square root of σ^2 gives us:

$$r = (1 - w)r_1 + (w)r_2$$

$$\sigma = (1 - w)\sigma_1 + (w)\sigma_2$$

The rate of change in the return and the risk with respect to the portfolio weight is:

$$\frac{dr}{dw} = r_2 - r_1$$

$$\frac{d\sigma}{dw} = \sigma_2 - \sigma_1$$

Therefore, the risk-return trade-off for Case I is:

$$\frac{dr}{d\sigma} = \frac{r_2 - r_1}{\sigma_2 - \sigma_1}$$

Thus, the return-risk trade-off falls along a positively sloping line in the risk-return space. It is positively sloped, since it must be that if r_2 is greater than r_1, then σ_2 must be greater than σ_1. Otherwise, there would be an arbitrage opportunity to sell the riskier asset with lower return and to buy the less risky asset with a higher return and earn an arbitrage profit. Arbitrage profit opportunities cannot persist.

Now assume the opposite limiting case that $\rho = -1$. Call this *Case II*. In this case, we have:

$$r = (1 - w)r_1 + (w)r_2$$

$$\sigma^2 = (1 - w)^2\sigma_1^2 + w^2\sigma_2^2 - 2w(1 - w)\sigma_1\sigma_2 = [(1 - w)\sigma_1 - w\sigma_2]^2$$

Taking the square root of the variance to get the risk relationship, we get the following two equations:

$$r = (1 - w)r_1 + (w)r_2$$

$$\sigma = |(1 - w)\sigma_1 - w\sigma_2|$$

For the risk to be defined (that is, positive), it must be that $(1 - w)\sigma_1 > w\sigma_2$. When the weight w is small, then this will be the case. Specifically, you can see that as long as $w < \frac{\sigma_1}{(\sigma_1 + \sigma_2)}$, then this condition is satisfied. When $w > \frac{\sigma_1}{(\sigma_1 + \sigma_2)}$, then the relationship becomes $\sigma = (w)\sigma_2 - (1 - w)\sigma_1$. Call this *Case III*. Therefore, there is a switching point at which $w = \frac{\sigma_1}{(\sigma_1 + \sigma_2)}$, and substituting this expression into σ, we solve for the switching point:

$$\sigma = \left[\frac{\sigma_2}{\sigma_1 + \sigma_2}\right]\sigma_1 - \left[\frac{\sigma_1}{\sigma_1 + \sigma_2}\right]\sigma_2 = 0$$

$$r = \left[\frac{\sigma_2}{(\sigma_1 + \sigma_2)}\right]r_1 + \left[\frac{\sigma_1}{(\sigma_1 + \sigma_2)}\right]r_2 = \frac{(r_1\sigma_2 + r_2\sigma_1)}{(\sigma_1 + \sigma_2)}$$

This is a point in risk-return space. It has zero risk and vertical intercept equal to the value of r just given. I now derive the rest of the efficient set.

We have these two additional cases beginning with Case II:

$$\frac{dr}{dw} = (r_2 - r_1)$$

$$\frac{d\sigma}{dw} = -(\sigma_2 + \sigma_1)$$

$$\frac{dr}{d\sigma} = -\frac{(r_2 - r_1)}{(\sigma_2 + \sigma_1)}$$

Case II, therefore, is a line with negative slope. Case III, however, is:

$$r = (1 - w)r_1 + (w)r_2$$

$$\sigma = (w)\sigma_2 - (1 - w)\sigma_1$$

$$\frac{dr}{d\sigma} = \frac{(r_2 - r_1)}{(\sigma_2 + \sigma_1)}$$

This is an upward sloping line in $r - \sigma$ space. Putting these ideas together, we derive the general shape of the feasible set of portfolios that can be constructed across these two assets. (See Figure 5.2.)

In general, the correlation coefficient between the returns is less than one in absolute value, and the actual value will determine the shape of the feasible set. From the preceding figure, we see that portfolios along the lower boundary are dominated by those directly above them. For example, for two portfolios with the same risk, we'd prefer the one with the higher return. Therefore, the *efficient set* consists of the top portion of the feasible

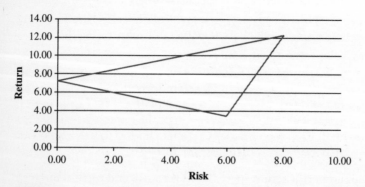

FIGURE 5.2   Feasible Set

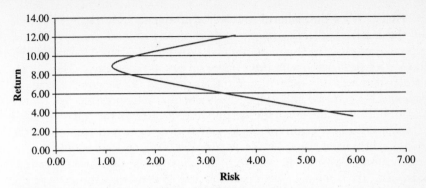

FIGURE 5.3 Feasible Set for Contingent Claim Example

set. When the correlation coefficient is less than one in absolute value, this frontier is convex. Figure 5.3 shows the feasible set using Figure 5.1, which depicted payouts to two assets, X and Y, which have correlation equal to –0.87.

MARKOWITZ PORTFOLIO SELECTION CRITERIA

Efficiency is about minimizing risk. The efficient frontier is the set of risk-minimizing portfolios for any given set of returns. The *mean-variance efficient portfolio* is the one with *minimum risk*. Markowitz's contribution was to give us the calculus to solve portfolio problems like this. The objective is to find the weightings (w_i) that minimize the risk for a given portfolio return. Achieving this would generate a weighting of the assets in a portfolio, which would occupy a point on the efficient frontier. How can one achieve this objective? Consider again the risk we solved earlier and reprint here:

$$\sigma^2 = \sum_{i,j=1}^{n} w_i w_j \sigma_{ij}$$

We desire to choose the weightings (the w_i and w_j) that minimize this quantity for a given portfolio return. There are several ways to set up this problem and I outline a few here that serve as a platform for our empirical work in Excel. I begin with a very intuitively appealing representation of the problem as a risk-adjusted return maximization in matrix format that solves for the vector w that maximizes the quadratic form given by:

$$\max_w w'r - \frac{(\lambda w' V w)}{2}$$

Here w is a k-dimensional row vector of weights $(1xk)$, where k stands for the number of assets in the portfolio, r is a conforming vector of expected returns $((kx1)$ column vector), V is the covariance matrix (kxk), and λ is a risk aversion parameter (more on risk aversion later). Thus, $w'r$ is a scalar that measures the return to the portfolio (it is a weighted average of the expected returns) and $w'Vw$ is a scalar that measures the risk on the portfolio. (This is the quadratic part because it involves the squared values of weights, variances, and covariances. We divide by two to account for the square, which we'll also see more clearly later. For now, understand that its presence doesn't affect the solution). Thus, we want a set of weights that *maximizes the risk-adjusted return*. A review of matrix operations is in the appendix to Chapter 6.

Differentiating with respect to w', setting this expression to zero and solving for the remaining w yields:

$$\frac{d}{dw} = r - \lambda Vw = 0$$

$$(\lambda V)^{-1}r = w$$

The solution w is a $(kx1)$ vector of weights that define this optimal portfolio. Ignoring the risk-aversion parameter for the moment (this serves only to scale the solution), assume that V is a diagonal matrix, meaning that the returns to the k assets are independent and that the diagonal elements of V are the returns variances. Then the solution is a portfolio whose weights (w) are their respective expected returns divided by their respective variances. The portfolio that minimizes risk chooses assets in proportion to their return per unit of risk, that is, the lowest risk-to-reward ratio.

If returns are not independent, then V contains covariances and the inverse of V is more complicated. Nevertheless, the optimal portfolio still has the same interpretation, only here the risk on each asset extends to the strength of its correlations with the other assets. In general, the more positive those correlations, the higher the risk (bad things can happen to more than one asset at the same time, so to speak) and the lower the weight assigned to that asset. We investigate this more closely in our empirical applications further on.

Let's now break apart the matrix algebra into the set of underlying equations so that we can get a better understanding of what's going on in the calculus. At the same time, let's address a few important constraints like forcing the sum of the weights to equal unity (fully invested portfolio) and that the desired portfolio return is known ahead. How do we do this? We do so by writing the *Lagrangian* (this is a constrained optimization problem) and using the first order conditions to solve for the weights. We'll set it up formally first and then talk about the intuition. We wish to optimize the following setup, which is to *find a portfolio w that minimizes the risk*:

$$\min_w = \frac{1}{2} \sum_{i,j=1}^{n} w_i w_j \sigma_{ij}$$

Subject to the two adding-up constraints:

$$\sum_{i=1}^{n} w_i \bar{r}_i = \bar{r}$$

and

$$\sum_{i=1}^{n} w_i = 1$$

The first constraint says that the weighted asset means in the fund must sum to the targeted return on the portfolio. The second says that the weights must sum to unity (we say that the fund is fully invested; there's no money left on the table, so to speak).

We now form the Lagrangian:

$$L = \frac{1}{2} \sum_{i,j=1}^{n} w_i w_j \sigma_{ij} - \lambda \left(\sum_{i=1}^{n} w_i \bar{r}_i - \bar{r} \right) - \mu \left(\sum_{i=1}^{n} w_i - 1 \right)$$

We differentiate this function with respect to each of the w_i in the portfolio and with respect to the Lagrange multipliers lambda (λ) and mu (μ). That means we will end up with k first order conditions (there are k assets, and therefore one derivative for each) and two derivatives for the constraints for a total of $k + 2$ first order conditions. We set each of these first order conditions equal to zero and solve this system of $k + 2$ equations simultaneously for the weights as well as λ and μ as the constraint parameters (we'll focus on the weights).

The first order conditions involve k equations, one for each w_i followed by the two constraints.

$$\sum \sigma_{ij} w_j - \lambda \bar{r}_i - \mu = 0 \, for \, i = 1, \ldots, k$$

$$\sum w_i \bar{r}_i = \bar{r}$$

$$\sum w_i = 1$$

To make the first of these three relations make sense, think of a two-asset portfolio and the covariance structure of its returns given by:

$$V = \begin{bmatrix} \sigma_1^2 & \sigma_{12} \\ \sigma_{21} & \sigma_2^2 \end{bmatrix}$$

The diagonal elements are the variances, and the off-diagonal elements, the covariances. The portfolio risk was derived earlier in this chapter. It must be, therefore, that the following two relations are equivalent:

$$\sum_{i,j=1}^{2} w_i w_j \sigma_{ij} = w_1^2 \sigma_1^2 + w_2^2 \sigma_2^2 + 2w_1 w_2 \sigma_{12}$$

This, incidentally, has the matrix equivalent:

$$w' V w = (w_1, w_2) \begin{bmatrix} \sigma_1^2 & \sigma_{12} \\ \sigma_{21} & \sigma_2^2 \end{bmatrix} \begin{pmatrix} w_1 \\ w_2 \end{pmatrix}$$

Either way, we can now see that differentiating the Langrangian with respect to the weights produces the following first order conditions:

$$\sigma_1^2 w_1 + \sigma_{12} w_2 - \lambda \bar{r} - \mu = 0$$

$$\sigma_{21} w_1 + \sigma_2^2 w_2 - \lambda \bar{r} - \mu = 0$$

$$\bar{r}_1 w_1 + \bar{r}_2 w_2 = \bar{r}$$

$$w_1 + w_2 = 1$$

As promised, there are $k + 2 = 4$ equations in four unknowns. One solution method is Cramer's Rule; the other is straightforward matrix multiplication, which I prefer to use since this is the method most suited to our spreadsheet work that will follow later. Our system is given directly further on. The data are in the first (4X4) matrix. The parameters we wish to solve for are in the second vector $(w_1, w_2, \lambda, \mu)'$, while the targeted values in the constraints are in the vector on the right-hand side of the equation.

$$
\begin{bmatrix}
\sigma_{11} & \sigma_{12} & -\bar{r}_1 & -1 \\
\sigma_{21} & \sigma_{22} & -\bar{r}_2 & -1 \\
\bar{r}_1 & \bar{r}_2 & 0 & 0 \\
1 & 1 & 0 & 0
\end{bmatrix}
\begin{bmatrix}
w_1 \\
w_2 \\
\lambda \\
\mu
\end{bmatrix}
=
\begin{bmatrix}
0 \\
0 \\
\bar{r} \\
1
\end{bmatrix}
$$

Solving this system is not hard. If we represent it as $Ax = b$, then $x = A^{-1}b$. Our minimum variance portfolio consists of the first two elements in x. The leftmost point on the efficient frontier is the minimum variance portfolio. We can solve this portfolio by eliminating the third row in A, x, and b and the third column in A and solve for $(w_1, w_2, \mu)'$.

CAPITAL MARKET LINE AND THE CAPM

We have been analyzing an optimization problem whose solution resolves the Markowitz problem, specifically, what combination of weights in a k-asset portfolio return a targeted portfolio mean return at minimum variance.

The *Two-Fund theorem* basically states that for any two efficient portfolios (hence, two sets of weights corresponding to two targeted returns $\bar{r}_1$ and $\bar{r}_2$), any other efficient portfolio can be constructed as a linear combination of these two.

Now, we derive the *One Fund*. Add a risk-free asset to our analysis earning a rate of return r_f. Then, suppose we have a proportion α in this asset and the remainder $(1 - \alpha)$ in the risky asset(s). The mean return on this portfolio will be

$$
\mu = \alpha r_f + (1 - \alpha)r
$$

where r is the mean return to the risky portfolio with variance

$$
\text{Var} = (1 - \alpha)^2 \sigma^2
$$

Var is a scalar because both the variance and covariance of returns on the riskless asset is zero by definition. The standard deviation on this new portfolio is then $(1 - \alpha)\sigma$. What is the relationship between the mean (u) and the risk in this portfolio as the relative share, α, changes? To find out, take two derivatives; $\frac{d\mu}{d\alpha} = (r_f - r)$ and $\frac{d\sigma}{d\alpha} = -\sigma$. Divide the first by the

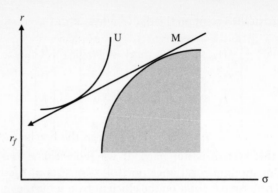

FIGURE 5.4   Capital Market Line

second to get $\frac{d\mu}{d\sigma} = \frac{(r-r_f)}{\sigma}$. This is the slope of a line in (r, σ) space. Its intercept is r_f (that is, the return on the portfolio when $\sigma = 0$ is r_f because with no risk, we cannot be holding any of the risky asset).

The shaded region in Figure 5.4 is the feasible set depicted in Figure 5.3 bordered by the efficient frontier. The line from r_f through M is the *capital market line*. M is the *One Fund* (the market portfolio below) and U represents a representative investor's utility. Note that utility is increasing to the northwest. The point at which U is tangent with the capital market line represents a combination of M and the riskless asset that maximizes utility. The inclusion of the riskless asset therefore permits lending (or borrowing); it allows the investor to purchase a single fund of the risky asset M and lend or borrow to maximize utility. Points to the right of M along the line represent borrowing (hence buying more of the risky asset M and therefore increasing risk). Points between M and r_f represent lending. Either way, points along the line dominate points on the efficient frontier since they generate higher utility.

What is the *One Fund?* The concept is a little abstract, but think of it this way: if all investors had the same beliefs about returns and risks associated with each risky asset, and all are aware of a risk-free asset with return r_f, and everyone is a mean-variance optimizer (like Markowitz), then M is a fund of risky assets that contain every asset in the market in proportion to that asset's market capitalization. For example, if the market consists of only two risky assets, X and Y, with valuations of \$100 and \$200, respectively, then the market has capital value of \$300 and X's capitalization weight is $\frac{1}{3}$ and Y's is $\frac{2}{3}$. In equilibrium, M will contain each of theseα assets in these proportions. If market participants' expectations change, then so will demand and supply of each asset, which, in turn, alters their respective values, and hence, their capitalization weights. Thus, M is still the market portfolio, the One Fund. All investors will buy shares of M and borrow or lend, or both, to maximize utility. (This is the logic of various index funds in the mutual fund industry.)

From our discussion of the capital market line, in slope-intercept form, the risk-return trade-off is $r = r_f + \left[\frac{(r_m - r_f)}{\sigma_m}\right]\sigma$. Here, σ_m is the risk on the portfolio M (the market portfolio). The term in the brackets is the price of risk and σ is the amount of risk. For zero risk, obviously, the return is $r = r_f$.

EXAMPLE 5.1

Suppose I ask you to invest $1,000 of venture capital into my business. My claim is that your investment will grow to $1,200 in one year. Historically, the standard deviation of my returns has been 36 percent and the market return has been 17 percent with a standard deviation of 12 percent. The risk-free rate is 10 percent. Show that this investment opportunity (which can be thought of as a single asset portfolio) lies below the capital market line and is therefore inefficient and that the rate of return required should be 31 percent.

The capital market line represents a set of portfolios consisting of the market portfolio M and the risk-free asset. It is silent, however, on informing us on how to *price* risky assets. The capital asset pricing model (CAPM) combines the capital market line with investors' mean-variance optimizing behavior to arrive at an equilibrium-inspired model that prices risky assets.

In a word, the CAPM implies that if M is efficient, then the mean return r_i for all securities i satisfies $r_i - r_f = \beta(r_m - r_f)$, where r_i and r_m are mean returns and $\beta = \frac{\sigma_{im}}{\sigma_m^2}$. The question CAPM addresses is this: if M is a diversified portfolio and r_i is the return to a risky asset, then for this risky asset to be included in the portfolio, it should have an excess return over the risk-free asset that is proportional to the excess return of M over the risk-free asset. The factor of proportionality is the asset's **beta** β. Generalizing, the returns to all risky assets should be proportional to their betas—this is the notion underlying the security market line that we will derive shortly.

The intuition is that there is a portfolio of asset i and the market portfolio M with weights α and $(1 - \alpha)$, respectively, given by:

$$r_p = \alpha r_i + (1 - \alpha)r_m$$

This portfolio has standard deviation (risk) given by:

$$\sigma_p = \left(\alpha^2\sigma_i^2 + (1-\alpha)^2\sigma_m^2 + 2\alpha(1-\alpha)\sigma_{im}\right)^{\frac{1}{2}}$$

As we saw while constructing the efficient frontier, changes in α will trace out a curve in return-risk space ($\alpha = 0$ in particular corresponds to M, the market portfolio). Since the capital market line contains M, then this bounded set of opportunities involving M and the risky asset, with portfolio weights α and $(1-\alpha)$ share a common point (M). Therefore, the capital market line is a tangent to this set of portfolios containing M and the risky asset. We want to find the relationship that satisfies this tangency because it will connect the concept of the risk-return trade-off between a diversified portfolio M and the riskless asset with the concept of the relationship between risky assets, in general, and the conditions for their conclusion in a well-diversified portfolio M. To begin with, the trade-off between the return to this *portfolio* of any risky asset and M with respect to small changes in α is defined by:

$$\frac{dr_p}{d\alpha} = r_i - r_m$$

Likewise, the trade-off between the risk and the allocation weight α is:

$$\frac{d\sigma_p}{d\alpha} = \frac{\alpha\sigma_i^2 + (1-2\alpha)\sigma_{im} + (\alpha-1)\sigma_m^2}{\sigma_p}$$

If we evaluate the risk at the point of tangency ($\alpha = 0$ meaning the location of M on the capital market line), then:

$$\left.\frac{d\sigma_p}{d\alpha}\right|_{\alpha=0} = \frac{\sigma_{im} - \sigma_m^2}{\sigma_m}$$

And finally, the risk-return trade-off:

$$\left.\frac{dr_p}{d\sigma_p}\right|_{\alpha=0} = \frac{(r_i - r_m)\sigma_m}{\sigma_{im} - \sigma_m^2}$$

This slope must be equal to the slope of the capital market line. Setting them equal:

$$\frac{(r_i - r_m)\sigma_m}{\sigma_{im} - \sigma_m^2} = \frac{r_m - r_f}{\sigma_m}$$

Finally, solving for the return on the risky asset that is to be added to the diversified market portfolio M, we get:

$$r_i = r_f + \frac{\sigma_{im}}{\sigma_m^2}\left(r_m - r_f\right)$$

That completes the derivation of the CAPM.

This means that the excess return $r_i - r_f$ to the risky asset is proportional to the excess market return $\left(r_m - r_f\right)$. The factor of proportionality is the asset's beta. For each asset i, we can plot the relation between the mean return r_i and the asset's beta. This relationship is the *security market line* and has slope equal to the excess market return. This is the same thing as saying that any risky asset return r_i is linear in its beta and the trade-off between the two is the market excess return. So if the market excess return is 5 percent, for example, then the excess return to the risky asset is five times whatever its beta is. As beta rises, so does this excess return. Why? Because beta is a normalized covariance between the asset return and the market. The more they covary in a positive way, the greater the contribution to risk in the portfolio through inclusion of the risky asset. The investor needs therefore to be compensated for this and that is why the CAPM indicates that the excess return to the risky asset must increase.

The CAPM is an idealized relationship. At any point in time, however, an asset's excess return is not always exactly equal to the product of its beta and the market excess return. That is, there is some mean zero error ε in the relationship that captures the asset's idiosyncratic error—the volatility of this error is its *specific* or *nonsystematic risk*. Unlike β, which is *systematic* and compensated risk, specific risk is uncompensated and must be diversified away. We write the *empirical* CAPM as

$$r_i - r_f = \alpha + \beta\left(r_m - r_f\right) + \varepsilon$$

Note that ε is the asset's idiosyncratic error (what we're calling specific risk) and is uncorrelated with the market excess return and $E(\varepsilon) = 0$. Therefore, the variance is:

$$\sigma_i^2 = \beta_i^2 \sigma_m^2 + \text{var}(\varepsilon)$$

The first term on the right-hand side is the systematic error (systematic risk), which must be compensated for if the asset is to be priced correctly. The second term, $\text{var}(\varepsilon)$, is the idiosyncratic error, which can be diversified away. Why can it be diversified away? Because it is uncorrelated with the market return. Any asset that lies on the security market line must, by

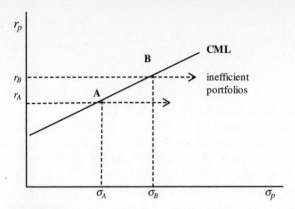

FIGURE 5.5 Capital Market Line with Inefficient Portfolios

definition, have risk equal to $\beta\sigma_m$. Therefore, assets that have nonsystematic risk will lie horizontally to the right of a point on the capital market line. This is illustrated in Figure 5.5.

PERFORMANCE EVALUATION

EXAMPLE 5.2

Consider a stock with mean return of 20 percent and standard deviation of 40 percent. The mean market rate of return is 20 percent, with standard deviation equal to 12 percent. The covariance of these two risky asset returns is assumed to be equal to 4 percent. The risk-free rate is 8 percent. With this information, we compute $\beta = \frac{0.04}{(0.12)^2} = 2.78$. Thus, we have:

$$(r_i - r_f) = \beta(r_m - r_f) + \varepsilon$$

$$(0.2 - 0.08) = 2.78(0.12) + \varepsilon$$

$$0.12 = 0.3336 + \varepsilon$$

This suggests that $\varepsilon = -21.36$ percent. This stock is not a good buy because it is performing below its CAPM risk-adjusted rate of return. What we've computed here is *Jensen's index,* the abnormal return on the risky asset, which, in this case, is about –21.36 percent. The intuition is that if the CAPM holds, then $E(\varepsilon) = 0$ and the actual excess return to the asset is proportional to the excess market return as indicated by $\beta = 2.78$ (this beta estimate says that this asset is about 2.78 times as risky as the market portfolio). In this example, however, the asset's excess return is too low, that is, its return lies below the capital market line. It is what we might call an underperformer. (Jensen's index—sometimes called Jensen's alpha in the empirical literature—is really a test of the CAPM.) Significantly nonzero estimates of the intercept α in a regression of the asset's excess return on the market excess return invalidates the CAPM.

The *Sharpe ratio,* on the other hand, examines the ratio of the excess return on an asset to its standard deviation (or risk). That is, $\frac{r_i - r_f}{\sigma}$ is the Sharpe ratio.

For pricing, recall that the one period return (ignoring dividends) is $r = \frac{P_1 - P_0}{P_1}$, where P is the asset's market price and the subscripts index time. Thus, $r_i = r_f + \beta(r_m - r_f)$ according to the CAPM, and substituting for r_i:

$$\frac{P_1 - P_0}{P_0} = r_f + \beta(r_m - r_f)$$

$$P_0 = \frac{P_1}{\left(1 + r_f + \beta(r_m - r_f)\right)}$$

What's interesting here is that the asset's beta and the market excess return together price the asset. If the asset has a beta of zero (indicating that it doesn't covary with the market), then P_0 is simply the discounted (at the risk-free rate) value of the payoff P_1.

The payoff, P_1 is usually not known with certainty. As such, it is a random variable that is state dependent. We are interested in its expected value $E(P_1)$. It is reasonable to think that the expected future price is a function of the stream of cash flows, or dividends, if we are thinking about a share of stock. Thus, we can write a simple dividend discount model as:

$$P_0 = \frac{E\left(\sum d_i\right)}{\left(1 + r_f + \beta(r_m - r_f)\right)}$$

More importantly, we can show how the CAPM extends interpretation of the discount rate used in the DDM of Chapter 4. There, the pricing model discounted expected future cash flows at a constant rate, r:

$$p_t = \frac{1}{(1+r)} p_{t+1}^e + \frac{1}{(1+r)} d_{t+1}^e$$

The capital asset pricing model produces a logically consistent result but uses a more meaningful discounting function—we replace r with $r_f + \beta(r_m - r_f)$.

SUMMARY

This chapter introduces the portfolio optimization problem as a solution to a specific objective function, namely, to find the portfolio (vector of asset weights) that minimizes portfolio risk. Variations abound in later chapters. Recognizing that a disciplined approach to this problem requires basic tools in statistics and calculus, I mix quantitative methods within a narrative describing the underlying intuition. In this manner, we see the role that expected returns, variances, and correlation play in constructing optimal portfolios and how one addresses concepts such as diversification with this framework. We derive from first principles the efficient frontier and the capital asset pricing model (CAPM), and then examine applications of each. The CAPM is then used in applications as a pricing model and we analyze its relationship to the dividend discount model of the previous chapter. Finally, we introduce for the first time basic performance evaluation criteria such as Jensen's alpha and the Sharpe ratio. Throughout, we refer technical arguments to the chapter appendix, which contains a review of statistics relevant to the concepts covered in this chapter.

APPENDIX 5.1: STATISTICAL REVIEW

Asset returns are not perfectly anticipated. Therefore, they are modeled as draws from an underlying probability distribution (for example, the Normal density with mean return μ and variance σ^2). The probability distribution describes the riskiness of returns. For example, if returns are normally distributed, then observed returns will have a relatively high likelihood of being close to the average, or central tendency of the distribution and, consequently, would have a low likelihood of taking on extreme values in the tails of the distribution. The following is a picture of the standard normal density for the random variable $z = \frac{x-\mu}{\sigma}$. The likelihood is higher for values of z closer to the mean (zero) than for extreme values.

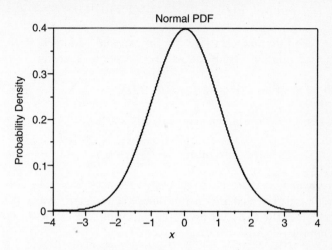

We can therefore think of a random draw as having an expected value that corresponds to some notion of central tendency. Thus, the expected value of a random variable is some kind of average of all its possible outcomes. Figure 5.1 is such an example—the expected values of the random payoffs are weighted averages of their possible outcomes. In repeated draws, we would expect an outcome to be represented by:

$$E(r) = \sum_{i=1}^{N} f_i r_i$$

Here, f_i is the relative frequency (probability) of observing return (or payoff) r_i, and there are N possible outcomes. If all N returns are equally likely as they would be in a *simple random sample,* then the return is expected to be:

$$\frac{E(r) = \sum \frac{1}{N} r_i = \sum r_i}{N}$$

Variances are also expected values, but for squared deviations of the possible returns from what we would expect them to be:

$$\text{Variance}(r_i) = E[r_i - E(r)]^2$$

Like an expected value, the expectation is simply the sum of the squared terms divided by N. Before we evaluate the expectation (E), let's first expand the square to get:

$$E[r_i - E(r)]^2 = E[r_i^2] - 2r_iE(r) + [E(r)]^2]$$

Now, recall that expectations are for random variables, so if c is constant and r is a random variable, then $E(cr) = cE(r)$. Therefore,

$$E[r_i - E(r)]^2 = E[r_i^2] - 2[E(r)]^2 + [E(r)]^2] = \frac{1}{N}\sum r_i^2 - [E(r)]^2$$

If we denote $E(r) = \mu$, then equivalently, we have

$$\text{variance}(r_i) = \frac{\sum r_i^2}{N} - \mu^2$$

This is a standard formula to estimate variances. Now take two random variables, r_1 and r_2, which are the random returns on two assets. What is the covariance? It is the expectation of the variation *across* these two returns over the sample.

$$\text{Cov}(r_1, r_2) = E[(r_1 - E(r_1))][r_2 - E(r_2)]$$

Let's denote $E(r_i) = \mu_i$. Therefore:

$$\text{Cov}(r_1, r_2) = E[(r_1 - \mu_1][r_2 - \mu_2]$$

$$\text{Cov}(r_1, r_2) = E(r_1r_2 - r_1\mu_2 - r_2\mu_1 + \mu_1\mu_2)$$

Now, passing the expectations operator through and evaluating the expected values of the random variables yields:

$$\text{Cov}(r_1, r_2) = \frac{\sum r_1r_2}{N} - \frac{\sum r_1}{N}\mu_2 - \frac{\sum r_2}{N}\mu_1 + \mu_1\mu_2$$

Since $\frac{\sum r_i}{N} = \mu_i$, then this simplifies to the following:

$$\text{Cov}(r_1, r_2) = \frac{\sum r_1r_2}{N - \mu_1\mu_2}$$

Correlations are closely related—they are standardized covariances. That is,

$$\rho = \frac{\text{Cov}(r_1r_2)}{\sigma_1\sigma_2}$$

Rho (ρ) is the correlation coefficient and σ_i are standard deviations (square roots of the variances). The denominator is always positive but the numerator can take positive or negative values. Therefore, ρ may be of either sign. It is, however, bounded by one in absolute value since $|\text{Cov}(r_1, r_2)| = \sigma_1 \sigma_2$ by the Cauchy-Schwartz inequality.

Extrapolation

Assume a security's returns are independently distributed over time; that is, the return today does not depend on the return in any other time. Over a period of time T, we observe total return

$$(1 + R_T) = (1 + r_1)(1 + r_2(1 + r_3) \cdots (1 + r_T)$$

Taking logarithms produces the sum:

$$ln(1 + R_T) = ln(1 + r_1) + ln(1 + r_2) + ln(1 + r_3) + \cdots + ln(1 + r_T)$$

For simplicity, let $r_t^* = \ln(1 + r_t)$. Then, the return for the entire period T is the sum:

$$r_1^* + r_2^* + r_3^* + \cdots + r_T^*$$

Since returns are assumed to be independent, the variance of the return over T periods is the sum of the individual variances (since independence requires the cross-product terms to be zero):

$$\sigma_T^2 = \sigma^2 T$$

This suggests that volatility over any time span T be a simple constant extrapolation of the single period volatility:

$$\sigma_T = \sigma \sqrt{T}$$

Diversification on the Margin

Suppose a portfolio consists of a single risky asset with variance $\sigma_1{}^2$. Does adding another risky asset always reduce risk as long as the correlation between the two assets is less than one? To answer this question, let's find out under which conditions the risk on the two-asset portfolio is less than the risk on the single risky asset. We express this relationship as an inequality:

$$w^2 \sigma_1^2 + (1 - w)^2 \sigma_2^2 + 2w(1 - w)\rho \sigma_{12} \leq \sigma_1^2$$

The left side of the inequality is the risk on the two-asset portfolio. With no loss of generality, assume that the second asset's risk is linear in the first asset's risk, so that:

$$\sigma_2 = \alpha\sigma_1$$

The constant α can be any number. Making this substitution into the first equation from before and collecting a few terms yields the following:

$$(1 - w)^2\sigma_2^2 + 2w(1 - w)\rho\sigma_{12} \leq \sigma_1^2(1 - w)^2$$

Now, if we isolate the correlation coefficient ρ, we can show that the risk on the expanded portfolio will depend on the relative values between the two assets' correlation, their weights, and their individual risks. Solving for ρ:

$$\rho \leq \frac{1 - w^2 - \alpha^2(1 - w)^2}{2\alpha w(1 - w)}$$

Therefore, whether diversification of risk occurs will depend on the strength of their correlation; in general, smaller correlations are required. If we were to examine this problem in a spreadsheet, we would quickly find that the correlation alone is not the arbiter of diversification. Rather, it is the risk on the second asset relative to the first asset, captured by α, as well as their relative weights. Diversification is not guaranteed simply because the asset being added to the portfolio has a low correlation to the existing assets. Rather, diversification depends on how risky the second asset is as well as how heavily weighted the bigger portfolio is to this asset. Therefore, as α gets larger, ρ will have to be smaller to compensate for the additional assets' higher risk.

APPENDIX 5.2: RISK-ADJUSTED PERFORMANCE

The basic CAPM result states that the excess return on any asset (portfolio) is proportional to the excess return on the benchmark portfolio where the factor of proportionality is the asset's beta:

$$r_i - r_f = \beta(r_b - r_f)$$

The Sharpe ratio is the excess return per unit risk. Thus, we rewrite the CAPM as follows:

$$\frac{r_i - r_f}{\sigma_i} = \frac{\sigma_{i,b}}{\sigma_b^2}\frac{(r_b - r_f)}{\sigma_i}$$

Noting that $\sigma_{i,b} = \rho\sigma_i\sigma_b$ and making this substitution, we have:

$$\frac{r_i - r_f}{\sigma_i} = \rho\frac{\sigma_i\sigma_b}{\sigma_b^2}\frac{(r_b - r_f)}{\sigma_i}$$

Collecting terms and assuming $\rho = 1$,

$$(r_i - r_f) * \frac{\sigma_b}{\sigma_i} = (r_b - r_f)$$

Equivalently,

$$(r_i - r_f) * \frac{\sigma_b}{\sigma_i} + r_f = r_b$$

And finally,

$$r_i * \frac{\sigma_b}{\sigma_i} + (1 - \sigma_b/\sigma_i)r_f = r_b$$

Thus, the return on a weighted average of the risky asset and the risk-free asset mimics the return to the benchmark portfolio. The weight scales the asset's return to reflect the risk difference between the benchmark and the asset. Thus, if benchmark risk is higher, then the asset's return is adjusted upward to reflect this difference. This is the basic result of the Modigliani risk-adjusted performance result (Modigliani 1997). What is interesting is that the risk on this portfolio is the same as the benchmark risk. This is particularly easy to estimate since the risk-free asset has zero risk. Therefore:

$$\text{Var}\left(r_i * \frac{\sigma_b}{\sigma_i}\right) = \frac{\sigma_b^2}{\sigma_i^2}\text{Var}(r_i) = \frac{\sigma_b^2}{\sigma_i^2}\sigma_i^2 = \sigma_b^2$$

REFERENCE

Modigliani, Franco 1997. Risk-adjusted performance. *Journal of Portfolio Management* 23 (Winter): 45–54.

CHAPTER 6

Optimal Portfolios

The essence of investment management is the management of risks, not the management of returns.

—Benjamin Graham

This chapter applies the principles of Chapter 5 toward the construction of portfolios that characterize specific optimization objectives, for example, minimum variance portfolios or portfolios that maximize risk-adjusted returns; perhaps satisfying specific constraints like no shorting, or bounded allocations to certain securities. It makes sense to start with simple cases to fix ideas. We will build from the discussion in Chapter 5 on the Markowitz selection criteria.

PORTFOLIO 1: MINIMUM VARIANCE PORTFOLIO (FULLY INVESTED)

Go to the companion website for more details.

There are two assets and we wish to solve for the portfolio (this is a vector of weights) that minimizes the portfolio's risk. Risk is the standard deviation of the time series of returns on the portfolio, which is a weighted average of the individual risks on the two assets and their covariances. That is, we want to minimize the scalar quantity (by scalar, I mean a single value, that is $w'Vw$ is a number; a 1×1 matrix) given by:

$$w'Vw = (w_1, w_2) \begin{bmatrix} \sigma_1^2 & \sigma_{12} \\ \sigma_{21} & \sigma_2^2 \end{bmatrix} \begin{pmatrix} w_1 \\ w_2 \end{pmatrix}$$

Expanding this as we did in Chapter 5 is equivalent to optimizing the following objective function:

$$\min_w = \frac{1}{2} \sum_{i,j=1}^{n} w_i w_j \sigma_{ij}$$

Written out, the summation is:

$$\sum_{i,j=1}^{2} w_i w_j \sigma_{ij} = w_1^2 \sigma_1^2 + w_2^2 \sigma_2^2 + 2 w_1 w_2 \sigma_{12}$$

This is the portfolio's risk for a given set of weights and covariances. We want to minimize this quantity subject to the constraint that the portfolio is fully invested, that is, that the weights sum to unity, $\sum w_i = w_1 + w_2 = 1$. We set this up as a Langrangian:

$$L = \frac{1}{2} \sum w_i w_j \sigma_{ij} - \lambda \left(\sum w_i - 1 \right)$$

Write out the summation and take derivatives with respect to the w_i to get the first order conditions as we did in Chapter 5. There are three first order conditions. The first two are:

$$\frac{\partial L}{\partial w_1} = \frac{1}{2} \left(2 w_1 \sigma_1^2 + 2 w_2 \sigma_{12} \right) - \lambda = 0$$

$$\frac{\partial L}{\partial w_2} = \frac{1}{2} \left(2 w_2 \sigma_2^2 + 2 w_1 \sigma_{12} \right) - \lambda = 0$$

And the third (with respect to the constraint λ is:

$$\frac{\partial L}{\partial \lambda} = w_1 + w_2 - 1 = 0$$

Factor the first order conditions and write them in matrix format (see Appendix 6.1 for a review of matrix operators and simple matrix algebra) as:

$$\begin{bmatrix} \sigma_{11} & \sigma_{12} & -1 \\ \sigma_{21} & \sigma_{22} & -1 \\ 1 & 1 & 0 \end{bmatrix} \begin{bmatrix} w_1 \\ w_2 \\ \lambda \end{bmatrix} = \begin{bmatrix} 0 \\ 0 \\ 1 \end{bmatrix}$$

We wrote this system as $Ax = b$. We want the vector x. Let's substitute the numbers from the spreadsheet, that is, from the sample data sheet assuming the two returns are uncorrelated for now:

$$\begin{bmatrix} \sigma_1^2 & \sigma_{12} \\ \sigma_{21} & \sigma_2^2 \end{bmatrix} = \begin{bmatrix} 0.15 & 0 \\ 0 & 0.20 \end{bmatrix}$$

The zero covariances imply that the returns are independent. (This makes the math more transparent, as you will see shortly.) With this information, the system is:

$$A = \begin{matrix} 0.15 & 0 & -1 \\ 0 & 0.2 & -1 \\ 1 & 1 & 0 \end{matrix} \qquad b = \begin{matrix} 0 \\ 0 \\ 1 \end{matrix}$$

The solution is (look at the formula bar in the spreadsheet for the Excel instructions):

$$A^{-1}b = x = \begin{matrix} 0.57 & w_1 \\ 0.43 & w_2 \\ 0.09 & \lambda \end{matrix}$$

It is easy to verify that these weights are the reciprocals of the variances on the two assets. For example: $(1/.15) = 6.67$; $(1/.2) = 5$; $6.67/(6.67 + 5) = 0.57$ and $5/(6.67 + 5) = 0.43$. Thus, the minimum variance portfolio selected assets in inverse proportion to their individual risks—the riskier, the lower the weight. That establishes the basic intuition of portfolio optimization. There are other ways of framing the objective as we shall see but the intuition remains unchanged. Constraints will, of course, restrict the space in which we look for the solution, but within that constrained space, we still seek allocations inversely proportional to their risks.

Recall that returns were assumed independent in the preceding example. This makes the covariances zero and highlights the relationship between optimization and individual asset risks. In general, however, covariances among asset returns are nonzero as asset prices evolve over the business cycle and respond to unanticipated shocks. As such, the off-diagonal elements in the covariance matrix are nonzero and the risk to each asset is a weighted average of its own risk and its covariance with the other assets in the portfolio. If, for example, the covariation in returns in the preceding example was 0.10, then the solution would change as follows:

$$A = \begin{matrix} 0.15 & 0.1 & -1 \\ 0.01 & 0.2 & -1 \\ 1 & 1 & 0 \end{matrix} \qquad b = \begin{matrix} 0 \\ 0 \\ 1 \end{matrix}$$

$$A^{-1}b = x = \begin{matrix} 0.67 & w_1 \\ 0.33 & w_2 \\ 0.13 & \lambda \end{matrix}$$

Verify this for yourself. The weight to the first asset has now increased at the expense of the weight to the second asset. The reason is that the positive covariance increases the total risk to investing in both assets but proportionately more for the second asset. Since the objective is to minimize portfolio risk, the optimizer now puts more weight on asset 1 and less on asset 2.

Note that portfolio 1 finds the left-most point on the efficient frontier.

PORTFOLIO 2: MINIMUM VARIANCE PORTFOLIOS WITH TARGETED RETURN

Whereas portfolio 1 did not stipulate a return (it earns a return but this is the return to the minimum variance portfolio), Portfolio 2 does. This stipulation takes the form of another constraint (see the example in Chapter 5), and therefore the Lagrangian has form:

$$L = \frac{1}{2}\sum_{i,j=1}^{n} w_i w_j \sigma_{ij} - \mu\left(\sum_{i=1}^{n} w_i \bar{r}_i - \bar{r}\right) - \lambda\left(\sum_{i=1}^{n} w_i - 1\right)$$

From the first order conditions, we write the system $Ax = b$ as:

$$\begin{bmatrix} \sigma_{11} & \sigma_{12} & -1 & -\bar{r}_1 \\ \sigma_{21} & \sigma_{22} & -1 & -\bar{r}_2 \\ 1 & 1 & 0 & 0 \\ \bar{r}_1 & -\bar{r}_2 & 0 & 0 \end{bmatrix} \begin{bmatrix} w_1 \\ w_2 \\ \lambda \\ \mu \end{bmatrix} = \begin{bmatrix} 0 \\ 0 \\ 1 \\ \bar{r} \end{bmatrix}$$

Suppose we stipulate the portfolio return as 0.036. This is not entirely arbitrary; from the spreadsheet, the two mean returns are 0.03 and 0.04. The portfolio return has to be a weighted average of these. Set it too high (above 0.04) and the optimizer will have to short the lower return asset in an attempt to achieve this higher return. You can demonstrate this using the spreadsheet. Assuming independence in the returns so that $\sigma_{12} = \sigma_{21} = 0$, we have the following setup:

$$A = \begin{array}{cccc} 0.15 & 0 & -1 & -0.03 \\ 0 & 0.2 & -1 & -0.04 \\ 1 & 1 & 0 & 0 \\ 0.03 & 0.04 & 0 & 0 \end{array} \qquad b = \begin{array}{c} 0 \\ 0 \\ 1 \\ 0.036 \end{array}$$

$$A^{-1}b = x = \begin{array}{cc} 0.4 & w_1 \\ 0.6 & w_2 \\ -0.12 & \lambda \\ 6 & \mu \end{array}$$

The calculations are in the spreadsheet. It makes intuitive sense that the portfolio would be tilted toward the higher returning asset since the portfolio return is greater than what the lower returning asset can deliver.

PORTFOLIO 3: MINIMUM VARIANCE PORTFOLIOS WITH NO SHORT SALES

Consider now the fully invested, minimum variance portfolio given by the solution to

$$L = \frac{1}{2} \sum_{i,j=1}^{n} w_i w_j \sigma_{ij} - \mu \left(\sum_{i=1}^{n} w_i - 1 \right)$$

but with the added (inequality) constraint that the weights must all be non-negative, that is,

$$w_i \geq 0, i = 1, \ldots, n$$

This is an example of an inequality constraint; in this case, short sales are prohibited. The portfolio that solves this constrained minimization problem cannot be solved directly as we did for portfolios 1 and 2. Rather, we must iterate using numerical procedures (variants of Newton's method, for example). Excel has a data tool called Solver, which we can use to solve problems such as this. (Recall, we used Solver to find a solution to the linear programming problem of hedging future pension liabilities by selecting among several bonds of varying duration.)

To illustrate, let's take a look at a hypothetical three-asset portfolio with covariances and expected returns given by:

$$A = \begin{array}{ccc} 0.15 & 0 & 0.2 \\ 0 & 0.2 & 0 \\ 0.2 & 0 & 0.3 \end{array}$$

Expected Returns   0.03   0.04   0.025

The diagonal of matrix A contains the asset return variances. The two off-diagonal elements indicate that asset 1 and asset 3 returns are positively correlated ($\rho = 0.94$, which you should verify) having covariance 0.2. I set this problem up purposely to show that without a no-shorting constraint, the optimizer will want to short asset 3. The intuition behind the short sale lies in the fact that asset 3 has both the highest risk and the lowest return, plus its risk is positively correlated with the risk on asset 1 (the lowest risk asset). Thus, it would be hard to make a case for taking a long position in asset 3 outside of a pure diversification argument (which, by the way is a powerful argument which you can see for yourself by experimenting with the covariances given in the spreadsheet to this chapter). The minimum-variance portfolio *without* a no-short sales restriction—that is, the solution using the method given in portfolio 1 is:

$$X = \begin{array}{cc} 1.45 & w_1 \\ 0.36 & w_2 \\ -0.82 & w_3 \end{array}$$

$$\sum w = 1 \quad 1.00$$
$$\mu \quad 0.038$$
$$\sigma \quad 0.262$$

Notice the negative weight (−0.82) on asset 3 and the long weight (1.45) on asset 1, indicating that asset 1 has more than 100 percent weight; the sale of asset 3 was used to fund an increased allocation to asset 1. The expected return on this portfolio is 3.8 percent with volatility (risk) equal to 26.2 percent.

Let's now restrict short sales using Excel's Solver. Here is a snapshot of Solver's window with cell references from the chapter spreadsheet. Solver is asked to maximize the Sharpe ratio, μ/σ, by changing the weights (named *wns* for weights, no shorting) and restricting these weights to be non-negative. Thus, the Solver Parameters window looks like this:

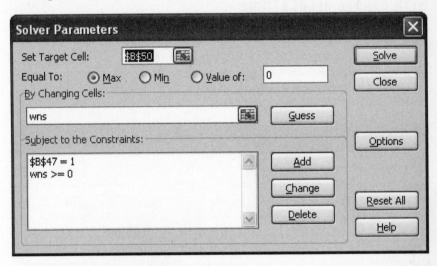

Solving gives the portfolio

$$X = \quad 0.50 \quad w_1$$
$$0.50 \quad w_2$$
$$0.00 \quad w_3$$
$$\sum w = 1 \quad 1.00$$
$$\mu \quad 0.035$$
$$\sigma \quad 0.296$$
$$\textbf{Sharpe} \quad 0.118$$

Notice that the allocation to asset 3 binds on the constraint at zero. The expected return on any constrained portfolio will, by definition, be lower than that for unconstrained portfolios and that is borne out here as well (the return has fallen slightly to 3.5 percent). Risk must also be higher on the constrained portfolio (29.6 percent in this case). Intuitively, the absence of constraints allows the optimizer to search the entire weight space for the allocation that minimizes risk. Constraints restrict the available space for this search and therefore produce allocations that, while not globally optimal, are optimal in the restricted space.

PORTFOLIO 4: MINIMUM VARIANCE PORTFOLIOS WITH CAPPED ALLOCATIONS

Suppose we extend our analysis of constrained optima to include restrictions on how much we can invest in certain assets. In practice, managers often cap allocations to certain asset classes so as to control their exposure to risk. Let's take as an example an allocation cap to asset 2 with a maximum of 30 percent while still restricting short sales. Solver then looks like this:

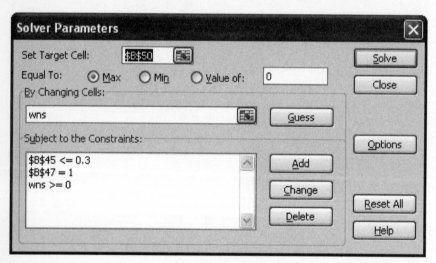

Notice the allocation constraint on asset 2 in cell B45. Solving yields:

$$
\begin{array}{rll}
X = & 0.70 & w_1 \\
& 0.30 & w_2 \\
& 0.00 & w_3 \\
\sum w = 1 & 1.00 & \\
\mu & 0.033 & \\
\sigma & 0.302 &
\end{array}
$$

Again, we see the impact of restricted optimizations in the form of higher risk (30.2 percent) and lower expected returns (3.3 percent).

By now, several intuitively appealing properties of minimum variance portfolios should be clear. First, the allocation weights are generally inversely proportional to the asset's risk. Second, nonzero covariances complicate risk but the intuition is unaffected. Third, the minimum variance portfolio is the left-most point on the efficient frontier. And fourth, constraints on the optimization problem do not come without a cost; for example, too high a targeted portfolio return will force the optimizer to short (hold a negative weight) in the lower-returning asset. Alternatively, too high a risk relative to the asset's return will do likewise. Restrictions, in general, force the optimization problem to locate solutions in a restricted parameter space. Naturally, this action will have implications regarding the portfolio risk. We turn to the issue of portfolio risk now.

PORTFOLIO 5: MAXIMUM RISK-ADJUSTED RETURN

We solved this portfolio previously but we did not examine its properties. We shall do that now. The objective is to find the portfolio that maximizes risk-adjusted return, that is,

$$\max_w w'r - \frac{(w'Vw)}{2}$$

The first term, $w'r$, is the portfolio return, while $w'Vw$ is the variance of the returns on the portfolio w. This is particularly straightforward to solve by differentiation with respect to w':

$$\frac{d}{dw'} = r - Vw = 0$$

Solving this first order condition yields the portfolio:

$$V^{-1}r = w$$

Let's examine the intuition here. If we revert to the two-asset case that we have been studying, then we would write the objective function as follows:

$$\max_w L = (w_1 r_1 + w_2 r_2) - \frac{1}{2}(w_1^2 \sigma_1^2 + w_2^2 \sigma_2^2 + 2w_1 w_2 \sigma_{12})$$

This has two first order conditions:

$$\frac{\partial L}{\partial w_1} = r_1 - \frac{1}{2}\left(2w_1\sigma_1^2 + 2w_2\sigma_{12}\right) = 0$$

$$\frac{\partial L}{\partial w_2} = r_2 - \frac{1}{2}\left(2w_2\sigma_2^2 + 2w_1\sigma_{12}\right) = 0$$

Simplifying, and rewriting in matrix format, we get the following two-equation system:

$$\begin{bmatrix} \sigma_{11} & \sigma_{12} \\ \sigma_{21} & \sigma_{22} \end{bmatrix} \begin{bmatrix} w_1 \\ w_2 \end{bmatrix} = \begin{bmatrix} r_1 \\ r_2 \end{bmatrix}$$

The covariance matrix is diagonal in our preceding applications and making the following substitutions:

$$\begin{bmatrix} \sigma_1^2 & \sigma_{12} \\ \sigma_{21} & \sigma_2^2 \end{bmatrix} = \begin{bmatrix} 0.15 & 0 \\ 0 & 0.20 \end{bmatrix}; \begin{bmatrix} r_1 \\ r_2 \end{bmatrix} = \begin{bmatrix} 0.03 \\ 0.04 \end{bmatrix}$$

which give us the solution by inverting the covariance matrix and post-multiplying it by the returns vector, yielding the vector $\begin{bmatrix} w_1 \\ w_2 \end{bmatrix} = \begin{bmatrix} 0.2 \\ 0.2 \end{bmatrix}$.
Since we did not impose an adding-up constraint, let us do so now. Dividing each weight by the weight sum 0.4 clearly shows that this portfolio equally weights the two assets at 0.5 each. This is not coincidental. Look again at the covariance matrix. Since it's diagonal, its inverse is also a diagonal matrix with elements equal to the reciprocals of the variances, that is:

$$V^{-1} = \begin{bmatrix} \dfrac{1}{0.15} & 0 \\ 0 & \dfrac{1}{0.2} \end{bmatrix}$$

When we post-multiply by the returns vector, we get a 2 × 1 vector of the returns divided by their respective variances (see the appendix for a review of matrix operations):

$$\begin{bmatrix} 0.03/0.15 \\ 0.04/0.2 \end{bmatrix} = \begin{bmatrix} 0.2 \\ 0.2 \end{bmatrix}$$

We are looking at return per unit risk and that is exactly what this portfolio maximizes. The diagonal covariance matrix adds a lot of transparency to this intuition. In the case for which the returns to these two assets are not independent of each other, then the inverse of the covariance matrix is more complicated because risks to each asset are a combination of their individual risks (variances) plus the contribution to risk carried by their covariation with the other asset. But the intuition holds nonetheless. You should confirm that this portfolio will have return equal to 3.5 percent, with risk 29.58 percent and Sharpe ratio of 0.118 and that this Sharpe ratio is the highest of any portfolio. We are assuming that the risk-free rate is zero. Referring back to the capital market line, this portfolio is the tangency point on a line with intercept equal to the risk-free rate and slope equal to r_p/σ_p, where the subscript p denotes this portfolio's return and risk. Stated differently, no other mean-variance efficient portfolio can have a higher Sharpe ratio than the tangency portfolio.

PERFORMANCE ATTRIBUTION

The preceding first two cases present us with two distinct optimal portfolios. The *portfolio returns* are simply the optimally weighted average of the expected returns on the individual securities, that is:

$$E(r) = w_1 E(r_1) + w_2 E(r_2)$$

where the w_i are the optimal weights. For portfolio 1, the mean return is 3.4 percent, while for portfolio 2, it is the stipulated 3.6 percent. The expected variance of the portfolio returns is given by $w'Vw$, and the *portfolio risk* (volatility) is the square root of this number. For portfolio 1, it is 29.3 percent (this is the left-most point on the efficient frontier) and a bit higher for portfolio 2 (31 percent) because this portfolio required a higher rate of return. See the spreadsheet for computational details.

Portfolio managers are interested in measuring the contribution to portfolio risk as the weight allocated to a specific security change. This is called the *marginal contribution to risk* (MCR), denoted by:

$$MCR = \frac{d\sigma}{dw} = \frac{Vw}{\sigma}$$

This is easily derived—recall that σ is the portfolio risk, which is equal to $(w'Vw)^{\frac{1}{2}}$. The derivative of this with respect to w' is MCR. The MCR is a therefore a vector; it shows the contribution to risk on the margin for a given change in the portfolio weights. Let's put this in perspective, using portfolio 2. Again, the computational details are provided on the spreadsheet. Since V is a 2×2 square matrix and w is a 2×1 column vector with σ a scalar, then MCR is a 2×1 vector. For portfolio 2, it is MCR = $(0.19, 0.39)'$. The interpretation is that if the allocation to asset 2 were to rise one unit, then portfolio risk rises 39 percent. Since our weights are in percents, then a 1 percent change produces 0.39 percent change in portfolio risk. More generally, however, we focus on the relative differences in MCR across assets—here, for example, the marginal contribution to portfolio risk is roughly twice as high for asset 2 relative to asset 1, and this has important implications for the portfolio manager contemplating tilting his portfolio in the direction of asset 2. We discuss the concept of overall portfolio risk in the chapter on risk budgeting.

Let me introduce you to one more risk measure—*Allocation Attribution*. This is a decomposition of total portfolio risk and is given by $w.*\left(\frac{Vw}{\sigma}\right)$. The notation ".*" denotes element wise multiplication (see the spreadsheet for details). This is the MCR that is weighted by the individual optimal allocations. For portfolio 2, it is $(0.25, 0.75)$, respectively, indicating that our portfolio risk is three times as concentrated in asset 2 relative to asset 1.

The impact that portfolio restrictions have on risk attribution can be significant, which I show in Table 6.1.

Allowing asset 3 to be shorted in portfolio 3 means that its allocation attribution—contribution to total risk on the portfolio (which was 26.2 percent)—is negative. On the other hand, asset 1 accounts for roughly three times the risk as asset 2 because of its overweighting. On the margin, however, asset 2 has the highest contribution to risk. When short sales are restricted (portfolio 3), this picture changes; clearly asset 3 can contribute nothing to risk since it has

TABLE 6.1 Risk Attribution—Portfolios 3 and 4

		Port 3*	Port 3	Port 4
Marginal Contribution	Asset 1	0.21	0.25	0.35
	Asset 2	0.28	0.34	0.20
	Asset 3	0.17	0.34	0.46
Allocation Attribution	Asset 1	0.30	0.13	0.24
	Asset 2	0.10	0.17	0.06
	Asset 3	−0.14	0.00	0.00

Port 3*—Short Sales Allowed
Port 3—No Short Sales Restriction
Port 4—No Short Sales and Allocation Cap to Asset 2 at 30%

zero weight. If we were to allocate to asset 3 on the margin, then risk would increase in the portfolio by 34 basis points for each 1 percent risk in asset 3 (and asset 2) allocation. Finally, when we restrict both short sales and cap the weight to asset 2, then the risk contribution from asset 2 must decline, which it does, while the contributions to risk on the margin from assets 1 and 3 rise. The allocation attribution is heavily concentrated on asset 1 because there is a zero allocation to asset 3 and a capped allocation to asset 2.

THE EFFICIENT FRONTIER (AGAIN)

 Go to the companion website for more details (see Efficient Frontier under Chapter 6 Examples).

We can use the two-fund theorem to construct our efficient frontier (see Figure 6.1). Recall that this theorem states that the set of efficient funds (portfolios) can be constructed as linear combinations of any two efficient portfolios. We have two minimum variance and, hence, efficient portfolios from portfolios 1 and 2. I form a bunch of new funds as linear combinations of these two funds on the Efficient Frontier sheet in Chapter 6 Examples. xlsx. To do this, I need the return and risks for the two portfolios and their correlation coefficient ρ. I also need a set of weights that I use to form linear combinations of these two portfolios. The only restriction is that the two weights must sum to one. The gradation of the weights is not important,

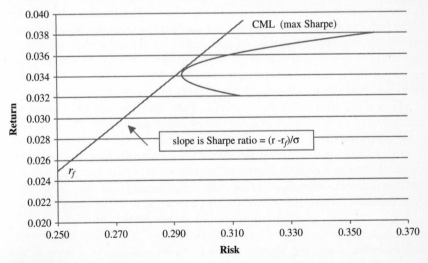

FIGURE 6.1 Efficient Frontier

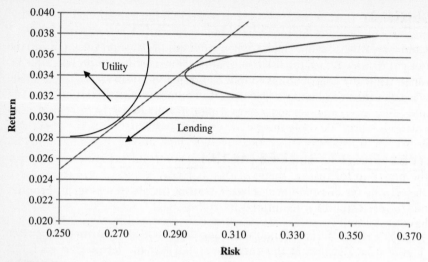

FIGURE 6.2 Maximizing Utility by Borrowing or Lending

but you can see from the spreadsheet that I generated enough to get a smooth graph of the frontier. Here it is:

I assume the risk-free rate is 2.5 percent. The line tangent to the efficient set is the capital market line. We already showed that it has slope $\frac{(r_p - r_f)}{\sigma_p}$ and intercept equal to the risk free rate r_f. It has maximum slope at the point of tangency with the efficient set—this is portfolio 5, with a risk-free rate of 2.5 percent; it is the portfolio with the maximum Sharpe ratio. If we refer to the Efficient Frontier spreadsheet, we see that the tangency portfolio consists of equal parts of Portfolios 1 and 2 that we derived earlier. This is an important result. It means that all we need own is this portfolio (the tangency portfolio) and lend or borrow at the risk-free rate to maximize utility. Everyone, regardless of the form of her utility functions, can do likewise.

Figure 6.2 illustrates this concept. The CML contains the tangency portfolio and includes a set of points all of which are preferred to any other point on the efficient frontier. That is, all points on the CML have higher return and risk. If we express peoples' utility functions in risk and return space—I impose a representative indifference curve that is tangent to the CML to illustrate—then we can see that, depending on individual risk appetites, the utility-maximizing investor can choose to hold the tangency portfolio (the market), lend by holding a mix of the market portfolio and the risk-free asset (as shown in Figure 6.2), or borrow by shorting the risk-free asset in order to achieve higher expected returns and risk by moving to the northeast along the CML.

SUMMARY

Here, we bring together and apply optimization principles using Excel as our platform, solving and analyzing four distinct optimization schemes for the purpose of highlighting the impact imposed by constraints. The purpose was to illustrate the impact that constraints have on the optimized solution and in particular to assess the cost of constraints in the form of portfolio risk and return. We study three constraints in particular—a targeted portfolio return, no short sales (no negative weights), and capped allocations to specific assets. Our results show that while constraints may be imposed on the portfolio for institutional reasons or to cap exposure to certain asset classes, the result is that they always restrict the space in which our optimizer can search for the optimal portfolio. That suggests that constraints have costs, and in particular, we find that two costs are higher risk (for sure) and possibly lower returns. We then take a fresh look at performance statistics, again, in the form of marginal contributions to risk and allocative risk, along with a fresh look at the efficient frontier.

APPENDIX 6.1: MATRIX OPERATIONS

In general, think of two matrices, A and B, and their (inner) product C:

$$\begin{bmatrix} 1 & 2 & 3 \\ 2 & 1 & 1 \end{bmatrix} \begin{bmatrix} 3 & 2 \\ 2 & 2 \\ 1 & 3 \end{bmatrix} = \begin{bmatrix} 10 & 15 \\ 9 & 9 \end{bmatrix}$$

$$A \quad x \quad B \quad = \quad C$$
$$(2x3) \quad x \quad (3x2) \quad = \quad (2x2)$$

The first element in the inner product ($C_{11} = 10$) is the product of the first *row* of A and the first *column* of B, that is, $(1 * 3) + (2 * 2) + (3 * 1) = 10$. Similarly, $C_{12} = 15$ is the inner product of the first row of A and the *second* column of B. C is the collection of inner products of the rows of A and the columns of B. Verify this for yourselves.

Excel requires that we know the dimension of C before we ask Excel to calculate the inner product. We first highlight a $(2x2)$ set of cells (do not press *Enter* yet). Type the command $= mmult(A,B)$ and then simultaneously press *CTRL-SHIFT-ENTER*.

You can also get the inverse of a matrix. It must be a square matrix. Take matrix C as an example. Its inverse is (a full discussion of this operation is given next):

$$adj\frac{\begin{bmatrix} 9 & -9 \\ -15 & 10 \end{bmatrix}}{\begin{bmatrix} 10 & 15 \\ 9 & 9 \end{bmatrix}} = \frac{\begin{bmatrix} 9 & -15 \\ -9 & 10 \end{bmatrix}}{-45} = C^{-1}$$

The denominator (-45) is the determinant of C. If this value is zero, then the inverse is undefined.

The Excel sequence that computes a matrix inverse again requires that we know the dimensions. We highlight a $(2x2)$ set of cells once again and then type the command $= minverse(C)$, followed by the $CTRL\text{-}SHIFT\text{-}ENTER$ sequence.

I want to show you a more meaningful multivariate regression application. Let Y be a set of N observations (for example, the returns to N stocks for the current month). Let X be a $(Nx(k + 1))$ matrix of regressors, including the column of ones associated with the intercept. The regressors can be thought of as factors like earnings growth, earnings surprises, firm size, and so on, that returns depend upon. Let β be a $((k + 1)x1)$ column vector of parameters that we wish to estimate and let ε be a $(Nx1)$ column vector of disturbances. Let's write our model as follows. (From now on, we will denote the dimension of β as $k \times 1$, understanding that k includes the intercept.)

$$Y = X\beta + \varepsilon$$

$$\begin{bmatrix} Y_1 \\ Y_2 \\ Y_3 \\ \cdot \\ \cdot \\ \cdot \\ Y_N \end{bmatrix} = \begin{bmatrix} 1 & X_{11} & \dots & X_{k1} \\ 1 & X_{12} & \dots & X_{k2} \\ 1 & X_{12} & \dots & X_{k3} \\ \cdot & \cdot & \dots & \cdot \\ \cdot & \cdot & \dots & \cdot \\ \cdot & \cdot & \dots & \cdot \\ 1 & X_{1N} & \dots & X_{kN} \end{bmatrix} \begin{bmatrix} \beta_0 \\ \beta_1 \\ \beta_2 \\ \cdot \\ \cdot \\ \cdot \\ \beta_k \end{bmatrix} + \begin{bmatrix} \varepsilon_0 \\ \varepsilon_1 \\ \varepsilon_2 \\ \cdot \\ \cdot \\ \cdot \\ \varepsilon_k \end{bmatrix}$$

This is how we visualize our data and our simple linear model. The usual assumptions apply (the errors are independent and identically distributed

[IID], meaning zero with constant variance and uncorrelated with the regressors). If we want to make inferences and test hypotheses, we add the assumption that the errors are $N(0, \sigma^2)$, understanding that the population variance is unknown and must consequently be estimated. Tests and inferences proceed under the t-distribution with degrees of freedom $(N - k)$.

We wish to estimate the $(kx1)$ vector $\boldsymbol{\beta}$. I will do this now. First, write the model in *matrix*

$$Y = X\boldsymbol{\beta} + \varepsilon$$

Note that $Y \sim (Nx1)$ and $X\boldsymbol{\beta} \sim (Nxk)$ times $(kx1)$, which by the rules of matrix algebra is conformable for multiplication, that is, $X\boldsymbol{\beta} \sim (Nx1)$. Finally, $\varepsilon \sim (Nx1)$.

The inner product $(X\boldsymbol{\beta})$ is the product of a (Nxk) matrix X and a $(kx1)$ matrix of parameters $\boldsymbol{\beta}$, which has dimension $(Nx1)$ (a column vector). As before, the first element in $X\boldsymbol{\beta}$ is the product of the first row in X and the vector $\boldsymbol{\beta}$, the second element in the second row in X and the vector $\boldsymbol{\beta}$, and so forth.

Now, multiply both sides by the *transpose* of X, which we call X'. If $X \sim (Nxk)$, then $X' \sim (kxN)$. Our model now looks like this:

$$X'Y = X'X\boldsymbol{\beta} + X'\varepsilon$$

$X'Y$ has dimensions $(kx1)$, $X'X$ is (kxk), and therefore $X'X\boldsymbol{\beta}$ is $(kx1)$, and finally $X'\varepsilon$ is $(kx1)$. In Excel, highlight a $(kx1)$ column of cells (do not press *Enter*) and follow this with the command *=mmult(transpose(X),Y)* and simultaneously press *CTRL-SHIFT-ENTER*.

Let's now solve this system for $\boldsymbol{\beta}$. First, eliminate $X'\varepsilon$. Since the regressors are assumed independent of the errors, then this term is zero, anyway (specifically, its expectation is zero). Now, we are looking at the system:

$$X'Y = X'X\boldsymbol{\beta}$$

To do this, we must eliminate $X'X$ (the square matrix) by dividing both sides by $X'X$, that is, we multiply by its inverse $\left(X'X\right)^{-1}$. Let's do that now.

$$\left(X'X\right)^{-1}X'Y = \left(X'X\right)^{-1}\left(X'X\right)\boldsymbol{\beta}$$

$$(X'X)^{-1}X'Y = b$$

The statistic b is the least squares estimate of population parameter $\boldsymbol{\beta}$. Here's how we would do this in Excel. First, we use Excel's naming convention by highlighting vectors and matrices, and giving them names. Alternatively, in Excel, click on Formulas and select appropriately among the Name Manager (you can change and delete names) and Define Name for new arrays. Let's highlight the $X'X$ matrix we solved for earlier and in the top left command window, name is XX. Likewise, highlight the vector $X'Y$ and name it XY. To estimate β, highlight a $(kx1)$ column of cells. Then type the command, $= mmult(XX,XY)$ followed by $CTRL\text{-}SHIFT\text{-}ENTER$.

This is what we need to know in Excel. But it seems to be a waste to stop here when we could use this framework to get a deeper understanding of the algebra of least squares (we will be doing a lot of regression in this book). Let's follow up with a simpler illustration, using a single regressor. What does $X'Y$ look like? How about $X'X$? The first is a cross-product matrix. For the case with a single regressor and an intercept, $X'Y$ is:

$$\begin{bmatrix} 1 & 1 & \cdots & 1 \\ X_{11} & X_{12} & \cdots & X_{1N} \end{bmatrix} \begin{bmatrix} Y_1 \\ Y_2 \\ \cdot \\ \cdot \\ \cdot \\ Y_N \end{bmatrix} = \begin{bmatrix} \sum Y \\ \sum YX \end{bmatrix}$$

The matrix $X'X$ is the inner product of the regressors (this is a quadratic form just like $\sum x_i^2$ in a bivariate regression). We build $X'X$ as follows:

$$\begin{bmatrix} 1 & 1 & \cdots & 1 \\ X_{11} & X_{12} & \cdots & X_{1N} \end{bmatrix} \begin{bmatrix} 1 & X_{11} \\ 1 & X_{12} \\ 1 & X_{13} \\ \cdot & \cdot \\ \cdot & \cdot \\ \cdot & \cdot \\ 1 & X_{1N} \end{bmatrix} = \begin{bmatrix} N & \sum X_1 \\ \sum X_1 & \sum X_1^2 \end{bmatrix}$$

What is the inverse of $X'X$? It is the adjoint matrix of $X'X$ divided by the determinant of $X'X$. The determinant is:

$$\begin{bmatrix} N & \sum X_1 \\ \sum X_1 & \sum X_1^2 \end{bmatrix} = N \sum X_1^2 - \left(\sum X_1 \right)^2$$

The inverse is then the adjoint of $X'X$ given in the numerator in the following equation, divided by the determinant, that is, it is a $(2x2)$ matrix $(k = 2)$.

$$adj \frac{\begin{bmatrix} \sum X_1^2 & -\sum X_1 \\ -\sum X_1 & N \end{bmatrix}}{N \sum X_1^2 - (\sum X_1)^2} = (X'X)^{-1}$$

We can generalize to the two-regressor case. You can see how the dimensionality of the problem increases. Here is the $X'X$ matrix:

$$\begin{bmatrix} 1 & 1 & \dots & 1 \\ X_{11} & X_{12} & \dots & X_{1N} \\ X_{21} & X_{22} & \dots & X_{2N} \end{bmatrix} \begin{bmatrix} 1 & X_{11} & X_{21} \\ 1 & X_{12} & X_{22} \\ 1 & X_{13} & X_{23} \\ \cdot & \cdot & \cdot \\ \cdot & \cdot & \cdot \\ \cdot & \cdot & \cdot \\ 1 & X_{1N} & X_{2N} \end{bmatrix} = \begin{bmatrix} N & \sum X_1 & \sum X_2 \\ \sum X_1 & \sum X_1^2 & \sum X_{12} \\ \sum X_2 & \sum X_{12} & \sum X_2^2 \end{bmatrix}$$

The $X'Y$ matrix is therefore:

$$\begin{bmatrix} 1 & 1 & \dots & 1 \\ X_{11} & X_{12} & \dots & X_{1N} \\ X_{21} & X_{22} & \dots & X_{21} \end{bmatrix} \begin{bmatrix} Y_1 \\ Y_2 \\ \cdot \\ \cdot \\ \cdot \\ Y_N \end{bmatrix} = \begin{bmatrix} \sum Y \\ \sum X_1 Y \\ \sum X_2 Y \end{bmatrix}$$

We multiply this by the inverse of $(X'X)$ to get the least squares estimate of β.

It is convenient that Excel has regression commands like *slope, linest,* and *trend* that do the algebra for us. In many cases, however, such as for portfolio optimization, we must do the dirty work ourselves. Fortunately, it is not too difficult and the process itself gives us deeper insight into the optimization problem.

CHAPTER 7

Data and Applications

Experience is the name everyone gives to their mistakes.

—Oscar Wilde

In this chapter, we analyze security level data at various reporting frequencies, extract returns, form minimum variance portfolios, construct efficient frontiers, apply the CAPM, and comment on several performance attribution measures. We also learn to work with statistical concepts in Excel, including estimation of covariances, correlations, betas to the market portfolio, means, variances, and risk measures. This work will be most closely related to the real-world applications that you will be required to analyze in subsequent study in this book.

ANALYZING RETURNS ON A 10-ASSET PORTFOLIO

 Go to the companion website for more details.

I present closing prices on 10 companies in monthly, weekly, and daily frequencies. These are given on mthly_p, wkly_p, and dly_p, respectively, for:

1. CitiGroup (C)
2. Cisco (CSCO)
3. Dell
4. Ford (F)
5. Home Depot (HD)
6. Intel (INTC)
7. Phillip Morris (MO)
8. Merck (MRK)

9. Microsoft (MSFT)
10. Time Warner (TWX)

I also give the benchmark, or market index, value on the S&P 500.

By closing, I mean the last price recorded for a specific time (for example, end of day closing price). I include a fourth sheet, mthly_r, on which I compute monthly returns using the monthly closing prices. Notice that I compute the monthly return as the natural logarithm of the ratio of the current over the previous month's closing price, $r = \ln\left(\frac{P_t}{P_{t-1}}\right)$. Recall that with continuous compounding, $P_t = P_{t-1}e^r$. Therefore, $\ln(P_t) = \ln(P_{t-1}) + r$, which is equal to $r = \ln\frac{P_t}{P_{t-1}}$. You can do it this way or, if you prefer, you can calculate month-over-month percentage changes, that is, $r = \frac{(P_t - P_{t-1})}{P_{t-1}}$. Monthly data range from March 1992 to December 2006. I have highlighted the first five years of monthly prices and that is where we begin our analysis.

In rows 180 and 181, I compute the average monthly returns and the volatilities (standard deviations). Then, I annualize them in rows 183 and 184. To annualize a monthly average, multiply it by 12. The logic is that if you earn 1 percent per month, then you earn 12 percent per year using an arithmetic averaging. Alternatively, if you geometrically link a 1 percent monthly return over the year, it grows to $(1.01)^{12}$, which is equal to $(1.01)^{12} - 1 = 12.68\%$ return for the year. I do the simpler arithmetic average. To annualize a variance, multiply it, too, by 12. To annualize a standard deviation, multiply it by $\sqrt{12}$. The logic here is that if returns are independent (that's a strong assumption, by the way), then over the year we have $(r_1 + r_2 + \ldots + r_{12})$. The variance of this sum is the sum of their individual variances $(\sigma_1^2 + \sigma_2^2 + \ldots + \sigma_{12}^2)$ *plus* their covariances. But if returns are independent, then the covariances are zero. If returns are identically distributed, then $\sigma_i^2 = \sigma^2$ for all i and thus, the annual variance is simply 12 times the monthly variance. The annualized standard deviation is therefore the square root.

If you check the formulas, you will see that I named the returns matrix (this is the (10x10) matrix of highlighted monthly returns) R_97, and I also name the monthly mean returns μ_m. The variance-covariance matrix V is therefore:

$$V = \text{mmult}(\text{transpose}(\text{R\_97}), \text{R\_97}) - \text{mmult}(\text{transpose}(\mu\_m), \mu\_m)$$

Note that I leave the benchmark out. Our objective is to try to find a minimum variance portfolio of the 10 stocks. We intend to compare the performance of this portfolio to the benchmark but we do not hold the benchmark in that portfolio.

Upon inspection, we can see that there appear to be some attractive diversification opportunities here—Ford, for example, is negatively correlated with HD and INTC as well as TWX. It will be interesting to see how our portfolio loads on these securities. To that end, let's solve the minimum variance portfolio first. Recall that this portfolio finds the vector w that minimizes risk $w'Vw$ for a fully invested portfolio ($\sum w_i = 1$). From the development of the Lagrangian in Chapter 6, I add a row of ones and column of minus ones (recall our first order conditions—we don't have to repeat the math here) to V (the matrix we referred to as A). These are highlighted in gray. I now name the extended covariance matrix A and I add in the vector b as we did in Chapter 6. These results are presented in the spreadsheet (click on the Clipboard at the top left of the spreadsheet to review these names). The optimal portfolio is the solution $A^{-1}b$.

PERFORMANCE ATTRIBUTION

I label this Port 1 (it is portfolio 1 in Chapter 6) and compute its monthly expected return (1.2 percent) and risk (3 percent). Their annualized counterparts, if you are interested, are 14.4 percent return and 10.4 percent risk. Notice that the portfolio is heavily weighted to Ford, Home Depot, and Intel (diversification opportunities) with a sizable allocation to Merck but short positions (negative weights) in the riskiest of assets (C, CSCO, and DELL) and a tiny position in TWX. You can see that even though these short positions were for assets with the highest returns, they were also very risky and had little diversification opportunity to exploit. On the other hand, although Ford does not have a particularly high return, its returns are negatively correlated with several other firms.

Portfolio 1 is the left-most point on the efficient frontier. Let's solve for another portfolio, one with a targeted return. Since there are an infinite number of them, the choice of return is somewhat arbitrary but still should be chosen with some care since it is important the current asset mix be able to deliver that return. Portfolio 1 earns a 1.2 percent return. We therefore target a portfolio 2 return that is higher (and therefore riskier) at, say, 3 percent monthly. Because portfolio 2 involves an additional constraint (mean return equal to 3 percent), I have highlighted the extension to the original matrix A and the vector b from the solution involving the first order conditions (again, see Chapter 6 for a review). The solution labeled Port 2 reflects these changes and is displayed in Table 7.1 for convenience:

TABLE 7.1   Two Mean-Variance Efficient Portfolios

	Port 1	Port 2	MCR 1	MCR 2	ATRB 1	ATRB 2
C	−0.024	0.171	0.030	0.044	−0.001	0.008
CSCO	−0.033	0.076	0.030	0.063	−0.001	0.005
DELL	−0.034	0.040	0.030	0.063	−0.001	0.003
F	0.357	0.228	0.030	0.015	0.011	0.004
HD	0.314	0.180	0.030	0.016	0.009	0.003
INTC	0.124	0.186	0.030	0.064	0.004	0.012
MO	0.028	−0.082	0.030	0.013	0.001	−0.001
MRK	0.166	0.026	0.030	0.017	0.005	0.000
MSFT	0.092	0.125	0.030	0.043	0.003	0.005
TWX	0.009	0.051	0.030	0.085	0.000	0.004
LagrMult	0.001	0.000				
μ_p	0.012	0.025				
σ_p	0.030	0.042				
ρ	0.706					

Port 2 is indeed riskier at 5.1 percent (monthly). This makes sense; there is a positive risk-return trade-off. The correlation between the two portfolios is 58.8 percent. Port 2 has a rather large short position in MO counterbalanced by larger exposures to C, INTC, MSFT, F, and HD. It appears to be more diversified in that regard and there are many stocks in this 10-stock universe that will help achieve that targeted return. Port 1, on the other hand, had the objective of minimizing risk and not achieving any stated return. Thus, Port 1 finds the least risky mix regardless of return.

It is interesting that the marginal contribution to risk (MCR) for Port 1 is the same across all assets. This may seem like a mistake at first, but it is not. Upon reflection, Port 1 is special; it is *the* minimum variance portfolio. The chapter on risk budgeting discusses this point in more detail, but this is the intuition. The MCR is a derivative, which in this case represents a gradient on the loss surface (a tangency to the risk surface). Since it is the minimum risk portfolio, it must be at a minimum point on the loss surface, and here the gradient has zero slope. Therefore, altering the weight by some fixed amount Δw to any asset will have the same impact on portfolio risk in any direction. The MCR for Port 2, on the other hand, differs across the portfolio; it is a minimum risk portfolio for the stated return, but not *the* minimum risk portfolio. Here, TWX has the highest marginal impact on risk, but it is also the riskiest of all the firms. Altering the weight vector in the direction of TWX will therefore increase risk the most.

Suppose instead that we are interested in decomposing risk across the portfolio. Attribution risk tells us the proportion of portfolio risk accounted for by each position in the portfolio. Since the sum of the attributions must equal the portfolio's risk, then we get a decomposition of risk. For example, the sum of ATRB 2 from before is equal to 5.1 percent. Therefore, INTC, at 1.4 percent, is the highest contributor to portfolio risk (about 27.4 percent of total risk is in this asset) and about 21.5 percent of total risk is in C. Together, these two positions account for almost half the portfolio risk despite the fact that risk is spread fairly evenly across the portfolio on the margin.

CHANGING THE INVESTMENT HORIZON
RETURNS FREQUENCY

Investors have different investment horizons for a variety of reasons— liquidity needs and risk management, to name a few. I have included both weekly and daily closing prices for these 10 stocks and the S&P benchmark so that we could study the frequency implications to portfolio construction. Sticking with the five-year period ending in February 1997, I have constructed on wkly_r.xlsx in Chapter 7 Examples.xlsx, a time series of weekly returns. These are highlighted and their corresponding weekly means and standard deviations are given in rows 261 and 262. The covariance matrix is denoted by V_w and I have constructed two new portfolios that are the weekly analogs to the portfolios found on mthly_r.xlsx.

The first question that comes to mind is how changing the frequency alters the sample statistics like means and variances, and therefore the portfolio. If you compound the weekly mean returns in row 261, for example, to get monthly returns, and compare these to those found on mthly_r.xlsx, you will see that they are very close. $(1 + rw)4 - 1$ should be close to the monthly mean return rm. Or, if you prefer, multiply rw by 4 to get the arithmetic monthly equivalent. Likewise, $\sigma w \sqrt{4}$ should be close to σm. The major point of interest, however, is in comparing optimal portfolios. I solve for both the minimum variance portfolio as well as a targeted return portfolio, in which the weekly targeted return compounds to the monthly targeted return of 3 percent solved for earlier. Table 7.2 shows the results.

The mean return for Port 1, when compounded to monthly, is $(1.0026)^4 - 1 = 0.0104$, which is slightly less than its monthly counterpart of 0.012. Comparing the risk to that on the minimum variance portfolio, we get $0.0186*2 = 0.0372$, which is slightly higher than the risk on the monthly counterpart. This is not supposed to be a big deal—we do not expect them to be the same—but it is important that they don't show wildly different results. More importantly, we ask how the allocation itself has changed. In this set of examples, there are significant differences. For

TABLE 7.2   Changing the Returns Frequency

	Port 1	Port 2	MCR 1	MCR 2	ATRB 1	ATRB 2
C	0.034	0.307	0.0186	0.0267	0.0006	0.0082
CSCO	−0.021	0.180	0.0186	0.0367	−0.0004	0.0066
DELL	−0.028	0.013	0.0186	0.0363	−0.0005	0.0005
F	0.247	0.056	0.0186	0.0088	0.0046	0.0005
HD	0.174	−0.140	0.0186	0.0090	0.0032	−0.0013
INTC	0.040	0.151	0.0186	0.0336	0.0007	0.0051
MO	0.201	0.072	0.0186	0.0098	0.0037	0.0007
MRK	0.222	0.087	0.0186	0.0108	0.0041	0.0009
MSFT	0.138	0.174	0.0186	0.0240	0.0026	0.0042
TWX	−0.008	0.100	0.0186	0.0450	−0.0002	0.0045
LagrMult	0.000	0.000				
μ_p	0.0026	0.0074				
σ_p	0.0186	0.0299				
ρ	0.62					

example, the higher frequency weekly returns have a long position in C compared to the short position in the monthly frequency portfolio. Whereas the monthly portfolio is heavily tilted to Ford and Home Depot, the weekly portfolio also holds relatively heavy exposures to MO and MRK. Naturally, these differences will have implications concerning the marginal contributions to risk and to risk attribution in general. Why is this? Should observing market prices more frequently alter the risk-return trade-off that much? The short answer is yes and the reason is that higher frequency data contain more noise, which is embedded in covariance estimates. So, while the mean returns and risks seem to be fairly consistent across frequencies, their covariances may not be.

It is hard to compare covariances across frequencies; instead, we resort to comparisons of correlations, which are standardized covariances and, therefore, can be compared across any unit of measure. Recall that the correlation coefficient between two returns series rho:

$$\rho = \frac{cov(r_1, r_2)}{\sigma_1 \sigma_2}$$

Since we have 10 return series and covariances are symmetric, that is, $cov(r_1, r_2) = cov(r_2, r_1)$, then we will have to estimate $\frac{(N^2 - N)}{2}$ covariances (and correlations) plus N variances (and standard deviations). The covariance matrices V_m and V_w each have 45 covariances and 10 variances (the latter along the diagonal). If we divide each element in the covariance matrix by the product of the standard deviations of the two relevant returns series, then we can construct a correlation matrix. I did this for both the monthly and the weekly returns series. The Excel command is to highlight a (NxN) area in the spreadsheet and then type the command:

$$= \mathbf{V\_m}/\text{mmult}(\text{transpose}(\sigma\_m)\sigma\_m)$$

Since σ_m is a row vector of standard deviations (I used STDEVP), then its transpose is a column vector and the product of an $(Nx1)$ and a $(1xN)$ vector is an (NxN) matrix, as you can see here:

$$\begin{bmatrix} \sigma_1 \\ \sigma_2 \\ . \\ . \\ . \\ \sigma_N \end{bmatrix} \begin{bmatrix} \sigma_1 & \sigma_2 & \cdots & \sigma_N \end{bmatrix} = \begin{bmatrix} \sigma_1^2 & \sigma_1\sigma_2 & \cdots & \cdots & \sigma_1\sigma_N \\ \sigma_2\sigma_1 & \sigma_2^2 & \cdots & \cdots & \sigma_2\sigma_N \\ \cdots & \cdots & \cdots & \cdots & \cdots \\ \cdots & \cdots & \cdots & \cdots & \cdots \\ \sigma_N\sigma_1 & \cdots & \cdots & \cdots & \sigma_N^2 \end{bmatrix}$$

This is what we call an outer product (as opposed to an inner product, which consists of product sums). You should be able to see clearly that dividing the covariance matrix by this matrix produces exactly what we are after—a matrix of standardized covariances with ones along the diagonal.

BENCHMARKING TO THE MARKET PORTFOLIO

All our work to this point made no reference to the market portfolio, in this case, the S&P 500 return. It is common, however, to compare the return to an asset or a portfolio of assets to the return on the market. There are many reasons, foremost of which is that the return to the market represents the opportunity cost of portfolio under management. For example, the return to Port 2 in the monthly data (weekly data) is 3 percent (0.742 percent) with risk 5.1 percent (2.99 percent). Had we invested in the market portfolio instead, we would have a return of 1 percent (0.3 percent) with risk 2.6 percent (1.3 percent). Does this look like a favorable risk-return trade-off to you? It depends on your risk preferences, but the return per unit risk is 3 percent/5.1 percent on the monthly Port 2 versus 1 percent/2.6 percent on the monthly S&P. This is a *Sharpe ratio* and it favors Port 2, at least from a risk-adjusted return perspective.

What about risk at the security level? Obviously, we can compare volatilities (standard deviations). But is there a measure of security risk relative to benchmark risk? The CAPM provides this measure in the form of the asset's β:

$$r_i = r_f + \beta_i(r_m - r_f)$$

Beta is a measure of the covariation in the asset's return to the market return, specifically:

$$r_i = r_f + \frac{\sigma_{im}}{\sigma_m^2}(r_m - r_f)$$

Actually, it is a very intuitive concept; a β of one means that the two return series are perfectly correlated, that is, a 1 percent change in the market excess return is matched by a 1 percent return in the asset's excess return. A beta of two means that the asset's return is twice as variable as the market return, and a beta of zero means that the asset's return is uncorrelated with the market. If $\beta > 1$, then we say the asset is riskier than the market. When portfolio managers talk about their beta exposure, they are generally referring to how correlated their portfolio is to the market or benchmark. The betas for the 10 firms under study here range as we would expect (you can find them in Chapter 7 Examples.xlsx on the mthly_r and wkly_r spreadsheets). I estimate betas using Excel's slope function. Citigroup (C) has a beta that is close to two in the monthly data, suggesting that is twice as risky as holding the market. It is no wonder that the optimizer tries to find risk-diversifying combinations of these firms in its search for the minimum variance portfolio.

We can tie our β measures into the CAPM as a pricing model. Recalling the dividend discount model that we developed in Chapter 4 and applied to the CAPM in Chapter 5, and using, say, Citigroup as a case in point, then the discount rate for C would be $(1 + r_f + \beta(r_m - r_f))$. To get at the point directly here, if we assume that the risk-free rate is zero, then $\beta = 2$ suggests that Citigroup's dividends should be discounted at *twice* the market rate. This is clearly a far cry from discounting at a bond rate of interest or the market rate of interest—the correct discount factor should account for the risk on the security, and the CAPM is a pricing model that accounts for that extra-market risk.

What about the portfolio's exposure to market risk? How is that risk compensated? I estimate the betas for Port 1 and Port 2 (see mthly_r) over the five-year period under scrutiny to be 0.85 and 1.24, respectively. Thus, the minimum variance portfolio has lower risk than the market portfolio, while Port 2 has higher risk relative to the market. Both results make intuitive sense.

Beta measures *systematic* risk because it shows the degree to which the asset's return covaries with the market return. Thus, the asset's return should reflect this risk, which we can see from the CAPM we developed in Chapter 5. In its empirical form, we add an error term to capture asset-specific pricing error:

$$r_i = r_f + \beta_i(r_m - r_f) + \varepsilon_i$$

Therefore, the expected return on the asset should be:

$$E(r_i) = r_f + \beta_i(E(r_m) - r_f) + E(\varepsilon_i)$$

The term ε_i is the asset's idiosyncratic risk and is also referred to as non-systematic risk, or the *firm's specific risk*. It is separate from and independent of the market return and is therefore not compensated. Since β is estimated by least squares and the standard assumptions of the classical linear regression model require that ε be independent of r_m with expected value $E(\varepsilon_i)$ equal to zero (meaning that on average these risks are zero), then $E(r_i)$ is simply linear in β. We will return to this point momentarily, but we must first understand that while market risk is compensated, idiosyncratic risk is not and, in fact, idiosyncratic risk can only be diversified away. We demonstrated this point in Chapter 5. Diversification rests on the assumption of idiosyncratic risks being distributed independently across assets. If the CAPM is specified correctly in the sense that the market excess return $(r_m - r_f)$ is the single factor sufficient to explain systematic movements in asset returns, then the ε_i must be distributed independently across assets. Adding assets to the portfolio will increase the chances that the average of the ε_i converge to zero. Thus, in the limit, the portfolio will contain only systematic risk, which is compensated.

Let's now return to the assertion that the CAPM posits a linear relationship between asset returns and beta. What this means is that higher beta stocks should have higher returns. We can demonstrate this relationship using the betas and observed mean returns from the 10 firms and the S&P 500 from the Chapter 7 Examples spreadsheet. Certainly, this sample is too small but it does give you something to fix ideas upon.

If we fit a trend line to these data points, we get the security market line (SML), as shown in Figure 7.1. This suggests a trade-off between return and risk as measured by beta. Assets (firms) with higher betas should also have higher returns. The CAPM is not only a pricing model—it also says something about the cross-section of returns. Tests of the CAPM focus on empirical tests of the slope and intercept of the SML, a topic that we explore in more detail in Chapter 8.

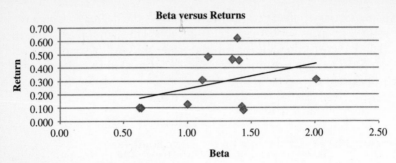

FIGURE 7.1 Security Market Line

THE COST OF CONSTRAINTS

The CAPM is an equilibrium model in which investors' supply and demand decisions defines the market portfolio, in which all investors possess identical information and preferences are mean variance optimizers, and for which there are no restrictions on selling. Restrictions make portfolios inefficient relative to the market portfolio. In reality, there are many practical instances of restrictions; institutional investors, for example, may face short-selling restrictions as risk controls and others (like you and me) may find it impractical to engage in short sales for a variety of reasons (brokerage fees, trade size limitations, and downside risk). These restrictions will necessarily push our portfolios off the efficient frontier.

The impact of no short-sales restrictions can be seen in the spreadsheet exercises for this chapter. In this application, we solve for the minimum variance portfolio subject to an additional restriction that all weights must be nonzero. The solution is not analytic as was the case for Port 1 and Port 2 given earlier. Instead, it is a search process requiring iteration toward a combination of asset weights that generate the minimum variance for a targeted return. In all cases, the risk on the no-shorts portfolio will be higher. If, for example, we refer to the sheet containing the monthly returns for our 10 firms and set the targeted portfolio return at 2.5 percent, we get the following minimum variance portfolio:

	Port 2
C	0.171
CSCO	0.076
DELL	0.040
F	0.228
HD	0.180
INTC	0.186

MO	−0.082
MRK	0.026
MSFT	0.125
TWX	0.051
LagrMult	0.000
μ_p	0.025
σ_p	0.042

There is but one short position in this portfolio and that is with Phillip Morris (MO). If we restrict short sales, then we must use Excel's Solver function (we used Solver in Chapters 2 and 6). You can view the Solver setup for the short sales by clicking on Solver under the Data tab on the spreadsheet. This restricted portfolio is:

	NoShorts
C	0.177
CSCO	0.075
DELL	0.046
F	0.198
HD	0.141
INTC	0.185
MO	0.000
MRK	0.000
MSFT	0.115
TWX	0.063
LagrMult	
	1.000
μ_p	0.025
σ_p	0.043
Sharpe R	0.587

Notice there are no negative weights, but that the risk is slightly higher at 4.3 percent, which is the cost of the restriction. Put differently, the loss of efficiency is borne by the additional risk. Since Port 2 purportedly lies on the efficient frontier, then the No Shorts portfolio must not; in fact, it lies interior to the frontier directly to the right of Port 2, having increased risk for the same return.

A BOND STRATEGY

Bond managers often target a portfolio risk that is also tied to their benchmark. As we discovered in Chapter 2, a bond's duration summarizes its risk in terms of interest rate sensitivity. Bond managers who manage to a benchmark will therefore constrain the duration on their portfolio to match the benchmark duration.

 Go to the companion website for more details (see Bond Strategy under Chapter 7 Examples).

The bond strategy spreadsheet in the Chapter 7 Examples workbook presents such an example. These are *daily* total percentage returns on the benchmark and six bond indices—Treasuries, agencies, asset-backed securities, commercial mortgage-backed securities, mortgage-backed securities, and high yield corporate credit (investment grade). We will estimate a vector of mean returns and a covariance matrix to use as arguments in our mean-variance optimization.

These daily returns span April 2006 through the close of 2010. We wish to optimize a portfolio of these six bonds having a maximum return per unit risk with no short sales and with a portfolio duration that matches the benchmark duration of 4.43 years. For perspective, we also solve the minimum variance portfolio without short sales restrictions. The covariance matrix, as before, is bordered with two rows (columns) consisting of the adding up and expected return constraints so that the basic problem looks like the following:

	tsy	agy	abs	cmbs	mbs	cred	E(return)	$\sum w$	
tsy	0.113	0.069	0.046	0.047	0.062	0.108	−0.024	−1.000	0
agy	0.069	0.050	0.033	0.051	0.045	0.069	−0.023	−1.000	0
abs	0.046	0.033	0.108	0.026	0.025	0.050	−0.018	−1.000	0
cmbs	0.047	0.051	0.026	0.549	0.063	0.089	−0.026	−1.000	0
mbs	0.062	0.045	0.025	0.063	0.063	0.066	−0.026	−1.000	0
cred	0.108	0.069	0.050	0.089	0.066	0.136	−0.026	−1.000	0
E(return)	0.024	0.023	0.018	0.026	0.026	0.026	0.000	0.000	0.024
$\sum w$	1.000	1.000	1.000	1.000	1.000	1.000	0.000	0.000	1.000
				H					b

We first solve for the portfolio $w_c = H^{-1}b$. This portfolio and its expected return and risk are given further on alongside the no-short, duration-restricted portfolio (wd). The latter was solved using Excel's Solver (see the spreadsheet for details). We target maximizing the Sharpe ratio subject to two constraints: that there are no short sales (negative weights) and that the portfolio duration matches the targeted duration on the benchmark (in this case, 4.43 years).

	Duration		wc	wd
Treasury	3.45		−0.685	0.000
Agency	7.94		1.097	0.244
ABS	3.96		0.027	0.121
CMBS	2.88		−0.040	0.000
MBS	3.18		0.550	0.635
Credit	6.16		0.051	0.000
			2.417	1.000
Target	4.436		−0.020	
		return	0.024	0.024
		risk	0.193	0.223
		Sharpe	0.123	0.109
		wd*Dur		4.436

The optimal daily return is 2.4 basis points on each with 22.3 basis points of risk on the duration-constrained portfolio, and somewhat less, 19.3 bps, on the unconstrained portfolio. These results should also reinforce our understanding of the cost of constraints; wd is riskier and, hence, has a smaller Sharpe ratio. Nevertheless, it tracks the constraints, especially the duration target.

A word is in order concerning return frequency. This bond portfolio is built using daily returns. Choice of frequency is not coincidental. Managers choose frequencies to match their investment horizon and its inherent risks. Quarterly and monthly frequencies, for example, will model into the co-variance matrix a much different set of risk factors than will daily frequencies, for example, business cycle factors in quarterly and monthly data, seasonal factors in monthly, and temporal shocks, noise, and trading activity in daily data.

SUMMARY

This chapter is a natural extension of the hypothetical applications in Chapter 6. Here, we begin with actual historical returns series on 10 firms. Estimating mean returns, covariances, and volatilities, we constructed three portfolios: (1) The minimum risk portfolio located at the left-most point on the efficient set (technically uncorrelated with the market portfolio), the (2) set of minimum risk portfolios lying on the efficient set, and (3) the restricted no-shorts portfolio. We have conducted risk attribution analysis, estimated betas, correlations, the Sharpe ratio, derived the security market line, and discussed the implications of the capital asset pricing model . We also introduced the concept of the benchmark portfolio and how we assess portfolio performance in the presence of an alternative passive benchmark. We return to this concept fully in Chapter 10, on active management. Finally, we demonstrated the impact of alternate returns frequencies on portfolio allocation and performance.

CHAPTER 8

Anomalies

I can calculate the motion of heavenly bodies but not the madness of people.

—Isaac Newton

If, as presented in Chapter 4, stock prices are basically a rational forecast of the present value of expected future dividends, then why do observed stock prices vary so much? In two influential papers, Robert Shiller (1981, 1984) argued that stock prices do not reflect values based solely on fundamentals. Had they, then the variability in stock prices would be roughly accounted for by the variability in the underlying fundamentals incorporated in earnings and dividends. Yet, stock prices often exhibit excessive volatility in the absence of news reflected in fundamentals (for example, the crash of October 1987). See Summers 1981 and Cutler et al. (1989) for more on this topic.

As we shall see further on, the documentation of significant departures in prices from fundamentals (so-called anomalies) and the attempt to attribute these departures to cognitive biases, limitations to arbitrage, and boundedly rational behavior has generated a large and diverse literature in behavioral finance. (For an excellent survey, see Barberis and Thaler 2003.) The seeds to this literature can be traced to tests of the CAPM, whose failure as a predictive model spawned the controversial literature on anomalies.

The CAPM that was developed in Chapter 5 posits a relationship between asset returns and the return to the market portfolio in an equilibrium setting in which supply and demand determine market capitalization weights that, in turn, define the market portfolio and where all investors share the same information set and preferences and are mean variance optimizers. These are a rigid set of assumptions. In fact, the observed market portfolio is, at best, a proxy; the S&P 500 for example, or the

Russell 3000, or even the Wilshire 5000, are not the universe of all assets and therefore not the market portfolio on which the CAPM rests. In fact, no observed index can pass as the true market portfolio if for no other reason than it cannot include some assets, such as human capital. The observed market portfolio is therefore imperfect—we can hope that it is at least an efficient portfolio—but, in general, the CAPM in theory may be quite different from the CAPM in practice.

DEVIATIONS FROM THE CAPM

If the CAPM held, then discussion of various investment strategies related to (for example) style analysis, low volatility, sector rotation, momentum, and reversal, would be moot academic exercises. But the empirical evidence against CAPM is overwhelming with the tests, themselves, giving rise to a host of alternative portfolio strategies that are regarded as anomalies because they should not work in the equilibrium state described by CAPM.

The central questions are why the CAPM fails as a pricing relationship and what we learn about the relationships between risk and returns from these tests. The elegance of the CAPM model lies in the linear relationship between the expected return on any security and its covariance (beta) with the market rate of return, that is, the familiar relationship given by:

$$E(r_i) = r_f + \beta_i (E(r_m) - r_f)$$

The asset's beta is determined by its covariance with the market return as a ratio to the market variance, that is, $\beta_i = \frac{cov(r_i, r_m)}{var(r_m)}$. The CAPM takes the empirical form given by:

$$r_i = r_f + \beta_i (r_m - r_f) + \varepsilon_i$$

Expected returns are replaced by observed returns and appended with the pricing error term, ε_i, representing the firm's (asset's) specific risk. Specific risk is, of course, diversifiable but otherwise uncompensated. Only the firm's risk relative to the market portfolio—its systematic risk—is compensated and the price of that risk is given by its beta.

Typically, the empirical model is supplemented with an intercept and estimated using least squares in the following regression format:

$$r_i - r_f = \alpha + \beta_i (r_m - r_f) + \varepsilon_i$$

If the CAPM holds, then it should explain the cross-section of returns in the sense that assets with higher betas will also have higher returns. Thus, the relationship between β_i and r_i (as given by the security market line) should be linear and the slope should be equal to the average excess market return with no intercept. Lintner (1965), and later Miller and Scholes (1972), published some of the early empirical studies rejecting the CAPM.

The basic methodology for these early studies used monthly returns for five-year periods on, say, the S&P 500 (proxy for the market portfolio), the one-month Treasury bill (risk-free rate), and the returns on a set of 100 stocks. In a first-pass regression, the set of individual security betas were estimated with 100 separate bivariate regressions. These constituted the estimates for the security characteristic line (SML). The SML is the graph of the linear relationship between individual returns and betas. In the second-pass regression, the set of average security excess returns were regressed on the beta estimates from the first-pass regression, that is,

$$(\overline{r_i - r_f}) = \gamma_0 + \gamma_1 \beta_i$$

The hypothesis tested was $(\gamma_0, \gamma_1) = (0, (\overline{r_m - r_f})$ that is, that the security market line would have slope equal to the market excess return and a zero intercept (no abnormal return). Adding specific risk estimates (from the SML regressions) gives us the following empirical model:

$$(\overline{r_i - r_f}) = \gamma_0 + \gamma_1 \beta_i + \gamma_2 \sigma_i^2$$

where we test the hypothesis that the excess return is determined solely by systematic risk captured by β, and therefore that γ_2 must be statistically zero. Lintner found the slope γ_1 to be too flat (less than the average market excess return for the period under study) with a significant and positive intercept γ_0. He also found that a significant part of the cross-sectional excess return is also explained by specific risk ($\gamma_2 > 0$).

Still, it was hard to accept these implications, and attention turned to the statistical properties of the empirical methodology. In particular, it was noted that stock return volatility introduces measurement error into the estimates of the β_i and that these bias the estimates of γ_0 up and γ_1 downward. The thought was that eliminating measurement error would bring the test results back in line with the predictions of the theory. They did not. Second, because the estimated β_i are not independent of the errors in the second-pass regression, then the coefficient on the specific risk term γ_2 is biased upward. Again, fixing this inconsistency would push the test results in the direction of the CAPM. This helped but the basic findings with respect to (γ_0, γ_1) went unchanged.

In their attempt to deal with measurement error and orthogonality problems, Black, Jensen, and Scholes (BJS) introduced a methodology based on the portfolio deciling that is standard practice today. Because this methodology also (inadvertently) illuminated many of the anomalies that drove style research, it is worth reviewing.

In the BJS methodology, the first-pass regression is used to generate the cross-section of β_i based on, say, a trailing 60-month window of monthly returns for each stock. Stocks are then ranked by their betas and placed into deciles. Thus: (1) βs are estimated each year from a trailing 60-month sample, (2) firms are assigned a decile based on the size of their β estimate, (3) the 10 portfolio's betas are estimated for the forward period. Figure 8.1 illustrates this procedure.

Ranking βs and combining stocks into deciles provides the diversification that essentially aggregates away the impact of the measurement error as well as the effects of specific risks. The BJS study used all available NYSE returns for the period 1931 to 1965 (Black et al. 1972). To the disappointment of many, their results were not much different—the SML was still too flat with a positive intercept but it also appeared that the decile approach diversified away the statistical impact of the unsystematic risk on excess returns. Subsequent attention was focused sharply on what these failures now seemed to imply about the characteristics of the cross-section of stocks.

The BJS methodology illuminated several key relationships.

- First, it appears clear that lower beta portfolios earned consistently better risk-adjusted returns than higher beta portfolios that defy the expected risk-return trade-off.
- Second, high beta portfolios had a greater proportion of volatility explained by nonsystematic, or firm-specific, risk. Thus, not all risk was being priced.
- Third, a pattern emerges showing that measured alphas are negative for large beta portfolios and positive for low beta portfolios. Thus, riskier stocks appear to have lower abnormal returns.

Fama and MacBeth (1973) use the BJS methodology expanded to 20 portfolios to include a squared beta term to test for nonlinearities (there weren't any) and still find that the slope of the SML is too flat with significantly positive intercept. In time, more evidence of anomalous behavior was published:

First Year:

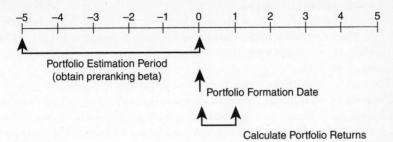

Second Year:

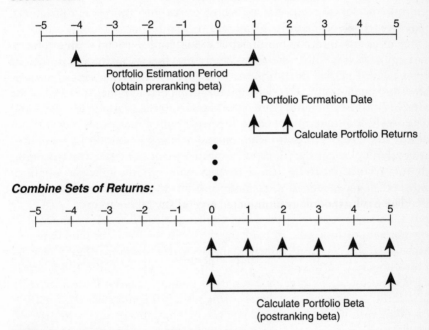

FIGURE 8.1 The Black-Jensen-Scholes Methodology

- Small firm effect—Kiem (1983)
- The p/e ratio effect—Ball (1992), Basu (1983)
- The leverage effect—Bhandari (1988)
- The book-to-market effect—Stattman (1980)

Fama and French (1992) sorted on size and then on beta and found that after controlling for size, the relationship between beta and return is negative. They concluded that the firm's size and book-to-market ratio together capture the cross-sectional variation in returns. In a word, Fama and French argue that beta is not compensated. This was the paper that spawned the style index work related to value (HML) and size (SMB); various indices sorted on these characteristics can be found on French's website.

The notion of beta not being compensated brings into question portfolio efficiency as we know it. Specifically, if all portfolios located on the efficient frontier are mean-variance efficient, but higher risk (beta) portfolios do not earn higher returns, then can we hold lower variance portfolios and earn essentially the same return as more risky positions do? Haugen and Baker (1991) question the claim that capitalization-weighted portfolios are indeed efficient, arguing that for a host of reasons (short-sale restrictions, inability to reliably estimate mean returns), large index holdings cannot be efficient except under very restrictive assumptions. Theirs is an argument not unlike Roll's, which questions the premise that we are indeed looking at the so-called market portfolio, for example, that the exclusion of alternatives and human capital render capitalization portfolios inferior to what the CAPM assumes investors are benchmarking to. Clarke, de Silva, and Thorley (2006) take this concept further, arguing that mean blur (our inability to measure precisely mean returns) makes it practically impossible to properly implement the Markowitz mean-variance criteria. The true minimum variance portfolio (the left-most point on the efficient frontier), however, is independent of our notions of mean returns; it is formed independently of expected returns or a targeted portfolio return. Clarke, de Silva, and Thorley (CST) therefore challenge the efficiency assumption of the market portfolio and, by studying the performance of the minimum variance portfolio over time, conclude that it delivers a lower volatility market portfolio–like return. Using the CRSP database, they study the 1,000 largest capitalization stocks over the time from January 1968 to December 2005 and construct a covariance matrix using principal component (PC) analysis on 60 months of excess returns over the one-month Treasury yield (the PC analysis allows them to identify various risk factors that aid in the formation of their optimal portfolios). The minimum variance portfolios is the solution to the quadratic programming problem (i is a conformable vector of ones for summing)

$$min_w i' V' i$$

Subject to:

$$i' w = 1$$

The portfolio that solves this is given by:

$$w = \frac{V^{-1}i}{i'V^{-1}i}$$

Thus, the minimum variance portfolio is solely a function of the covariance matrix V. It should be noted, however, that this is not the true minimum variance portfolio since CST impose long-only constraints. They also explore cases that selectively impose market neutrality constraints with respect to market capitalization (size), book to market (value), and momentum (prior year less prior month return) as well as the implications of different return frequencies (daily returns). Their basic findings are that (1) minimum variance portfolios generate returns that are at least as high as the cap-weighted portfolio but with (2) significantly lower risk and that (3) the minimum variance portfolios display a value and small-size bias. Thomas and Shapiro (2009) confirm and strengthen the robustness of the Haugen and Baker as well as the CST findings using the BARRA USE3L model in place of PC. Blitz and van Vliet (2007) don't even use a risk model to select their stocks; rather, each month they simply construct equally weighted decile portfolios by ranking stocks on the past three years' volatility using weekly returns (using FTSE World Developed Index). They show that stocks with low historical volatility have higher risk-adjusted returns using either Sharpe ratios or CAPM alphas and extend the CST results to a global universe, where they find particularly strong global performance (with a strong negative alpha for U.S. stocks).

BEHAVIORAL FINANCE

Why does the CAPM fail? Surely, if prices deviate from fundamentals, then mispricing will be profitably exploited by rational agents. If mispricing persists, then this anomaly may reflect something else; for example, the notion that the book-to-market factor (HML) in the Fama and French three-factor model explains the overreaction anomaly that the single-factor CAPM cannot. The anomalies discussed in the previous section suggest that either the model is misspecified in the sense that risk factors are missing (Eugene Fama's argument) or that the behavior implicit in the model—rational agents with identical preferences acting as mean variance optimizers—is not representative of the underlying market dynamic.

The theory of rational expectations posits that agents' subjective distributions of outcomes coincide with nature's objective distribution of outcomes, that is, that agents' models are correctly specified. This is a strong assumption. In fact, agents' information sets are asymmetric and their models are at best incomplete. Even with learning, agents' behavior may not be able to adjust adequately to ensure convergence to rational expectations equilibria. In short, equilibrium pricing models like the CAPM as well as the notion of efficient markets may fall victim to various imperfections in the rational paradigm.

Mainstream economics finds comfort in the argument that markets are self-correcting; that irrational agents will present arbitrage opportunities to rational agents and that inefficiencies will effectively be arbitraged away. Fisher Black presented an intriguing counterexample of agents who think they are trading on information but are, in fact, trading on transitory noise (Black 1986). The traditional model of arbitrage suggests that noise traders provide liquidity to the market that is exploited by rational arbitrageurs who, acting on superior information, absorb noise traders' capital, thus eliminating them from the market. Under these circumstances, noise traders cannot rationally persist. But Shiller (1984, op cit.) argues that there is little evidence to suggest that rational arbitrageurs dominate markets commonly and others such as Delong, Shleifer, Summers, and Waldmann (1990) introduce models showing that because noise traders systematically underestimate risk, they invest relatively greater fractions of their wealth in risky assets, driving up asset prices, allowing them to not only survive, but to dominate markets. In effect, overconfident noise traders taking long positions may be able to outlast rational arbitrageurs who are short the market. It is therefore possible to see persistent mispricing.

Behavioral finance argues that mispricing can persist because of limits to arbitrage and psychological biases. This is not a surprising claim from the perspective of regular market participants who see traditional money managers as poster children for a host of cognitive failures, including, for example, representativeness, overconfidence and overreaction, heuristics, confirmation bias, framing, and mental accounting. These present themselves as evidence that there are limits to arbitrage.

Representativeness, first introduced by Tversky and Kahneman (1974) is related to the law of small numbers, in which agents make decisions based on how much a choice resembles available data rather than a more careful analysis requiring mixing available facts and new information in an optimal way using Bayes's rule. Representativeness would suggest that when equity returns have been high for some time, like they were during the recent bull market, then agents begin to believe that high returns are normal. To take an example, suppose a top analyst named Mark has a reputation for correctly calling market moves and Mark is currently calling for a positive market movement not seen in some time. Suppose further that an independent analysis of market movements clearly shows that movements of this magnitude occur less than 1 percent of the time. When asked whether they wish to invest money on Mark's advice, many investors will, ignoring the base line probability; that is, investors will overweight the likelihood that Mark is correct and returns will be abnormally high. Instead of combining data on market movements with Mark's track record in an optimal way—which, incidentally, would suggest a much smaller probability of Mark being correct—they chose to invest on the basis of the advice being representative of Mark and not the underlying statistical evidence.

Overconfidence is both contagious and of epidemic proportions in financial markets. There is certainly ample self-selection as well, since entrepreneurs and money managers in general are neither timid nor overly reflective in general. Lack of diversification and hence overexposure to unsystematic risks, are an expected outcome. In general, men tend to be more overconfident than women, which Barber and Odean (2001) tie to their finding that men not only tend to trade more than women, they also tend to do worse.

Heuristics make decision making easier in a complex world. How many investors, when confronted with a choice of N mutual funds to invest in their defined contribution retirement plans simply use the $1/N$ allocation rule? Benartzi and Thaler (2001) refer to this as naïve diversification.

Go to the companion website for more details.

Consider the following example using the monthly returns data on the broad market indices for U.S. equity index, fixed income (FI), non-U.S. equity, high yield bonds (HY), convertible bonds, and REITs given in Chapter 8 Examples.xlsx. I began with the five-year sample of returns beginning in January 1988 through December 1992 and constructed two portfolios. The first simply diversifies investment across the six asset classes using the $1/N$ rule and holds this allocation going forward. The second portfolio uses the five-year trailing returns to estimate the covariance matrix and estimates the mean-variance efficient portfolio, rebalancing in each successive month using the trailing five-year returns through the close of 2009. Figure 8.2 compares the portfolio returns on the two strategies.

Clearly, failing to rebalance does a poor job of controlling risk, and the naïve strategy generates returns that reflect the broad market movements, especially during the tech crash of 2001 and the credit crisis that began in 2007. The MV efficient portfolio, by contrast, has a less erratic return history that mitigates downside risks but also caps participation in upside swings such as those experienced in the runup to the recent credit crisis. Volatilities bear this out, as we see in Figure 8.3.

The risk of the naïve strategy dominates through the sample accelerating to historic highs after 2007. A comparison, then, of risk-adjusted

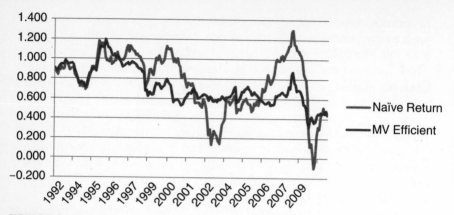

FIGURE 8.2 Returns

returns would indicate that the MV efficient strategy may produce uniformly superior performance, which it does as depicted in Figure 8.4, using Sharpe ratios (return per unit of risk):

The takeaway from this is the difficulty in accepting the hypothesis that markets are efficient. One of the biggest challenges for administrators of defined contribution pension funds is how to give useful advice in a world in which investors diversify across a menu of available fund choices using the 1/N rule. It is precisely this type of behavior that has led to various lifestyle and target date funds as default choices (investors don't opt out of good advice but they hardly ever opt in to it).

Framing and mental accounting, such as compartmentalizing losses and gains helps explain why people make mistakes when analyzing situations in isolation that would be better viewed together and why they hold losers too

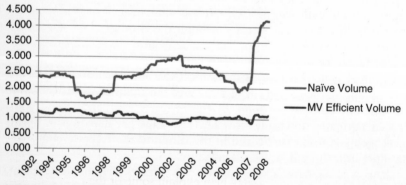

FIGURE 8.3 Volatilities

FIGURE 8.4 Sharpe Ratios

long and sell winners too early (Thaler 1985; Shefrin and Statman 1985). Framing is a powerful cognitive manipulator. Early-bird specials as opposed to peak time surcharges and survival probabilities instead of mortality rates are strong examples that decisions are sensitive to the way choices are framed. The disposition effect can explain why British Petroleum investors, in the wake of the Global Horizon explosion in the Gulf of Mexico in 2010, held their shares despite evidence indicating that BP's liability costs would almost certainly drive down expected returns into the indefinite future. Investors in this case were reluctant to sell shares bought at, say, $60, even though they quickly fell in value based on fundamentals to $30, in the hope that prices would eventually rebound. Framing also produces variations in attitudes toward risk. Value at risk (VaR), for example, is typically stated as the likelihood or not losing more than some specified amount. For example, 95 percent VaR indicates that the portfolio will lose no more than, say, $L 95 percent of the time. An equivalent statement, but one that is framed quite differently, is that the portfolio will lose more than $L 5 percent of the time. Thus, framing may elicit quite different responses on how risk should be managed.

Confirmation bias occurs when agents actively seek data supporting a closely held hypothesis. Self-deception, in which individuals think they are smarter than they really are (the Lake Wobegon effect), contributes to overconfidence and self-attribution biases. Individually or together, these biases can drive a wedge into the pricing mechanism, causing persistent mispricing (Daniel 2001).

These are examples of cognitive departures from the rational model of asset price determination that may help explain some of the anomalies discussed earlier. Others include hot-hands fallacies, in which we wrongly believe that events, which are truly independent, are not. For example, it is an empirical fact that hot hands or hot streaks in scoring in basketball do not exist, yet ample evidence confirms the belief in the importance in getting the ball into the hands of someone who has just scored several points in a row (Gilovich et al. 1985). The hot hands fallacy may help explain mutual fund flows to those hot funds having recent outperformance. This could explain in part why momentum is a statistically important factor explaining movements in asset returns.

How many of us know individuals who play the lottery and are sure not to use numbers of past winners? These same individuals are aware that lottery numbers are *independent* random draws, yet their behavior clearly indicates otherwise; indeed, the probability that yesterday's winner is also today's winner is just as likely as any other number being today's winner. Efficient markets hypotheses require that price changes are unanticipated or independent. Perhaps it is no coincidence that rejection of this hypothesis occurs in a world in which so many agents' behavior displays some rather radical departures from the rational cognitive model. Still, other cognitive departures suggest that loss aversion encourages people to value what they already have a lot more than others do, that they tend to hold losers too long and that they tend to be asymmetrically risk-seeking with losses and risk-averse with gains. And finally, there is ample evidence that individuals don't understand the fundamentals of probability as most famously displayed in the Monty Hall puzzle in which an individual is asked to pick which of three doors is hiding a valuable prize. After making a selection, one of the remaining two doors is opened that does not contain the prize. Contestants are then asked if they would like to change their choice. Most do not. They correctly surmise that the probability that the prize is behind their original choice is still one-third. But they incorrectly conclude that the probability that the prize is behind the remaining door is also one-third. They do not fully understand how conditional probabilities depend upon the set of possible outcomes. The correct choice is always to change the choice to the remaining door. To understand why, let me reframe the problem. Suppose you lost a diamond ring while out walking in a field. You don't have time to search the entire field so you divide the area into a grid consisting of one hundred equally sized squares. You select one at random to search knowing that there is a 1 percent chance that the ring is contained in this square and that there is a 99 percent chance that it is contained somewhere in the remaining 99 squares. Now, suppose that I reveal to you information identifying which 98 of the 99 remaining squares do not contain the ring. The field has clearly shrunk as there is only one square left besides your original choice that could contain the ring. But there is a 99 percent probability that the ring is in that square! Should you choose to search your original square or change if given the opportunity? Clearly, you will change squares.

This example shows how deficient we are in processing new information that may alter the likelihood of outcomes. Thus, while there is a propensity to hold losers (risk-seeking in losses), there may also be a predilection to holding losers because we incorrectly process new information, indicating that we should reallocate so as to avoid higher probabilities of losses.

One of the primary findings in cognitive science is that the human brain did not evolve to process probabilities; rather, it evolved in directions that increased the chances of survival and probabilities were not an essential feature of that behavior. Research in cognitive science using fMRI has also located the region within the brain that governs how we discount future costs and rewards (cerebral cortex) (McClure et al. 2004). Importantly, we find that discount rates are variable across individuals, age groups, and cultures. This is a fascinating concept. For example, younger societies having lower discount rates (emerging markets?) while older demographics in developed economies having inherently higher discount rates. In any case, it would be a mistake to think that we all discount to the same value, for example, future environmental costs from carbon emissions.

SUMMARY

There are vast anomalies in the literature. This chapter was not an attempt to survey that literature. Rather, my objective was to balance the presentation of rational pricing models of the preceding chapters with their inability to adequately incorporate the impact of cognitive failures. Pricing models are by nature restrictive so they may be tractable. The CAPM is one such model that fails statistically to adequately explain the cross-section of returns. Neither are markets as efficient as proposed by the efficient markets hypothesis. Since these models abstract away the complexities of human behavior, it is no real surprise that they fall short. However, these failures should not be construed as a reason to discard these models. The CAPM, for example, is a powerful tool to help organize our thinking about how markets price assets, and extensions of the CAPM can go a long way in improving our understanding of the pricing mechanism. The new generation of multifactor models, which are covered in Chapter 9, explicitly recognize perceived cognitive failures by extending the single-factor model beyond the Fama-French three-factor model to include variables explicitly designed to account for cognitive traits such as overreaction and momentum as well as early anomalies attributed to size, value, and liquidity.

REFERENCES

Ball, Ray. 1992. The earnings-price anomaly. *Journal of Accounting and Economics* 15.

Barber, Brad, and Terry Odean. 2001. Boys will be boys: Gender, overconfidence, and common stock investment. *Quarterly Journal of Economics* 116.

Barberis, Nicholas, and Richard Thaler. 2003. A survey of behavioral finance. In *The Handbook of the Economics of Finance*, eds. George M. Constantinides, Milton Harris, and Rene Stulz. Amsterdam: Elsevier.

Basu, Sanjoy. 1983. The relationship between earnings yield, market value and return for NYSE common stocks: Further evidence. *Journal of Financial Economics* 12.

Benartzi, Shlomo, and Richard Thaler. 2001. Naïve diversification strategies in defined contribution savings plans. *American Economic Review* 91.

Bhanddari, Laxmi. 1988. Debt/equity ratio and expected common stock returns: empirical evidence. *The Journal of Finance* 43.

Black, Fisher. 1986. Noise. *Journal of Finance* 41.

Black, Fisher, Michael Jensen, and Myron Scholes. 1972. The capital asset pricing model: Some empirical tests. In *Studies in the theory of capital markets*, ed. Michael Jensen. New York: Praeger.

Blitz, David, and Pim van Vliet. 2007. The volatility effect. *Journal of Portfolio Management*.

Clarke, Roger, Harinda de Silva, and Steven Thorley. 2006. Minimum-variance portfolios in the U.S. equity market. *Journal of Portfolio Management*.

Cutler, David, James Poterba, and Lawrence Summers. 1989. What moves stock prices? *Journal of Portfolio Management* (Spring).

Daniel, Kent, Hirshleifer, David, and Avanidhar Subrahmanyan. 2001. Mispricing, covariance risk, and the cross-section of security returns. *Journal of Finance* 56.

Delong, J. Bradford, Andrei Shleifer, Lawrence Summers, and Robert Waldmann. 1990. Noise trader risk in financial markets. *Journal of Political Economy* 98.

Delong, J. Bradford, Andrei Shleifer, Lawrence Summers, and Robert Waldmann. 1991. The survival of noise traders in financial markets. *Journal of Business* 64.

Fama, Eugene, and Kenneth French. 1992. The cross-section of expected stock returns. *Journal of Finance* 47.

Fama, Eugene, and James MacBeth. 1973. Risk, return, and equilibrium: Empirical tests. *Journal of Political Economy* 81 (March).

Gilovich, Thomas, Robert Vallone, and Amos Tversky. 1985. The hot hands in basketball: On the misperception of random sequences. *Cognitive Psychology* 17.

Haugen, Robert, and Nardin Baker. 1991. The efficient market inefficiency of capitalization-weighted stock portfolios. *Journal of Portfolio Management*.

Kiem, Donald. 1983. Size-related anomalies and stock return seasonality: Further empirical evidence. *Journal of Financial Economics* 12.

Lintner, John. 1965. Security prices, risk and maximal gains from diversification. *Journal of Finance* 20.

McClure, Samuel, David Laibson, George Loewenstein, and Jonathan D. Cohen. 2004. Separate neural systems value immediate and delayed monetary rewards. *Science* 306: 503–507.

Miller, Merton, and Myron Scholes. 1972. Rate of return in relation to risk: A re-examination of some recent findings. In *Studies in the theory of capital markets*, ed. Michael C. Jensen. New York: Praeger.

Shefrin Hersh, and Meir Statman. 1985. The disposition to sell winners too early and ride losers too long. *Journal of Finance* 40.

Shiller, Robert. 1981. Do stock prices move too much to be justified by subsequent changes in dividends? *American Economic Review* (June).

Shiller, Robert. 1984. Stock prices and social dynamics. *The Brookings Papers on Economic Activity* 2.

Stattman, Dennis. 1980. Book values and stock returns. *The Chicago MBA: A Journal of Selected Papers* 4.

Summers, Lawrence. 1981. Does the stock market rationally reflect fundamental values? *American Economic Review.*

Thomas, Rick, and Robert Shapiro. 2009. *Managed volatility: A new approach to equity investing.* Boston: SSgA Capital Insights.

Thaler, Richard. 1985. Mental accounting and consumer choice. *Marketing Science* 4.

Tversky, Amos, and Daniel Kahneman. 1974. Judgement under uncertainty: Heuristics and biases. *Science* 185.

CHAPTER 9

Factor Models

An economist is someone who sees something in the real world and wonders if it would work in theory.

—Ronald Reagan

The CAPM can be interpreted as a *single index* factor model, and since we are already familiar with it, I will use the CAPM to introduce this important class of pricing models.

Factor models can be thought of as models of the *conditional* mean return to an asset (or portfolio of assets). We used *unconditional* mean return estimates as inputs to the optimal mean-variance efficient portfolios solved for in Chapters 6 and 7. To understand the difference, let r_{it} be the return on asset i at time t. Then the asset's unconditional mean return is simply the average return, that is, $E(r_i) = \sum \frac{r_i}{T} = \bar{r}$. Now, think of the CAPM model:

$$r_i - r_f = \alpha + \beta_i(r_m - r_f) + \varepsilon_i$$

For ease of exposition, drop the risk-free rate (that is, assume that cash earns no return) and take expectations (see the statistical review in the appendix to Chapter 5) noting that $E(\varepsilon_i) = 0$ by definition. Then,

$$E(r_i) = \alpha + \beta_i E(r_m)$$

Simply stated, this says that the expected return is now *conditional* on the market return. The market return is therefore the single factor and beta is the return (sometimes called the *factor loading*) to that factor.

There are several attractive features of factor models that are developed in this chapter, but the first and most obvious feature is that factors help attribute the asset's return to movements in specific underlying sources of risk and return. The Fama-French three-factor model introduced in Chapter 8, for example, decomposes the asset's return into three component parts—the return attributable to the value portfolio (HML), the return attributable to market capitalization or size (SMB), and the market return:

$$r_i = \alpha + \beta_1 HML + \beta_2 SMB + \beta_3 r_m + \varepsilon_i$$

Since the factors themselves are returns, then the factor returns (the betas) measure the return attributable to the asset's exposure to each of these factors. Thus, a 1 percent change in the factor is expected to move the asset's return by the amount of its beta with respect to that factor. The parameters of factor models are generally estimated by ordinary least squares available in virtually all spreadsheet and statistical software packages. Thus, collecting a time series of returns on the asset and the factors (the latter are available at French's website) then regressing r_i on the factors will generate estimates of the parameters. We explore some applications further on.

 See Kenneth French's website at http://mba.tuck.dartmouth.edu/pages/ faculty/ken.french/index.html.

ARBITRAGE PRICING THEORY (APT)

Let's digress a bit on the underlying theory of factor models. Under some fairly general assumptions and using a no-arbitrage argument, we can show that the factor returns (betas) in factor models must be related across assets and that the asset's return is linear in the factors. The seminal work is Ross (1976).

 Other references on APT and multifactor models can be found at www .kellogg.northwestern.edu/faculty/korajczy/htm/aptlist.htm.

Not only is the no-arbitrage argument less restrictive than the equilibrium requirement underlying CAPM, arbitrage pricing theory (APT) expands the number of factors beyond just the market return. This is a powerful result, as we see further on where we try to estimate parameters for large portfolios of assets; APT requires estimating several factor returns that can then be used to model the covariance matrix of returns across assets. This greatly reduces the data requirements necessary for estimation purposes. Recall that in the N asset case, we need to estimate $\frac{N^2 - N}{2}$ covariances and N variances. For large portfolios, we will see that there are insufficient observations available to do so as N begins to overwhelm the number of time periods T. The S&P 500, for example, requires estimates for 500 variances and 124,750 covariances. This would require about 10,000 years of monthly returns, which, obviously, are not available. On the other hand, a k-factor model basically reduces the dimensionality of the problem to the k factors. So, in a sense, APT provides the basis for multifactor models that extend the concept of the CAPM as a pricing model but with fewer restrictions. We develop these ideas more fully further on. I am going to borrow liberally from Luenberger (1998). To begin, let's focus on a single linear factor model, letting f stand for some factor (for example, the return to the market portfolio) and write the return to asset i as $r_i = \alpha + \beta_i f$. Do the same for asset j: $r_j = \alpha + \beta_j f$. Now form a portfolio of these two assets with weights w and $(1 - w)$ having return r equal to:

$$r = wr_i + (1 - w)r_j$$

$$r = w\alpha_i + (1 - w)\alpha_j + \left[w\beta_i + (1 - w)\beta_j\right]f$$

Here is where the no-arbitrage argument comes in. The factor f is the source of systematic risk. Suppose we solve for the weight that makes this risk zero. Doing so will then imply that the return on the portfolio is risk free. A little algebra easily shows that the weight that makes $[w\beta_i + (1 - w)\beta_j]f = 0$ is:

$$w = \frac{\beta_j}{\beta_j - \beta_i}$$

Substituting this into the previous equation and solving for the portfolio return confirms that it is risk free. For example, it is no longer a function of the systematic risk embodied in the factor.

$$r = \alpha_i\left(\frac{\beta_j}{\beta_j - \beta_i}\right) + \alpha_j\left(\frac{\beta_i}{\beta_i - \beta_j}\right)$$

This return must be equal to the risk-free return, r_f. Otherwise, an arbitrage opportunity presents itself, since we could borrow at the risk-free rate and fund this portfolio earning the premium $(r - r_f)$. Therefore it must be true that:

$$r_f = \alpha_i\left(\frac{\beta_j}{\beta_j - \beta_i}\right) + \alpha_j\left(\frac{\beta_i}{\beta_i - \beta_j}\right)$$

Rearranging terms indicates that the relationship between the parameters across assets in the portfolio is not arbitrary:

$$r_f\left(\beta_j - \beta_i\right) = \alpha_i\beta_j - \alpha_j\beta_i$$

$$\frac{\alpha_j - r_f}{\beta_j} = \frac{\alpha_i - r_f}{\beta_i}$$

Indeed, the no-arbitrage argument establishes that the risk-adjusted premium (the parameter α is the asset's *alpha*—its return in excess of its risk-adjusted return) over the risk-free rate of return must be constant across assets. The numerator is therefore a premium over the riskless rate, which is standardized by the return to the systematic source of risk from the factor) over the riskless rate of return must be constant across assets:

$$C = \frac{\alpha_j - r_f}{\beta_j} = \frac{\alpha_i - r_f}{\beta_i}$$

This is a powerful and subtle result. Solving for α on asset j:

$$\alpha_j = r_f + \beta_i C$$

Substituting this in for α in the factor model and taking expectations produces the expected return to the asset, given the factor f:

$$E(r_i) = \alpha_i + \beta_i\bar{f} = r_f + \beta_i C + \beta_i\bar{f}$$

$$\bar{r}_i = r_f + \beta_i\left(C + \bar{f}\right)$$

Thus, the expected return is the risk-free rate plus a risk premium (scaled by the constant C) where β measures the return to being exposed to the source of risk embodied in the factor. Statistically, β is the covariance between the asset's return and the risk factor f scaled by the factor variance:

$$\beta_i = \frac{\sigma_{if}}{\sigma_f^2}$$

We can generalize APT to many factors. The multifactor model takes the general form:

$$r_i = \alpha_i + \sum_{k=1}^{K} \beta_{ik} f_k$$

whereupon substituting the no-arbitrage constraint implications for α yields:

$$\bar{r}_i = r_f + \sum_{k=1}^{K} \beta_{ik} \left(C + \bar{f}_j \right)$$

In practice, analysts are interested in estimating the parameters of this model to help them form an expectation of the asset's return. For estimation purposes, the APT is written as the linear multiple regression model, with error term ε, which captures the asset's idiosyncratic (or specific) risk, that is, the variance in return not explained by the systematic sources of risk represented in the factors.

$$r_i = \alpha_i + \sum_{k=1}^{K} \beta_{ik} f_k + \varepsilon_i$$

Specific risk is unsystematic and can therefore be diversified away. To see why, let's construct a portfolio of N assets with weights indicating that the portfolio is fully invested, that is,

$$\sum_{i=1}^{N} w_i = 1$$

and write the return to the portfolio as follows:

$$r = \alpha + \sum_{k=1}^{K} \beta_k f_k + \varepsilon$$

$$\alpha = \sum w_i \alpha_i$$

$$\beta_k = \sum w_i \beta_{ik}$$

$$\varepsilon = \sum w_i \varepsilon_i$$

$$\sigma_\varepsilon^2 = \sum w_i^2 \sigma_{\varepsilon i}^2$$

In general, we diversify by adding assets to the portfolio. If we assume that the weights are all approximately the same (note that we are not assuming naïve investing as discussed in the chapter on anomalies), that is, w_i is approximately equal to $1/N$, then if the idiosyncratic risks $\sigma_{\varepsilon i}^2$ are bounded (they aren't infinite), then clearly, as N increases, σ_ε^2 must go to zero in the limit. In practice, factor selection can be designed to maximize the explanatory power of the model so that $\sigma_{\varepsilon i}^2$ is minimized as well.

I made the claim earlier that CAPM is a single-factor model with the market rate of return as the factor. Let's establish now the link between APT and CAPM. Suppose we have an asset whose returns are determined by two factors:

$$r_i = \alpha_i + \beta_{i1}f_1 + \beta_{i2}f_2 + \varepsilon_i$$

In the CAPM, we would be interested in the covariance between r_i and r_m, that is, in estimating the asset's beta.

$$\text{cov}(r_i, r_m) = \beta_{i1}\text{cov}(f_1, r_m) + \beta_{i2}\text{cov}(f_2, r_m) + \text{cov}(\varepsilon_i, r_m)$$

If we divide both sides by σ_{rm}^2, we get the asset's beta as follows:

$$\beta_i = \beta_{i1}\frac{\sigma_{f_1, r_m}}{\sigma_{rm}^2} + \beta_{i2}\frac{\sigma_{f_2, r_m}}{\sigma_{rm}^2}$$

The connection to APT is that the CAPM beta is a weighted average of the underlying factor returns. The weights are a function of the covariances between the factors and the market return. We can generalize this to show that the CAPM beta is a weighted average of factors in any factor model. Therefore, CAPM is a special case of APT.

The parameters of the Fama-French three-factor model would be estimated using the following regression specification:

$$r_{it} = \alpha + \beta_{it}HML_t + \beta_{2i}SMB_t + \beta_{3i}r_{mt} + \varepsilon_{it}$$

FACTOR SELECTION

There are several commercially available factor models that provide useful insights into methodological differences regarding both estimation and factor selection. The BARRA, BIRR, and RAM multifactor models all offer a multidimensional view of risk analysis. BARRA was developed by Bar Rosenberg; BIRR by Burmeister, Ibbotson, Roll, and Ross, while RAM was a proprietary *risk attribute model* of Salomon Brothers. That is, each models asset returns as a function of several sources of risk, some emanating from macroeconomic sources, while for others, namely BARRA, company fundamentals.

BIRR and RAM are macroeconomic factor models motivated by arbitrage pricing theory. As we have just demonstrated, that theory maintains that factor sensitivities are determined in such a way as to preclude arbitrage opportunities. For example, in the single-factor CAPM model, estimated alpha and beta values must generate a relationship between excess returns to the asset and the market portfolio sufficient to eliminate riskless short-selling of one asset for a certain gain on the other. If it is believed that there are relatively few factors that account for the variation in asset returns, then a multifactor model will produce factor sensitivity estimates that meaningfully represent the pricing relationship to the factor in an arbitrage-free and hence, efficient, market. Of course, the objective is to determine what these factors are and no one has yet resolved this issue; hence, the multitude of proprietary models. For now, let us assume that each of these models is correctly specified.

The macroeconomic models offered by BIRR and RAM use historic stock returns and macroeconomic variables as descriptors. These are given next. More specifics can be found at their websites.

BIRR descriptors

- Investor confidence (confidence risk)
- Interest rates (time horizon risk)
- Inflation (inflation risk)
- Real business activity (business cycle risk)
- A market index (market timing risk)

RAM descriptors

- Change in expected long-run economic growth
- Short-run business cycle risk
- Long-term bond yield changes
- Short-term Treasury bill changes
- Inflation shock
- Dollar changes versus trading partner currencies

Let's set up the RAM methodology, which uses a 3,500-stock universe. This method generalizes to BIRR and macroeconomic factor models in general. I describe the methodology in four steps and follow with an interpretation.

MODEL ESTIMATION

(1) Factors are first standardized. These are time series, so standardization for a factor involves differencing the time-t value from the time series mean and dividing by the standard deviation of the macro factor. (2) Then a time series for each stock's returns is regressed on the standardized factors (also called factor exposures) and the estimated factor sensitivities (also referred to as beta, factor return, or factor loading) are saved. (3) This time series regression is then repeated for the universe of stocks. The resulting population factor sensitivities are saved. (4) Individual factor sensitivities are standardized, that is, the standardized factor sensitivity for the ith asset on the jth factor is given by (b_{ij} − b_j)/s_{bj} where b_j and s_{bj} are the estimated sensitivity and standard error for the jth factor, using the universe of stocks.

A factor sensitivity with value zero means that the stock has average sensitivity to that particular factor. Standardized factor sensitivities can be positive or negative. Output from this model is called a *score*. For example, output is the sum of the standardized factors and sensitivities products for a firm. For the ith firm,

$$\hat{r}_i = \beta_{i1} f_1 + \cdots + \beta_{i6} f_6$$

where $\hat{r}$ denotes the score, β_{ik} are the factor returns or sensitivities, and the factors, f_i, are standardized exposures across time. This is a predicted return, conditional on the factor exposures and their estimated sensitivities and, in principle, can be used as the mean return in the mean-variance portfolio optimization. If the factors are orthogonal, then the covariance matrix is diagonal; in this case, the variance of the asset's return is the sum of the factor variances weighted by the squares of their betas (see the following discussion on principal components).

Factor sensitivities measure the estimated response to a one-standard deviation in the factor. Standardized factor sensitivities can be ranked across factors to ascertain which factors are more or less important in driving returns. Scenarios can then be devised whereupon the manager takes action based on the estimated response in the stock's return to contrived factor values. Essentially, the same analysis can be conducted using BIRR (though for BIRR, the output is an expected excess return). Both methodologies use time series. The entire set of factor sensitivities is the portfolio's risk profile—the weighted average of the factor sensitivities of the individual stocks that compose the portfolio. This analysis is then replicated for the benchmark, or index portfolio (for example, S&P 500), and risk profiles can be compared allowing managers to assess relative risk exposures, compute expected returns, and reallocate accordingly.

The BARRA methodology is cross-sectional. Although factors are still standardized (for the current time cross-section of firms) and factor sensitivities are still ordinary least squares (OLS) estimates, there are econometric implications for cross-sectional models, which differ from time series methods. Some of these are covered in the next section. BARRA begins with firm fundamentals, not macroeconomic variables, as raw descriptors, and combines them to obtain risk indices to capture company attributes. For example, debt-to-asset ratio, debt-to-equity ratio, and fixed rate coverage can be combined to obtain the risk index for financial leverage. BARRA's GEM2 global model, for example, covers 54 countries and currencies, 34 industry groups, and a host of risk factors, including value, growth, size, momentum, volatility, liquidity, and leverage.

As with the macroeconomic factor models, the raw descriptors are standardized and then the indices are standardized (as functions of the standardized raw descriptors). Factor sensitivities are standardized as well after estimation. In general, estimation is a cross-sectional regression across n firms at time t. If, for example, data are of monthly frequency, then we could write the model as follows:

$$r_{it} = \quad \alpha + \beta_i f_{1i,t} + \cdots + \beta_k f_{ki,t} + \varepsilon_{it}$$

$$\cdot$$
$$\cdot$$
$$\cdot$$

$$r_{jt} = \quad \alpha + \beta_i f_{1j,t} + \cdots + \beta_k f_{kj,t} + \varepsilon_{jt}$$

$$\cdot$$
$$\cdot$$
$$\cdot$$

$$r_{nt} = \quad \alpha + \beta_i f_{1n,t} + \cdots + \beta_k f_{kn,t} + \varepsilon_{nt}$$

The factor sensitivities are OLS estimates from a cross-sectional regression of the n firms' returns at time t. While all firms share the factor sensitivity, they have different exposures. Therefore β_k measures the impact of a one-standard deviation change in firm i's exposure to factor k.

It is convenient to work with this model in matrix format, which we can write as:

$$
Y_t = \begin{bmatrix} r_{1t} \\ r_{2t} \\ \cdot \\ \cdot \\ \cdot \\ r_{nt} \end{bmatrix}; \quad
X_t = \begin{bmatrix} f_{11} & \cdots & f_{k1} \\ \cdot & & \cdot \\ \cdot & & \cdot \\ \cdot & & \cdot \\ f_{1n} & \cdots & f_{kn} \end{bmatrix}; \quad
\beta_t = \begin{bmatrix} \beta_1 \\ \beta_2 \\ \cdot \\ \cdot \\ \beta_k \end{bmatrix}; \quad
\varepsilon_t = \begin{bmatrix} \varepsilon_{1t} \\ \varepsilon_{2t} \\ \cdot \\ \cdot \\ \varepsilon_{nt} \end{bmatrix}
$$

It follows therefore that:

$$
Y_t = X_t \beta_t + \varepsilon_t
$$

The vector β_t is estimated using least squares. This is a cross-sectional regression model whose factor sensitivities are estimated for each time period. We can collect these vectors over time T into a matrix,

$$
\beta = \begin{bmatrix}
\beta_{1,t} & \beta_{1,t+1} & \cdots & \beta_{1,T} \\
\beta_{2,t} & \beta_{2,t+1} & \cdots & \beta_{2,T} \\
\cdot & & & \cdot \\
\cdot & & & \cdot \\
\cdot & & & \cdot \\
\beta_{k,t} & \beta_{k,t+1} & \cdots & \beta_{k,T}
\end{bmatrix}
$$

These factor sensitivities have a covariance relationship over T given by:

$$
V_\beta = \mathrm{cov}(\beta) = E\left[\beta \beta^T\right] = \begin{bmatrix}
\sigma_{\beta_1}^2 & \cdot & \cdot & \cdot & \sigma_{\beta_{1k}} \\
\cdot & \cdot & & & \cdot \\
\cdot & & \cdot & & \cdot \\
\cdot & & & \cdot & \cdot \\
\sigma_{\beta_{k1}} & \cdot & \cdot & \cdot & \sigma_{\beta_k}^2
\end{bmatrix}
$$

Therefore, the cross-sectional variation in returns is closely tied to the covariances of the β's. Let's write the total variance in returns as follows:

$$
\mathrm{Var}(Y_t) = X_t \mathrm{var}(\beta) X'_t + \mathrm{var}(\varepsilon_t)
$$

$$
= X_t V_\beta X'_t + V_\varepsilon
$$

Think about the dimensions of this result and what they mean. Since there are n firms and k factors, we first note that X_t is an $n \times k$ matrix of standardized factor exposures observed at time t, and V_β is the estimated $k \times k$ covariance matrix of factor sensitivities using information up to time t. Therefore, $X_t V_\beta X'_t$ is of dimension $n \times n$. Likewise, V_ε is the $n \times n$ idiosyncratic risk matrix (referred to also as specific risk):

$$V_\varepsilon = \begin{bmatrix} \sigma^2_{\varepsilon_1} & \cdot & \cdot & \cdot & 0 \\ & \cdot & & & \cdot \\ & & \cdot & & \cdot \\ & & & \cdot & \cdot \\ 0 & \cdot & \cdot & \cdot & \sigma^2_{\varepsilon_n} \end{bmatrix}$$

Therefore, $\mathrm{Var}(Y_t)$—the cross-section variation in returns—is the sum of a systematic component, $X_t V_\beta X'_t$, which is conditional on the standardized factor exposures plus an unsystematic component embodied in the cross-section of specific risks. Furthermore, $X_t V_\beta X'_t$ merely scales V_β with the current observed factor matrix.

Now, of what importance is this to mean-variance optimization? Well, first recall that any minimum variance portfolio (for a stated return) is also the maximum return portfolio for a stated level of risk. We therefore want the vector w (the portfolio) that solves the following problem:

$$\max_w w'r - \frac{1}{2} w'Vw$$

This problem takes two arguments (r, V), the vector of N returns to the assets and the covariance matrix of those returns: the risk matrix. In previous chapters, these parameters were estimated using sample means and variances. For example, $\bar{r}$ was the simple sample mean returns and V was the returns covariances. Two problems arise with this approach. First, these are unconditional moment estimates and are therefore entirely driven by historical data. Factor models yield conditional moments for us. For example, instead of the unconditional mean return, we use the estimated factor model return:

$$\hat{r}_i = \hat{\beta}_1 f_{i1} + \cdots + \hat{\beta}_k f_{i,k}$$

The second problem relates to estimating V. For small portfolios, V is estimated using historical returns, as we've shown in previous chapters. However, if the number of firms N exceeds the length of the time series t, then V cannot be estimated from sample returns at all. Recall that V has

$\frac{N^2 - N}{2}$ covariance estimates as well as N variances along the diagonal. Monthly historical data going back 50 years will consist of roughly 600 observations, which is insufficient to estimate the required 780 covariances in a 40-asset portfolio! Portfolio analysts who estimate V under this condition will find that their optimizations routinely return computational errors based on V having less than full rank, the end result being that V is not invertible. The factor model, however, gives an estimate of V, which consists of two components, $X_t V_\beta X'_t$ that are tied to estimating the $K \times K$ matrix V_β and V_ε, which is a diagonal matrix requiring N individual specific risk estimates. Since K is small relative to T, then V_β will not violate the rank condition based on any degrees of freedom restriction. And, since the specific risk estimates are often estimated from the residuals of the factor model, then V_ε will also have full rank. Therefore, we substitute for r and V using:

$$\hat{r}_i = \hat{\beta}_1 f_{i1} + \cdots + \hat{\beta}_k f_{i,k}$$

$$V = X_t V_\beta X'_t + V_\varepsilon$$

This is a powerful result and one that we need to fully comprehend. Factor models have moved portfolio management from unconditional moment estimates to estimates conditional on the underlying risk factors. This development allows managers to condition returns estimates on subsets of factors, effectively tilting the portfolio in the direction of, or away from, chosen factors (that is, basing $\bar{r}$ on a subset of factors) and, more importantly, provides a methodology to handling large portfolios. Nonetheless, these improvements do not come without their own set of problems, foremost of which is estimation of specific risks. In most applications, specific risk dominates V. The reason is that factors often leave much of the cross-sectional variation in returns unexplained, which means that residual variation (the source of specific risk) must now be modeled. This is not an easy task, as these residuals often do not have ideal time series properties. Approaches to specific risk estimates are varied and complicated. One time series approach would be to collect the time series of factor model residuals for each firm and then model these using GARCH. On the other hand, a naïve estimate would be the firm-specific residual variances. Managers must be aware that optimal portfolios may be quite sensitive to the properties of V, a topic beyond the scope of this book but a very important one nevertheless.

Manager performance can then be evaluated by comparing the risk profile of the portfolio to that of the benchmark, say the set of risk exposures to the S&P 500. Differences in factor sensitivities highlight bets and identify their sources vis-à-vis the risk factor. Managers can then rebalance or tilt the portfolios according to their investment objectives.

PRINCIPAL COMPONENTS

Think of a set R of T historical returns on k assets so that $R \sim T \times k$. There are, at best, k independent sources of variation in this set of returns. If, for example, one of the asset's returns can be expressed as a linear combination of another asset's returns, then there are only $k - 1$ independent sources of variation. In that case, the $k \times k$ covariance matrix would not be invertible since it has less than full rank; its rank is $k - 1$. Without full rank, we could not solve for the minimum variance portfolio. The reason is that we are asking too much of our data: it can provide us with only $k - 1$ weights, not k. At the other extreme, if the asset returns are independent, then there are k independent sources of variation (called factors) and the covariance matrix has full rank, whose diagonal elements contain variances of the individual asset returns and zeros otherwise.

The idea of the diagonal covariance matrix is intriguing for two reasons: first, it would suggest that returns are independent and that has important implications for diversification. Second, it simplifies the math; for example, solving the minimum variance portfolio is a matter of ranking the individual variances (or Sharpe ratios), giving highest weight to the lowest variance (highest Sharpe ratio).

Principal components analyzes the covariance properties of a set of returns or factors and finds the set of orthogonal factors that best explains the covariation of returns. Orthogonality means that the return vectors are at right angles—therefore, their inner products are zero. Thus, orthogonality implies independence. These orthogonal factors are the eigenvectors of the covariance matrix. There are k of them. Thus, for $R \sim T \times k$ there are k eigenvectors, with each eigenvector corresponding to a single eigenvalue or characteristic root (we will derive these shortly). In the preceding case in which one asset's return depends upon another asset's return, then there would be a single eigenvalue equal to zero. As such, there would be $k - 1$ eigenvectors and only $k - 1$ factors to be recovered.

Let's talk a bit about the intuition here before getting into the mathematics of eigenvalues. As demonstrated in previous sections of this chapter, factor models, in general, endeavor to describe the variation in returns, whether that is a cross-sectional variation or a time series variation. The factor model projects the asset's returns into the space spanned by the factors using a regression model, and the coefficients are used to weight the factors generating an expected, or conditional, return. Principal component analysis finds the set of independent factors that accounts for the cross-sectional variation in the set of returns R.

I will first introduce you to the principal components using a simple example to fix ideas and then expand the method using observed historical data. Suppose we have the following 2×2 matrix V (financial economists study covariance matrices, so keep that in mind as we move through this example).

$$V = \begin{pmatrix} 2 & 2 \\ 2 & -1 \end{pmatrix}$$

We want to find the eigenvalues, associated eigenvectors, and principal components associated with this covariance matrix. The first step is to find the eigenvalues or roots λ by solving the determinant:

$$V = \begin{pmatrix} 2 - \lambda & 2 \\ 2 & -1 - \lambda \end{pmatrix}$$

The determinant is $-(1 + \lambda)(2 - \lambda) - 4 = (\lambda - 2)(\lambda - 3)$, which we set to zero and solve for λ. Thus, we want the solution to the quadratic equation: $\lambda^2 - \lambda - 6 = 0$. The solution involves two roots, which are (λ_1, λ_2) $(-2, 3)$. The second step substitutes each root in turn to solve for the two eigenvectors. This gives us, first, for $\lambda = 3$:

$$V = \begin{pmatrix} 2 - \lambda & 2 \\ 2 & -1 - \lambda \end{pmatrix} = \begin{pmatrix} -1 & 2 \\ 2 & -4 \end{pmatrix}$$

The eigenvector associated with this root is solved using the form:

$$\begin{pmatrix} -1 & 2 \\ 2 & -1 \end{pmatrix} \begin{pmatrix} x_1 \\ x_2 \end{pmatrix} = \begin{pmatrix} 0 \\ 0 \end{pmatrix}$$

Here $\begin{pmatrix} x_1 \\ x_2 \end{pmatrix}$ is the eigenvector that projects the matrix into the null space. This can be solved by inspection to be $x_1 = 2x_2$. To get a unique solution, we normalize by restricting the sum $x_1^2 + x_2^2 = 1$. Substituting $x_1 = 2x_2$ produces the restricted sum $5x_2^2 = 1$, or $x_2 = 1/\sqrt{5}$. Therefore, $x_1 = 2/\sqrt{5}$. With that, we find the first eigenvectors associated with the eigenvalue $\lambda = 3$ to be:

$$v_1 = \begin{pmatrix} 2/\sqrt{5} \\ 1/\sqrt{5} \end{pmatrix}$$

Repeating this process for the second root, $\lambda = -2$, we solve the second eigenvector:

$$v_2 = \begin{pmatrix} -1/\sqrt{5} \\ 2/\sqrt{5} \end{pmatrix}$$

We now transform the original matrix V into a diagonal matrix consisting of two independent (orthogonal) vectors, using these two eigenvectors:

$$\begin{pmatrix} 2/\sqrt{5} & -1/\sqrt{5} \\ 1/\sqrt{5} & 2/\sqrt{5} \end{pmatrix} \begin{pmatrix} 2 & 2 \\ 2 & -1 \end{pmatrix} \begin{pmatrix} 2/\sqrt{5} & 1/\sqrt{5} \\ -1/\sqrt{5} & 2/\sqrt{5} \end{pmatrix} = \begin{pmatrix} 3 & 0 \\ 0 & -2 \end{pmatrix}$$

Let's label matrix $\begin{pmatrix} 3 & 0 \\ 0 & -2 \end{pmatrix} = P$. The columns of P are orthogonal and the trace of this matrix is the sum of the eigenvalues. Therefore, if we let X denote the matrix of eigenvectors, then we have $XVX' = P$. Note that the columns of X are orthogonal as well as those of P. Thus, these two eigenvectors form a basis in two-dimensional space R^2.

I illustrate using monthly returns data from 1988 to 2009 given in the Chapter 9 examples spreadsheet on the *princomp* tab. Columns B to G contain monthly returns on benchmarks for six asset classes: U.S. equity, fixed income, non-U.S. equity, high yield, convertible bonds, and REITs. The covariance matrix is $V \sim 6 \times 6$:

	18.632	0.922	15.777	6.263	13.079	13.113
	0.922	1.506	0.474	0.633	0.672	0.849
V=	15.777	0.474	26.543	6.251	12.155	12.418
	6.263	0.633	6.251	5.938	6.226	7.243
	13.079	0.672	12.155	6.226	12.481	9.941
	13.113	0.849	12.418	7.243	9.941	27.485

The covariance matrix of returns V has eigenvalues (roots):

roots
63.428
15.279
7.590
3.460
1.592
1.236

The roots are all strictly greater than zero, indicating a positive definite covariance matrix with full rank (it is therefore invertible). Dividing each root by the sum of the six roots gives the proportion of the total variation in the six returns that is accounted for by the eigenvector associated with that root. The first root, therefore, will account for 68.5 percent of the total cross-sectional variation in returns and succeeding roots less. Following our example, the eigenvectors are:

v1	v2	v3	v4	v5	v6
−0.487	−0.163	0.487	−0.572	0.274	−0.312
−0.025	0.016	0.066	0.059	0.735	0.672
−0.547	−0.547	−0.628	0.080	0.017	0.030
−0.220	0.060	0.223	0.765	0.327	−0.455
−0.384	−0.137	0.497	0.271	−0.524	0.489
−0.518	0.807	−0.261	−0.074	−0.061	0.060

Letting R be the $T \times k = 264 \times 6$ returns matrix, then Rv_i for $i = 1, \ldots,$ 6 is a $T \times 1$ principal component vector. Each element in this principal component is a linear combination of the six returns for a given month times the elements in the eigenvector:

$$PC_{1,t} = r_{t,1}v_{11} + r_{t,2} * v_{12} + r_{t,3} * v_{13} + \cdots + r_{t,6} * v_{16}$$

Repeating for each eigenvector generates a $T \times k$ matrix of principal components, which are given in rows I–N of the spreadsheet. One observation worth noting is that more often than not, it is difficult to discriminate among principal components because they are linear combinations of all the original factors. Thus, while we may have a set of orthogonal principal component factors, we may have difficulty interpreting them. The covariance matrix for the principal components will be a 6×6 diagonal matrix containing the eigenvalues along the diagonal.

Now, relating these results to the discussion at the beginning of this section, we find that the first principal component is a factor that accounts for 68.5 percent of the total variance in the cross-section of returns. Thus, these six asset returns share a common factor that accounts for the majority of their cross-sectional variation. If returns were truly independent, then V would be diagonal and the eigenvalues would account for shares of the cross-sectional variation, depending only on the returns' relative variances.

Extending this thinking to a matrix of factors $X \sim T \times k$, we use principal components to generate a $T \times k$ matrix of orthogonal factors, with each factor a linear combination of the eigenvectors. In this case, we have the factor model $r = F\beta + \varepsilon$, where r is a $T \times 1$ vector or returns, but where F is now a matrix of principal components derived from X. Decomposing the variance of returns yields:

$$\text{var}(r) = \beta'\text{cov}(F)\beta + \text{var}(\varepsilon)$$

Since cov(F) is diagonal, then the variance of the return can be decomposed into the scalar weighted sum of the variances of the orthogonal factors (the scalars being the estimated factor sensitivities in β) plus the idiosyncratic risk that is orthogonal to F. Therefore, for the nth firm,

$$\text{var}(r_n) = \sum_{i=1}^{k} \beta_i^2 \sigma_i^2 + \sigma_n^2$$

Here, σ_n^2 is the firm's idiosyncratic, or specific, risk. The systematic risk is composed of the sum of independent factor variances weighted by the squares of their factor sensitivities.

APPLICATIONS AND EXAMPLES

Example 9.1: The Fama-French Three-Factor Model

Recall that I presented this model as an extension of the CAPM single index model. The factors represent the return premiums on mimicking portfolios constructed on value (HML) and size (SMB) as well as the market portfolio (r_m).

$$r_{it} = \alpha + \beta_1 HML_t + \beta_2 SMB_t + \beta_3 r_m + \varepsilon_{it}$$

Notice that this is a time series regression (indexed by t) whose parameters are estimated for each stock or portfolio of stocks (indexed by i). This is fundamentally different from the cross-sectional regressions developed in the previous section, as I will make clear shortly.

Go to the companion website for more details.

Chapter 9 Examples.xlsx estimates the parameters of this factor model using the returns on the minimum variance portfolio solved for in Chapter 7. (Because I want to focus on the factor sensitivities, I will ignore the standard errors of the parameter estimates and statistical tests of significance in these examples). Since this portfolio was constructed on 10 large capitalization stocks, it is no surprise that it has a beta close to one with the market

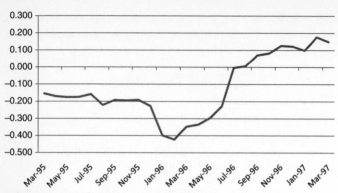

FIGURE 9.1 Fama-French Value (HML)

portfolio. Here is the model estimated on the first three years of data (through March 1997).

$$r_{it} = 0.192 - 0.155HML_t - 0.179SMB_t + 0.969r_{mt}$$

The returns to the portfolio are negatively related to value and small firms as we'd expect; after all, these are large cap growth firms. To get at some dynamics, I rolled these regressions forward in a three-year moving window through March 1997 (see Figure 9.1). As the following charts indicate, the portfolio's style appears to change dramatically over this period leading into the tech bubble of the late 1990s.

This portfolio begins to track the value portfolio in mid-1996 and, at approximately the same time, starts to become relatively neutral to size (see Figure 9.2).

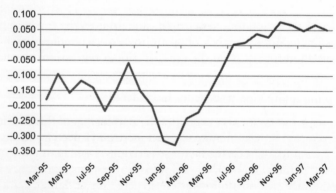

FIGURE 9.2 Fama-French Size (SMB)

The style drift we are witnessing here is likely the impact of the runup in tech stocks during this time—earnings-to-price ratios as you will recall, had reached historical highs on the S&P 500 index late in the decade—as some of the firms in this portfolio were beginning to perform more like small value stocks. These data in the spreadsheet extend through 2006, so it is possible to track these factor sensitivities past March 1997. I will leave that as an exercise. One caveat worth mentioning at this point is that the portfolio returns are calculated on the minimum variance portfolio as of March 1995. This portfolio was then allowed to drift and hence the portfolio we are analyzing after this point in time is likely not the minimum variance portfolio. In practice, we would reoptimize, or rebalance, this portfolio periodically. See Chapter 21 on Optimal Rebalancing.

Example 9.2: Macro Factors

This model decomposes an assets's return into four risk-factor contributions. We look at volatility (implied volatility, captured by the VIX index), inflation risk, default risk (AAA corporate spread over Treasuries) and liquidity risk, which is proxied by the TED spread (LIBOR over the 90-day T-bill). Again, this is a time series model. Each asset's return is regressed separately, since there is no informational gain to pooling returns into a panel regression because they all share identical exposures to the risk factors. We therefore estimate the parameters of the following model for asset i using least squares:

$$r_{it} = \alpha + \beta_1 Default_t + \beta_2 VIX_t + \beta_3 INFL_t + \beta_4 TED_t + \varepsilon_{it}$$

Refer to the second tab on the Chapter 9 Examples spreadsheet to view data and the results. Using the same procedure we used earlier for the Fama-French three-factor model, I estimated the parameters for the same minimum variance portfolio with a trailing three-year window beginning in March 1995.

$$r_t = -9.12 - 2.723\,Default_t + 0.0231\,VIX_t + 3.512\,INFL_t - 0.369\,TED_t$$

This says that the minimum variance portfolio return is expected to fall by 2.723 percent for each 100 basis point increase (1 percent) in the default spread but only 37 basis points (bps) for an equivalent increase in the TED spread. Returns tend to increase with inflation—an effect that is established in the literature but only for moderate and low inflation; high inflation will drive returns down—which is consistent with the claim that equity is a natural inflation hedge. Returns are also predicted to be higher in volatile markets as indicated by the positive sign on the VIX, which also makes sense. Although this effect is weakest in magnitude, keep in mind that the VIX can change a lot compared to the spread instruments. For example, the VIX can go from 15 to 45 in the time it takes the default spread to change by 100 bps. In fact, in our data, the VIX has roughly 25 times the volatility of the default spread.

In either model, we could forecast the asset's return conditional on our views regarding the factors. If, for example, we believed that the default spread was going to tighten by 50 bps over the holding period for this asset, then we might raise our expected return estimate by 1.35 percent. In general, we estimate factor models over all the assets in the portfolio (say, each of the 10 firms comprising these data) and use our views to forecast expected returns, which are then input as arguments in our optimizer. Therefore, given a covariance matrix V and a vector of expected returns conditional on specific factor exposures, we solve the mean-variance efficient portfolio as outlined in Chapters 6 and 7.

Factor models give us some perspective on how asset returns are influenced by and respond to movements in various factors that influence risk and return on the portfolio. They also provide an alternative to using the unconditional mean return, which is, by definition, an equal weighted average of past returns and not necessarily indicative of future returns. If we are confident in the model specification (choice of factors) and the estimates of the factor sensitivities, then the factor model serves as a means to generate more realistic forward returns estimates.

Example 9.3: Fundamental Factor Model

Here is an example that more closely tracks the methodology of the MSCI-BARRA fundamental model. Using monthly data from January 2001 through November 2009, I constructed a panel data set (cross-sectional time series) on the MSCI All World Index for the following major GICS: Energy, Consumer Staples, Materials, Health Care, Industrials, Financials, Consumer Discretionary, Information Technology, Telecommunications, and Utilities.

To keep the model tractable, I selected five fundamental factors. These factors are called *fundamental factors* since they are factor exposures unique to each sector at each point in time: Dividend yield, value, size, momentum, and volatility.

In each month, each fundamental factor is standardized across the assets in the portfolio, which, in this example, is the 10 sectors. (This example is illustrative. In practice, we would be working with hundreds or thousands of assets for which statistical properties would be much more robust.) Therefore, the estimated factor sensitivities measure the expected response in the asset return, given a one standard deviation change in the fundamental factor. The final data set consists of 107 monthly observations on 10 sectors. We are therefore estimating the $k = 5$ parameters on $t = 1, \ldots, 107$ observations.

The methodology requires estimating a cross-sectional regression involving $N = 10$ observations in each of the 107 months. This is a bit cumbersome in Excel, so I did it in Matlab. The results, however, were written to the tab labeled Fundamental Factors in the spreadsheet. There, you will find first a 107×5 matrix of factors sensitivities followed by a 107×10 matrix of the conditional expected returns. The covariance matrix V for the betas follows. This example is small enough that we can use it to highlight the power of fundamental factor models in helping us generate the covariance matrix that we need for the mean variance optimization problem. Recall that for large N, this covariance matrix is impossible to estimate from returns data alone. The factor model, however, provides an avenue to arrive at a full-rank covariance estimate, and that matrix is given on the spreadsheet as Vx. Again, I abstract some details for simplicity. In this case, I am ignoring $V\varepsilon$, which is the diagonal matrix of specific risks estimated using the residuals collected from the 107 cross-sectional regressions. Compare this matrix to that estimated using the actual returns, V (which we can do in this example since T is sufficiently large relative to N). The optimizer takes as arguments Vx for the minimum variance portfolio, or Vx, and some expected return vector (from the matrix of estimated factor-based returns) for the minimum variance portfolio with targeted return. It is interesting to see what the minimum variance portfolios would have looked like in both cases. See Table 9.1.

These are not identical; nor should they be. The fundamental portfolio using Vx is estimated using a covariance matrix that is a function of the last observation on X, that is, $XV_\beta X'$, with X being the exposures from the most recent month. Therefore, we see that Vx contains a dynamic element not typically present in V by weighting the covariance matrix more heavily on the most recent factor exposures.

Fundamental quant managers will sometimes tilt their portfolios in the direction of certain factors, for example, by estimating expected returns off of a subset of factor exposures and factor sensitivities. On the other hand, they may restrict weights to certain sectors, thereby overweighting the remaining sectors. Overweights to certain sectors are sometimes based on macro factor models like those outlined in Example 9.2, discussed earlier.

TABLE 9.1 Minimum Variance Portfolios

V	Sector	Vx
–0.221	Energy	–0.249
0.856	ConStap	1.036
–0.786	Materials	–0.051
0.162	HealthCare	–0.142
–0.048	Indust	–0.143
0.106	Fin	0.269
–0.053	ConDis	–0.049
–0.009	IT	–0.108
0.227	TeleCom	–0.209
0.766	Util	0.644

SUMMARY

I use Ross's theory of arbitrage pricing (APT) to motivate factor models and show that the CAPM—the single index model—is a special case of APT. Factor models can be specified as either cross-sectional (BARRA) or time series (BIRR); in either case, they attribute the variation in asset returns to risk-and-return factors whose contribution to return is measured by their factor sensitivities (the β_i). In cross-sectional models for which the number of assets exceeds the number of degrees of freedom available in the time series of returns, then factor models are essential to estimating the covariance matrix. The BARRA model is one such remedy to this problem. As we saw, factor selection appears to be somewhat arbitrary. While there is some comfort in appealing to the theory of fundamentals offered up by, say, dividend discount models, factor selection remains a challenging task. Principal components address this issue from two perspectives: first, principal components analysis helps locate the number of independent sources of variation, or number of factors, that help explain the cross-sectional variability in a collection of asset returns and, second, principal components are useful in finding a subset of independent factors to use in the factor model and in decomposing the variation in returns across this set of independent factors. However, since principal components are linear combinations of the original factors, it is often difficult to clearly discriminate among principal components.

REFERENCES

Luenberger, David. 1998. *Investment science*. New York: Oxford University Press.
Ross, Stephen. 1976. The arbitrage theory of capital asset pricing. *Journal of Economic Theory* (December).

CHAPTER 10

Active Portfolio Management

To whom men commit much, of him, they will demand the more.
—Luke 12:48, *The New Testament*

Portfolios can be managed passively or actively. Passive allocations are typically investments in an index fund. This management style is attractive because it minimizes trading costs and eliminates most management fees while earning the return on the index. The popularity of index funds has increased geometrically as evidenced by the staggering array of choices offered as retirement investment vehicles in various 401(k) and defined contribution plans. Active allocations, on the other hand, are made by managers who believe they can beat the index, presumably because they have superior information or skills, or both, relative to other market participants. Clients hire active managers and pay fees with the anticipation that the active manager will produce risk-adjusted returns above the index (the opportunity cost of funds) net of fees. These returns, referred to as *alpha,* are the returns to skill—stock selection, superior information, models, and so on—and are uncorrelated with the index return (and therefore beta). Active managers are alpha seekers who measure their performance relative to an agreed-upon benchmark.

Active management can be thought of as shorting the benchmark and going long the active portfolio. The active allocation therefore generates a return differential, relative to the benchmark, as well as a risk differential, referred to as the active portfolio's tracking error. A very simple, yet intuitively clear, model is the single-index model we developed from the CAPM, again, where r_i indexes the return to portfolio i and r_m the return on the market (benchmark):

$$r_i = \alpha + \beta r_m + \varepsilon$$

where ε denotes pricing error that we assume to be zero on average (that is, we assume the single-index model is correctly specified). Subtracting r_m from both sides and taking expectations $(E(\varepsilon) = 0)$ creates the portfolio's expected return premium over the benchmark:

$$r_i - r_m = \alpha + (\beta - 1)r_m$$

This is what I was alluding to earlier when I suggested that the observed premium may be misleading as an alpha measure. Only in the case for which the portfolio's beta is one is the premium pure alpha. As you can see, if the portfolio's beta exceeds one, then the observed return premium is due in part to taking on incremental systematic risk in the amount $(\beta - 1)r_m$.

To continue the example, consider the case of a pension fund whose assets are managed actively across two classes—stock and bonds. Suppose the trustees of the fund establish a long-term 70/30 mix of stocks and bonds as the fund's benchmark. A passive investment would therefore consist of investing 70 percent of the fund in an equity index and 30 percent in a bond index. On the other hand, if the trustees have faith in a manager's professed ability to beat the benchmark, net of fees, then they will fund the manager to deviate from the benchmark weights (obviously, it would make no sense to pay fees if the manager were to maintain the benchmark weights). In making that decision, the trustees will consider the foregone opportunity loss by not investing in the benchmark, that is,

$$r_b = w_{b1}r_1 + w_{b2}r_2$$

where r_1 and r_2 index the two asset classes with respective benchmark weights w_{b1} and w_{b2} and compare this to the return on the manager's investment in the active portfolio:

$$r_p = w_{p1}r_1 + w_{p2}r_2$$

The return premium, now called the *active return,* is the difference:

$$r_p - r_b = (w_{p1} - w_{b1})r_1 + (w_{p2} - w_{b2})r_2$$

The *active risk,* or *tracking error,* can be thought of as the standard deviation of the active return:

$$\sigma_a = \left[(w_{p1} - w_{b1})^2 \sigma_1^2 + (w_{p2} - w_{b2})^2 \sigma_2^2 + 2(w_{p1} - w_{1b})(w_{p2} - w_{2b})\sigma_{12} \right]^{1/2}$$

It is more compact to express these terms in matrix form as we first did in Chapter 5. The active return r_a is therefore the scalar:

$$r_a = (w_p - w_b)' r$$

where w_p, w_b, and r are vectors (in this case 2×1 vectors). This return is what the client is paying for. The active risk, on the other hand, is the risk the client must bear to receive the active return. In matrix form, it is expressed as:

$$\sigma_a = \left[(w_p - w_b)' V_a (w_p - w_b) \right]^{1/2}$$

where V_a is the active returns covariance matrix.

Construction of V_a is a bit tricky and it pays to understand how to do it correctly. Recall my claim from before that the active portfolio can be thought of as a short position in the benchmark and a long position in the active portfolio. We can therefore think of the covariance matrix as covariances across both the benchmark returns and the active portfolio returns. In our two-asset case, we have covariances between returns on stocks and bonds in the benchmark, covariances between returns on stocks and bonds in the actively invested portfolio, and covariances between stocks and bonds across the benchmark and the active portfolio (denoted with the subscripts b and p, respectively). Thus, for the two-asset case:

$$V_a = \begin{bmatrix} \begin{pmatrix} \sigma_{b1}^2 & \sigma_{b1b2} \\ \sigma_{b2b1} & \sigma_{b2}^2 \end{pmatrix} & \begin{pmatrix} \sigma_{b1p1} & \sigma_{b1p2} \\ \sigma_{b2p1} & \sigma_{b2p2} \end{pmatrix} \\ \begin{pmatrix} \sigma_{p1b1} & \sigma_{p1b2} \\ \sigma_{p2b1} & \sigma_{p2b2} \end{pmatrix} & \begin{pmatrix} \sigma_{p1}^2 & \sigma_{p1p2} \\ \sigma_{p2p1} & \sigma_{p2}^2 \end{pmatrix} \end{bmatrix}$$

Generalizing to k-assets implies that V_a will have dimension $2k \times 2k$. The elements of V_a are estimated using the benchmark and the portfolio returns. Recognizing again the short benchmark position, we construct the weight vector w_a such that:

$$w_a = \begin{bmatrix} -w_{b1} \\ -w_{b2} \\ w_{p1} \\ w_{p2} \end{bmatrix}$$

We then estimate the tracking error (active risk) using the following:

$$\sigma_a = [w_a' V_a w_a]^{1/2}$$

So, the client takes risk σ_a in return for expected return r_a. What exactly does this mean? Clearly, any return premium is due to tilts away from the benchmark, that is, $(w_p - w_b) \neq 0$, and this is reflected in the active risk estimate. Of interest, therefore, is the price in terms of active risk of deviating from the benchmark:

$$\frac{d\sigma_a}{dw_a} = \frac{V_a w_a}{\sigma_a}$$

This is the marginal contribution to active risk (MCAR). Suppose, for example, the two assets were stocks and bonds and the benchmark was a 70/30 mix of these two assets. The client has the choice of investing in this passively or investing with the active manager. Suppose the active manager invests in a portfolio having weights 75/25, indicating a tilt away from the benchmark with an overweight to stocks and an underweight to bonds. Suppose, furthermore, that the manager contemplates taking even more exposure to stocks, that is, by increasing the allocation to stocks beyond 75 percent. MCAR will estimate the contribution to active risk. Let's see now how this works in practice.

ACTIVE PORTFOLIO CONSTRUCTION AND ATTRIBUTION ANALYSIS

 Go to the companion website for more details.

Chapter 10 Examples.xlsx contains historical monthly percentage returns for the Citi BIG bond index (CitiGroup Broad Investment Grade) and the S&P 500 equity index, which serve as benchmarks. There are also returns to the 10 large cap firms we studied in Chapter 7 as well as the four sectors comprising the Citi BIG bond index: Treasuries (TSY), agencies (AGY), collateralized (COLL), and corporate credit (CRED). We are going to construct a fund consisting of two mean-variance efficient portfolios—a bond portfolio and an equity portfolio—and compare their performance to their respective benchmarks. Consider then the following scenario.

It's December 30, 2001. The trustees of a large pension fund are contemplating departing from a passive 70/30 benchmark allocation to the S&P 500 and the Citi BIG indices. They cite their desire to reclaim the fund's losses during the crash of the tech bubble that began in late 2000 and the subsequent decline in the pension's funded status. Hoping to enhance the fund's return performance, the trustees increase the exposure to equities to 80 percent. *This move indicates a departure from their strategic bench-mark weights. The trustees are now actively managing the fund to the 70/30 benchmark with an active 80/20 allocation. Suppose the trustees hire two active managers to carry out their new mandate. One is a bond man-ager claiming to deliver 50 basis points annually over the BIG. The second manager runs an active equity strategy and purports that his skill at picking winners will produce an annual 100 basis points in active return over his benchmark, the S&P 500.*

Assume that both managers are mean-variance optimizers. Using re-turns data through December 2001, they estimate covariances and mean returns (monthly mean return plus their monthly alpha estimates) that they then input to their optimizers. There are no short sales and managers must remain fully invested. They solve for their optimal portfolios and invest for the following month (beginning in January 2002). Since they rebalance their portfolios monthly, they repeat this process for the next 60 months, creating a five-year sample of active portfolio returns that we will use to evaluate their performances.

On the sheet labeled "Active Portf," the first line gives the observed re-turns to the two benchmarks for the month January 2002. The next two cells (Equity_A, Bonds_A) are returns for January 2002 on two active mean-variance efficient portfolios formed using information through De-cember 2001. Equity_A was built from the returns to the 10 firms, and Bonds_A was built from the four sectors of the Citi BIG. The arguments for the optimizers consisted of the mean returns (plus monthly alpha) and the covariance matrices also using information through December 2001. Subse-quent lines report active returns to these portfolios as they are rebalanced. Columns G and H report the returns to two funds: the first, RpA is the ac-tive portfolio consisting of an 80/20 mix of Equity_A and Bonds_A while Rb is simply the long-term benchmark 70/30 mix of the two benchmarks. We are interested in the performance of RpA relative to Rb.

The combined active covariance matrix for the evaluation period begin-ning in January 2002 and ending December 2006 is estimated using the four returns streams given in columns B through E:

	Active Cov - Va			
	S&P 500	Citi Big	Equity_A	Bonds_A
S&P 500	12.96	−1.11	15.44	−0.74
Citi Big	−1.11	1.23	−0.18	0.79
Equity_A	15.44	−0.18	27.51	−0.13
Bonds_A	−0.74	0.79	−0.13	0.58

These statistics say that the variances on the returns to the S&P 500 and Citi BIG benchmarks were 12.96 percent and 1.23 percent, respectively, with a negative covariance −1.11 percent. The actively managed portfolios are quite different; notice especially that the variance on the equity portfolio, consisting of positions in the 10 firms, is now much higher at 27.51 percent. This is due to two facts: first, 10 stocks don't necessarily offer the diversification opportunities of the broad index consisting of 500 stocks and, second, the manager is forced to take larger positions in the higher returning (and therefore riskier) stocks in order to achieve his aggressive alpha target. With no short positions permitted, this likely means that he is holding just a few stocks with zero weights on the others.

Note that these returns are monthly frequency. Their annualized equivalents would be higher by a factor of 12, for example, the annualized volatility on the active equity portfolio would be $\sqrt{27.51} * \sqrt{12} = 18.17\%$. Finally, we note that the off-diagonal covariances are between benchmarks and active portfolios. In any case, there is a negative correlation between stocks and bonds, a characteristic that all optimizers will exploit.

PERFORMANCE ATTRIBUTION

The following summarizes some relevant parameter values and performance statistics.

The first column obviously shows the short position in the benchmark and the equity tilt in the active portfolio. The second column shows the average monthly returns to the benchmark and active portfolios during the evaluation period. Note the negative return to the active equity portfolio. The third column contains the marginal contributions to active risk (MCAR). These tell us how active risk changes on the margin for a 1 percent increase in the allocation to the portfolio in question. The active risk σ_a is equal to 2.55 percent (monthly). The allocation to equity in the active

TABLE 10.1 Performance Summary and Parameter Values

	w_a	μ_{return}	MCAR	AllocAttr	MCRb	MCRp
S&P 500	−0.7	0.35	1.36	−0.95	3.47	
Citi Big	−0.3	0.42	0.17	−0.05	−0.58	
Equity_A	0.8	−0.21	4.41	3.53		5.24
Bonds_A	0.2	0.4	0.11	0.02		0.00
σ_p	4.19	μ_p	−0.9			
σ_b	2.45	μ_b	0.37			
σ_a	2.55	μ_a	−0.46			

portfolio is 0.8. Since MCAR is a derivative, $^d\sigma_a/_dw_a$, it returns the change in active risk (from 2.55 percent) for a one-unit change in the active weight (0.8 to 1.8). We need to rescale this weight change for it to make sense. Thus, a change from 0.8 to 0.9 ($dw_a = 0.10$, in this case) implies a change in active risk of 0.441, which bumps σ_a to 2.99 percent.

This is a powerful feature of risk management. It tells us how our portfolio risk changes along the margins. Obviously, active risk is much more sensitive to small changes in the allocation to the active equity portfolio; for example, an equivalent allocation increase to active bonds (from 0.2 to 0.3) would raise active risk from 2.55 percent to about 2.56 percent. This shows us just how much riskier the equity manager is relative to the bond manager. That's a lot of risk for 50 bps of annualized return over the benchmark!

The allocation attribution (AllocAttr) simply parses risk across the portfolio. Summing the elements in this column give us 2.55 percent. Obviously, the active equity portfolio accounts for more than 100 percent of this (3.53 percent) but is offset somewhat by the short position in the benchmark (−0.95 percent).

The last two columns are there to illustrate that marginal contributions to risk are not confined to the active portfolio; we can compute these derivatives for the benchmarks and the active portfolios separately as:

$$MCAR_b = \frac{d(w'_a V_b w_a)}{dw_a}; \quad w'_a = (0.1, -0.1)$$

Notice that w_a is 2×1, showing the deviations in the active portfolio from the long-run benchmark. This measure informs us of the cost of deviating from the benchmark. Similarly, we can compute marginal risk directly on the active portfolio:

$$MCAR_p = \frac{d(w'_p V_p w_p)}{dw_p}$$

Each measure is a gradient-measuring slope along the risk surface. Chapter 11 develops these concepts in greater detail. For the moment, recognize that there are measures of total risk (for example, $\sigma_a = 2.55$ percent), which is a static concept, as well as risk sensitivity along the margins, which gives a clear picture on what our risk function looks like in the neighborhood of the current allocation.

One big question remains—how good did the active managers do? Clearly, there's a lot of unwelcome risk carried in the active equity portfolio, but did it pay off? The simple answer is no. We see that the mean return to the active portfolio (0.8*Equity_A + 0.2*Bonds_A) is negative at −0.9 per month while the benchmark portfolio (0.7*S&P 500 + 0.3*Citi BIG) is 0.37 per month. The difference between them is −0.46 per month, which translates into about -0.46^*12, or -5.52 percent per year under performance. That's because of the aggressive equity style. In fact, if we were to regress RpA on Rb, we'd get the following result:

$$RpA = -0.62 + 1.43\,Rb$$

The t-statistics are -2.03 and 11.45, respectively, indicating that they are both statistically significant. Thus, the trustees did not get the alpha they anticipated. Rather, the active portfolio underperformed by 0.62 percent per month while the beta estimate of 1.43 says that the active portfolio had 43 percent more risk than the benchmark portfolio. This means that the active managers were not contributing skill per se, but were simply taking more equity risk relative to the benchmark. Using the mean benchmark return of 0.37 percent per month, I estimate that the expected annual return attributable to this active strategy would have been -1.09 percent.

This is admittedly a contrived example, but it is instructive nevertheless. The mean-variance efficient portfolios are given on the "Active Positions" tab. You can see here that the equity portfolios are heavily tilted toward HD, MO, and MRK and F, of which only MO had a positive average return over the evaluation period. The two remaining firms with average positive returns, C and CSCO, by contrast, had much smaller allocations. The covariance estimates were steering the optimizer toward these exposures in 10 firms that had essentially little to offer in the way of return. That and the aggressive strategy forced a highly risky allocation that could not outperform the benchmark, which, itself, had a comparatively good track record. For the bond fund, performance was somewhat more muted, but clearly, the allocation was almost entirely COLL (not surprising since the risks are so much closer together for these bonds sectors compared to the 10 equities). The active bond portfolio missed out on the relatively better return record offered by CRED over the evaluation period. Nevertheless, let's not read into these results too much. The purpose of the exercise was to demonstrate performance attribution methodologies and not portfolio selection.

SUMMARY

I introduced active management somewhat obliquely in Chapter 7 with the concept of managing to a benchmark. Active management is important to understand because virtually all managers manage relative to a bogey, that is, some notion of an opportunity cost embodied by a passive portfolio. Since investors have the option of investing in the passive benchmark, then the decision to invest with a manager who departs from that benchmark (a necessary condition for investors *not* holding the benchmark) is implicit confidence that the manager can beat the benchmark on a risk-adjusted basis net of fees. This chapter outlines how active management changes the objective function in the solution to the optimal mean-variance efficient portfolio, how the notion of risk is transformed to tracking error, returns to the notion of risk-adjusted alpha, and the decomposition of risk in active space.

APPENDIX 10.1: ACTIVE SPACE

For active portfolios consisting of many benchmarks, it is often convenient to compress the various benchmarks into a single composite benchmark. That way, we compare k active portfolios to a single benchmark. It not only reduces the dimensionality of the problem from $2k \times 2k$ to a $(k+1) \times (k+1)$ problem, but simplifies computations and interpretations of active risk. What we need to do, therefore, is to somehow aggregate the benchmarks into a single overall benchmark and compare all the active holdings to this single benchmark. Admittedly, that is not intuitive, but we can hope that it will make more sense after I develop the concept for you.

First, I construct a special matrix that will aggregate the benchmark variances and covariances into a single row and column. For the two-asset case it looks like this:

$$
m = \begin{bmatrix} w_{b1} & 0 & 0 \\ w_{b2} & 0 & 0 \\ 0 & 1 & 0 \\ 0 & 0 & 1 \end{bmatrix}
$$

Recall V_a:

$$
V_a = \begin{bmatrix} \begin{pmatrix} \sigma_{b1}^2 & \sigma_{b1b2} \\ \sigma_{b2b1} & \sigma_{b2}^2 \end{pmatrix} & \begin{pmatrix} \sigma_{b1p1} & \sigma_{b1p2} \\ \sigma_{b2p1} & \sigma_{b2p2} \end{pmatrix} \\ \begin{pmatrix} \sigma_{p1b1} & \sigma_{p1b2} \\ \sigma_{p2b1} & \sigma_{p2b2} \end{pmatrix} & \begin{pmatrix} \sigma_{p1}^2 & \sigma_{p1p2} \\ \sigma_{p2p1} & \sigma_{p2}^2 \end{pmatrix} \end{bmatrix}
$$

Aggregating the benchmarks is accomplished by $m'V_a m$, which reduces to:

$$V_c = \begin{bmatrix} (w_{b1}^2\sigma_{b1}^2 + w_{b2}^2\sigma_{b2}^2 + 2w_{b1b2}\sigma_{b1b2}) & w_{b1}\sigma_{b1p1}^2 & w_{b2}\sigma_{b1p2} \\ (w_{b1}\sigma_{b1p1} + w_{b2}\sigma_{b2p1}) & \sigma_{p1}^2 & \sigma_{p1p2} \\ (w_{b1}\sigma_{b1p2} + w_{b2}\sigma_{b2p2}) & \sigma_{p2p1} & \sigma_{p2}^2 \end{bmatrix}$$

Thus, where we started with a $2k \times 2k$ active covariance matrix, we now work with a matrix of dimension $k + 1$, in which the first row and column summarize the covariances between the benchmarks and portfolios (or assets). The 2×2 diagonal submatrix in the lower right section summarizes the risks associated with the actively managed portfolio positions. This setup generalizes to any given $2k \times 2k$ active covariance matrix. That is, the combined active covariance matrix V_c will consist of a $k \times k$ covariance matrix for the actively managed assets bordered by a single row and column summarizing the benchmark and actively managed covariances.

Likewise, we similarly compress the active weight vector such that the first element in the combined weight vector simply represents the short position in the benchmark.

$$w_a = \begin{bmatrix} -w_{b1} \\ -w_{b2} \\ w_{p1} \\ w_{p2} \end{bmatrix} ; \quad w_c = \begin{bmatrix} -1 \\ w_{p1} \\ w_{p2} \end{bmatrix}$$

It is not difficult to prove the following equivalency:

$$w_a V_a w'_a = w_c V_c w'_c$$

CHAPTER 11

Risk

The lucky person passes for a genius.

—Euripedes

Crises have a way of inviting reassessment. Ex post, we ask ourselves what went wrong, how we failed to anticipate events, and how we might refocus our efforts so as to manage events better in the future. Sometimes this requires newly innovated methodologies and sometimes it simply means incorporating things we had known all along but had somehow de-emphasized.

One such de-emphasis has been the distinction between *uncertainty* and *risk*. The University of Chicago economist Frank Knight first distinguished between these two terms as far back as 1921. And yet, as events began to unfold at the onset of the 2008 credit crisis, we still talked about risk for the most part as if it were a set of "known unknowns." In this case, hubris had a rather high cost.

In general, risk involves choices we make in a world in which outcomes are random but their probabilities are known in advance. Gambles are examples—they involve risk but there is no uncertainty. Uncertainty, rather, deals with unknown risks. To extend our gambling analogy, uncertainty is a poker game in which the risk, which can be modeled precisely in a deck of cards, is elevated because of the behavior of other players (for example, bluffing). Risk, therefore, is amplified by uncertainty. Still, despite knowing this, the great moderation of the Greenspan years nevertheless lulled us into complacency until we found that standard risk models didn't work well in a world complicated by increasing uncertainty.

Uncertainty tends to operate in a feedback loop during crises in which peoples' decisions are not self-regulating. As a result, we get extreme outcomes (Taleb's Black Swans) that are generated by increased uncertainty and hyperelevated risk. Short selling, for example, can produce unstable results through self-reinforcing feedback. Some crises, then, are reminiscent of regimes in which risk becomes endogenous to the system. Moving from exogenous to endogenous risk is a very difficult transition to make in modeling—one from a world of known unknown risks to one in which risk itself is a product of the system.

Exogenous risks are always present—they are the roll of the die, so to speak, and the forces of nature independent of our own behavior that affect outcomes. Endogenous risks arise because of uncertainty and are intimately related to how our behavior is affected by the behavior of others. Manias, bubbles, panics, and cascades all occur because of the dynamics of human behavior. As events of the credit crisis unfolded, we realized quite clearly that we had moved beyond the capacity of standard risk models to manage the challenges that confronted us.

"But this time is different" (Reinhart 2009). Is it? The history of speculation can be traced at least as far back as the Roman Empire. Relatively recent episodes include the South Sea Bubble of 1720, the railroad mania of the 1840s, the crash of 1929, the Japanese bubble of the 1980s, the tech bubble in the 1990s, and the housing bubble that ended abruptly in the summer of 2006. The answer to the question why we did not seem to learn from these experiences is not entirely obvious. One possibility, however, is that there always seem to be different players with no existing collective social memory of previous crises, and therefore the mentality that, indeed, this time *is* different. Regardless, the relevant question is what have we learned from the current crisis? Without question, we learned that risks can be endogenous, that volatility is but one aspect of risk, that other risk sources such as liquidity, leverage, counterparty, and systemic risks (to name a few) can be just as important, and that complexity, though wonderfully elegant, often harbors hidden risks.

THE FAILURE OF VaR

Reactions from risk managers are varied. Before the crisis, Basel II capital requirements focused on value at risk (VaR) methodologies. Standard VaR assumes returns are normally distributed, when, in fact, they generally are not. Moreover, during financial turmoil, the tails of returns distributions are much fatter than indicated by normality; hence, losses are underestimated during these periods. Countless empirical studies find the normality assumption applied to asset returns to be excessively restrictive. Heavy-tailed distributions (distributions with more mass under the tails attach higher likelihoods to extreme events. Examples include the T-distribution, Pareto, and lognormal) have been used as an alternative.

VaR debuted as a risk measure by informing us about what proportion of the portfolio is at risk during any given time interval. If, for example, returns were assumed normally distributed with mean return 7 percent and volatility equal to 15 percent, then *95 percent of the time the portfolio would lose less than* (7% – 1.645*15% =) –17.175 percent. Depending on how we want to frame risk, an equivalent statement would be that returns would be even less than –17.175 percent, but only *5 percent of the time*. That's a lower bound. Unfortunately, it leaves open the question of how large losses may be, which is precisely the question of interest during a financial crisis. In any case, VaR is not a coherent risk measure, that is, one cannot cap-weight the VaR across programs to get the plan-level VaR. Expected tail losses (ETL) provide a more complete picture of what the loss distribution actually looks like. As the name *expected* suggests, observed losses are weighted by their likelihoods and summed. With respect to non-normality, we can use maximum likelihood procedures to determine the best candidate probability function describing returns, a point to which we return later. In any case, it should not be surprising that different asset classes should use different distributional assumptions.

We care about downside risk. So, why not model the lower tail of the returns distribution independently? The literature on extreme value theory (EVT) does exactly this. Thus, depending on the asset class, we would have custom distributions informing us of return risks in general, and tails risks specifically. We could then extend these insights to develop tools that identify portfolios that minimize downside risk, another point to which we shall return.

During crises, correlations often align, signaling highly contagious market risks as returns across asset classes begin to move in lockstep. Standard methods track correlations using rolling windows, consisting, for example, of the trailing three months, or one year, or three years of returns. The problem with these measures is that they will always lag changes in volatility. Thus, when volatility shifts higher and correlations follow, these measures will underestimate risk. Our response could be to fit distributions to the returns data whose parameters capture the volatility regime more precisely because these parameters are measured using maximum likelihood methods. Examples include GARCH and EGARCH (asymmetric risk) and multivariate GARCH. The research is unequivocal—GARCH produces a more efficient and unbiased forecast of risk.

These methods were either unavailable or impractical a generation ago. Advances in mathematics, computing power, and data availability have now put these on the front line of risk management tools. Still, many risk managers have failed to adopt them. Others tools include the use of copulas to model and simulate the joint probability of risks across asset classes and Monte Carlo techniques used to simulate scenario analyses on various risks. I include an application using copulas further on that minimize downside risk.

Risks change dynamically, suggesting that exposures to tail losses are conditional through time. Sullivan, Peterson, and Waltenbaugh (2010) developed a set of models that estimate hazards—the probability that an asset class will experience a threshold event (tail loss event) conditional on the values of factors that influence loss events like default or liquidity risk. They extended this thinking to estimate a systemic risk index that estimates the probability that two or more asset classes will simultaneously experience threshold losses. Systemic risks are the topic of the next chapter. A by-product of these analyses is a time-to-failure measure, which signals the number of days between threshold events.

Hubris creates its own risk. No risk management process will succeed in fully anticipating what are essentially unsystematic risks. Because risk management is basically a systematic monitoring process, the tools we have developed and described herein serve that end. Therefore, while our risk programs may identify profiles that match historical systemic risk episodes, we must be vigilant in our efforts to recognize the signs that may signal uniquely different episodes. This is the challenge as I see it going forward. To meet this challenge, we need to focus our efforts on understanding the operation of the global economy and, especially, behavioral signs and patterns among agents that will signal distress that may lead to systemic events. Even during normal times, the complexion of risk is constantly changing with leverage, liquidity, market, operations, counterparty, credit, and political risks competing for attention. Moving forward, risk management needs to monitor a global market environment that will become increasingly competitive and more diversely regulated.

TAXONOMY OF RISK

Investment decisions are intertemporal choices that trade off present and future consumption. Because the future can only be anticipated, then these choices must rest upon some expectation of uncertain future payoffs. If we admit the possibility that future payoffs are state-dependent (for example, the asset pays a dollar on a rainy day and zero otherwise), then we allow, in principle, the possibility that an uncertain future can be modeled as a set of contingent claims whose payoffs (receiving a dollar) depend on whether certain future conditions are met (a rainy day) with respect to a set of related factors (humidity, barometric pressure). This suggests that there is a distinction, a la Frank Knight, between uncertainty and risk with risk as a refined state of uncertainty in the sense that although future outcomes may not be known, their probabilities are.

Knight didn't mean that the difference between risk and uncertainty was an arbitrary set of probabilities. Markets, after all, are not card decks whose outcomes, though uncertain, can be modeled with a well-defined probability distribution and whose risks are perfectly known. Instead, market models will necessarily contain *model risk* in varying degrees, depending on our inability to model the problem's structure precisely. Attempts to model risk in market environments must therefore incorporate an awareness of this additional source of risk. Value at Risk (VaR), for example, is a flawed model, and to the extent that return distributions are non-normal with time dependent correlations, the advice from static risk models will often prove inadequate. Models that incorporate alternative distributional assumptions and more dynamic correlation structures can help minimize predictive errors but, ideally, *model risk* is best mitigated by using a broad array of risk models, which, while not necessarily independent of each other, bring different perspectives of risk to the end user.

Risk managers use a broad range of models. Several models are often tasked to the same problem (for example, competing volatility models) while simultaneously, other models address the cross-section of risks (for example, credit, counterparty) in an attempt to create a network of mutually supportive diagnostic tools that provide management a more complete picture of plan-level risks.

For pension funds, there are four readily agreed-upon sources of liability risk—*solvency, longevity, inflation,* and *interest rate risk.* The last two are applicable to the asset side of the balance sheet as well. Pension plan asset liability modeling (ALM) analyzes, for example, funded status under stress environments with variable discount rates, inflation scenarios, and mortality assumptions, as well as volatility regimes.

On the *asset* side of the balance sheet, we need to address three broad risk classes: *market risk, counterparty risk,* and *model risk.* We must also recognize the challenges posed by operational risk, and endogenous risk. *Market risk* is extensive, incorporating macro risks, including inflation and interest rates, exogenous shocks such as spiking oil prices, return volatilities at various frequencies, correlations, and various dynamics. In an efficient market, risks would be reflected in the time series of returns. Hence, the volatility of returns would be a primary risk signal. Virtually all portfolio managers examine returns volatility, usually in discrete historical examples. Attempts to uncover evolving volatility usually entail using some type of simple moving average of returns. RiskMetrics, for example, uses an exponentially weighted moving average of returns to estimate volatilities and applies this basic methodology to various returns frequencies. More efficient models of returns volatility include GARCH methods, which are optimally weighted exponential weightings that describe volatility regimes (high and low periods of volatility). Generalized autoregressive conditional heteroscedasticity (GARCH) and ARCH models are developed in most time series texts. Extensions to multivariate GARCH models help uncover dynamic correlations in returns across assets. GARCH methods provide a window onto volatility regimes at the asset level as well as correlation spikes across assets, strategies, managers, and programs. These are powerful tools that support the risk manager's objective in capturing changes in absolute and relative risks as the market incorporates new information into observed returns.

VISUALIZING RISK

In previous chapters, we analyzed market and interest rate risks and generated detailed risk-attribution statistics that decomposed and allocated total measured risk across the portfolio. In this chapter, I hope to provide a basis for thinking about risk and to develop a more rigorous set of risk management tools based upon that thinking. Let's begin by developing conceptually how we see risk geometrically.

Optimal portfolios are all conceptually related in that they provide a risk-minimizing allocation across assets—a set of weights that minimize portfolio risk. Risk, itself, is a weighted average of the individual asset risks as well as their covariances. For example, risk is essentially the sum $w'Vw$. We have already covered this ground. Covariances are estimated from historical returns that incorporate information about future expected returns and future risks in general; that is, we believe that markets are at least efficient aggregators of information. That is why we think covariances are informative. With this in mind, think of a two-asset portfolio again and the minimum variance portfolio. The minimum variance portfolio is the solution to the familiar quadratic form (usually subject to constraints):

$$\min_w \frac{1}{2} w'Vw$$

For a two-asset portfolio, this problem can be visualized in three dimensions (x,y,z), where x and y are the two weights and z is the level of risk (dependent on the covariances V and the weights). If we vary weights like we did when we constructed the efficient frontier in Chapter 6, we can show the risk function and conceptualize how the weights are determined that minimize this risk. Figure 11.1 illustrates risk, using four distinct covariance structures. The covariance matrices that these represent are given above each case. V1, for example, represents two assets with identical variances equal to 5 percent but whose returns are independent (zero covariances). This loss surface is symmetric and rises monotonically in the direction of either asset. V2, on the other hand, shows the case in which the returns are correlated which, in general, shifts risk up as measured along the vertical axis, but notice as well that the risk surface loses some of its convexity. V3 illustrates the case in which returns are negatively correlated, thus reducing risks, and V4 shows a case, not unlike the stocks and bonds case in the previous chapter in which one of the asset risks dominates. In this case, the return variance to asset 1 (w_1) is three times that of asset 2. The risk contours are projected onto the horizontal (x,y) plain showing how risk changes on the margins as the respective weights are altered. For V4, we see that these trade-offs become more extreme as represented on the ellipsoids—risk is minimized definitely by moving out of the riskier asset.

I first introduced the optimization problem in Chapter 5, where I wrote out the first order conditions as the derivatives to the quadratic given earlier (with constraints using the Lagrangian). These first order conditions (derivatives) are the gradients, or slopes of tangent planes along these risk surfaces. Imagine, for example, having to try to find the minimum variance portfolio by hand, so to speak. You would start with an arbitrary weight vector—a value for w_1 and another for w_2. These two weights, with the given covariance matrix, would define a point on the loss surface. You would look at that point, see it was not at the lowest point on the surface, and then change the weights *in the direction of the minimum* as illustrated in Figure 11.1.

This is how the gradient functions in the computer optimization algorithm we would we using. We compute the value of the gradient using the first order condition and then change the weight vector values in the direction of the gradient toward the minimum (see Figure 11.2).

Constraints such as being fully invested (the weights sum to one) and no short sales restrict the region in weight space that we are allowed to optimize. No shorting would restrict optimization to the positive quadrant while the adding up constraint would restrict it further to weight combinations along the diagonal in the plot in the figure shown here.

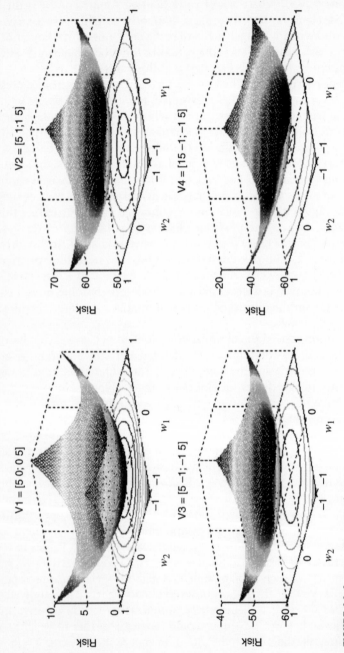

FIGURE 11.1 Four Loss Surfaces

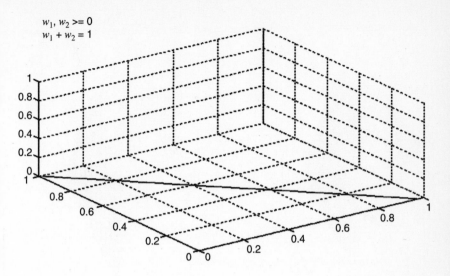

The effects of no shorting relegate the search for the minimum portfolio in the positive quadrant as depicted in Figure 11.3 for these four risk surfaces.

The adding-up constraint requiring full investment ($w_1 + w_2 = 1$) basically restricts the search further to a slice perpendicular to the diagonal line given earlier. As such, the region over which the optimal portfolio is found can be seen to be predetermined in large part by the constraints. The

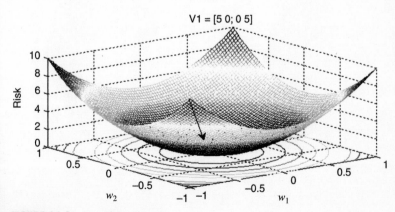

FIGURE 11.2 Gradient Descent

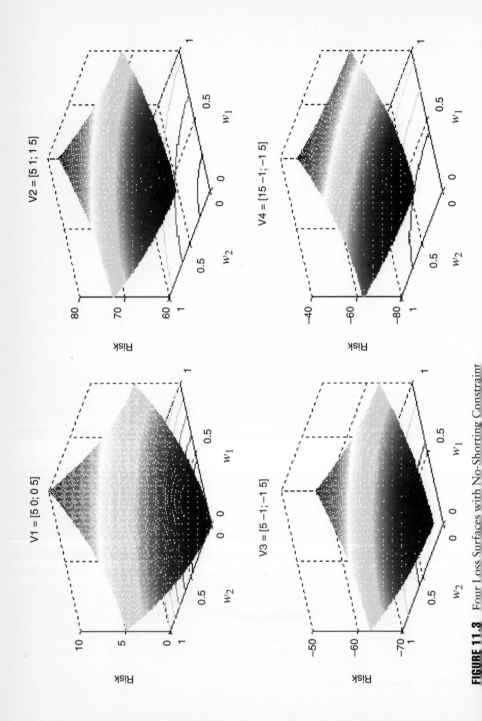

FIGURE 11.3 Four Loss Surfaces with No-Shorting Constraint

gradients we are interested in moving along are in this area as depicted in the next figure (this was constructed using V1).

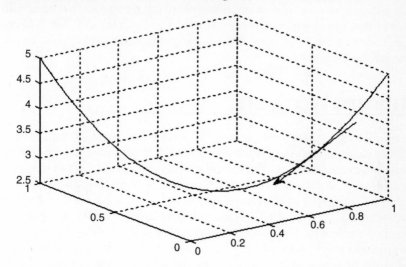

You can readily see how V4 further pushes the search in the direction away from the high-risk asset and toward asset two (increasing w_2 relative to w_1 in the process).

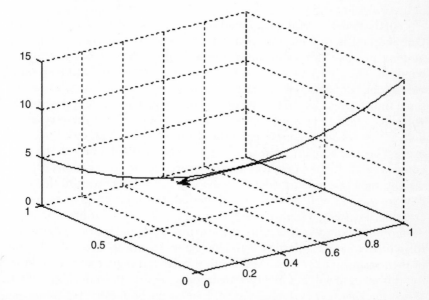

As it happens, the minimum variance portfolio for V4 has $w_2 = 73$ percent and $w_1 = 27$ percent. V1 is a 50/50 mix, as are V2 and V3. These last two results may seem somewhat nonintuitive but remember that equal allocations don't necessarily imply equal risk. The risks for (V1, V2, V3) are, respectively (1.58, 1.73, and 1.41), which should make perfect sense to you. The risk on V4 is 1.83.

ESTIMATING VOLATILITIES

I can observe an asset's return; it is the percentage change in the observed market value of the asset between two well-defined points in time. Strictly speaking, I cannot observe the volatility of the return. I can only estimate it. In Chapter 5, volatility—or standard deviation—was a sample statistic. It was the square root of the return variance. The variance was the mean of the squared deviations of returns from their sample mean. We didn't discuss N—the sample size. The implicit assumption was that N was the size of the historical example. As statisticians, we prefer N to be large, as more information is preferred to less when estimating statistics. The annualized volatility of the return on the S&P 500 since 1950 is 14.7 percent. That is a volatility averaged over 60 years ($N = 721$). But what if I think that the market *today* is not average, that is, what if the market is clearly in a high or low volatility regime?

Analysts use several cheap methods to deal with changing volatility. One method is to measure volatility over a short trailing horizon as a *moving average,* for example, using a trailing three-year or five-year window. The choice of window width is arbitrary but the idea is to provide a long enough window to generate meaningful estimates while at the same time trying to keep the window short enough to capture the present volatility regime. This method is clearly suboptimal for three reasons: first, it throws away data outside the window while the moving average process creates a highly correlated series. Second, it still gives all the data equal weight. If the point was to give more recent observations greater weight, then this method doesn't really work. Analysts then roll this window forward as well, so that in each period, the volatility is reestimated, creating, in effect, a highly correlated time series of volatilities. Using a 36-month rolling window will create a time series of monthly volatilities for which adjacent volatility estimates have 35 observations in common in their respective samples. And third, if there is a regime shift in volatility, this method will not incorporate it for some time to come. Figure 11.4 shows the volatility cycling of the S&P 500 using both three-year and five-year windows.

FIGURE 11.4 S&P 500 Volatility

The five-year moving average (MA) provides more smoothing since the series is being averaged over a longer period of time. Higher volatility regimes should be obvious surrounding the crash of October 1987, the default of Long-Term Capital Management in 1989, the tech bubble crash in 2001, and the credit crisis beginning in 2008. Clearly, assuming volatility is equal to a constant long-term average of 14.7 percent would appear too restrictive as volatility obviously has time series properties that we would like to exploit.

Figure 11.5 imposes the GARCH(1,1) volatility estimate (I use a GARCH(1,1) process that I derive further on) on top of these two MA estimates using S&P 500 price returns from 1980 to the present. I will provide an intuitive derivation of GARCH in a moment, but to fix ideas, I think it is interesting to contrast this maximum likelihood volatility estimator to the three- and five-year MA estimators. I mentioned earlier that the MA would lag volatility developments in the market. Take the 2008 credit crisis, for example. The five-year MA volatility estimate relies on *equal weighting* of

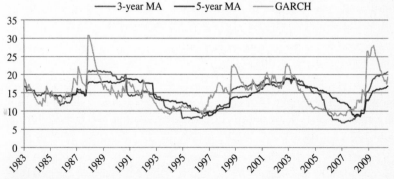

FIGURE 11.5 S&P 500 Volatility

the trailing 60 months of return, that is, it smoothes the impact of more recent events across this longer time horizon. We see quite clearly that it is underestimating what true volatility must surely be to the extent that its volatility estimate has barely budged above the long-term unconditional mean volatility of 14.7 percent. The same is true for the three-year MA estimate but more muted since it is smoothing returns over a shorter trailing 36-month period. The GARCH estimate, on the other hand, is much more responsive, showing a sharp spike up in risk at the beginning of the crisis in 2008.

Smoothed MA estimates of volatility also have the property of creating a memory where none is deserved. Notice, for example, that both MA volatilities remain artificially high after the crash of October 1987 as well as the 2001 tech bubble crash. In contrast, the GARCH estimate recovers from these transitory shocks more quickly. And while GARCH volatility estimates have come down in 2010 (consistent with other market measures of risk like the VIX), the MA estimators will remain artificially high for some time to come.

These are clearly undesirable properties—MA estimators use less information, treat the distant past as if it were as important as the present, and produce biased forecasts. One response to simple MA estimators is to use all of the available data (instead of a moving window) and weight observations so that more recent returns have higher weight. These are still moving averages, but they are *exponentially weighted* so that the most recent observation has a weight of one and weights decline exponentially to zero (but not exactly zero) into the past. This has a certain intuitive appeal. I will develop this idea now and use it to derive the GARCH estimator.

As in Chapter 1, we define the one-period return to an asset as:

$$r_t = \frac{(P_t - P_{t-1})}{P_{t-1}}$$

Assuming a sample size of m, then a consistent estimator—this is the maximum likelihood estimator—for the return variance is

$$\sigma_t^2 = \frac{1}{m} \sum_{i=1}^{m} (r_{t-i} - \bar{r})^2$$

Notice that the weight $1/m$ is equal for all observations and that the sum of the weights is one. With no loss of generality, assume the mean return is zero and allow for the weights to vary across time but still sum to one as in:

$$\sigma_t^2 = \sum_{i=1}^{m} \alpha_i r_{t-i}^2 \quad ; \sum \alpha_i = 1, \alpha_i > 0$$

We will focus now on the weights α_i. First, let's assume further that the variance has a long run mean β_0, and add this to the process:

$$\sigma_t^2 = \beta_0 + \sum_{i=1}^{m} \alpha_i r_{t-i}^2$$

Finally, assume that the weights exponentially decline according to $(0 < \lambda < 1)$:

$$\alpha_{i+1} = \lambda \alpha_i$$

Making this substitution gives us the exponentially weighted moving average (EWMA):

$$\sigma_t^2 = \beta_0 + \sum_{i=1}^{m} \alpha \lambda^{i-1} r_{t-i}^2$$

The weights $\alpha \lambda^{i-1}$ are time dependent with decay parameter λ. A word on exponential weighting is in order here. If we wanted to construct an exponentially weighted series of returns, for example, we would need to choose a value for λ. One way to do this is to think of a half-life, that is, the point in time going back in the sample for which that observation has a weight equal to 0.5. If we set, for example, a half-life of 36 months, then what we are imposing is that the return at that point has half the weight of the current return (and exponentially continues to decay thereafter toward zero). More explicitly, we seek a value for the decay rate, in this case, such that, in general, $\lambda^t = 0.5$. Taking natural logarithms on each side gives us:

$$t\ln(\lambda) = \ln(0.5)$$

Therefore, given a value for t, say, 36 months, we solve for λ, which in this case is 0.992. Substituting this parameter into the preceding equation provides the required weight decay pattern.

There are two problems with EWMA. The first and more obvious concerns the arbitrary choice of half-life, which is subjective. We will return to this point in a moment. The second problem is subtler; it has to do with the properties of the EWMA variance model. In particular, this model of volatility is not mean-reverting. That means that we are not guaranteed that the volatility process will return to a long-run equilibrium and, in fact, it could be nonstationary. In a word, nonstationary means that the mean and variance (and higher moments) of the returns series are functions of time. A random walk is one such example. Properties of nonstationary series include inconsistent test statistics (the usual t and F statistics). In many cases, first differences generate stationarity. For econometricians, this is a hugely significant weakness to the model. Fortunately, GARCH shares none of these weaknesses, and in fact, the EWMA can be shown to be a special case of GARCH. Let me try to develop the GARCH intuition from the EWMA model.

Once again, let's simplify whenever possible. First, we will assume that the long-run mean variance β_0 is zero and that $\alpha = 1$. Now, we can focus on the decay parameter. We have the following:

$$\sigma_t^2 = \sum_{i=1}^{m} \lambda^{i-1} r_{t-i}{}^2$$

If we then expand the resulting variance specification by writing the summation out, we get:

$$\sigma_t^2 = r_{t-1}^2 + \lambda r_{t-2}^2 + \lambda^2 r_{t-3}^2 + \ldots + \lambda^m r_{t-m-1}^2$$

Lagging this one period gets us the following:

$$\sigma_{t-1}^2 = r_{t-2}^2 + \lambda r_{t-3}^2 + \lambda^2 r_{t-4}^2 + \ldots + \lambda^m r_{t-m-2}^2$$

Now, multiply this last equation by λ on both sides:

$$\lambda \sigma_{t-1}^2 = \lambda r_{t-2}^2 + \lambda^2 r_{t-3}^2 + \lambda^3 r_{t-4}^2 + \ldots + \lambda^m r_{t-m-1}^2 + \lambda^{m+1} r_{t-m-2}^2$$

subtract it from the previous equation, and simplify to get:

$$\sigma_t^2 = \lambda \sigma_{t-1}^2 + r_{t-1}^2 - \lambda^{m+1} r_{t-m-2}^2$$

This is basically the result we want, but this can be simplified further because the last term goes to zero as m gets large, that is,

$$\lim_{m \to \infty} \lambda^{m+1} r_{t-m-2}^2 = 0$$

If we restrict the weights on the two remaining terms to sum to one, then we can write our new variance formula as follows:

$$\sigma_t^2 = \gamma \sigma_{t-1}^2 + (1 - \gamma) r_{t-1}^2$$

· Those of you who have studied time series analysis recognize this as the GARCH(1,1) process. It has one autoregressive component $(1 - \gamma)r_{t-1}^2$ and one moving average component, $\gamma\sigma_{t-1}^2$. The final specification, which includes the long-run mean variance is specified as:

$$\sigma_t^2 = \beta_0 V_L + \alpha r_{t-1}^2 \beta\sigma_{t-1}^2$$

where $(\alpha+\beta) < 1$ for stationarity and $(\beta_0 + \alpha + \beta) = 1$. Estimation is by maximum likelihood. Most software packages return estimates for α, β, and the long-run mean V_L. What is especially attractive is that the decay parameters is a maximum likelihood estimate and therefore optimal. I have found that during the crisis beginning in 2008, GARCH(1,1) estimates of the half-life are much shorter than those used by EWMA and that these parameters can be quite variable over time.

The GARCH(1,1) estimates that were presented in the preceding graphic for the S&P 500 can be found on the Chapter 11 spreadsheet. This specification is convenient since it provides a *one-step ahead forecast* for the volatility of the series. That is, the current forecast is computed given values for the lagged volatility σ_{t-1}^2 and last period's squared return deviation r_{t-1}^2, and the maximum likelihood parameter values. Forecasts for $t + k$ can be derived by recursive substitution. For example, the k-step ahead forecast is a function of the $t + 1$ through $t + k - 1$ forecasts. Most software packages that estimate GARCH volatilities also have commands available for out-of-sample forecasts.

MAXIMUM LIKELIHOOD ESTIMATION (OPTIONAL)

Although solving for MLE GARCH is beyond the scope of this book, it is instructive to see how MLE works for variance estimates in the homoscedastic case (single variance for all time). The intuition is that if we have a sample of returns r_i for $i = 1, \ldots, m$, and that returns are independent and normally distributed, then the likelihood is the joint probability of seeing this particular sample. The parameters are then estimated to maximize this likelihood. For a sample of size m, the likelihood function can be written as the product of the individual likelihoods, since this is a joint likelihood (again, assuming the mean return to be zero)

$$\prod \left[\frac{1}{\sqrt{2\pi\sigma^2}} \exp\left(\frac{-r_i^2}{2\sigma^2}\right) \right]$$

Taking logarithms turns this product into a sum that is easier to work with and it does not affect the solution (note that we drop the constant $\sqrt{2\pi}$, which has no impact on the solution).

$$\sum_{i=1}^{m} \left[-\ln\sigma^2 - \frac{r_i^2}{\sigma^2} \right]$$

To maximize this likelihood, take the derivative with respect to σ_2:

$$\frac{dL}{d\sigma^2} = 0 = \frac{-m}{\sigma^2} + \sum \frac{r_i^2}{(\sigma^2)^2}$$

Solving this gets:

$$\sigma^2 = \frac{\sum r_i^2}{m}$$

which is the familiar MLE of basic statistics courses. GARCH extends this logic to σ_i^2.

Multivariate GARCH models can estimate time-varying correlations and covariances. Figure 11.6 shows the correlation between fixed income and U.S. equity using a multivariate GARCH(1,1) setup. I used Matlab's UCSD toolbox and the dcc_mvgarch.m function.

The time-varying nature of the correlation is obvious, but the points in which it turns negative may be a bit more subtle to some observers. Historical returns are provided on the spreadsheet labeled "Benchmark Correlations." Notice, in particular, that during equity shocks such as the crash of October 1987, the bottom after the tech bubble crash, and the beginning of the credit crisis in early 2008 the correlations turn negative.

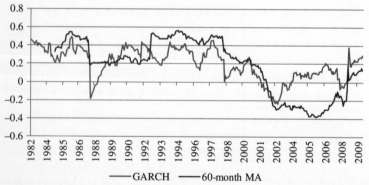

FIGURE 11.6   Equity-Fixed Income Correlation

During the "great moderation" of the latter part of the Greenspan Fed the correlation is rising (2001 to 2008), falls quickly below zero around the time that Bear Stearns failed and then spiked up again in the fall of 2008 when markets were locked into a systemic risk episode. It should be clear that the moving average correlation lags events considerably and in some cases misses them altogether.

The importance of changing volatilities and correlations should be obvious—portfolio optimization requires a covariance matrix. Up until now, we have been happy with a recursive covariance estimate using a sample of equal weighted returns history up to the present date. In this case, we are getting an average of the covariances. If, on the other hand, covariances and risk in general are regime-dependent, then standard recursive covariances are misspecified. That suggests that the optimized portfolio is as well. To see the intuition, consider again a two-asset portfolio of stocks and bonds. Using equal weighting, the covariance between these two asset classes is a historical average. If, however, we are in a phase in which the correlations have gone below zero but do not recognize that state, we are going to miss out on the diversification opportunities offered by negative covariances. Similarly, during periods in which correlations spike, standard covariance estimates will underestimate risk and overallocate as a result to the more risky assets. This is an excellent exercise to undertake as a test of your understanding on how covariance estimates affect asset allocation. Using the data in the spreadsheet to this chapter on fixed income (FI) and U.S. equity, use the MV GARCH correlations to construct a covariance matrix each month and, alongside the standard recursive covariance estimates, generate two optimal portfolios, rebalance each monthly, and compare their performance to a 70/30 benchmark of bonds and stocks.

CREDIT RISK

Credit risk is the likelihood that the borrower will default. Rating agencies like Standard & Poor's, Fitch, and Moody's all rate bonds, and these ratings (AAA, AA, BBB, and so on) signal the underlying credit risk of the issuer. Credit risks can be quantified by looking at spreads over Treasuries (which are considered to be risk-free). So, for example, if the investment grade corporate bond yield is 7 percent and the 10-year Treasury yield is 3 percent, then the spread of 4 percent can be thought of as the expected loss on the corporate bond. A simple model of default is therefore the *credit spread* over the risk-free yield on Treasuries.

The holder of the corporate bond is compensated for the expected loss and the 400 basis points is the risk premium. If we consider, too, that with default comes less than full recovery, then a more precise estimate of default likelihood is the spread adjusted for the expected recovery. For example, suppose the recovery rate is 50 percent where, upon default, the bondholder expects to recover half of the bond's value when the assets of the firm are liquidated. Then the expected credit risk is equal to the spread divided by $(1 - R)$, where R is the recovery rate. In this case, the expected default rate is 8 percent per year.

We can estimate more accurate default probabilities. Using the spreadsheet developed in Chapter 2, suppose we have a five-year corporate bond paying a 6 percent coupon with a yield to maturity of 7 percent and that the yield on the five-year Treasury (also paying a 6 percent coupon) is 5 percent. The corporate bond is therefore priced at 95.84, while the Treasury is priced at 104.38. The difference is $8.54, and this must be the expected loss on the corporate bond. With continuous compounding, this value would be slightly higher than $8.75. The expected probability of default would appear to be 8.54/95.84 or about 8.9 percent (9.1 percent in the continuously compounded case).

This is a useful approximation to expected default loss but it doesn't provide a guide to default probabilities over the life of the bond. To get at default probabilities, we need to estimate the present value of expected losses over the life of the bond, and using this number, solve for the probability of default. Let's look at this by way of an example provided in Hull's text (2008). Suppose we are analyzing the same five-year corporate bond with the expected loss to default equal to $8.75. On the credit risk spreadsheet for this chapter, I show the cash flows for this bond discounted forward at a 5 percent risk-free rate. The risk-free value is therefore the value of the bond paying the corporate coupon discounted using the risk-free yield to maturity. We assume that losses occur on the half-year directly preceding coupon payment (these are the green shaded cells in Table 11.1).

The risk-free value at any given time is the present value of the current coupon of $3 plus the future cash flows on that bond until maturity. We assume a recovery rate of 40 percent in the table and sum the PV of expected losses to $288.48 over the life of the bond. If the expected default loss is $8.75, then this must equal the probability weighted value of the total expected loss. For example, $8.75 = ρ $288.48 where ρ, the default probability, is solved to be 3.03 percent. This is the annual *default hazard* for this bond. (See Chapter 13 for a deeper discussion of hazard rates.)

This can be improved upon further. Consider three corporate bonds—a three-, five-, and seven-year bond and their Treasury equivalents. We use the three-year bond to derive a default probability for the first three years. Then we use the five-year bond to estimate the default probability for years four and five and the seven-year bond for default probabilities in years six

TABLE 11.1 Estimating Default Probability

Time	r_f	cf(t)	d(t)	Risk-Free Value	PV E(loss)
0.5	0.05	3	0.975	106.73	65.08
1	0.05	3	0.951	106.35	63.12
1.5	0.05	3	0.928	105.97	61.20
2	0.05	3	0.905	105.58	59.34
2.5	0.05	3	0.882	105.17	57.52
3	0.05	3	0.861	104.76	55.74
3.5	0.05	3	0.839	104.34	54.01
4	0.05	3	0.819	103.90	52.32
4.5	0.05	3	0.799	103.46	50.67
5	0.05	103	0.779	103	49.06
recovery	0.4			Total E(loss)	288.48
				Prob(default)	0.0303

and seven. Doing this gives us a more realistic and complete picture of default risk over time. In principle, given available bond data, we could bootstrap out the term structure of default risks.

ADJUSTING FOR LEVERAGE

Leverage is insidious. Suppose I have $100 of my own equity to invest and I supplement that amount with $900 in borrowed funds. That's 9:1 leverage. Colloquially, this is sometimes referred to as *nine turns* of leverage. I now have $1,000 in working capital. If my investment earns 10 percent, then my dollar return is $100. That's a 100 percent return on my equity. That's the power of leverage. Now, imagine, instead, that my investment lost 50 percent. I now default on my loan but my equity loss is limited to my original $100. Of course, I am abstracting away a few details but the example illustrates how leverage permits me to enjoy all the upside while limiting my downside exposure. Before the credit crisis, U.S. investment banks were leveraged at around 30:1, meaning that every dollar in equity invested was accompanied by 30 dollars of borrowed funds. The historical average was closer to 15:1. By way of contrast, Long-Term Capital Management, at the time of their default, was leveraged about 90:1! By way of contrast, Long-Term Capital Management, at the time of their default, was leveraged about 90:1!

First, some definitions: Leverage is the fraction ω of total working capital that is debt financed:

$$\omega = \frac{D}{D + E}$$

This implies that $D = \omega E/(1 - \omega)$, where D and E are debt and equity, respectively. The leveraged return, r_L, is the growth rate of working capital, net of financing costs, over equity:

$$r_L = \frac{[\Delta(D + E) - r_d D]}{E}$$

We can rewrite this to get an expression in returns and leverage as follows. Making the substitution for the definition of $D = \omega E/(1 - \omega)$ we can show that:

$$r_L = \frac{r - \omega r_d}{(1 - \omega)}$$

Here, r is the observed return on equity and r_D is the cost of capital. Obviously, an unleveraged position has a return equivalent to the return on equity. The higher leverage is, the smaller is $(1 - \omega)$ and the greater is r_L relative to r. That suggests an incentive to use borrowed funds. Highly leveraged positions enjoy all the benefits of the upside with none of the risk on the downside. Leverage, in effect, allows us to put other people's money at risk. If we lose it, then we walk away; otherwise, we get the gain, which we don't have to share (we just pay back the borrowed capital).

Now, what about risk? The variance of the leveraged return is straightforward:

$$\sigma_L^2 = \frac{\sigma_E^2 + \omega^2 \sigma_D^2 - 2\text{cov}(r, r_d)}{(1 - \omega)^2}$$

This is a bit complicated. A spreadsheet will illuminate the relationship between risk and leverage. The one here is copied from the chapter spreadsheet labeled Leverage. To keep things simple, I have assumed that the covariance between the return on equity and the cost of capital is zero and that the cost of capital is constant (zero variance). If so, we get the following leverage adjustments for risk (ignore the liquidity adjustment ρ).

This trade-off is illustrated more clearly graphically in Figure 11.7.

Now, we see the true impact of leverage—it increases risks exponentially. You can use the spreadsheet to experiment with various leverage ratios as well as cost of capital parameters. The bottom line is that leverage escalates downside risk. The lesson here is that if the rest of the market is running unleveraged portfolios with 8 percent returns and 8 percent

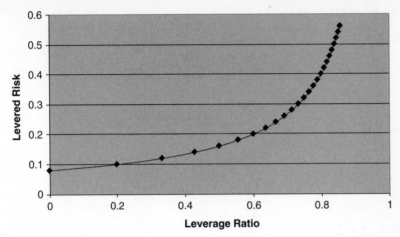

FIGURE 11.7 Levered Risk

volatility as shown in Table 11.2, and your portfolio is levered 2:1, in which case two-thirds of working capital is borrowed, then you are operating with the equivalent of 24 percent volatility. Now, think back to our earlier observation that investment banks were running 30:1 leverage. That is equivalent to 248 percent volatility. The relationship derived here between risk and leverage is also known as *levered beta*. Suppose, for example, that we hold the market portfolio. This portfolio, by definition, will have a beta of one. If we purchased the portfolio with six dollars of borrowed funds for each dollar of our own money, then we have a debt-to-equity ratio of 6:1. Ignoring taxes, the beta on this levered portfolio is:

$$\beta_L = \beta \left[1 + \frac{debt}{equity} \right]$$

which, in our example, is equal to seven times the beta on the market portfolio. If the market portfolio has volatility equal to 8 percent, then the levered portfolio must have volatility equal to 56 percent, which is exactly what Table 11.2 confirms. Intuitively, if each dollar in equity is matched with a dollar of debt, then levered beta must be twice the unlevered beta. Incorporating taxes represented by the tax rate τ, the levered beta is a bit more complicated but still transparent:

$$\beta_L = \beta \left[1 + (1 - \tau) * \frac{debt}{equity} \right]$$

TABLE 11.2   Risk Adjusted for Leverage

One dollar borrowed per dollar equity (e.g., 7:1).

Liquidity	E(return)	E(risk)	CostCap
ρ	r	σ_E	r_d
0	0.08	0.08	0.06
Rate_levered[1]	v	r_L	σ_L
0	0.00	0.08	0.08
0.25	0.20	0.085	0.1
0.5	0.33	0.09	0.12
0.75	0.43	0.095	0.14
1	0.50	0.1	0.16
1.25	0.56	0.105	0.18
1.5	0.60	0.11	0.2
1.75	0.64	0.115	0.22
2	0.67	0.12	0.24
2.25	0.69	0.125	0.26
2.5	0.71	0.13	0.28
2.75	0.73	0.135	0.3
3	0.75	0.14	0.32
3.25	0.76	0.145	0.34
3.5	0.78	0.15	0.36
3.75	0.79	0.155	0.38
4	0.80	0.16	0.4
4.25	0.81	0.165	0.42
4.5	0.82	0.17	0.44
4.75	0.83	0.175	0.46
5	0.83	0.18	0.48
5.25	0.84	0.185	0.5
5.5	0.85	0.19	0.52
5.75	0.85	0.195	0.54
6	0.86	0.2	0.56

With these facts in mind, it is important to leverage-adjust the volatility estimate we would be using in our covariance estimates. This task requires a little foresight—a private real estate portfolio that is leveraged six times over needs to be adjusted for this leverage if it is to be compared to an unleveraged benchmark like the NAREIT. On the other hand, most firms in the publicly traded Russell 3000 are leveraged around four or five times. As such, it may be better not to leverage adjust these returns because, if these stocks are publicly traded, their return volatilities probably already show the effects of leverage. My point is similar to the one made at the beginning of this chapter, which is that information on publicly traded assets in high volume markets tend to be more efficient—that is, they aggregate diverse information more completely into reported returns than privately traded assets with low liquidity.

ADJUSTING FOR ILLIQUIDITY

Conceptually, illiquidity is difficult to compensate. Getmansky, Lo, and Makarov demonstrate that illiquidity causes serial correlation in observed returns due to stale pricing. The degree of illiquidity can be modeled as the proportion ρ of the previous period's return that is carried forward to the current return:

$$r_t = \rho r_{t-1} + \varepsilon_t$$

The variance of this return is:

$$\sigma_E^2 = \frac{\sigma_\varepsilon^2}{(1 - \rho^2)}$$

A model of liquidity-modified leveraged risk is therefore:

$$\sigma_L^2 = \frac{\dfrac{\sigma_\varepsilon^2}{(1 - \rho^2)} + \omega^2 \sigma_D^2 - 2\text{cov}(r, r_d)}{(1 - \omega)^2}$$

OTHER RISKS

This section is small, not because these risks are unimportant, but because it is difficult to integrate them into a comprehensive measure of risk that we can allocate to. *Counterparty risk,* for example, is contractual exposure to other agents, for example, uncollateralized derivatives exposure with custodians and investment banks or managers. This risk is captured through a credit default swap (CDS), which is the interest rate spread we pay to insure our positions. If the CDS spread is rising, then that means that the market is pricing in more risk of default. As an example, suppose our portfolio has a position with a counterparty that is currently earning us 5 percent. We want to insure against our counterparty defaulting and so look to buy a CDS. Suppose the spread is currently 300 bps. If we were to buy the CDS, then our net return would fall to 2 percent. As the risk rises, so does the spread, which draws our return down further.

The notional market for credit default swaps was estimated to be around $50 trillion in 2008, and a lot of that was in short positions, that is, insurers like AIG wrote or sold these, meaning that AIG was on the hook to pay up in the case of default. That's another story but the point is that the market for CDS has expanded to include counterparties of all types, including sovereign and state governments.

SUMMARY

The lessons learned from the recent credit crisis taught us that traditional risk measures like VaR, which were largely dependent on the assumption that returns are normally distributed, significantly underestimated portfolio risks. Risk managers are quickly adopting alternatives to VaR, such as expected tail loss (ETL) as well as alternatives to normal distributional assumptions such as extreme value theory (EVT). Highly volatile episodes in markets over the period from 2008 to 2010 also refocused attention on volatility and correlation methodologies. On a simple level, moving average volatility measures may be intuitively appealing but, as discussed earlier, these are biased estimates and we introduced GARCH as an efficient, mean-reverting measure of volatility and multivariate GARCH as a powerful method in modeling dynamic correlations.

Not all risk is adequately captured by returns volatility, and the credit crisis taught risk managers to look beyond returns to liquidity, leverage, and counterparty (credit) risk as well and we explored adjusting risk estimates in the presence of these sources of risk. Finally, we discussed the implications of endogenous risk in which risks are outcomes of underlying behavior rather than exogenous shocks (known unknowns). In the next chapter, we study the concept of systemic risk, which takes up the concept of endogenous risk.

REFERENCES

Getmansky, Mila, Andrew W. Lo, and Igor Makarov. 2003. An econometric model of serial correlation and illiquidity in hedge fund returns. Working paper, MIT Laboratory for Financial Engineering.

Hull, John. 2008. *Options, futures, and other derivatives*, 7th ed. Upper Saddle River, NJ: Prentice-Hall, 501.

Reinhart, Carmen, and Kenneth Rogoff. 2009. *This time is different: Eight centuries of financial folly.* Princeton, NJ: Princeton University Press.

Sullivan, Rodney, Steven Peterson, and David Waltenbaugh. 2010. Measuring global systemic risk: What are markets saying about risk? *Journal of Portfolio Management* 37(1).

Taleb, Nicholas Nassim. 2007. *The black swan: The impact of the highly improbable.* New York: Random House.

CHAPTER 12

Monte Carlo Methods

Out of intense complexities intense simplicities emerge.
—Winston Churchill

Many problems in finance do not have deterministic solutions because of the inherently stochastic nature of the problems' underlying behaviors. In these cases, solutions are interpreted probabilistically and our interest centers on the statistical properties of the conclusions we draw from studying certain statistics of interest. Monte Carlo methods are algorithms that perform repeated random samplings in which sample properties provide us insight into the sampling distributions of these statistics of interest. One particular application, for example, relates to credit risk and the sensitivity of joint default on bonds to changes in the correlation across bonds—the probability, say, that bonds A, B, and C default at the same time. The relationship of interest in this case is the dependence of joint default risk on the correlation of returns across the bonds. We study this problem in detail further on.

Monte Carlo methods are the topic of a voluminous literature in the sciences and my intent here is not to cover that literature but to introduce you to this important class of models as they relate to our study of risk. Although there is no hard consensus on what exactly constitutes a Monte Carlo study, they all share some common elements: Given a set of known parameters—means, volatilities, and correlations, for example—we generate samples of new observations consistent with the distributional properties of these parameters using random draws from a known distribution and then compute deterministic solutions to a stated problem. This process is repeated, generating samples of solutions whose properties are the object of our study. In this introductory section, I present three examples, in increasing order of complexity, that develop some basic elements of the Monte Carlo method. We then move on to address directly the distributional properties of the random number generation process and, in particular, non-normal distributions. This will set us up to discuss and develop copulas. Our applications in this chapter are directly relevant to our discussion on risk.

EXAMPLE 12.1: GENERATING RANDOM NUMBERS—ESTIMATING π

A simple computational application that estimates the value of pi will serve as an introduction to this technique (Kalos 2008). Figure 12.1 shows the unit circle circumscribed within a unit square. The diameter, d, of the circle and the width of the square are both equal to one. The area of the square is therefore d^2 and the area of the circle is $\pi r^2 = \pi (d/2)^2$. The ratio of the area of the circle to that of the square is therefore $\pi/4$.

Now, suppose we were to draw a sample of pairs of numbers from the *uniform distribution* defined over the unit interval (between zero and one). Each pair is a coordinate in the x-y plane depicted in Figure 12.1, that is, a point within the unit square. There is a sample of 100 draws provided in the Chapter 12 worksheet examples on the sheet titled "Estimating pi." We will use these random draws to estimate pi. But, first, some background. The equation for a circle is given by $(y - a)^2 + (x - b)^2 = z^2$. In Figure 12.1, the lower left coordinate is the origin $(y,x) = (0,0)$, the midpoint is $(a,b) = (0.5,0.5)$, and the radius $z = 0.5$. We can therefore locate the sample points within

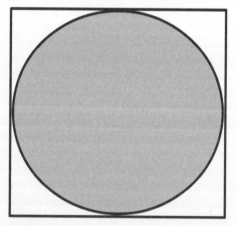

FIGURE 12.1   Circle within the Unit Square

the circle by counting those points (*x-y* coordinate pairs) that satisfy the following inequality: $(y - 0.5)^2 + (x - 0.5)^2 \leq 0.25$. To do this in Excel, we use the IF function in column C of the spreadsheet, specifically, =IF($(a^2 - 0.5)$^2 + $(b^2 - 0.5)$^2 $\leq$ 0.25,1,0). The count of all these points is the sum of column C. We divide the count by the total points (all of which fall in the square) and multiply by 4. This provides an estimate of pi. This value is given in cell D2 on the spreadsheet. Pressing F9 refreshes the sheet, generating another estimate. Larger samples give a more precise estimate.

Clearly, we do not need to go to this effort to estimate pi, whose value we already know. Rather, this simple example illustrates how random sampling from a known distribution can be used to estimate the value of an unknown parameter and, in that sense, it serves as an introduction to the intuition on Monte Carlo procedures.

EXAMPLE 12.2: CONFIRMING THE CENTRAL LIMIT THEOREM

Let's expand our method. Consider a problem whose solution is now a function of the size of the randomly drawn sample. In this case, we want to demonstrate a result of the central limit theorem, which states that the distribution of the sample mean is normally distributed as the sample size increases. Figure 12.2 illustrates this result, using four sample sizes with the normal density overlaid.

The central limit theorem is one of the most powerful results in statistics. It states that no matter what the underlying distribution a random sample is drawn from, the distribution of the sample mean follows a normal distribution. Think of this for a moment. It says that no matter what the shape of the probability distribution we draw data from, the mean of that sample will follow the bell-shaped normal density. This is an asymptotic result, as $N \rightarrow \infty$, which I intend to show further on. That means that we can safely appeal to test statistics for hypotheses involving means using a single distribution—the normal distribution. The results in Figure 12.2 were generated from a Monte Carlo experiment drawing from the *uniform distribution* defined over the range 0 to 10 (which assigns *equal* probability of drawing any number in the 0 to 10 interval).

(continued)

(continued)

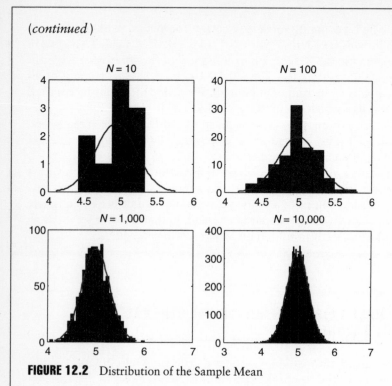

FIGURE 12.2   Distribution of the Sample Mean

The experiment draws 100 values from the uniform distribution and estimates the sample mean. The population mean of uniform distribution in our example is equal to $(b - a))/(2) = ((10 - 0))/2 = 5$. The central limit theorem states that if we repeat this experiment N times, drawing new samples of size 100 and estimating the mean, then the distribution of these means is normal. With $N = 10$, we see from Figure 12.2 that we are far from normality. However, it is clear that as N increases, the distribution of the sample mean indeed becomes normal in the limit around its true population mean. Asymptotically, the distribution of the sample mean collapses to the population mean as N approaches infinity. The central limit theorem justifies the use of sample statistics based on the normal density function (z, t, χ^2, and F statistics) and although it, too, is proved in mathematics, the Monte Carlo demonstration used here helps illustrate the usefulness of sampling experiments to derive properties of various estimators.

EXAMPLE 12.3: CREDIT DEFAULT RISK

Let's shift to an application that has more significance to finance. Consider three bonds (A, B, and C) which have mean *monthly* default probability, in percent, $\mu = (0.25, 0.33, 0.42)$, respectively, with *monthly* volatilities of $(1.5, 2, 2.6)$ percent, respectively. For example, the probability that bond A will default in any given month is one-quarter of 1 percent. A two-standard deviation positive shock to that probability puts default risk at 3.25 percent per month. We are interested in the joint default sensitivity of these bonds to the correlations in their returns. To that end, we begin with a correlation matrix that shows default rates to be highly correlated as shown in the following correlation matrix:

$$C = \begin{bmatrix} 1 & .99 & .989 \\ .99 & 1 & .99 \\ .989 & .99 & 1 \end{bmatrix}$$

We showed previously that the covariance matrix V can be expressed as the product: S^*C^*S, where S is a diagonal matrix of volatilities:

$$V = \begin{bmatrix} 1.5 & 0 & 0 \\ 0 & 2 & 0 \\ 0 & 0 & 2.6 \end{bmatrix} \begin{bmatrix} 1 & .99 & .989 \\ .99 & 1 & .99 \\ .989 & .99 & 1 \end{bmatrix} \begin{bmatrix} 1.5 & 0 & 0 \\ 0 & 2 & 0 \\ 0 & 0 & 2.6 \end{bmatrix}$$

$$= \begin{bmatrix} 2.25 & 2.97 & 3.86 \\ 2.97 & 4.00 & 5.15 \\ 3.86 & 5.15 & 6.76 \end{bmatrix}$$

$$V = \begin{bmatrix} 1.5 & 0 & 0 \\ 0 & 2 & 0 \\ 0 & 0 & 2.6 \end{bmatrix} \begin{bmatrix} 1 & 0 & 0 \\ 0 & 1 & 0 \\ 0 & 0 & 1 \end{bmatrix} \begin{bmatrix} 1.5 & 0 & 0 \\ 0 & 2 & 0 \\ 0 & 0 & 2.6 \end{bmatrix}$$

$$= \begin{bmatrix} 2.25 & 2.97 & 3.86 \\ 2.97 & 4.00 & 5.15 \\ 3.86 & 5.15 & 6.76 \end{bmatrix}$$

(continued)

(*continued*)

Our objective is to try to determine how many times in a 10-year period that this market will fail. *Failure* is defined here as a joint occurrence that all three bonds default jointly. We arbitrarily define a bond default if its monthly default probability exceeds an arbitrary upper bound exceeding the ninety-seventh percentile of its default distribution. If all three bonds default simultaneously in any given month, then we have joint failure (what is called *systemic failure*). Since we are simulating 10 years of monthly default probabilities, we are interested in estimating the incidence of systemic failure over a decade and, moreover, the sensitivity of systemic failure to changes in the correlations given in C.

How do we go about accomplishing this task? Well, clearly we wish to generate a series of default probabilities for these three bonds that have means μ, volatilities given by the diagonal matrix S, and correlations consistent with C. The Cholesky decomposition of V is the upper triangular matrix P such that $V = P'^{*}P$. For the V given here, P is equal to:

$$P = \begin{bmatrix} 1.5 & 1.98 & 2.574 \\ 0 & 0.2821 & 0.1825 \\ 0 & 0 & 0.3182 \end{bmatrix}$$

This suggests that multiplying P times a 3×1 vector of random draws from the standard normal density $(z_1, z_2, z_3)'$ and adding μ will give us a simulated set of returns with expected value equal to μ and variance-covariance equal to V. The important assumption here (and one that is perhaps quite restrictive) is that defaults are multivariate normal. Thus, the z's are draws from a multivariate normal distribution with mean μ and covariance V. That is,

$$E[\mu + P'z] = E(\mu) + P'E(z) = E(\mu) = \mu$$

This holds because $E(z) = 0$, since the individual z_i are independent draws from the standard normal distribution. Likewise, the variance is:

$$E[\mu + P'z]^2 = P'E(zz')P = P'IP = V$$

which holds because the variance of μ is zero (it is a parameter) and the variance of z is one (more precisely, $E(zz')$ is the identity matrix). The Monte Carlo design therefore consists of repeated draws z from

$N(0,1)$. For our first trial, therefore, we draw 120 triplets from N $(0,1)$, where the simulated return in each of the 120 draws is a 3×1 vector $x_i = \mu + P'z_i$ for $i = 1, \ldots, 120$. There will be 120 cases—one for each month in our 10-year experiment. The entire sample is a 3×120 matrix of probabilities, in which each column represents a joint probability of default and each row corresponds to a single bond. Thus, each triplet (column) is a realization under the multivariate normal density with parameters μ and V. The probability of seeing these values can be computed using the normal cumulative density—that is, the probability that z is greater than or equal to the simulated value. In Excel, this is done with the NORMDIST(x) function. Applying this function to our simulated returns yields probabilities. We care about those that lie above the ninety-seventh percentile and count the total number of columns for which all three bond default probabilities jointly exceed this cutoff point and divide by 120.

The experiment is then repeated, changing the off-diagonal elements (the correlations) given in C. Let's assume for simplicity of exposition here that the correlations are the same across bonds A and B, B

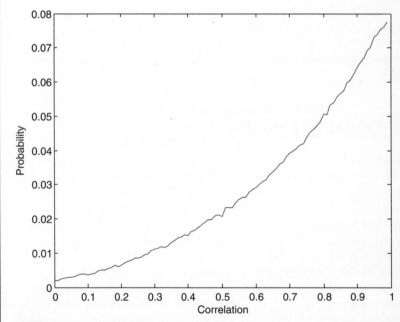

FIGURE 12.3 Credit Default Systemic Risk

(*continued*)

(*continued*)
and C, and A and C. In this manner, we need only change a single value in the correlation matrix. We range this single value from 0 to 0.99 in increments of one basis point, creating 100 cases over which the correlation matrix varies and counting up the proportion of the 120 cases in each that have joint default events. Figure 12.3 shows the relationship between the joint probability of credit default and returns correlation. In this example, the probability is convex in the correlations.

The experiment can be summarized in the following steps:

- Define the parameters (means, correlations, volatilities, covariances).
- Solve for the Cholesky decomposition of the covariance matrix.
- Using the mean vector and the Cholesky decomposition, generate a sample of size $T \times k$, where k is the number of assets, by repeating $x_i = \mu + $ Cholesky*randn(0,1), where randn(0,1) is a $k \times 1$ vector of standard normal random numbers and μ is a $k \times 1$ vector of mean returns and Cholesky is a $k \times k$ matrix. Repeat T times.
- Convert these simulated returns to cumulative probabilities using NORMDIST(x).
- Count the cases that fall into the appropriate tail region.
- Change the correlations and repeat all of the preceding steps.

NON-NORMAL DISTRIBUTIONS

In the previous example, we generated samples conditional on a set of parameters given by μ and V assuming that these default probabilities were distributed multivariate normal. Next, we use this basic setup again in the form of a Gaussian copula. But, for now, let's revisit the experiment once again and focus on the last step, which involves NORMDIST. Recall that this step produced a cumulative probability under the normal cumulative density that we used in our subsequent analysis on credit defaults. Let's change the object of interest to portfolio loss, specifically the probability that returns would be less than or equal to some critical loss value. The underlying assumption again is that returns are multivariate normal. What if, instead, we felt that they were distributed non-normally?

Consider, for example, the possibility that the returns have fat tails implying the likelihood of more extreme returns compared to the normal density.

This is illustrated conceptually further on for the case in which the normal density underestimates the likelihood of losses in general and extreme losses in particular. In this case, the normal density would underestimate both VaR and ETL if the true distribution of returns followed some type of extreme value distribution (in this case, one that is skewed left with a fatter tail).

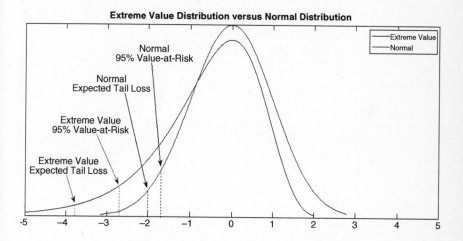

Extreme Value Distribution versus Normal Distribution

Suppose we felt that distributions of returns were more consistent with a heavy-tailed distribution such as the *t*-distribution? What implications would this assumption have on our loss measures? Intuitively, our answer would hinge on understanding that heavier tails make losses observed under the normal distribution more likely under the alternative heavy-tail distribution. Therefore, we'd expect that there would be fewer observed returns falling below some critical percentile in the left tail. For example, NORMINV(.05,0,1) = -1.645, which states that the fifth percentile of a standardized normal distribution is located 1.645 standard deviations below the mean. Suppose instead, that, in truth, returns were distributed under the *t*-distribution with six degrees of freedom. This suggests TINV(.05,6) = -1.943 as the fifth percentile, which is further into the tail than would otherwise be under the normal density. The important conclusion here is that with heavier tails, heretofore extreme events are no longer so extreme and that the assumption of normality will underestimate risks. This was the case as the world entered the credit crisis in 2008; risk managers, who were locked into VaR based on the normal density, began to experience losses at frequencies that were supposed to be virtually impossible. This prompted the turn of phrase *Black Swans*.

THE GAUSSIAN COPULA

The idea of studying portfolio risk in a world in which returns may follow different distributions, perhaps depending on the asset class, is an intriguing one. After all, there is ample evidence to suggest that returns, in general, are not well modeled by the normal density (fat tails, excess kurtosis, negative or positive skew, and so forth). The following example shows the empirical distribution of U.S. equity returns over the period 1970 to 2009 fit to both the normal and t-distribution with six degrees of freedom. The t-distribution maximizes the likelihood of the observed data. Notice that while the normal density would tend to overestimate mid-range losses, it also tends to underestimate tail losses and that there is also an asymmetry embodied in the lower tail of the distribution of returns. Chapter 13 models the distribution of the tail directly, using extreme value theory.

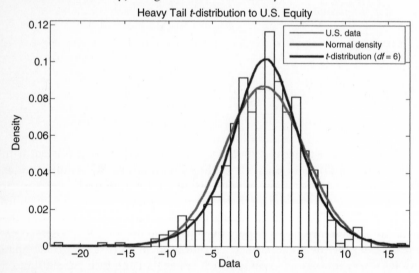

Therefore, while we may reject normality in favor of an alternative distributional assumption, these alternatives are generally the result of empirical models fit to specific return streams using maximum likelihood methods, which would suggest that return distributions will vary across asset classes. High yield credit, for example, is likely to have fatter tails than investment grade bonds, and bond returns, in general, will behave differently from equity returns. Moreover, it is also likely that asset return distributions are sensitive to the business cycle as well as shock, for example, financial crises. The point is that the assumption of normality may be overly restrictive and the cost of that restriction could be quite high from the perspective of risk management.

The problem we face is that while we can generate a multivariate distribution of returns conditional on a vector of means, a correlation matrix, and the individual asset volatilities as in the preceding example, we have no method at this point of being able to combine different marginal distributions into a coherent joint distribution. In the credit default example discussed earlier, the three bonds were assumed to all have a multivariate normal distribution. In the immediately preceding discussion, however, we are entertaining the notion of possibly three different distributions. In general, we may have k assets with wide-ranging marginal distributions (log normal, beta, gamma, t, and so forth). It is mathematically intractable to solve for the joint distribution in these cases. This is where copulas come in.

A copula is a function that joins together marginal distributions into a multivariate distribution. In a theorem proposed by Sklar (Rachev 2003), it was proved that for any set of marginal distributions, there exists a copula that joins these into a multivariate distribution. Sklar's theorem was published in 1959. Since then, a large literature on copulas has formed and interest in copulas has increased dramatically since the onset of the credit crisis in 2008. Copula functions have now become standard fare in several software packages, including Matlab. I will state this result for the bivariate case but leave the mathematical details to a set of recommended references. (A comprehensive survey can be found in Rachev 2003.) Sklar's theorem states that given two distinct marginal distributions on the random variables x and y, given by $F(x)$ and $G(y)$, and a joint distribution on x and y given by $H(x,y)$, then there exists a copula C such that $H(x,y) = C(F(x), G(y))$. I will develop the Gaussian copula and apply it in the discussion that follows.

To fix ideas, let's refer to the monthly returns data on U.S. equity and non-U.S.-developed equity spanning 1970 to 2009 and presented in the chapter spreadsheet under the copula tab. Our objective is to model tail risk, VaR, and ETL by constructing a viable model of the underlying dynamics between these two returns series. We can then use this model to simulate bivariate returns for these two asset classes in subsequent work. Figure 12.4 is a scatterplot of the returns, which have a Pearson correlation of 63 percent over this period. Here are some summary statistics on these returns:

U.S.	Non-U.S.	
0.89	0.98	μ
4.58	5.06	σ
-9.76	-10.80	VaR (1%)

The monthly returns are 89 bps and 98 bps, respectively, with monthly volatilities 4.58 percent and 5.06 percent. The 1 percent VaR is computed using $\mu - 2.326\sigma$, where $\text{Prob}(z < -2.31) = 0.01$. The seven dots located in the far lower left denote the joint occurrence of returns exceeding the VaR cutoffs. These seven events occur in a sample size of 480.

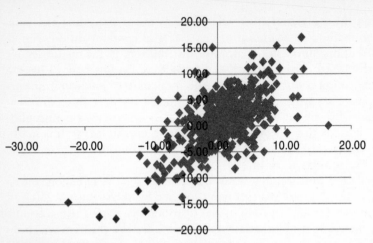

FIGURE 12.4 U.S. versus Non-U.S. Equity Returns

Let us now fit these returns empirically to a t-distribution using the method of maximum likelihood (I used Matlab's *dfittool* function to do this). The marginal distribution for U.S. equity was already shown earlier with six degrees of freedom. The maximum likelihood distribution for non-U.S. equity was likewise t-distributed with six degrees of freedom and is presented directly here.

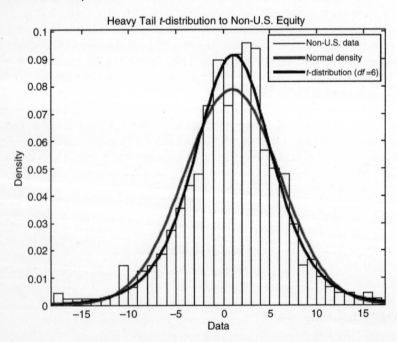

Let's spend a little time analyzing these two distributions. On the copula spreadsheet, we summarize the tail experience for both the *t*-distribution (with six degrees of freedom) and the normal distribution. The one percentile cutoffs are −3.143 (*t*) and −2.326 (normal). Columns M to P contain a few cases for which observed returns fell below the first percentile. These results are summarized here:

U.S.	Non-U.S.	
3	4	*t*-dist(df=6)
0.60%	0.80%	
8	7	normal
1.70%	1.50%	

Under the normal distribution, for example, the incidence of extreme U.S. equity returns is about 1.7 times expected (8/480 = 1.7 percent) and 1.5 times expected for non-U.S. equity. This is evidence supporting the propensity of the normal assumption, when improperly applied, to lead to underestimates of risk. Under the *t*-distribution, on the other hand, the incidence of extreme returns is less than expected but still closer to the 1 percent expected incidence. In any case, we note that these observations are based on a single sample.

The objective is to use a copula to generate a joint distribution using these two marginal *t*-distributions, each with six degrees of freedom. We can follow the six-step procedure given previously but with a few modifications:

- Define the parameters (means, correlations, volatilities, covariances). Substitute the Spearman rank order correlations for Pearson correlations (see the discussion further on) and using the volatilities, compute the new covariance matrix.
- Find the Cholesky decomposition of the covariance matrix.
- Using the mean vector μ and the Cholesky decomposition P', generate a $T \times k$ sample, where k is the number of assets, by repeating $x_i = \mu + P'^*\text{randn}(0,1)$, where $\text{randn}(0,1)$ is a $k \times 1$ vector of standard normal random numbers and μ is a $k \times 1$ vector of mean returns and P' is a $k \times k$ matrix.
- Convert these simulated returns to cumulative probabilities u, using NORMDIST(x).
- The matrix u can be thought of as random draws from a uniform distribution. Construct the marginal distributions tinv(u,6). By Sklar's

theorem, these marginal distributions will have a joint density given by the Gaussian copula with rank correlation given by Spearman and co-variance V.

Spearman correlations are used because the copula does not preserve the Pearson product-moment correlations in the transformation of the marginal distributions. We therefore use the rank order correlations in place of the Pearson correlations, since rank order is preserved under the transformation. Note that we could use Kendall's τ instead of Spearman.

We can review the copula construction process by reviewing the spreadsheet. Columns R and S on the spreadsheet generate two vectors of 480 random draws from the standard normal density. Columns U and V pre-multiply these draws by the Cholesky decomposition of the covariance matrix. These are values under the normal distribution, which are then evaluated as probabilities using the normal (NORMDIST)—this is the matrix u in step 4. The copula then transforms these uniform values using the TINV $(u,6)$ function, producing a multivariate set of random returns consistent with the covariance given by V and, specifically, the Spearman correlations. The scatterplot provided in Figure 12.5 seems to match the original returns quite well. Pressing F9 will refresh the spreadsheet.

Suppose now that we invest in an equal-weighted portfolio of U.S. and non-U.S. equity. The returns to this portfolio are given in column AC on the spreadsheet and the ranks are provided in column AD. There are 480 realizations from the experiment. Pressing F9 generates another

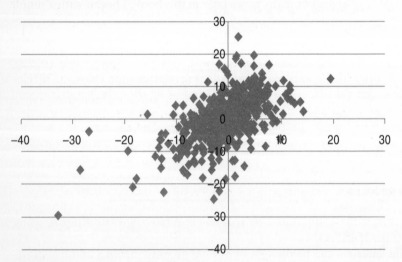

FIGURE 12.5 Gaussian Copula for U.S. versus Non-U.S. Simulated Returns

sample. Columns AF and AG provides the results from one such simulation. These portfolio returns are ranked in ascending order. Rows 1 to 25, for example, correspond to the tail comprising the 5 percent lowest returns (given in green). The average of these returns is −12.52 percent. This is the expected tail loss (ETL), where the tail is defined by the 5 percent VaR, which under $t(df = 6)$ is equal to −10.0221. The VaR says that this portfolio is expected to lose at least −10.0221 percent 5 percent of the time. The ETL, which is a *coherent* risk measure, is equal to −12.52 percent and gives the expected loss based upon the returns that exist in the tail, the largest loss on this particular simulation being −21.36 percent. In principle, we could generate a sampling distribution of ETL and study the statistical properties of this distribution under the structure imposed by our copula. Thus, the copula permits the introduction of virtually any marginal distribution. A large negative shock, for example, may lead us to adopt even fatter tail *t*-distributions (lowering the degrees of freedom parameter) or perhaps substituting more skewed distributions from the beta family. The resultant structures produce scatterplots like those in Figures 12.4 and 12.5, which are reminiscent of observed returns but with specific marginal distributions. It is also straightforward to expand the dimension to include many assets.

SUMMARY

In this chapter, I introduce the very important Monte Carlo methodology, which we will appeal to many times later in this book. I began with a simple application of the technique and extended that simple model to cover increasingly complex problems ranging from a simple experiment to confirm the central limit theorem, to joint credit defaults, to value at risk with non-normal returns, and finally to copulas. Each of these problems is accompanied by a spreadsheet application included in the chapter examples.

Monte Carlo is an important class of simulation models and we shall appeal to these models later when we study options and derivatives as well as models of stock price dynamics, hedging tail risk, and many other applications.

REFERENCES

Kalos, Malvin H., and Paula A. Whitlock. 2008. *Monte Carlo methods*. Hoboken, NJ: John Wiley & Sons.
Rachev, Svetlozar T., ed. 2003. *Handbook of heavy tailed distributions in finance*. Amsterdam: Elsevier.

CHAPTER 13

Systemic Risk

Markets can remain irrational longer than you can remain solvent.
—J. M. Keynes

Financial markets on occasion experience abrupt and sometimes severe disruptions. As a consequence, market returns are more appropriately modeled using heavy-, or fat-, tailed distributions rather than standard Gaussian (normal), or log normal, distributions. During these episodes, risk models, such as traditional VaR, often fail to predict the duration and magnitude of extreme losses because they are parametrically ill suited to that task. Standard symmetric, two-parameter densities like the normal density do not produce the extreme outcomes of recent experience, and during periods of turmoil, these restrictions are especially costly as behavior becomes more complex as displayed by distributional asymmetries, skewness, and kurtosis (fat tails).

Systemic risks arise on the confluence of many factors and are accompanied by widespread losses and spikes in correlations across asset classes. The common factors frequently underlying market bubbles are discussed in Sullivan (2009). These include speculative leverage, investor emotions, and a misunderstanding of the true consequences of financial innovation, to name a few. The failure of Lehman Brothers, for example, announced on Sunday, September 14, 2008, signaled the severity of the collapse in credit markets, which precipitated a series of extreme losses that spread across asset classes as well as geographic boundaries. I demonstrate in this chapter the degree of non-normality of returns with particular attention to the shape of the left tail of the distribution of returns recently witnessed across various global markets. We also cover multivariate models of risk that condition on three common factors (liquidity, volatility, and default risk) giving us probabilities of instantaneous failure (hazard rates) as well as joint failure across markets (systemic risk). A failure event is defined as a *threshold exceedance.* Together, these models form a basis of monitoring tail risk and providing conditional forecasts of extreme returns both within and across markets.

EXTREME VALUE THEORY

I begin by applying extreme value theory (EVT) to model fat-tailed return distributions, specifically, the distribution of losses exceeding a prespecified lower threshold. Extreme value theory has received much attention in the insurance industry to predict rare events such as floods, earthquakes, and other natural disasters and has a large devoted literature. See for example, the text by Embrechts, Kluppelberg, and Mikosch (1997). Our interest centers not only on applying extreme value theory to predict rare market events but, more importantly, monitoring changes in the parameters of the extreme value distributions themselves, which may signal a fundamental shift in downside risks. There is also a deep and rich literature on applying EVT to financial markets. See, for example, Cotter (2006), Longin and Solnik (2001), LeBaron, Blake, and Samanta (2004), Malevergne, Pisarenko, and Sornette (2006).

There is a related literature on extreme outcomes, specifically, the distribution of order statistics (see, for example, Mood et al. 1974 for an introduction, and the related quantile regression theory developed by Koenker and Basset [1978], which models specific extreme quantiles, for example, the fifth percentile of the distribution of returns). EVT, on the other hand, models the likelihood function for the tail density and not a quantile, which in our case, is the set of minimum returns found in the left-hand tail. The challenge with EVT is to estimate the tail parameters from a finite sample of data using either maximum likelihood (as in this chapter) or Monte Carlo simulation (Longin and Solnik 2001). Thus, we will model downside risks, where *downside* is taken to be those observed returns that fall below a specific loss threshold—in our case, the fifth percentile. Our choice of the empirical quantile that determines the threshold is subjective but sensible (Ledford and Tawn 1996).

Graphs such as those shown in Figure 13.1, illustrate this process.

Let's define the distribution of interest as the extra-threshold returns— what we call the *fail event criteria* (losses beyond the defined threshold). More formally, we model the likelihood function for these returns using the generalized extreme value (GEV) probability density and estimate its parameters using the method of maximum likelihood. We assume intervals are independent with exponential distribution. The generalized extreme value distribution is a three-parameter family: scale (σ), a measure of the

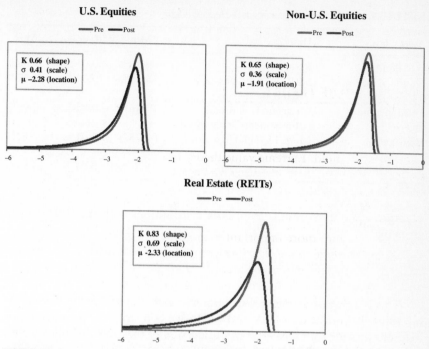

FIGURE 13.1 Pre- and Post-Lehman Tail Densities

dispersion of return events, location (μ), which shows the average position of the extreme within the distribution, and shape (κ), a measure of skewness. In general, these loss distributions will be skewed to the left but their specific shapes will depend on the values of their specific shape ($\kappa > 0$), and scale (σ), parameters. Denoting daily returns by r, the density function for the GEV distribution is defined as (Embrechts, Kluppelberg, and Mikosch [1997]):

$$f(r|\mu, \sigma, k > 0) = \frac{1}{\sigma} \, exp\left(-\left(1 + k\frac{(r-\mu)}{\sigma}\right)^{-1/k}\right)\left(1 + k\frac{(r-\mu)}{\sigma}\right)^{-1-\left(\frac{1}{k}\right)}$$

Malevergne, Pisarenko, and Sornette (2006) show that estimates of the GEV are inefficient in the absence of the independence of returns and that this inefficiency confounds the precision of point estimates of the distribution's parameters. They show that the generalized Pareto (GPD) performs somewhat better but suffers likewise in the presence of strong dependence

TABLE 13.1 Daily Total Return Series Descriptions

Asset Class	Description	Min	Average	Max
U.S. Equities	Russell 3000	−9.28%	0.01%	11.48%
Non-U.S. Equities	S&P Developed ex-U.S. Large-Mid Cap	−8.19%	0.02%	8.42%
Fixed Income	Citigroup U.S. Broad Investment Grade (BIG)	−1.46%	0.02%	2.00%
High Yield	Merrill Lynch High Yield Master II	−4.73%	0.01%	2.52%
Real Estate (REITs)	Dow Jones Wilshire REIT	−19.77%	0.04%	18.99%

in returns. We show results from both distributions with the GPD density given by:

$$f(r|\theta, \sigma, k > 0) = \frac{1}{\sigma}\left(1 + k\frac{(r - \mu)}{\sigma}\right)^{-1-\left(\frac{1}{k}\right)}$$

This is a three-parameter distribution as well, but where θ is the threshold value. In both cases—GEV and GPD—we bootstrap the parameter estimates to provide standard errors. A discussion of these results follows with Tables 13.1, 13.2, and 13.3.

Let's now bring this together through an examination of the recent volatile market events. The five asset classes analyzed are U.S. equities, non-U.S. equities, U.S. fixed income, high yield bonds, and REITs. They're all described in Table 13.1.

We compare results across two periods. The pre-Lehman period is estimated from February 1, 1996, through August 31, 2008, and the post-Lehman period has the same start date but is estimated through December 2008. These periods serve to demonstrate the impact of the turbulent markets witnessed in the fall of 2008. Table 13.1 shows a large post-Lehman shift in the GEV parameters (location, shape, and scale) and this, in turn, clearly reveals the increased likelihood of downside risks.

The parameter estimates for virtually all of these return distributions appear to have degraded into higher risk states; average tail losses are higher (μ has declined), dispersion has increased (σ) and losses have become more skewed (κ). Nevertheless, a higher risk state does not necessarily follow from these changed parameter values for the reasons cited in Malevergne et al. (2006), that is, in the presence of low parameter precision, these values may be statistical artifacts from the same distribution. We therefore bootstrapped 1,000 samples from both the pre-Lehman and post-Lehman histories (pre-Lehman is a subset of the post-Lehman set). We estimated the

TABLE 13.2 GEV Parameter Estimates and Confidence Intervals

GEV		Pre-Lehman			Post-Lehman		
		Shape	Scale	Location	Shape	Scale	Location
U.S.	2.5%	0.26	0.27	2.00	0.50	0.33	2.12
	50%	0.44	0.32	2.12	0.66	0.40	2.28
	97.5%	0.67	0.37	2.25	0.87	0.48	2.44
Non-U.S.	2.5%	0.23	0.24	1.66	0.49	0.30	1.78
	50%	0.40	0.29	1.78	0.65	0.36	1.91
	97.5%	0.60	0.34	1.90	0.83	0.44	2.04
FI	2.5%	0.29	0.06	0.44	0.34	0.06	0.45
	50%	0.48	0.07	0.46	0.52	0.07	0.47
	97.5%	0.71	0.09	0.49	0.72	0.09	0.50
HY	2.5%	0.44	0.07	0.35	0.64	0.10	0.40
	50%	0.64	0.08	0.38	0.83	0.12	0.45
	97.5%	0.88	0.10	0.41	1.03	0.15	0.49
RE	2.5%	0.37	0.33	1.81	0.64	0.52	2.06
	50%	0.59	0.41	1.97	0.85	0.67	2.32
	97.5%	0.85	0.52	2.17	1.09	0.86	2.62

TABLE 13.3 GPD Parameter Estimates and Confidence Intervals

GPD		Pre-Lehman			Post-Lehman		
		Shape	Scale	Threshold	Shape	Scale	Threshold
U.S.	2.5%	−0.11	0.52	1.70	0.12	0.61	1.80
	50%	0.09	0.63	1.81	0.27	0.77	1.91
	97.5%	0.23	0.76	1.91	0.43	0.96	2.03
Non-U.S.	2.5%	−0.22	0.51	1.40	0.11	0.54	1.46
	50%	−0.03	0.63	1.47	0.25	0.69	1.56
	97.5%	0.11	0.78	1.57	0.41	0.86	1.69
Fixed Income	2.5%	−0.17	0.12	0.36	−0.19	0.13	0.37
	50%	0.01	0.16	0.39	0.01	0.17	0.40
	97.5%	0.18	0.20	0.42	0.17	0.21	0.43
High Yield	2.5%	−0.02	0.12	0.28	0.23	0.16	0.31
	50%	0.24	0.15	0.30	0.43	0.22	0.34
	97.5%	0.48	0.19	0.33	0.62	0.29	0.38
REITs	2.5%	−0.15	0.69	1.44	0.21	0.90	1.63
	50%	0.03	0.91	1.61	0.40	1.21	1.75
	97.5%	0.20	1.17	1.70	0.62	1.61	1.92

parameters of the likelihood function for each sample and then located the 2.5 percent and 97.5 percent percentiles along with the median across the bootstrapped samples. These results are presented in Table 13.2 for the GEV and in Table 13.3 for the GPD.

From Table 13.2, we see that the median value for the location parameter, post-Lehman, lies outside the 95 percent band constructed from the pre-Lehman returns data for all markets but fixed income. The same conclusion holds for the scale parameter, but only for non-U.S. equity and REITs regarding the shape parameter. Table 13.3 echoes these results for the threshold parameters but shows somewhat weaker results for scale and shape. In all cases, equity and REITs show the strongest divergence from the pre-Lehman downside risks.

While these may not constitute formal tests, they do support the empirical evidence of increased incidences of extreme losses and at the very least are useful monitoring devices. Failure to recognize shifts in these risk parameters would result in an underestimation of the probability of larger losses occurring in the future. This cost, in percent, is approximated in Figure 13.1 by the area between the *pre* and *post* distribution functions; if we believe that these distributions have changed, then for REITs, this cost amounts to an 8.44 percent underestimate of the mass to the left of the fifth percentile while that for high yield would have been 7.5 percent. Furthermore, losses would be underestimated by 7.25 percent for non-U.S. equity and 6.67 percent for U.S. equity. REITs, especially, experienced a large parametric shift in risk with expected downside loss increasing by roughly 20 percent, (μ changes from -1.97 percent to -2.32 percent) and with volatility nearly doubling (σ changes from 0.41 percent to 0.67 percent).

ESTIMATING THE HAZARDS OF DOWNSIDE RISKS

Monitoring sample movements in the parameters of extreme value distributions are uninformative in that we do not know why a parameter, say, location has shifted further into the tail of the distribution of returns. For this reason, we next devise a hazard function for downside risk conditional on a set of three factors we believe to influence this risk. The hazard rate is the probability of instantaneous failure—the likelihood that a return will exceed the threshold, right now, conditional on the risk state embodied in the values of the risk factors (see Kiefer 1988). We assume the hazard follows an exponential distribution so that the probability of failure is not duration dependent, that is, it is not a function of the length of time elapsed since the last failure; rather it is conditioned only on the level of market liquidity, volatility, and general default risk. There is no reason to restrict the analysis to these three risk factors. We did so for purely illustrative purposes but otherwise encourage more careful study of factors in general. The objective is to attribute the likelihood of extreme returns to changes in factors that we believe drive risks and that we can also observe. Thus, with a forward view on the underlying risk factors, we can form forward views on the probability of failures. A change in this particular risk barometer would, for example, lead portfolio managers to adjust the risk levels targeted in their portfolios if not their allocations. In this section, we demonstrate how such models can be constructed and used to better understand and predict the complex and adaptive return patterns that were depicted in the prior section.

Conditioning the probability of extreme loss on risk factors provides both a model of risk attribution as well as a basis for forecasting downside risk. The hazard model identifies the probability (risk) of a downside event (which we refer to as a fail event) based on the relationship to our three selected risk factors. Because risk factors change daily, our hazard model provides a time-varying probability of instantaneous failure, that is, the probability that the threshold will be exceeded today. See Appendix 13.1 for a discussion of hazard models. The presence of these conditioning covariates can be thought of as shifting the hazard up or down contemporaneously as these variables change. For example, an increasing VIX shifts the hazard up, meaning higher market risks. Our risk hazard model is therefore a probability (λ) of failure conditional on a set of risk factors—the option implied volatility (VIX), the LIBOR spread over Treasuries (TED), and the spread in investment grade credit (AAA corporate rate) over the 10-year Treasury note (DEF) and modeled using an exponential hazard:

$$\lambda(t, x, \beta) = \exp(\beta_0 + \beta_1 \text{VIX} + \beta_2 \text{DEF} + \beta_3 \text{TED})$$

The parameters of the hazard function are estimated by maximum likelihood. Substituting in values for the covariates in conjunction with the parameter estimates gives estimates of the hazard conditional on the respective values for the VIX and the two spreads. This is referred to as the baseline hazard in the survival literature.

The resulting hazard function coefficient estimates for the five asset classes, pre- and post-Lehman, are presented in Tables 13.4 and 13.5. For ease of exposition, we report hazard ratios (with corresponding z-statistics in italics). Hazard rates are the exponentiated coefficient estimates, for example, $\exp(\beta k)$ (see Appendix 13.1). A hazard ratio of unity, for example, means that a one-unit change in the risk factor has no impact on the hazard. A hazard ratio of 1.5 means the hazard function rises by a factor of 1.5 for a one-unit change in the risk factor, while a hazard ratio of 0.5

TABLE 13.4   Hazard Ratios (data through August 31, 2008)

	Hazard Ratio		
	VIX	Liquidity	Default
U.S.	1.11	2.14	2.49
	5.69	3.62	3.59
Non-U.S.	1.13	1.61	0.88
	6.93	2.05	−0.41
Fixed Income	0.95	1.75	3.52
	−2.74	2.97	4.99
High Yield	1.06	1.14	1.57
	3.27	0.57	1.65
REITs	1.03	4.86	0.49
	2.13	7.7	−2.54

z-statistics italicized

suggests the same change in the risk factor lowers the hazard function by half. Thus, hazard ratios less than unity mean hazard risk falls as the related risk factor rises (and hence the negative z-statistic) while hazard ratios above unity means higher hazard risk for the same change in risk factor. Hazard ratios close to unity mean that hazard risk is relatively unresponsive to the risk factor. From Table 13.4, for the period before the fall of 2008, we can see that for U.S. equity, the default spread has the greatest impact on failure, indicating that a 1 percent increase in the default spread raises the risk of failure by a factor of almost 2.5. For non-U.S. equity, liquidity has the greatest impact; an equivalent increase in the TED spread raises the hazard by a factor of 1.6. All five asset classes have risks relatively neutral to the VIX. REITs have the biggest sensitivity to liquidity with a hazard ratio of 4.86, but for which an equivalent increase in the default spread actually cuts the risk of failure in the REIT market in half.

Table 13.5 updates the hazard model parameter estimates for the period that includes the last four months of 2008. The changes are economically meaningful and demonstrate the importance of updating the models' parameters. For U.S. equity, the default spread becomes even more important, completely subsuming the influence of liquidity, now statistically insignificant. On the other hand, downside risk in the high yield market is now very sensitive to default and liquidity.

During the fall of 2008, the default spread, as proxied by DEF, remained at its high through the end of the year while the TED spread fell back to its pre-Lehman level later during October 2008. This may explain

TABLE 13.5 Hazard Ratios (data through December 31, 2008)

	Hazard Ratio		
	VIX	Liquidity	Default
U.S.	1.03	1.12	3.22
	2.81	*0.87*	*5.29*
Non-U.S.	1.04	1.21	1.45
	3.68	*1.35*	*1.47*
Fixed Income	0.97	1.76	3.00
	–2.12	*4.06*	*4.73*
High Yield	1.03	1.48	2.19
	2.54	*3.47*	*3.38*
REITs	1.03	2.49	0.64
	3.06	*8.76*	*–1.87*

z-statistics italicized

why the liquidity factor carries less weight in the full period analysis—fail events and hazards were both peaking by late October as the TED spread was actually declining.

Plots of recursive baseline hazards for the five asset classes are presented in Figure 13.2. The hazard models are estimated over a one-year *trailing* moving window beginning January 4, 2008, and ending March 30, 2009.

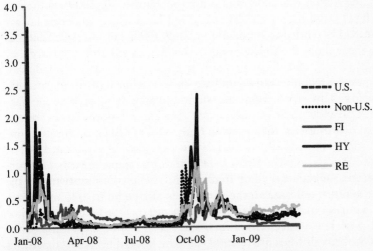

FIGURE 13.2 Baseline Hazards January 2008 to March 2009

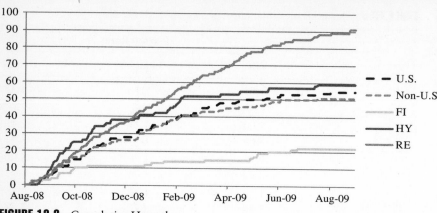

FIGURE 13.3   Cumulative Hazards

The January 4, 2008 hazards are estimated using the prior one year of daily returns and factor observations, and then the oldest observation is dropped as the January 5, 2008 data are added. This one-year window is moved forward through March 31, 2009. One can see a clear transition to higher tail risks across asset classes between September 2008 and October 2008, and declining thereafter but with resurgence in early 2009 as equity markets reached their lows.

Alternatively, we can observe cumulative fail events across asset classes. These are given in Figure 13.3 as the observed sums of threshold exceedances, beginning August 30, 2008, and ending September 30, 2009. By the end of 2008, REITs and high yield (HY) had the highest incidences of failure and all but REITs tended to moderate in 2009. REIT tail losses continue to accelerate throughout the spring of 2009 ahead of their baseline hazard (see Figure 13.2).

The question remains: How good are these baseline hazards at forecasting fail events? This is a difficult question to answer because baseline hazards do not provide point estimates that give exact failure dates. For the exponential distributions, the expected time to failure $E(T)$, or duration until the threshold is breached, is equal to the reciprocal of the hazard $\lambda(t, x, \beta)$ estimated in equation (3). Thus, $E(T) = 1/\lambda$. A baseline hazard of 10 percent, therefore, suggests a spell of 10 days until the next failure event. In the case of the exponential hazard, the variance is also equal to $1/\lambda$, and therefore, the exponential has standard deviation of $(1/\lambda)^{1/2}$. To get an idea of predictive power, we selected for each asset class all the days from January 4, 2008, through March 31, 2009, on which a fail event occurred. As investors, we care about forecasting the time to failure for the next such event. Thus, for each of those days, we compute $E(T)$ from that day's baseline hazard estimate and find the difference between duration predicted by the model on that day and the subsequent observed duration until failure. There was, for example, a fail event (threshold exceedance) in U.S. equity on January 4, 2008. The baseline hazard updated using the data through January 4, 2008, predicted the next event to occur in 10 days, indicating a standard deviation of $\sqrt{10}$. The observed duration turned out to be seven days, which showed that the prediction was three days too long but still well within a 2-sigma band (the error −3 days was less than $-2*\sqrt{10}$). There were 59 threshold exceedances for U.S. equity between January 4, 2008, and March 31, 2009. Of these, the baseline hazard predicted 76.27 percent of the subsequent durations to failure, that is, the observed durations lie within 2-sigma of $E(T)$ estimated from the previous failure date. Note that these results do not use revised baseline hazards. Revisions would imply that if, for example, the observed duration was 14 days from the current failure, we would get to revise our baseline hazard 13 more times until that event occurred. This was not the case. We forecast instantaneous durations conditional on information available on the current day and therefore represent unrevised forecasts. We summarize these results in Table 13.6.

In general, baseline hazard forecasts are more accurate the higher the incidence of threshold exceedance because they condition their likelihood estimates from an increasing incidence of failures. While this is an attractive property, it is also true that for asset classes characterized by a small number of failures, baseline hazards may have a less accurate forecasting record as well as increased incidence of false positives.

To summarize the analysis thus far, EVT is a univariate procedure; its objective is to model the distribution of extreme negative returns and provide some diagnostics on the stability of the distributions of these returns. We use EVT here to monitor tail risks. The baseline hazard, on the other hand, is a multivariate model of time to failure. Its role is to signal the risk of instantaneous failure and help risk managers monitor this particular risk conditional on a set of risk factors. It also provides a forecast of time to failure that can

TABLE 13.6

	Accuracy
U.S.	76.27%
Non-U.S.	63.64%
Fixed Income	23.68%
High Yield	66.15%
REITs	78%

be used to anticipate future fail events. The power of this model depends on factor selection and the asset class itself. Clearly, we have expended little effort on factor selection; rather, our focus is on method. Our primary interest in baseline hazards is to assess the impact on the hazard from changes in risk factors, that is, to conduct sensitivity analysis and to monitor the evolution of these risks through time and across asset classes.

These two methods represent an important extension to the typical, Gaussian VaR model. Moreover, because standard VaR models use Gaussian distributions, VaR estimates change with the standard deviation of the entire distribution of returns and not the downside tail risk that we wish to focus on. Because standard deviation weights all returns equally, it will tend to evolve more slowly in response to realized extreme losses. Thus, standard VaR tends to *underweight* extreme values just as our attention is necessarily focused on the left tail of the distribution of returns. Contrary to standard VaR, our EVT model adjusts its risk parameters with high frequency in accordance with market dynamics. We then use our EVT scaffolding to build a robust daily risk hazard model with dynamic linkages to the capital markets. The linkages include volatility, liquidity, and default risk, and can be expanded further in future research efforts. With these attributes, our hazard model gives us the relationship between the market environment and the probability that the environment is either entering (or already in) a crisis.

A SYSTEMIC RISK INDICATOR

We now turn to our main objective, which is to model systemic risk. The importance of systemic risk is well understood; it manifests itself in the form of higher positive correlations between returns, thereby reducing benefits from diversification, which could lead to significant losses. We define a systemic event as the simultaneous failure of numerous markets or asset classes. For our purposes, we settle on a specific definition of a systemic risk event as one in which three or more of the five asset classes fail on any given day (that is, their returns all exceed their respective thresholds). We can also use the markets of countries to define systemic risk. For example, systemic risk could be defined as the simultaneous failure of three countries.

To describe this mathematically, the systemic event, y is a binary dependent variable that takes the value 1 on a day in which there is a systemic event, and zero otherwise. We use a logistic regression to model the relationship between the likelihood of the systemic event, y, conditional on our three covariates: volatility (specifically, the daily growth rate in the VIX as well as its daily change), default risk (AAA spread over the 10-year Treasury), and liquidity (TED spread). See Greene (2002) for an introduction to

TABLE 13.7 Systemic Risk Index Model

	β	z	Odds Ratio
G_VIX	0.27	*5.91*	1.304
ΔG_VIX	−0.1	*−3.22*	0.9056
Liquidity	*1.03*	2.32	2.813
Default	2.09	*4.09*	8.069
Constant	−9.46	*−8.58*	

logit and probit models and Maddala (1983) on general limited dependent variable models. We therefore estimate the parameters of the following logistic function by maximum likelihood (qualitative differences weren't found by using a probit (normal density). Logistic density was chosen because it has fatter tails:

$$P(y = 1 | G\_vix, \Delta G\_vix, \text{default}, \text{liq}) = \exp(z)/[1 + \exp(z)]$$

$$z = \beta_0 + \beta_1 G\_vix + \beta_2 \Delta G\_vix + \beta_3 \text{default} + \beta_4 \text{liq}$$

The parameters for this equation are estimated using daily data through August 31, 2008, and are presented in Table 13.7. Perfect foresight forecasts are generated through September 30, 2009, and are depicted in Table 13.8. Our intent is to present the model as we would have seen it as risk managers on August 31, 2008. Perfect foresight assumes we know the factors' values one day forward. Clearly, we do not, but the point here is to illustrate the model and to examine the odds ratios.

As with the hazard models, interpretation of the systemic risk model's parameters are easier after exponentiating the coefficient estimates that, in the case of the logistic function, transforms the analysis to odds ratios in which odds refers to the ratio $P/(1 - P)$, where P is the probability that at least three markets simultaneously exceed their thresholds on any given day. In Table 13.7, therefore, we see that by far, the default factor has the greatest impact in determining the probability that three or more of these markets will experience joint extreme returns on any given day. Furthermore, the model suggests that a 1 percent increase in the default spread increases the odds of a systemic event by a factor of eight. Liquidity is also a highly important covariate. A similar 1 percent increase in the TED spread (liquidity) would produce an odds ratio close to three. Changes in the daily growth of the VIX are more benign but nevertheless significant as well.

For our systemic risk index, given in Figure 13.4, we estimated the parameters of the logit model as of August 31, 2008, and then predicted the

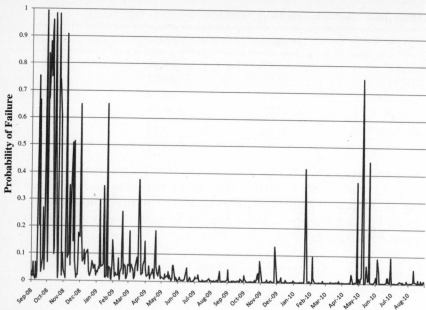

FIGURE 13.4 Probability of Systemic Failure

probability of systemic risks going forward conditional on the observed daily values of the three risk factors. The index appears to track well the actual experience, spiking in September 2008, peaking in October 2008, and then tailing off in the fourth quarter only to resurge as the market bottomed in March 2009. One can see the Flash Crash as well in the spring of 2010.

Month-by-month counts of systemic events during the crisis along with the average value of the systemic risk index are summarized in Table 13.8. The risk index reached a peak in October 2008, coinciding with eight systemic events. The default spread in October of 2008 was fully 50 bps higher on average compared to September 2008 and the TED spread (liquidity) jumped from an average of 200 bps to 343 bps over the same period. Even if one could not have forecasted these factor changes, sensitivity analysis based on projections concerning default spreads, liquidity, and volatility would have been very useful in monitoring the likelihood of joint tail risk.

The systemic risk indicator developed here identifies structural changes in markets across a time series of returns and is simultaneously applied to a variety of markets. This high frequency systemic risk indicator reacts in real time to how information and shocks feed back into the evolution of

TABLE 13.8 Systemic Risk Index and Corresponding Systemic Events

Year	Month	Index	Events
2008	7	0.90%	0
2008	8	0.90%	0
2008	9	17%	4
2008	10	50.40%	8
2008	11	22%	6
2008	12	11.80%	3
2009	1	11.60%	4
2009	2	5%	2
2009	3	9.70%	4

markets. In other words, we effectively explore how stochastic market returns depend on both time and the state of capital markets. In short, this framework provides investors with a picture of the changing nature of risk during crises and provides a valuable guide to helping manage that risk.

SUMMARY

Systemic market events arise with increasing frequency in our complex, adaptive, and highly interconnected markets. Distributions of returns in these markets show leptokurtic and asymmetric characteristics, which are particularly ill-suited to the standard Value at Risk methods. Appealing to extreme value theory, we model the incidences of extreme losses witnessed recently across various global markets. Specifically, we generate maximum likelihood estimates of the generalized extreme value and generalized Pareto distributions and show how risk migrated further into the tails of these distributions as the financial crisis unfolded after the collapse of Lehman Brothers in September of 2008. We then extend our analysis to a multivariate framework using hazard models to track the instantaneous risk that returns will fall into the extreme region of the tail conditional on movements in underlying risk factors such as market volatility, liquidity, and credit risk. Finally, we use a logistic model to estimate the probability of systemic risk—the joint probability that returns across markets simultaneously cross the threshold into the left tail. In sum, we present evidence of parametric shifts toward more extreme downside risks across many asset classes during the crisis with sharply rising hazards that are sensitive to market volatility, changes in liquidity, and credit risk. Also, we present a barometer of systemic risk, also conditional on these same risk factors. We believe that these three models offer a potentially useful framework for monitoring risk as well as for conducting sensitivity and scenario analyses. Our research effort aims to provide tools for a better fundamental understanding of dynamic portfolio risk from an empirical standpoint. This approach presents a plausible set of models that help identify market risk across the global financial system and monitor the evolution of market risk across time.

REFERENCES

Bookstaber, Richard. 2007. *A demon of our own design*. Hoboken, NJ: John Wiley & Sons.

Cotter, John. 2006. Modelling catastrophic risk in international equity markets: An extreme value approach. *Applied Financial Economics Letters* 2(1): 13–17. (www.informaworld.com/smpp/content~content=a741568766~db=all).

Embrechts, Paul, Claudia Klüppelberg, and Thomas Mikosch. 1997. *Modelling extremal events for insurance and finance*. Berlin: Springer-Verlag.

Greene, William H. 2002. *Econometric analysis*. 5th ed. Upper Saddle River, NJ: Prentice-Hall.

Kiefer, Nicholas M. 1988. Economic duration data and hazard functions. *Journal of Economic Literature* 26(2): 646–679.

Koenker, Roger, and Gilbert Bassett Jr. 1978. Regression quantiles. *Econometrica* 46(1): 33–50.

LeBaron, Blake, and Ritirupa Samanta. 2004. *Extreme value theory and fat tails in equity markets*. Working Paper.

Ledford, Anthony W., and Jonathan A. Tawn. 1996. Statistics for near independence in multivariate extreme values. *Biometrika* 83(1): 169–187.

Longin, François, and Bruno Solnik. 2001. Extreme correlation of international equity markets. *Journal of Finance* 56(2): 649–676.

Maddala, Gangadharrao S. 1983. *Limited-dependent and qualitative variables in econometrics*. New York: Cambridge University Press.

Malevergne, Yannick, Vladilen Pisarenko, and Didier Sornette. 2006. On the power of generalized extreme value (GEV) and generalized Pareto distribution (GPD) estimators for empirical distributions of log-returns. *Applied Financial Economics* 16(3): 271–289.

Mood, Alexander M., Franklin A. Graybill, and Duane C. Boes. 1974. *Introduction to the theory of statistics* 3rd ed. New York: McGraw-Hill.

Sullivan, Rodney N. 2008. Taming global village risk. *Journal of Portfolio Management* 34(4): 58–67.

Sullivan, Rodney N. 2009. Taming global village risk II: Understanding and mitigating bubbles. *Journal of Portfolio Management* 35(4): 131–141.

Waldrop, Mitchell. 1992. *Complexity*. New York: Simon & Schuster.

CHAPTER 14

Incorporating Subjective Views

Not everything that can be counted counts and not everything that counts can be counted.

—Albert Einstein

The fictional trustees from Chapter 10 established a strategic allocation to stocks and bonds (70/30) and then actively managed around that with the assistance of two managers. By definition, active management produces active risk. Because active risk is viewed as a cost over the benchmark risk of a passive-only strategy, prudence suggests that the trustees establish an upper bound on the acceptable amount of active risk and allocate that risk across the active positions in the portfolio. This is the basis of risk budgeting.

A strategic asset allocation is a set of weights that target a portfolio's asset mix consistent with some predetermined policy goal. This portfolio generates variable risk and return through time, which require management if the strategy is to remain optimal. Risk management operates on two levels: an allocation across strategic asset classes (70/30) and an allocation within programs (the 80/20 mix as well as the risk at the manager level). Aggregating manager-level risk within and across programs produces an estimate of total risk. It is total risk that is the management objective.

The measure of risk we are interested in is the covariation in asset returns. Risk, in general, is estimated as the portfolio-weighted average of these covariances. With given covariances, risk management reduces to managing a set of portfolio weights. In a passively managed portfolio especially, there is little room for budgeting outside of finding a mean-variance efficient portfolio; all risk is benchmark risk and there is nothing to budget without fundamentally altering the risk-return profile.

A more realistic depiction has investment managers pursuing both passive and active strategies. Because active returns are the difference between the manager's strategy and the benchmark return, active risk is a combination of risk associated with movement in the market as well as the residual return associated with nonmarket moves (the strategy). As such, risk management is now the act of allocating passive *and* active risk and it is the presence of active risk that makes risk budgeting an interesting problem. Why? The mean of the residual return, after the active return is adjusted for the market exposure, measures the manager's contribution over the purely passive benchmark return, that is, alpha. That is, $\alpha = (r\_i) - \beta(r\_m)$ in our simple CAPM. As such, it is uncorrelated with market risk and, hence, there will always be a demand for active risk in the plan as long as the ratio of return to the marginal contribution to active risk across programs is not equal. Recall that the marginal contribution to active risk MCAR is generated by incrementally allocating (cash) to a program (manager). If the ratios of returns to MCAR vary across programs, then risk can be budgeted to exploit these differentials until equilibrium is restored. The allure of active risk suggests that it be allocated much like any other asset in the portfolio. The challenge is do it efficiently.

Active risk is therefore the raison d'être to risk budgeting. The process of risk budgeting can take various forms, such as porting alpha and devising active risk overlays. *Portable alpha,* for example, is an attempt to exploit differences in the ratios of active returns to active risk. To see this conceptually, consider a case in which we are very confident that a particular small cap manager will generate relatively high active returns. Hiring that manager exposes the fund to active risk, for which there is a positive demand, but the increased small cap market exposure will violate the plan's strategic allocation to size. Independently budgeting a short small cap index position simultaneously with a long large cap index position in futures ports the small cap manager's alpha (active return) to the large cap index. Although he still manages to the small cap benchmark, the long-short futures position effectively eliminates the increased small cap exposure with the large cap index futures position. The plan gets exposure to the desired active risk without violating its strategic allocation.

METHODOLOGICAL CONCEPTS

Seen in this light, risk budgeting is a method for allocating active risk. In times in which valuations in general are falling or stagnant and plans must face funding shortfalls, active risk is a commodity that can be allocated along with the remaining assets in the portfolio.

What does it mean to be confident in a view that a particular manager will generate relatively superior active returns? Budgeting active risk is predicated on ranking relative likelihoods of success among active managers. On an intuitive level, confidence in a view is inversely related to the level of active risk (or just returns volatility). More formally, confidences can be implied using the estimated moments of the returns distribution (sample covariances and mean returns) in conjunction with a set of views concerning relative asset performance (for example, small cap stocks will outperform large cap stocks by 50 basis points). Similarly, a set of views and their respective confidences will produce a set of expected returns that reflect a mix of sample information (covariances and mean returns) and prior information (views and associated confidences). Black and Litterman (1992) describe these expected returns as the mean of the posterior distribution in a Bayesian setup in which sample information is mixed with prior information in an optimal way. We cover this topic in more detail further on. This so-called Black-Litterman model was refined further in He and Litterman (1999); more accessible versions can be found in Idzorek (2003). We use the Black-Litterman model as well in our approach to risk budgeting as a formal method of incorporating views and risks in a risk budgeting framework. Mean-variance optimizers require a covariance matrix and a vector of expected returns. Up to now, we have seen how variances can be decomposed to highlight the impact of small changes in individual asset contributions to portfolio risk. We now develop in more detail the expected return assumption. In the introduction, we discussed briefly an example in which we wanted to gain exposure to the active risk in a hypothetical small cap strategy by porting its alpha onto a large cap futures position. The important point to make here is the *belief* that this active strategy would work.

Mixing Subjective Beliefs with the Historical Record

All portfolio managers have beliefs about forward expected returns, and these beliefs do not necessarily need to be consistent with the historical record. (The manager may have insight into future developments not in the historical record.) And because expected returns are generally more difficult to estimate than volatilities and covariances, debate centers less on covariance estimates and more on return estimation. One question that arises is how a meaningful discussion can be facilitated concerning differences in expected returns and their impact on portfolio allocation and risk. The Black-Litterman model provides a platform for constructive debate.

Suppose we have a vector of expected returns generated from either historical data or a factor model and a covariance matrix. Assume covariances are taken as given. Now, suppose that, *independent* of expected returns, a manager opines the *view* that asset class X (for example, the small cap strategy) will outperform asset class Y by some stated amount. As a consequence of this view, he proposes an increase in the allocation to asset X. (Forget about their respective volatilities for now and just assume that the volatility for X is no more than for Y.)

How do we assess this view? Is it risky? How confident should we be in the view itself? What are the implications for plan-wide risk? To answer this question, we must consider first the relative confidence in the view and the impact this has on our existing covariance matrix. The covariance matrix summarizes our current beliefs about risk. Views complicate that picture. More specifically, unless we are 100 percent confident in the view(s), then we must update our estimates of risk by adding to our covariance matrix another matrix summarizing confidences in our views. If we have only a single view (there are no limits to the number of views, however), then that simply means we have zero views on the remaining asset returns, and the matrix summarizing confidences in views is populated mostly by zeros. The point is that the revised covariance matrix is a combination of the original covariances and the view confidences. Lower confidences imply revising the original covariances upward by proportionately more.

What does this have to do with assessing the impact of the view? The view itself almost never replaces the expected return unless we have 100 percent confidence. Rather, the view modifies the expected return. Black-Litterman provides an optimal method for modification. More specifically, the modified expected return vector is a weighted average of the original expected return and the view(s). The weights are a function of the original covariance matrix and the matrix of view confidences. In Bayesian probability theory, the revised returns are the means of the posterior distribution. The views can be thought of as being combined with the priors (original covariances and expected returns) to form the posterior. It is the mean of this posterior and the posterior covariance matrix that find their way into the mean-variance optimization problem. Solving this yields an allocation reflecting the views and the risk or tracking error on the revised portfolio along with associated measures of risk decomposition and attribution discussed in the previous section.

Some detail will illuminate these ideas. Since the Black-Litterman method is covered in so many other citations, for example, Idzorek, that we leave many of the details to those papers. Think of priors as composed of the sample vector of expected returns and the covariance matrix that are estimated from historical returns. Expected returns, for example, could be the plan's long-run forward returns expectations. Denote these as Π. Therefore, observed returns are distributed around Π with error ε_u, according to:

$$\mu = \Pi + \varepsilon_u \; ; \Pi = E(r)$$

and assume that returns are normally distributed, that is, $\mu \sim N(\Pi, \tau V)$, where V is the covariance matrix of returns and the parameter τ simply scales this matrix. (We can ignore τ's contribution in the discussion that follows, so let us set it equal to 1.)

As an aside, Black and Litterman argue that market capitalization weights wm satisfy demand and supply equilibrium at any moment in time, thus suggesting a set of implied returns. That is, if the objective is to find the mean-variance efficient portfolio by maximizing:

$$\Pi w\_m - \lambda \left(w\_m^{\wedge'} V w\_m \right)$$

(λ is the risk aversion parameter) with respect to wm, yielding $\Pi^{\wedge} = \lambda V w\_m$. The $\Pi^{\wedge}$ are implied by the equilibrium cap weights (hence, implied returns). As a further aside, if V is ill conditioned, then small changes in wm will generate large swings in implied returns. This suggests that close attention be paid to the eigenvalues in V.

Note that expected returns—our forward-looking returns expectations that appear under the heading $E(r)$ in the risk budgeting spreadsheet are the same as Π; these are the returns we expect to prevail in equilibrium.

Views can be captured in an $m \times k$ matrix P (m may be any size), which has one row for each view. For example, with $k = 3$, a view about the sum of the returns to assets one and two is captured by putting the first row in P equal to $(1 - 1\ 0)$. A second view that targets the average return to assets two and three is represented by setting the second row in P equal to $(0, .5, .5)$. The vector μ' is (μ_1, μ_2, μ_3) for this example and the product $P\mu$ is therefore a 2×1 vector of returns consistent with these views. For example, if view one is that the sum of the returns to assets one and two is zero and the second view is that the average return across assets two and three is 3 percent, then we have $P\mu = Z = (0, 3)'$. Now model view uncertainty by including a normally distributed error term such that:

$$P\mu = Z + \varepsilon_v$$

Then, $Z|\mu$ is distributed $N(P\mu, \Omega)$, meaning that the conditional distribution of view-consistent returns has mean $P\mu$ and that ε_v has covariance matrix Ω. This last matrix captures the confidences associated with the views that we discussed earlier. Application of Bayes's rule yields the posterior distribution of returns with mean and variance given by:

$$\mu^* = \left[V^{-1} + P'\Omega^{-1}P \right]^{-1} \left[P'\Omega^{-1}Z + V^{-1}\Pi \right]$$

$$V^* = \left[V^{-1} + P'\Omega^{-1}P \right]^{-1}$$

The first term in $\mu*$ is $V*$—the posterior covariance matrix. Notice that it includes the old covariance matrix (the prior) and is supplemented by a matrix-weighted average of view confidences given by Ω. The second term is a combination of the prior returns given in Π weighted by their prior covariances plus the views Z weighted by their covariances. Thus $\mu*$ is the sum of two expected returns: the prior Π and the views Z with weights given by:

$$\left[V^{-1} + P'\Omega^{-1}P \right]^{-1} P'\Omega^{-1}, \left[V^{-1} + P'\Omega^{-1}P \right]^{-1} V^{-1}\Pi$$

Hence, the revised (posterior) mean reflects the prior information and the views in an optimal way in the sense that the weighting maximizes the likelihood of seeing $\mu*$.

Altering views changes P (and therefore Z) while view confidences are adjusted within Ω. In this way, the Black-Litterman methodology supports any number of views and the effect on the expected return and risk that optimally incorporates both view information and risk. Portfolio implications are the direct result of solving the mean-variance optimization problem with these new parameters. MCAR and attribution statistics can then be extracted in the manner outlined in the previous section. In sum, management has at its disposal, a platform for analyzing differing risk and return assumptions.

That leaves one additional point, which pertains to calibrating the values in the matrix Ω.

Intuitively, one would believe that view confidence would be inversely related to the underlying volatilities in the assets comprising the view. For example, our earlier view that the sum of the returns to the first two assets would be zero would ostensibly depend inversely upon their relative volatilities. Typically, these confidence are captured by making Ω a diagonal matrix with elements $p_i V p_i' = \Omega_i$. For example, in the two-asset case with a single view indicating that the sum of returns to assets X and Y is zero, this entry would consist of a function of the differences between the variances and covariances between the first two assets (since p_i is a row vector associated with this one view and has all other elements equal to zero). Specifically, $p_i V p_i'$ is now:

$$[1 - 1] \begin{bmatrix} \sigma_x^2 & \sigma_{xy} \\ \sigma_{yx} & \sigma_y^2 \end{bmatrix} \begin{bmatrix} 1 \\ -1 \end{bmatrix}$$

which, upon solving, yields:

$$\Omega_i = \sigma_x^2 + \sigma_y^2 - 2\sigma_{xy}$$

This is intuitively appealing; the risk of being wrong is linear in the sum of the variances of the underlying returns. As this quantity gets large, the weight on the view, that is,

$$\left[V^{-1} + P'\Omega^{-1}P \right]^{-1} P'\Omega^{-1}$$

in forming the prior goes to zero and the posterior expected return $\mu*$ converges to the prior. Increasing confidence, on the other hand, drives the weight on the prior to zero, leaving the view to determine the posterior $\mu*$. This is an appealing result. Nevertheless, there is no requirement that Ω reflect linear combinations of the underlying asset covariations. Alternatively, this matrix might reflect a more independently determined set of distributional assumptions and we leave that open to further debate, as it is beyond the scope of this book.

AN EXAMPLE USING BLACK-LITTERMAN

To illuminate concepts but minimize the size of the problem and associated math, consider a portfolio of stocks and bonds with returns data beginning monthly in June of 1978. Stocks are U.S. equity with a custom benchmark (R3000, S&P 500) and the benchmark for fixed income is the Lehman Aggregate. Let's ignore the benchmarks for now and concentrate on the program returns. Suppose that the forward-looking returns assumptions are that, in equilibrium, these will earn 7.10 and 5.30 percent, respectively. Thus $\Pi = (7.10, 5.30)'$. Using the historical returns, we estimate the covariance matrix to be:

$$V = \begin{bmatrix} 275 & 29 \\ 29 & 68 \end{bmatrix}$$

Volatilities are the square roots of the diagonal elements and indicate that stocks and bonds have volatilities equal to 16.57 percent and 8.27 percent, respectively, since 1978. Consider now a meeting in which two views are proposed. View one is that stocks will outperform bonds by 300 basis points. View two is that bonds will earn 6.0 percent. (Thus, view one implies that the stocks will earn 9.0 percent). Returns are thereby expected to change to:

$$Q = \begin{bmatrix} 9.0 \\ 6.0 \end{bmatrix}$$

The view matrix is now

$$P = \begin{bmatrix} 1 & -1 \\ 0 & 1 \end{bmatrix}$$

Simply adopting these views would suggest we have 100 percent confidence in each. Suppose we do not. Instead, we relate confidence in a view to the volatilities contained in V by computing the diagonal matrix:

$$\Omega = \begin{bmatrix} \Omega_1 & 0 \\ 0 & \Omega_2 \end{bmatrix}$$

We link views P to underlying volatilities V by setting:

$$\Omega_1 = p_1 V p_1' = \begin{bmatrix} 1 & -1 \end{bmatrix} \begin{bmatrix} 275 & 29 \\ 29 & 68 \end{bmatrix} \begin{bmatrix} 1 \\ -1 \end{bmatrix} = 286$$

and where p_1 is the first row of P. The second row operation produces $\Omega_2 = 68$. Replacing these values into Ω, we get:

$$\Omega = \begin{bmatrix} 268 & 0 \\ 0 & 68 \end{bmatrix}$$

Recall that whereas V models uncertainty with respect to the prior Π, Ω models uncertainty with respect to views. Note that the view and prior uncertainty associated with the bond return are identical at 68. This reflects the confidence in the bond return view being tied to the historical volatility in V but which is unrelated to volatility in stocks. The confidence in the view on stocks, however, does involve the view on the bonds and, because of their positive covariation, the confidence in the view on stocks suffers somewhat ($\Omega_1 = 286 > V_1 = 275$).

Solving equation $\mu*$ for the posterior expected returns yields:

$$\mu^* = \begin{bmatrix} 10.61 \\ 5.39 \end{bmatrix}$$

with posterior covariance matrix:

$$V^* = \begin{bmatrix} 153.12 & 23.36 \\ 23.36 & 33.47 \end{bmatrix}$$

V^* has no zero or negative eigen values and its condition number is 5.42, implying that the posterior covariance matrix is positive semi-definite and invertible. (Actually, as long as V and Ω are each positive semi-definite, then the sum of two positive semi-definite matrices is itself positive semi-definite.)

These posterior parameter estimates can then be substituted into the (unconstrained) mean-variance optimization problem:

$$w'\mu - \frac{\lambda}{2}(w'Vw)$$

from which the view portfolio w is solved. Using $\mu*$ and $V*$ (and assuming $\lambda = 2.25$), the view portfolio consists of a (0.28, 0.72) mix of the stocks and bonds. Compare this allocation with the prior allocation at $\Pi = (7.1, 5.3)'$ and V, which requires a mix of (0.21, 0.79), respectively. The view, therefore, shifts the portfolio in the direction of stocks. Most of this shift is due to the 300 bps expected spread between stock and bond returns but which is attenuated by the (lack of) confidence in the view itself.

Had we simply substituted the views Q for μ earlier and retained the prior covariances in V, the allocation would not have shifted far enough (it would now be 0.24, 0.76, respectively) because the covariance matrix V does not account for how our confidence in the views affect returns covariances. This is a very important point. *A view implicitly, but fundamentally, alters the return stream and* its covariances with the remaining assets. While it is tempting to insert one's view on returns, it is wrong to blithely assume that risks don't change to reflect those views. In essence, V alone is misspecified.

ACTIVE SPACE

Let's consider now an application in active space. To do so, we now need to include benchmark returns for stocks (US) and bonds (FI). We estimate the covariance matrix Q for all four returns series, which we will refer to as the combined covariance matrix V_c:

$$V_c = \begin{bmatrix} 275 & 29 & 269 & 23 \\ 29 & 68 & 31 & 58 \\ 269 & 31 & 270 & 24 \\ 23 & 58 & 24 & 51 \end{bmatrix}$$

Again, the top left quadrant is the 2×2 covariance matrix (V) for the program returns while the bottom right 2×2 matrix are benchmark covariances. The top right and bottom left 2×2 matrices estimate covariances across programs and benchmarks. The covariances in active space can be estimated by transforming V_c as in equation (8) generating $V_a = m'V_c m$:

$$V_a = \begin{bmatrix} 7.29 & -1.04 \\ -1.04 & 3.34 \end{bmatrix}$$

Thus, the *active* risks on stocks and bonds are the square roots of the diagonal (2.70, 1.83).

In the previous example, equilibrium returns were the forward-looking expectations $\Pi' = (7.1, 5.3)$. Since these returns are what managers expect to prevail over the long run, then they are, in essence, managers' expectations of equilibrium. Views, on the other hand, denote short-run deviations from equilibrium. From the previous example, the return view vector $Q' = (9, 6)$ suggests active returns equal to (2.9, 0.7).

Now, suppose management targets an alpha on the portfolio equal to 2 percent. Then the minimum variance active portfolio that achieves the target return (but with active weights constrained to sum to zero) is the solution to the system:

$$\begin{bmatrix} 7.29 & -1.04 & -2.9 & -1 \\ -1.04 & 3.34 & -0.7 & -1 \\ 2.9 & 0.7 & 0 & 0 \\ 1 & 1 & 0 & 0 \end{bmatrix} \begin{bmatrix} w_{a1} \\ w_{a2} \\ \lambda \\ \mu \end{bmatrix} = \begin{bmatrix} 0 \\ 0 \\ 2 \\ 0 \end{bmatrix}$$

where λ and μ are Lagrange multipliers. Notice the presence of V_a in the left-most matrix. On the right-hand side, the third element equal to 2 is the targeted alpha. We wish to solve this system and extract the solution for the active weights (w_{a1}, w_{a2}). Inverting the matrix and multiplying by the vector on the right-hand side yields $(0.87, -0.87) = w_a$. The active portfolio, in the presence of the views, overweights stocks relative to its benchmark (likewise, it underweights bonds). This makes sense in light of managers expecting a 300-basis point spread over equilibrium between stock and bond returns.

What is the active risk on this portfolio? It is $(w_a V_a w_a')^{1/2} = 3.10$. (Had we instead targeted a 1 percent active return on the portfolio, w_a would have been $(0.43, -0.43)$ with active risk equal to 1.55.)

RISK ATTRIBUTION

Keeping the targeted active return at 2 percent, the marginal contribution to active risk for this portfolio is:

$$\text{MCAR} = \frac{d\sigma_a}{dw_a} = \frac{V_a w_a}{\sigma_a} = \begin{bmatrix} 2.33 \\ -1.23 \end{bmatrix}$$

This clearly indicates that, because bonds are underweight relative to the benchmark, then marginal weight increments toward this asset class will lower active risk. Stocks, on the other hand contribute relatively more to active risk, both because they are riskier and because they are overweight relative to their benchmark. Moreover, we can attribute almost twice as much of the active risk ($\sigma_a = 3.10$) to stocks over bonds by estimating attribution risk:

$$\text{Attribution} = w_a. * \frac{V_a w_a}{\sigma_a} = \begin{bmatrix} 2.03 \\ 1.07 \end{bmatrix}$$

Recall that the sum of these must equal the tracking error. Therefore, the active position in stocks comprises about two-thirds of the tracking error. What about the effects of active allocations that deviate from the benchmark? Allocative risk is estimated to be roughly 14.36 percent:

$$\sigma = \left(w_a' V_b w_a \right)^{\frac{1}{2}} = 14.36$$

due primarily to stock overweighting to which we attribute 12.93/14.26, or 91 percent, to the position in stocks:

$$\text{Allocation Attribution} = w_a. * \frac{V_b w_a}{\sigma} = \begin{bmatrix} 12.93 \\ 1.43 \end{bmatrix}$$

Moving to the program weights (recall, the view portfolio was 0.28, 0.72 stocks and bonds), we estimate portfolio risk to be

$$\sigma_p = \left(w_p' V_p w_p \right)^{\frac{1}{2}} = 8.28$$

This is not active risk. It is the risk associated with the view portfolio. Decomposing it into the program level attributions give us:

$$\frac{d\sigma_p}{dw_p} = \frac{V_p w_p}{\sigma_p} = \begin{bmatrix} 11.79 \\ 6.91 \end{bmatrix}$$

Again, most of the risk is tied to stocks, but in this particular portfolio:

$$\text{Portfolio Attribution} = w_p. * \frac{V_p w_p}{\sigma_p} = \begin{bmatrix} 3.30 \\ 4.98 \end{bmatrix}$$

$4.98/8.28 = 60$ percent is accounted for by the 0.72 weight on bonds.

SUMMARY

Risk budgets force us to control the level of risk, and to budget that risk across assets in the portfolio. In this chapter, I tried to illustrate this task in a world in which managers have views about forward returns that may differ from the historical record. Fisher Black and Robert Litterman provide a method that mixes observed returns and risks from historical data with managers' beliefs in an optimal way. I then complicate this picture by introducing active portfolio management in which managers deviate from an established passive portfolio (the so-called benchmark portfolio) in their effort to produce an active return to their perceived skill. However, active management is not without its constraints; therefore, I show how principals such as trustees of funds restrict managements' departure from the benchmark allocation by imposing a risk budget. The result is that managers are allowed to take on tracking error (active risk) but the amount and allocation of this risk is now evident not only to them (agents) but to their principals as well. Risk budgets have profound implications on the amount of tracking error managers take. Trustees therefore may find that they can control agents through risk budgets and locate active risk sensitivities in the optimal allocation to small deviations in active weights within the risk budget.

REFERENCES

Black, Fisher, and Robert Litterman. 1992. Global portfolio optimization. *Financial Analysts Journal* 48 (September/October).

He, Guangliang, and Robert Litterman. 1999. *The intuition behind Black-Litterman model portfolios.* New York: Goldman Sachs Investment Management Research.

Idzorek, Thomas. 2003. *A step-by-step guide to the Black-Litterman model.* Unpublished Working Paper.

CHAPTER 15

Futures, Forwards, and Swaps

All that glisters is not gold.
—William Shakespeare, *The Merchant of Venice*

INSTITUTIONAL DETAIL AND FUTURES MECHANICS

Futures markets exist because of fundamental uncertainty about how future events will unfold and the concomitant risk that events may turn against us. Uncertainty breeds two types of futures market participants—hedgers, who lock in prices in an effort to eliminate future price volatility and speculators, who bet on their beliefs about future directional movements in prices.

A cattle rancher, for example, may have 120,000 pounds gross weight in a herd that he intends to bring to market in three months. The rancher wants to hedge the uncertainty that cattle prices may fall in the interim. He could enter a contract with a counterparty to sell his cattle *forward* for a price agreed upon today, thereby locking in a price. Alternatively, he could sell *futures* contracts. As we'll see, forwards are simpler versions of futures, not in how they are priced but in how they are managed. If we assume that the live cattle futures contract on the Chicago Mercantile Exchange (CME) is for delivery of 40,000 pounds, the rancher could sell (short) three contracts to deliver his cattle in three months at a price determined today. His short futures position locks in the price of cattle, thereby eliminating the risk of a price decline. The other side of this trade could be taken by a beef processor (or a speculator) who buys the futures contract (goes long), agreeing to take delivery of the cattle at the futures price and thereby eliminating the risk that cattle prices may rise in the interim.

One difference between forwards and futures is that participants generally take delivery in forward markets. In futures markets, this is rarely the case. With a futures hedge, the cattle rancher will still transport his herd to market in three months and receive the spot price (S). Separately, he will close out the short futures position by taking an equal and opposite position; in this case, by buying three long contracts with the same delivery date at price F_1. His cash flow will be the sum of the spot price received plus the gain or loss on his futures position, that is, $S_1 + (F_0 - F_1)$. The futures position will therefore offset the spot price if the price of the futures contract falls by the time he closes out his position. The futures position was just an overlay, whereby the gain or loss on the futures position countered any impact from a change in the spot price. To see this, suppose the spot (market) price for cattle today is $1 per pound and that the rancher sells three futures contracts at $1 per pound. If the spot price three months from now is $0.50 per pound, then the gain on the short futures position offsets the loss in the spot market. That is, he closes out the short futures position (worth $1 per pound) by buying the long futures contract just before delivery at $0.50 per pound. The net $0.50 per pound gain in the futures position in this case exactly offsets the loss in the spot market.

Delivery months differ by commodity type. Corn futures, for example, traded on the Chicago Board of Trade (CBOT) have delivery in March, May, July, September, and December. Crude oil futures, on the other hand, that are traded on the New York Mercantile Exchange (NYMEX) and Treasury bond futures, traded on the CBOT, are quoted in dollars and trade continuously.

Futures are traded on established exchanges using standardized contracts with daily settlement (contracts are marked to market daily) and with a range of settlement dates. As we saw earlier, contracts are typically closed out prior to delivery. Futures also have virtually no credit risk because participants are required to post margin. Table 15.1 illustrates how margin works. Suppose you were taking the long end of the cattle futures trade outlined earlier, obligating you take to delivery at $1 per pound for a total of $120,000. The broker who sold you this contract is exposed to credit risk in the event that you decide to walk away from your end of the deal if spot prices fall. Suppose the broker requires 20 percent ($24,000) margin to be posted and imposes a 75 percent maintenance margin (minimum margin balance in the account) equal to $18,000. Margins are set by the exchange and are generally proportional to the price volatility of the underlying. Each day, the futures position is marked to market, and if the margin balance falls below the maintenance level, there is a margin call whereby the broker requests the investor to post additional margin. The following table illustrates the process of daily settlement over a fictional 14-day period.

On day six, the futures price has fallen enough to deplete the margin account to the point at which the broker calls for the investor to deposit $6,000 in the margin account. On the tenth day, the maintenance margin is again

TABLE 15.1 Futures Mechanics

Day Count	Futures Price	Gain (Loss)	Cumulative Gain (Loss)	Margin Account Balance	Margin Call
	$1.00			$24,000.00	
1	$0.98	–$2,400.00	–$2,400.00	$21,600.00	
2	$0.99	$1,200.00	–$1,200.00	$22,800.00	
3	$0.98	–$1,200.00	–$2,400.00	$21,600.00	
4	$0.97	–$1,200.00	–$3,600.00	$20,400.00	
5	$0.96	–$1,200.00	–$4,800.00	$19,200.00	
6	$0.90	–$7,200.00	–$12,000.00	$12,000.00	$6,000.00
7	$0.91	$1,200.00	–$10,800.00	$19,200.00	
8	$0.90	–$1,200.00	–$12,000.00	$18,000.00	
9	$0.90	$0.00	–$12,000.00	$18,000.00	
10	$0.88	–$2,400.00	–$14,400.00	$15,600.00	$2,400.00
11	$0.89	$1,200.00	–$13,200.00	$19,200.00	
12	$0.88	–$1,200.00	–$14,400.00	$18,000.00	
13	$0.87	–$1,200.00	–$15,600.00	$16,800.00	$1,200.00
14	$0.79	–$9,600.00	–$25,200.00	$8,400.00	$9,600.00

breached, whereby another $2,400 is called and on the thirteenth day, $1,200 is called. By the end of the fourteenth day, the futures price has fallen to $0.79, requiring a margin call of $9,600. The investor then decides to close out the position and sell the three contracts for a total loss of $25,200.

Forward contracts differ from futures on several levels—they are typically nonstandardized, nonexchange, private contracts between parties that are traded over the counter (OTC) with a single delivery date and are usually held to the delivery date. More importantly, since forwards are settled only at the end of the contract period, there exists some credit risk. A typical example would be the case in which an exporter has a contract to sell goods to a foreign buyer at some specific future date and will get paid in foreign currency. The exporter may wish to enter into a forward trade with a counterparty by selling forward the foreign currency today. If, for example, the sale will be paid in euros, the exporter risks receiving fewer dollars if the euro falls against the dollar in the interim (that is, the dollar appreciates and the dollar cost of the euro declines between now and the time the euros are to be exchanged). Shorting a forward contract to deliver euros hedges the risk of a stronger dollar in the future. In this case, if the euro depreciates, meaning it exchanges for fewer dollars, then the short position will increase in value, exactly offsetting the loss. Table 15.2 illustrates the case for a short position taken in January against 500,000 euros to be received in May.

TABLE 15.2 Short Futures

	Short Forward		Short Futures		
	$/euro	Profit	Profit	Interest	Balance
1-Jan	$1.52	$0.00	$0.00	$0.00	$0.00
1-Feb	$1.40	$0.00	$60,000.00	$0.00	$60,000.00
1-Mar	$1.32	$0.00	$40,000.00	$600.00	$100,600.00
1-Apr	$1.30	$0.00	$10,000.00	$1,006.00	$111,606.00
1-May	$1.27	$125,000.00	$15,000.00	$1,116.06	$127,722.06

For illustrative purposes, I include an identical futures position that is settled monthly.

Clearly, the dollar has strengthened against the euro—in this case, by $0.25 per euro. With no forward or futures position, the exporter would have lost $125,000 when exchanging the 500,000 euros for dollars; that is, whereas euros became cheaper in dollar terms, dollars on the other hand became more expensive in euro terms. Thus, the 500,000 euros would have bought, not $1.52 × 500,000 = $760,000, but $1.27 × 500,000 = $635,000. As shown in the table, shorting euros in the forward market, therefore, would have generated a $125,000 profit that would exactly offset the loss to being long euros in May.

A similar position in futures would produce the same qualitative result. The distinction is that futures are settled monthly in this example and interest paid on margin balances at 12 percent annually. Thus, over the course of the contract, the margin account grows in principal and interest, and that explains why the short futures position is worth more. It also shows why margin is important to protect against credit risk; after all, had the dollar depreciated, then the short futures position would have had to adjust margins accordingly to provide protection while no such action would be taken regarding the forward position.

THE RELATIONSHIP BETWEEN SPOT PRICES AND FORWARD (FUTURES) PRICES

Suppose we buy one unit of the commodity at price S on the spot market and simultaneously enter a forward contract to deliver at time T one unit at price F (that is, we short one unit). We store the commodity for a period T and deliver it at price F. The cash flow is $(-S, F)$ which is fully determined at $t = 0$. This cash flow must be fully consistent with the interest rate over that period. Here's why.

Let's let $d(0,T)$ represent the discount rate over the period of the contract. That is $d(0,T) = (1 + r)^{-T}$ where, typically, r is the annual risk-free interest rate. Buying the commodity for future resale at price F must be exactly the same as lending an amount S with ending value equal to S/d $(0,T)$. This implies that $S = F\, d(0,T)$, which is the discounted value of the future payment for the time in question. Thus, the contract is priced so that it has zero value relative to a loan S at the market rate of interest.

If $F > S/d(0,T)$, then an arbitrage profit could be earned by shorting the contract. We could borrow S right now to buy the asset and deliver it at time T for F, keeping $F - S/d(0,T)$. That is, if the future value is higher than what you could earn if you were to invest S at $1/d(0,T)$, then you'd want to receive F later, at time T. To receive F, you store the asset. If, on the other hand, $F < S/d(0,T)$, then clearly it would pay to short the asset and use the proceeds to invest at $1/d(0,T)$. At the same time, we'd go long in the forward contract, agreeing now to purchase the asset at T for F and keeping the difference.

This logic suggests that as the delivery date nears, the forward price F and the spot price S must converge. The reason is that $1/d(0,T)$ must converge to one as T converges to zero. This is illustrated in Figure 15.1. Stated differently, the cash flow $(-S,F)$ must be fully consistent with the existing term structure of interest rates, or else investors will exploit arbitrage opportunities by borrowing and lending at the market rate, either storing the asset for future delivery or shorting the asset, investing the proceeds and taking delivery of the asset for a price less than the value of the investment.

Thus, while at $t = 0$, $F(t)$ and $S(t)$ may be quite different, but as $t \rightarrow T$, these two quantities must converge. The only reason they would not is because either the hedged asset is not the same as the asset used to hedge in the futures market, for example, we hedge our \$/euro exposure using forward

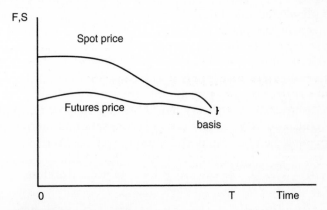

FIGURE 15.1 Basis Risk

contracts on yen, or that the futures contract may need to be closed out before the delivery month. The difference $F(t) - S(t)$ is referred to as the *basis*, and a nonzero basis is a risk, as we shall shortly demonstrate. The diagram shows $S(t) > F(t)$, but it is understood that $S(t) < F(t)$ may hold as well.

HEDGING BASIS RISK

Let's study the case of the hedger who takes a short position in futures at time $t = 1$ and knows that he will close out this position at time $t = 2$. The basis at $t = 1$ is therefore $b_1 = S_1 - F_1$, while the basis at $t = 2$ is $b_2 = S_2 - F_2$. In the case of our cattle rancher, the market price received for selling his herd would be S_2 and the profit on his futures position when he closes it out would be $F_1 - F_2$. The effective price he receives is therefore $S_2 + (F_1 - F_2)$, which by definition equals $F_1 + b_2$.

The value of F_1 is known at $t = 1$, but the basis b_2 at $t = 2$ is not. Were it so, then we would have constructed the perfect hedge. In fact, for the case in which the futures position is closed out on the delivery date and the hedging asset is the underlying, then the basis would be zero at $t = 2$. Since this is not always the case, then the final profit or loss includes b_2 as a risk. To see this more clearly, let S_2' be the spot price of the asset used for hedging. Adding and subtracting this from the effective price the hedger receives at $t = 2$, which from before, is $S_2 + (F_1 - F_2)$, we get:

$$S_2 + (F_1 - F_2) = F_1 + (S_2' - F_2) + (S_2 - S_2')$$

The two terms in parentheses are the components of the basis risk. $S_2 - S_2'$ is the part of the basis represented by the imperfect hedging choice, and $S_2' - F_2$ represents the nonconvergence in the spot to the futures price. If the asset hedged were identical to the hedging asset, then $S_2 = S_2'$ and the two basis components disappear, leaving F_1.

Let's return to our dollar/euro trade as an example. Suppose on January 1 the exporter knows she will receive 500,000 euros on May 1. Suppose euros futures contracts traded on the CME are for 100,000 euros with delivery dates at the close of every month. The exporter therefore decides to short five contracts with delivery date April 30. Suppose that the futures price on January 1 is $1.30 per euro and the spot and futures prices for euros turn out to be $1.275 and $1.27, respectively, on April 30.

The gain on the futures contract is $F_1 - F_2 = \$1.30 - \$1.27 = \$0.03$. The basis $b_2 = \$0.005$. The effective price obtained is therefore:

$$S_2 + (F_1 - F_2) = \$1.275 + (\$1.30 - 1.27) = \$1.305$$

Looked at differently, it is also equal to:

$$F_1 + b_2 = \$1.30 + \$0.005 = \$1.305$$

The total amount received by the exporter is therefore $\$1.305*500,000$ = $\$652,500$. That is, the exporter's hedged position consisted of the spot sale of her euros on April 30 at S_2 along with the (in this case) positive impact of the hedge $(F_1 - F_2)$.

Cross-Hedging

The hedging asset is oftentimes not the same as the asset being hedged. In these instances, the investor must select a hedging asset that is a close substitute (for example, orange juice futures to hedge grapefruit exposure). More specifically, the investor chooses a hedge position that is a function of the correlation between the asset being hedged (the underlying) and the hedging instrument. It should be obvious that if these are the same assets, then the correlation is one and the optimal hedge is to take an equal and opposite position in the futures market for the underlying. If they are not the same asset, then the investor desires to minimize the risk of an imperfect hedge.

Intuitively, the problem lies in the fact that changes in the spot price for the asset being hedged (S) do not vary one for one with changes in the futures price of the hedging instrument (denoted by F). That is, their correlation coefficient (ρ) is not 1. If the investor knew the correlation between S and F, then she would be able to adjust the size of her hedge to minimize the misfit caused by using an imperfect hedging asset.

If the investor had at her disposal a history of futures prices on the hedge instrument as well as the spot prices for the asset being hedged, then regressing S on F would give her the information she'd need to size the hedge. To see this, suppose she estimates the parameters of the following regression:

$$S = \alpha + \beta F + \varepsilon$$

In standard statistics texts it is demonstrated that (also see the appendix to Chapter 5):

$$\beta = \frac{\text{cov}(S, F)}{\text{var}(F)} = \frac{\sigma_{S,F}}{\sigma_F^2} = \rho \frac{\sigma_S}{\sigma_F}$$

If the asset hedged and the hedging asset were the same (no basis risk), then it should be clear that β would equal 1 and we'd hedge using an equal and opposite position in the futures market. Consider then, the case in which β is estimated to be equal to 2. In that case, the covariation between the two assets would be twice the variation in the hedging asset alone. This would imply that a hedge would need to consist of twice the normal position in the futures market because the variation in the underlying futures is half the covariation between it and the underlying asset. Thus, β is the optimal hedge ratio.

Let's prove this. In our livestock futures case, the rancher will go to market and sell his Q pounds of cattle at S_2 per pound. His hedge position has value equal to $(F_1 - F_2) h$, where h is the amount of the hedge (assume this is unknown for the moment). The total cash flow, C, at the time of sale is therefore equal to:

$$C = QS_2 + (F_1 - F_2)h$$

Note that $(F_1 - F_2) h$ represents the profit on the futures position. Absent futures, the cash flow at $t = 2$ will simply be QS_2. We seek the value of h that minimizes the variance of this cash flow. The variance is equal to the sum of the variance of QS_2 denoted as $Q^2 \text{var}(S)$, the variance of $(F_1 - F_2) h$, which we'll denote by $h^2 \text{var}(F)$, and twice their covariance denoted as $2 \text{cov}(S,F)$. This can be written as:

$$\text{Var}(C) = Q^2\text{var}(S) + h^2\text{var}(F) + 2hQ\text{cov}(S,F).$$

Taking the derivative with respect to h and solving yields $h = -Q\beta = -Q\text{cov}(S,F)/\text{var}(F)$. Thus, the optimal hedge is the asset's beta to the hedging asset scaled by the size of the position Q.

HEDGING PORTFOLIO RISK

As an example, recall from Chapter 7 that we estimated $\beta = 2$ against the S&P 500 for Citigroup. Suppose an investor wants to hedge downside risk on an investment in this stock. Suppose there is no futures contract available for Citigroup, but there is a liquid futures market for the S&P 500. This investor could short S&P futures contracts to hedge tail risk on a 2:1 basis. So, if she has a portfolio $P = \$100,000$ in Citigroup stock and one-month S&P 500 futures are at $F = \$1,000$, then she needs to short 200 futures contracts on the S&P 500. That is, the required short futures position N is equal to $-\beta\frac{P}{F}$, where P is the value of the Citigroup portfolio and F is the futures price on the S&P 500.

It is worthwhile noting that short hedges like the one just described effectively change the portfolio's beta. In this case, the portfolio had a beta of 2, which was reduced to zero with the hedge. Thus, the hedge effectively eliminated the portfolio's exposure to broad market movements. In fact, investors can use short and long futures exposures to achieve any desired beta and, with it, the associated risk and return. In the previous example, shorting 100 futures contracts on the S&P 500, for example, would result in hedging out half the downside risk, effectively pulling beta back to 1 on the portfolio. On the other hand, a long futures position equal to 100 contracts will increase the portfolio beta to 3. In general, if $\beta*$ is the desired beta on the portfolio and $\beta > \beta*$, then the investor needs to adopt a short position equal to:

$$(\beta - \beta^*)\frac{P}{F}$$

If, on the other hand, $\beta < \beta*$, then the investor adopts a long futures position equal to:

$$(\beta^* - \beta)\frac{P}{F}$$

Forward with Cost of Carry

Commodities generally cannot be stored at zero cost. Oil for example, was stored in offshore tankers during the runup in oil futures in the summer of 2008. Grain must be siloed in a conditioned environment to prevent spoilage, and livestock require a carrying cost to cover feed, water, grazing, and vet costs. These costs of carry must therefore be reflected in the futures price. Let $c(k)$ equal the per unit per time carrying costs. Then the price of the forward contract F will be the sum of $S/d(0,M)$ plus carry costs compounded over the carry period reflecting the opportunity cost of those expenses, that is, $\Sigma c(k)/d(k,M)$ over $k = 0, \cdots, M - 1$ (M periods). Therefore, the spot price must be $S = d(0,M)$ $F - \Sigma c(k)/d(k,M)*d(0,M) = d(0,M)F - \Sigma c(k)d(0,k)$. This says that the spot price is the sum of the discounted value at time M minus the discounted carrying costs.

EXAMPLE 15.1   Cost of Carry

Assume, for example, that the current cost of oil is $12 per barrel. We wish to find the forward price to be delivered in six months. Carrying costs are 0.10 per barrel per month paid at the beginning of each

(continued)

(*continued*)

month. Suppose the discount rate is calculated from a six-month Treasury bill with a yield of 5 percent. Then $1/d(0,1 \text{ mo.}) = (1 + .05/12) = 1.004$. Given these facts, $F = \$12(1.004)^6 + \Sigma(0.10)(1.004)^k$ for $k = 1, \ldots, 6$, which solves for $F = 12.91$.

FUTURES PRICING

In the previous section, we established the relationship between spot (S) and futures (F) prices as $S = F\, d(0,T)$, where $d(0,T)$ is the discount rate over the period of the futures contract. If it is observed that $S < F\, d(0,T)$ for which the current spot price is below the present value of the futures price there will be an incentive to short the futures contract, buy and store the asset, and then deliver it at time T for F. If, on the other hand, $S > F\, d(0,T)$, there is an incentive to short the asset, invest the proceeds at $d(0,T)$ and go long the futures, taking delivery of the asset at time T for a price F. Either way, there is an arbitrage profit to be made, and since these opportunities will be driven from the market, we conclude that the relationship between spot and futures prices must be fully consistent with the existing term structure of interest rates. Let's now take a closer look at this logic.

Suppose you borrow an amount S, buy one unit of the underlying asset on the spot market at price S, and take a short position in the futures market (to deliver this asset at price F). The total cost of this portfolio is zero, that is, the portfolio is $[-S/d(0,T), F]$. At time T, you deliver the asset for F and repay the loan amount $S/d(0,T)$. This is an equilibrium result. This relationship says that the current spot price is equal to the discounted present value of the futures price. If there were storage costs involved, then F must compensate for those as well as described earlier. Whereas the basic relationship is:

$$S/d(0,T) = F$$

we now have with storage costs:

$$S/d(0,T) = F - \Sigma c(k)/d(k,T)$$

The summation is over the k times in which the cash flows (storage cost payments) occur. Notice that storage costs are compounded, meaning that the futures price must necessarily be higher to compensate for these additional costs. Stated equivalently, the spot price must equal the discounted present value of the future price minus the *compounded* storage costs. We can solve this relation for F:

$$F = S/d(0,T) + \Sigma c(k)/d(k,T)$$

EXAMPLE 15.2   Oil Futures with Storage Costs

Taking the previous example, $S = \$12$ and $d(0,1 \text{ mo.}) = (1 + 0.05/12)^{-1}$. We therefore have the equilibrium relationship given by:

$$12 = \frac{F}{(1.004)^6} - 0.10\{1.004^6 + 1.004^5 + 1.004^4 + 1.004^3 + 1.004^2 + 1.004\}$$

$$F = 12 * (1.004)^6 + 0.10\{1.004^6 + 1.004^5 + 1.004^4 + 1.004^3 + 1.004^2 + 1.004\}$$
$$= 12.90$$

The intuition here is that the current spot price is the discounted futures price adjusted for all of the costs of storage up to the time of delivery. The individual storage costs are compounded, reflecting the opportunity cost of these funds.

EXAMPLE 15.3   Bond Forward

Now consider the following variation on this theme. The current price of a $10,000 face value bond paying an 8 percent coupon with several years yet to go to maturity is $9,260. Assume the yield curve is flat at 9 percent. Find the forward price for delivery in one year.

First recognize that coupons are inflows, whereas storage costs are outflows, so they will get the opposite sign. Since an 8 percent coupon on $10,000 is $400 semiannually, then we have the following equilibrium relationship:

$$9260 = \frac{F + 400}{1.045^2} + \frac{400}{1.045}$$

That is, the current spot price is the discounted present value of all the cash flows including the forward price (or forward valuation). Solve this for $F = \$9,294.15$.

EXAMPLE 15.4   Bond Forward

A 10-year bond is currently selling for $920. A pension manager owns a forward contract of this bond for delivery in one year at a price of
(continued)

(*continued*)
$940. Notice that these past two examples involve forwards, and not futures, since the objective is to take delivery of the asset. The bond pays coupons of $80 every six months with two coupons to be received—one at the end of the current six-month period and another when the contract is delivered. The current interest rates on six-month and one-year Treasury bills are 7 percent and 8 percent, respectively. What is the value of the forward contract?

The logic from the previous example suggests the following

$$F = S/d(0,2) - \Sigma d(0,k)c(k)/d(0,2)$$

where $T = 2$ is for two six-month periods, and $k = 2$ are the two coupons. Making the necessary substitutions, we get the following:

$$F = 920(1.04)^2 - 1.04^2 \left\{ \frac{80}{1.035} + \frac{80}{1.04^2} \right\}$$

We get the first coupon at the end of six months, so 3.5 percent applies as the discount factor to this cash flow and we get the second coupon at the end of the year, which indicates that 4 percent is the appropriate discount factor. The futures price is the compounded value of the spot price and the two discounted coupons. The solution is therefore $F = \$831.47$. The value of the forward contract is the difference between the current value and the delivery price updated (compounded) for one year, for example,

$$F(t) - F(0) = (831.47 - 940) * 1.04^2 = -100.34$$

The intuition underlying these examples should now be clear—the futures or forward price of the asset is the compounded value of the current spot price plus or minus the compounded value of any storage costs or coupons.

EXAMPLE 15.5   Oil Futures

The current spot price for oil is $53.15 per barrel. Assuming that storage costs are $1 per barrel per quarter (payable at the beginning of the quarter) and a flat term structure at 9 percent, what is the forward price of a barrel of oil deliverable in nine months?

The solution should be modeled as follows. The futures price is the compounded spot price for the nine months plus the compounded cost of storing oil beginning in the first quarter for the rest of the nine months, plus the storage costs of the second quarter compounded for the remaining six months and, finally, the storage costs for the last quarter compounded for the last quarter. Thus, we have:

$$F = S/d(0, 9\text{m}) + c(0)/d(0, 9\text{m}) + c(1)/d(3\text{m}, 9\text{m})$$
$$+ c(2)/d(3\text{m}, 9\text{m})$$

We therefore need to solve for the appropriate discount rates. These are, respectively:

$$\frac{1}{\left(1 + \dfrac{0.09}{4}\right)^3}, \frac{1}{\left(1 + \dfrac{0.09}{4}\right)^2}, \frac{1}{\left(1 + \dfrac{0.09}{4}\right)}$$

Substituting these for $d(0,9\text{m})$, $d(3\text{m},9\text{m})$, and $d(6\text{m},9\text{m})$, respectively, along with the spot and storage costs solves $F = \$59.95$.

Futures Returns and the Futures Term Structure

We dealt with a few cases earlier that computed the return to the futures contract. In general, we showed that the effective price paid by the hedger was the sum of the realized spot price plus the return to the futures contract: $S_2 + (F_1 - F_2)$. Let's focus on the latter term. The hedger shorts (sells) the futures contract at time $t = 1$ for F_1 and when he closes out his position at $t = 2$, he realizes the gain $F_1 - F_2$. As a short seller, a profit is earned when the futures price declines. As a hedger taking a long position, a profit is earned if $F_2 > F_1$. The profit or loss in either case is the result of closing out the contract.

In practice, futures positions are often rolled forward, especially in cases in which the hedger wishes to maintain a futures exposure over a period of time. Rolling the futures contract means selling the current contract before expiration and replacing that contract with the next available contract. Table 15.2 illustrates how futures are rolled forward. So, for example, if we desire to maintain exposure to oil futures through long one-month futures contracts then we must sell the current contract before it expires (to avoid taking delivery) and replacing it with the next available one-month contract. Using the following table, let's assume that contracts are rolled on the twenty-fourth day of the month. To maintain front-month exposure

TABLE 15.3 Rolling Futures Contracts

	Contract ($)				
Date	December	January	February	Front Month Contract	Roll Yield
Wed, Nov. 11, 2009	50.00	55.00	52.00	50.00	
Thu, Nov. 19, 2009	50.82	55.87	52.16	50.82	
Fri, Nov. 13, 2009	50.32	56.14	52.29	50.32	
Sat, Nov. 14, 2009	50.84	56.46	52.60	50.84	
Sun, Nov. 15, 2009	50.46	56.67	52.81	50.46	
Mon, Nov. 16, 2009	51.60	57.11	53.41	51.60	
Tue, Nov. 17, 2009	51.23	57.28	54.39	51.23	
Wed, Nov. 18, 2009	51.91	58.11	54.55	51.91	
Thu, Nov. 19, 2009	51.93	58.70	55.38	51.93	
Fri, Nov. 20, 2009	52.11	59.62	56.15	52.11	
Sat, Nov. 21, 2009	52.33	60.29	56.81	52.33	
Sun, Nov. 22, 2009	52.21	61.03	57.22	52.21	
Mon, Nov. 23, 2009	52.51	61.23	58.12	52.51	
Tue, Nov. 24, 2009	52.91	61.68	58.81	52.91	
Wed, Nov. 25, 2009	53.14	62.21	59.39	62.21	−14.22%
Thu, Nov. 26, 2009	53.18	62.34	59.95	62.34	
Fri, Nov. 27, 2009	53.48	62.88	60.37	62.88	
Sat, Nov. 28, 2009	53.60	63.11	61.34	63.11	
Sun, Nov. 29, 2009	53.40	63.40	61.20	63.40	
Mon, Nov. 30, 2009	53.50	64.16	61.76	64.16	
Tue, Dec. 01, 2009	54.16	64.37	61.78	64.37	
Wed, Dec. 02, 2009	54.21	67.73	62.42	67.73	
Thu, Dec. 03, 2009	54.26	65.35	62.20	65.35	
Fri, Dec. 04, 2009	55.03	66.04	63.10	66.04	
Sat, Dec. 05, 2009	54.52	66.75	64.07	66.75	
Sun, Dec. 06, 2009	55.98	67.03	64.55	67.03	
Mon, Dec. 07, 2009	55.37	67.91	65.41	67.91	
Tue, Dec. 08, 2009	56.06	68.82	65.59	68.82	
Wed, Dec. 09, 2009	55.72	69.04	65.98	69.04	
Thu, Dec. 10, 2009	56.26	69.53	66.49	69.53	
Fri, Dec. 11, 2009	55.83	70.42	67.42	70.42	
Sat, Dec. 12, 2009	57.17	71.25	67.49	71.25	
Sun, Dec. 13, 2009	56.35	71.32	68.45	71.32	
Mon, Dec. 14, 2009	57.82	71.60	69.41	71.60	
Tue, Dec. 15, 2009	56.85	72.79	69.72	72.79	
Wed, Dec. 16, 2009	58.10	72.86	69.92	72.86	
Thu, Dec. 17, 2009	57.30	73.01	70.75	73.01	
Fri, Dec. 18, 2009	58.75	73.10	70.90	73.10	
Sat, Dec. 19, 2009	57.35	73.85	71.82	73.85	
Sun, Dec. 20, 2009	58.82	74.73	71.89	74.73	

Mon, Dec. 21, 2009	57.60	75.22	72.79	75.22	
Tue, Dec. 22, 2009	58.85	75.67	72.81	75.67	
Wed, Dec. 23, 2009	57.76	76.03	73.65	76.03	
Thu, Dec. 24, 2009	59.65	76.87	74.45	76.87	
Fri, Dec. 25, 2009	58.03	77.21	75.08	75.08	3.25%

then, the current month contract is sold and the proceeds (and any additional funds if necessary) are used to buy the next month's contract.

The December contract in the table is therefore sold for $52.91 on November 24th. This is the analog to F_2 from before, and if $F_2 > F_1$, then a profit is recorded on the futures position when closed. We maintain our front month exposure by buying the January contract for $61.68. When the contract is cleared the following day, we record a roll yield of −14 percent. We do the same on the 24th of December for a roll yield of 3.25 percent by selling our January contract for $76.87 and buying the February contract for $75.08.

You will undoubtedly notice that the roll yield depends on the relationship between futures prices across contracts—the so-called term structure. The futures term structure can be seen by looking across a given row; we can see that it is humped in the preceding table, rising from the December to the January contract and then falling off when rolling to the February contract. An upward-sloping futures term structure is referred to as *contango*, while a downward-sloping term structure is called *backwardation*. (Contango is said to be a corruption of the English word *continue* and was thought to arise from the practice of buyers of commodities asking sellers for a continuation in the contract date. The sellers would do so only if they were compensated for the time value, or opportunity cost, of forgoing payment for the continuation period. Thus, longer continuations [contracts further out] sold at a premium.) Erb and Harvey (2005) and Gorton and Rouwenhorst (2004) argue that the realized historical positive returns to long futures exposures to commodities are explained in large part to backwardation and resultant positive roll yields and not to growth in commodity prices. Contango, on the other hand, produces negative roll yields that can quickly wipe out any positive returns from the futures position itself and, as a result, we are naturally interested in which factors affect the shape of the futures term structure.

Strictly speaking, if futures prices exceed expected spot prices, for example, $F(t) > E[S(t)]$, then the futures market is said to be in *contango* and roll yields will be negative. Contango is often identified if $F(t + 1) > F(t)$, ostensibly due to the belief that the expected spot price is not observed. For this to occur, the futures market has to have an imbalance of hedgers who are naturally short the commodity relative to hedgers with long positions. Speculators who are willing to take long positions will enter into contracts with short hedgers only if they are adequately compensated. For example, the futures prices must compensate them for storage costs and the risk that prices may fall. Contango is normal for nonperishable commodities with costs of carry (storage costs). In this situation, the longer-term contracts sell at a premium to nearer-term contracts due to the costs of carry. Theoretically, the size of the contango should be limited by the costs of carry but that has not always been the case, especially when the imbalance between short hedgers and long speculators is high and spot prices are volatile and uncertain.

On the other hand, when the prompt (nearest-term) contract sells at a premium to contracts further out, the market is said to be in backwardation. Backwardation in futures is normal in markets dominated by long hedgers; hedgers and speculators can be induced to take the short position (taking delivery) if the futures price is below the expected spot price. The longer the time to delivery, the greater the spread $F(t) < E[S(t)]$ necessary to protect against possible increases in spot prices. On the other hand, expectations of impending shortages can cause the holder of a commodity to charge a convenience yield that reflects the benefit of having the commodity in hand now than having to wait for it later. Similar thinking explains backwardated markets for commodities that pay dividends. Therefore, backwardated commodity markets have a declining term structure (see the December 24th January to February roll discussed earlier).

In 2008, crude oil futures were backwardated until early summer when they suddenly shifted into contango. This could happen as traders bought oil on the spot market and sold it forward. They would store the oil until delivery and the costs of carry contributed to the contango. The contango built into the market for commodities has exceeded the costs of carry in general; that is, future prices have exceeded the costs of owning physical commodities, which helps explain the increased interest from traders in owning inventories or warehousing and storage facilities. This behavior, in turn, has incented overproduction of commodities through the recession that began in 2008 while having only minimal impact on declining prices. But, as storage availability declined, making it more difficult to absorb and store the excess supply, the contango eventually eroded until it was equal to the actual costs of finance, returning contango to the cost of carry upper bound.

Agents who had access to lower financing costs could effectively exploit contango opportunities, creating a cash and carry trade that allowed them to sell futures with much lower storage costs. Institutional investors, like pension funds, with their interests in commodity investments as a natural inflation hedge, acted as natural counterparties to these trades by establishing the required long positions. Because they rolled their positions regularly they were the perfect counterparty to the cash and carry trade characterized by short futures positions with no intention of making delivery.

Since commodity prices are generally positively correlated with inflation, they then become natural candidates as inflation hedges (although there are probably more direct hedges such as TIPS and CPI swaps). There has been an active interest in commodities as portfolio diversifiers as well as hedging instruments but controversy still exists as to the effectiveness of these strategies. Some of that controversy is linked to the fact that outside of supply and demand, commodities do not possess a set of underlying fundamentals (for example, dividends and earnings) on which to base trading strategies.

SWAPS

Let me motivate this important class of derivatives with an example. Suppose a mining company receives spot price for bauxite (an aluminum ore) but would like to hedge out the risk of prices falling. Since the mining company is naturally long bauxite, it could engage in a continuing sequence of short forward contracts with an aluminum producer who takes the long forward position. Alternatively, if there was an active futures market for bauxite, the company could hedge their price exposure by writing short futures contracts for delivery every period (which they would close out before the delivery date). In either case, the company would need to manage their exposure to price risk continuously and assume the administrative costs of doing so. More importantly, if output from the mine is variable, then the amount of exposure to hedge would be unknown ahead of time, further complicating the hedging strategy. In truth, what the mining company wants to receive is a fixed price of bauxite. They could achieve this by entering into an agreement with a counterparty to swap their variable spot price for a fixed price. Thus, they receive spot, which they trade for fixed. Their cash flows would therefore become $(S_1 - x)$, $(S_2 - x)$, . . . , $(S_T - x)$, which they can scale by any desired notional amount N. This *commodity swap* would have value therefore, equal to:

$$V_0 = [(S_1 - x) + (S_2 - x) + \cdots + (S_T - x)]N$$

Since future spot prices are unknown, we use the futures relationship to value this contract, for example:

$$V_0 = \left[\sum_{i=1}^{T} (F_i - x)d(0, i) \right] N$$

Now consider a *plain vanilla interest rate swap*. Imagine that you are making payments on a variable rate loan in which the rate is tied to an index of Treasury yields (or LIBOR) and you desire to hedge the risk of rising rates. An interest rate swap would entail you receiving the floating rate (which offsets your variable loan payment) and paying a fixed rate. Letting c represent the floating rate and r the fixed rate, then this swap has a theoretical value equal to:

$$V_0 = \left[\sum_{i=1}^{T}(c_i - r)\right]N$$

The problem again is that c_i is unknown; its value, however, can be derived from the forward rate structure. Intuitively, we can value the floating leg of the swap contract by appealing to the algebra of floating rate bonds. To see this, think of a standard bond formula but one in which the coupon rate floats across the life of the bond, to wit:

$$P = \frac{c_1}{(1+r_1)} + \frac{c_2}{(1+r_2)^2} + \cdots + \frac{c_M}{(1+r_M)^M} + \frac{M}{(1+r_M)^M}$$

To simplify further, assume the price P and the face value M are both \$1 (equivalent to a \$1 notional amount). Then, immediately, we have the value of the floating portion:

$$1 - d(0,M) = \frac{c_1}{(1+r_1)} + \frac{c_2}{(1+r_2)^2} + \cdots + \frac{c_M}{(1+r_m)^M}$$

It follows that the value of the vanilla interest rate swap is:

$$V_0 = \left[1 - d(0,M) - \sum_{i=1}^{M} d(0,i)r\right]N$$

Notice that we are computing the discounted present value of the fixed interest payments that we pay, given by $\sum_{i=1}^{M} d(0,i)r$ and subtract those from the floating rate portion that we receive. This difference is scaled by the notional N. It is instructive to think about what fixed rate you would be willing to pay to make this a fair swap, sometimes referred to as the *break-even rate*. That is, given the forward rate structure, which fixed rate payment r makes us indifferent between the fixed and floating legs of the swap? This is easy to solve—I will do the algebra first and then follow with a

TABLE 15.4 Swaps Discount Rates

Rate	Time	$d(0,i)$
0.07	1	0.934579
0.073	2	0.868561
0.077	3	0.800484
0.081	4	0.732314
0.084	5	0.668119
0.088	6	0.602874
	$\sum d(0, i)$	4.606932

numerical example. The fixed rate that makes us indifferent between floating and fixed is:

$$r = \frac{1 - d(0, M)}{\sum_{i=1}^{M} d(0, i)}$$

Suppose, now, that we add some details, which are summarized in Table 15.4. Specifically, let's study a six-year swap and assume that the forward curve is given in the first column and the discount rates in the third column.

Substituting $d(0,6) = 0.602$ and $\sum_{i=1}^{M} d(0, i) = 4.606$ suggests that the fixed rate we'd be willing to pay would be 8.62 percent. Since we receive floating, then any fixed rate below 8.62 percent would generate positive value to us; otherwise, the swap would have positive value to the counterparty receiving fixed and paying floating. To prove this, we can compare the net present value of the sum of the difference in the cash flows as shown in Table 15.5. (The spreadsheet can be found in Chapter 15 Examples.xlsx.)

The net present value of the swap computed using 8.62 percent for the fixed payment is about 2.9 cents. You can confirm from the chapter

TABLE 15.5 Vanilla Swap

Rate	Time	$d(0,i)$	Fixed	Float	Fix-Float	NVP	Short Rate	
0.07	1	0.934579	8.62	7	1.62	1.514019	0.07	0.07
0.073	2	0.868561	8.62	7.6	1.02	0.885933	0.076	0.08
0.077	3	0.800484	8.62	8.5	0.12	0.096058	0.085	0.09
0.081	4	0.732314	8.62	9.3	−0.68	−0.49797	0.093	0.1
0.084	5	0.668119	8.62	9.6	−0.98	−0.65476	0.096	0.1
0.088	6	0.602874	8.62	10.8	−2.18	−1.31427	0.108	0.11
	$\sum d(0, i)$	4.606932				0.029014		

spreadsheet that the floating payment is computed from the short rates (last column), which are estimated from the forward rate structure given in the first column. The short rates are the rate earned on money during the period in question (one year in this example) and are given by the forward rate algebra discussed in Chapter 3. For example, the short rate for year two is computed (assuming continuous compounding) as:

$$0.076 = \frac{t_2 * r_2 - t_1 * r_1}{t_2 - t_1} = \frac{2 * 0.073 - 1 * 0.07}{2 - 1}$$

As a final swap example, let's think about a U.S. mining company that ships bulk ore to Japan and receives yen. (I am going to illustrate this type of swap using an example from Hull 2008.) The mining company is exposed to currency risk, specifically, that the yen may depreciate against the dollar. Rather than short the yen forward to hedge this risk, let's explore the possibility of achieving the same objective using a *currency swap*. Intuitively, the mining company wants to construct a swap that neutralizes its exposure and it does that by paying yen to a counterparty in exchange for dollars through a separate swap agreement. Here's how they might set up this trade.

The mining company approaches an investment bank to find a counterparty to a currency swap. Suppose the company agrees to deposit $10 million in an account paying 8 percent with the counterparty agreeing to deposit 1,100 million yen in an account paying 5 percent interest. (These rates are negotiated by the parties to the swap.) Thus, the mining company agrees to pay the counterparty $0.05(1100) = 55$ million yen annually, which is swapped for the counterparty's annual payment of $0.8 million. Broadly speaking, then, the mining company is paying yen and receiving dollars on these notional amounts. So, for example, if the mining company were receiving 55 million yen annually from the Japanese firm, it is now also paying that amount back out through the swap agreement to the counterparty. Let's add a few more details. Suppose that dollars cost 110 yen, the annual rate of interest in the United States is 4.5 percent and 4 percent in Japan and that the swap agreement is for three years. The mining company therefore pays yen for three years while receiving dollars and at the end of the swap term, it collects the $10 million it deposited and simultaneously reimburses the 1,100 million yen. That way, the transactions consist solely of the swap payments. We can present the value of the respective cash flows as given in Table 15.6.

The present value of the dollar portion of the swap is $10.93 million, while the present value of the yen portion is $1128/110 = $10.25 million.

TABLE 15.6 Three-Year Currency Swap

Time	USD cf	$d(0,i)$	PV	Yen cf	$d(0,i)$	PV
1	0.8	0.956	0.765	55	0.961	52.843
2	0.8	0.914	0.731	55	0.923	50.771
3	0.8	0.874	0.699	55	0.887	48.781
3	10	0.874	8.737	1,100	0.887	975.612
			10.932			1128.008

Since the mining company pays yen and receives dollars, the net present value of the swap is $10.93 – $10.25 = $0.68 million.

A couple of items of interest center on the interest rate differential and the exchange rate. In this example, because the interest rate is higher in the United States, the swapped dollars are going to be discounted more heavily. Put differently, the opportunity cost of dollars is relatively high and the mining company is bearing that cost. If U.S. interest rates were to fall, then so would this cost and that would improve the value of the swap to the counterparty receiving dollars. Secondly, if the exchange rate rises (yen/USD), then so would the value of this swap. This is the major point of the example, as it illuminates to us why the mining company would engage in the swap to begin with. That is, the mining company wants to lay off yen, so to speak, as they are received in exchange for dollars. This swap achieves that purpose directly. In any case, it is important to realize that the value of the swap is symmetric (one party's gain is the other's loss) depending on a host of parameters, including the payment rates, the cost of money in each country, and the exchange rate.

SUMMARY

Futures markets exist to facilitate the hedging of price risk. If there is an imbalance of hedgers, short and long, then speculators need to enter the futures market to correct these imbalances and futures prices will reflect this activity (for example, contango). This chapter introduces the mechanics of futures and forwards along with some institutional detail and provides a sound theoretical basis for pricing these derivative securities. We introduce as well plain vanilla swaps and develop their pricing and apply all of these models to practical applications targeted to portfolio management. The development of these models link up well to the concept of hedging risk, which has been a recurrent theme throughout this book and is the subject of Chapter 18.

REFERENCES

Erb, Claude B., and Campbell R. Harvey. 2005. *The tactical and strategic value of commodity futures.* Working Paper.

Gorton, Gary, and Geert Rouwenhorst. 2004. *Facts and fantasies about commodity futures.* Cambridge, MA: NBER Working Paper 10595.

Hull, John. 2008. *Options, futures, and other derivatives* 7th ed. Upper Saddle River, NJ: Prentice-Hall, 501.

CHAPTER 16

Introduction to Options

Money is made by discounting the obvious and betting on the unexpected.

—George Soros

I introduce options as hedging instruments in the next chapter. It is instructive, therefore, to develop some basics on option valuation so that we can better understand how to formulate portfolio strategies using this very flexible set of securities. This chapter is not intended to substitute for a more comprehensive treatment of this important class of derivatives; for that, I would suggest a book such as John Hull's *Options, Futures, and Other Derivatives* or David Luenberger's *Investment Science*. I borrow liberally from both in the discussion that follows. Like futures, forwards, and swaps, options are derivative securities whose values are tied to the value of some underlying security. For that reason, I include a section on asset price dynamics—models of derivative securities are only as good as the models of the underlying price dynamic.

In general, options are contracts that give the holder the right but not necessarily the obligation to sell or purchase a security over some interval into the future for a price agreed upon today. The price is referred to as the strike price (K) and if the option can be exercised at any time over its life, then it is an American option. If, on the other hand, the option can be exercised at a single specific date, it is a European option. We will study European options.

There are two general types of options, calls and puts. A call (put) option gives the holder the right to buy (sell) a security in the future at a known strike price. In the case of a call option, if the spot (S), or market, price of the security in question is greater than the strike price at the exercise date, then the option has value and will be exercised. In general, when the spot price exceeds the strike price, the call option is said to be in the money.

Otherwise, the option is either at the money (spot equals strike) or out of the money (spot is less than the strike price). Out of the money options will not be exercised. Puts, on the other hand, have value when the spot price falls below the strike price. An example, which we develop in the next chapter, involves portfolio insurance in which the portfolio manager buys a put option to hedge the risk of his portfolio losing value. The put gives him the option of selling his portfolio at some agreed-upon price; therefore, if the market price of the portfolio falls below the strike price, this put has value. We will learn how to value these options.

OPTION PAYOFFS AND PUT-CALL PARITY

Suppose you own a call option on a stock that you can exercise at time T at strike price K. If the spot price S is less than K, the call has zero value and will not be exercised. If, on the other hand, the spot prices exceeds K, then the call will have value equal to the difference $S - K$. The value of this option is depicted in Figure 16.1. As S exceeds K, the option value C exceeds zero. Thus, the call option is worth either zero because it goes unexercised if $S < K$ or it has positive value equal to the difference $S - K$ in the event $S > K$.

Put value is positive when the spot price is less than the strike price. In the limit, if the spot price were zero, then the value of the put would be equal to the strike price. As the spot price increases, then value declines and when $S > K$, the put has zero value and will not be exercised. Figure 16.2 depicts this relationship.

These two simple relationships were used by Robert Merton and Fischer Black and Myron Scholes to describe the capital structure of the firm. Those arguments are now standard fare in all corporate finance texts. Consider the example of a firm whose assets are financed by equity (shares)

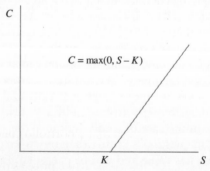

FIGURE 16.1   Call Value at Expiration

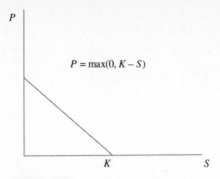

FIGURE 16.2 Put Value at Expiration

and debt (bonds). With no loss of generality, assume the bonds are zero coupon bonds. When the debt matures, a principal payment equal to K is due. The owners of the firm (shareholders) compare the value of the firm's assets to K. If the asset value exceeds the debt obligation, they pay off the debt. Otherwise, they default on the debt and turn the assets over to the bondholders. Shareholders therefore have a European call option on the assets of the firm. To see this, let's denote the value of the bonds at maturity (time T) by K and the value of the firm's assets by A_T. Shareholders therefore receive max $(A_T - K, 0)$ while bondholders receive min (A_T, K), which is the same as $K - \max(K - A_T, 0)$. The value of the debt K represents the strike price for the call option. At time $t = 0$, shareholders have a call option on the firm's assets while bondholders have the present value of the debt K minus a European put option on the firm's assets with a strike price of K. If the value of the firm's assets at time T exceeds K, the option will not be exercised. Otherwise, if $K > A_T$, bondholders get $K - (K - A_T) = A_T$, the value of the firm's assets.

In sum, the value of the equity is identical to a call option while the value of the firm's debt is the present value of the debt minus the put option. Thus, if we denote the call and put, respectively, by c and p, then we can write the value of the firm's assets at time $t = 0$ as:

$$A_0 = c + [Ke^{-rT} - p]$$

This says that the value of the assets must equal the total value of the securities used to finance the firm. Rearranging, we get the *put-call parity* condition:

$$c + Ke^{-rT} = p + A_0$$

Put-call parity therefore requires that a portfolio consisting of a call option on a share and a risk-free loan must equal the value of a portfolio consisting of a put option (with the same strike price as the call) and a share. The payout structure on this portfolio is illustrated in Figure 16.3.

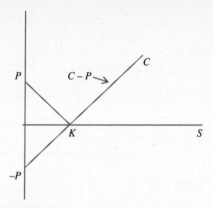

FIGURE 16.3 Combination of Put and Call

More formally, put-call parity says that a *combination of a put, a call, and risk-free loan have the same payout as the underlying stock*. Using the parity relationship described earlier, we get a condition for stock prices:

$$A_o = c + Ke^{-rT} - p$$

That is, buying one call on a share of stock, selling one put (both at the same strike price), and lending an amount Ke^{-rT} constitutes a portfolio that replicates the value of the stock. The combination of the put and call has the payout shown in Figure 16.3.

Adding the loan to the replicating portfolio produces a payout that is identical to S, as shown in Figure 16.4.

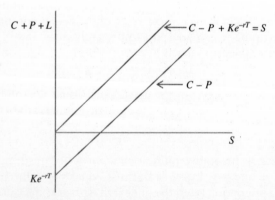

FIGURE 16.4 Put, Call, and Loan

FIGURE 16.5   Single Period Payout Space

PRICING EUROPEAN CALL OPTIONS

Let's use the idea of a replicating portfolio to derive the value of a call option. We'll begin with a single period problem depicted in Figure 16.5. Think of a stock whose spot price S can go up at the end of one period by a factor u to the level uS or can go down by a factor d to dS. I will derive the parameters u and d in Chapter 17. Moreover, suppose that the return on a risk-free loan is $R = (1 + r)$. Thus, we have the payout shown in Figure 16.5.

The call option will have the payout space given in Figure 16.6.

We want to use a combination of an investment in the stock and the risk-free asset to mimic the value of the call option. Letting Cu and Cd stand for the value of the call should the stock price rise or fall, respectively, then our aim is construct a riskless portfolio consisting of a long position of \$x in the stock and \$b in the risk-free asset plus a short position in one call option. If stock prices rise, we get the first of the following two equations; if they fall, we get the second equation. No arbitrage means that these will hold (otherwise, we can profit with no risk by selling calls in exchange for stock and vice versa). The question is how much of the stock do we need (x) and how much do we lend (b)? Thus, we solve the following for x and b:

$$ux + Rb = Cu$$
$$dx + Rb = Cd$$

We can solve the following system for x and b:

$$\begin{bmatrix} u & R \\ d & R \end{bmatrix} \begin{bmatrix} x \\ b \end{bmatrix} = \begin{bmatrix} Cu \\ Cd \end{bmatrix}$$

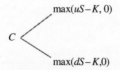

FIGURE 16.6   Call Payout Space

This has the solution given by:

$$x = \frac{Cu - Cd}{u - d}; b = \frac{uCd - dCu}{R(u - d)}$$

Therefore, the replicating portfolio is the sum:

$$x + b = \frac{1}{R}\left[\frac{(R - d)}{(u - d)}Cu + \frac{(u - R)}{(u - d)}Cd\right]$$

Substituting $q = \frac{(R-d)}{(u-d)}$ and recognizing that $(1 - q) = \frac{(u-R)}{(u-d)}$ simplifies this as:

$$x + b = \frac{1}{R}[qCu + (1 - q)Cd]$$

Finally, realizing that $x + b$ must equal the value of the call, we immediately have the result:

$$C = \frac{1}{R}[qCu + (1 - q)Cd]$$

Here the parameter q plays the role of a probability in determining the expected value. This says that the current period value of the call option is the discounted expected value of the next period valuations (see Figures 16.5 and 16.6). Notice that q does not include the stock's expected return and this feature is what makes this *risk-neutral pricing* because it does not depend in any way on our preferences toward risk. This is our major result. As an example, take the case of a one-month call option with current underlying share price $S = \$1$ and a strike price $K = \$0.9$. Note that the option is currently in the money. Assume that the annual risk-free rate is 10 percent, implying that the monthly risk-free rate return is $R = (1 + 0.1/12) = 1.0083$ and let's assume the up and down movement multipliers are $u = 1.06$ and $d = 1/u = 0.94$. From these values, we solve $q = 0.557$. Figure 16.7 illustrates the possible share prices one month out along with the call option values. Let's discuss how these numbers were arrived at.

		Cu		0.16
C			0.11	
		Cd		0.04
		uS		1.06
S			1.00	
		dS		0.94

FIGURE 16.7   One-Period Call Option on a Stock

					u^5S
				u^4S	
			u^3S		u^4dS
		u^2S		u^3dS	
	uS		u^2dS		u^3d^2S
S		udS		u^2d^2S	
	dS		ud^2S		u^2d^3S
		d^2S		ud^3S	
			d^3S		ud^4S
				d^4S	
					d^5S

FIGURE 16.8 Multiperiod Price Lattice

It's easy to see how the two share prices are arrived at. $uS = 1.06 * \$1$ and $dS = .94 * \$1$. The call option values corresponding to these two prices are derived from $C = \max(S - K, 0)$. If the share price rises to \$1.06, then the call has value $\$1.06 - \$0.9 = \$0.16$. Otherwise, if the share price falls to \$0.94, the call has value \$0.04. The value of the call presently is a weighted average of these two terminal call option values with weights q and $(1 - q)$. This gives us:

$$C = \frac{1}{1.0083}[.557 * 0.16 + (1 - .557) * 0.04] = \$0.11$$

This says that the fair price for the option to buy a currently priced \$1 share of stock one month from now for \$0.9 is 11 cents. A multiple-period model of stock prices is a natural extension, which we see in Figure 16.8.

EXAMPLE 16.1

Let's extend our one-period example to a five-month call option on the same stock with the same parameter values used in the previous example. Again, stock price dynamics are binomial; they either go up by a factor of $u = 1.06$ or down by a factor of $d = 1/u = 0.94$. We are now looking at the following stock price mapping:

(continued)

(continued)

```
                                                    1.33
                                          1.26
                                1.19                1.19
                       1.12              1.12
              1.06               1.06               1.06
     1.00              1.00              1.00
              0.94               0.94               0.94
                       0.89              0.89
                                0.84                0.84
                                          0.79
                                                    0.75
```

FIGURE 16.9   Multiperiod Stock Dynamic

Working from the highlighted terminal nodes in Figure 16.9, we get the terminal nodes for the call values as max $(S - K, 0)$. For example, the call value corresponding to a stock price outcome of $1.33 (with strike price $0.90) will be max $(1.33 - 0.90, 0) = 0.43$ which is the highest value of the call option given by the top entry in the last column of Figure 16.10. After filling in the remaining elements of this column, we work backward, computing the call value at each interior node as the discounted weighted average of the two possible immediate future call values. So, for example, conditional on the terminal period's prices being $1.33 or $1.19 with corresponding call values $0.43 and $0.29, respectively, the penultimate period value of the call option is:

$$C = \frac{1}{1.0083}[.557 * 0.43 + (1 - .557) * 0.29] = \$0.37$$

```
                                                    0.43
                                          0.37
                                0.30                0.29
                       0.24              0.23
              0.19               0.17               0.16
     0.145             0.13              0.11
              0.09               0.07               0.04
                       0.04              0.02
                                0.01                0.00
                                          0.00
                                                    0.00
```

FIGURE 16.10   Call Option Value

Completing the tree backward to the current period says that the five-month call option on a one dollar stock is worth about 15 cents at present. It's a lot easier to work computationally with spreadsheets if we construct our lattices as depicted here. We'll use this lattice format here on out.

		Call Value						Stock Value			
0	1	2	3	4	5	0	1	2	3	4	5
0.15	0.19	0.24	0.30	0.37	0.43	1.00	1.06	1.12	1.19	1.26	1.33
	0.09	0.13	0.17	0.23	0.29		0.94	1.00	1.06	1.12	1.19
		0.04	0.07	0.11	0.16			0.89	0.94	1.00	1.06
			0.01	0.02	0.04				0.84	0.89	0.94
				0.00	0.00					0.79	0.84
					0.00						0.75

 Go to the companion website for more details.

PRICING EUROPEAN PUT OPTIONS

Let's take the same $1 stock and price a five-month put with strike price $0.90, implying that the put is currently in the money. The put option will have value $\max(K - S, 0)$ at the terminal nodes as shown in Figure 16.11.

Again, I refer you to the Chapter 16 spreadsheet for specifics but the process is identical to call valuation, that is, we still work backward, discounting the weighted average of the relevant two front-running node values. Note that $\max(K - S, 0) = 0$ for all but the two lowest spot prices in

		Put Value						Stock Value			
0	1	2	3	4	5	0	1	2	3	4	5
0.01	0.00	0.00	0.00	0.00	0.00	1.00	1.06	1.12	1.19	1.26	1.33
	0.02	0.00	0.00	0.00	0.00		0.94	1.00	1.06	1.12	1.19
		0.03	0.01	0.00	0.00			0.89	0.94	1.00	1.06
			0.06	0.03	0.00				0.84	0.89	0.94
				0.10	0.06					0.79	0.84
					0.15						0.75

FIGURE 16.11   Five-Month Put Option Value

the fifth month. Because the exercise price is $0.90, then the spot price needs to be below this level for the put to have value. Valuation mechanics are otherwise the same as for call options. For example, at the penultimate node for the put for which the two possible terminal spot prices are $0.84 and $0.75, we get, for example:

$$P = \frac{1}{1.0083}[.557 * 0.06 + (1 - .557) * 0.15] = \$0.10$$

We conclude that a five-month put on a $1 stock has value today equal to $0.01.

OPTION STRATEGIES

Go to the companion website for more details (see Options Simulator under Chapter 16 Examples).

The Excel workbook titled *options simulator* contains examples of several options strategies that can be simulated and their payoffs graphed. The option spreadsheet in this workbook consists of several lattices for pricing up to three independent call options and two put options along with a Black-Scholes pricing model that provides a continuous time check against the discrete form lattices. The Black-Scholes-Merton pricing model is derived in Chapter 17. These options are linked to the payouts provided on the Strategy spreadsheet (columns A to G). For example, consider a six-month call option on a share with current spot price at $100 and with annual volatility 20 percent. The strike price of the call is $K_1 = \$90$ and with annual risk-free rate of 5 percent. This option is priced at $13.44, using the lattice, and $13.50, using Black-Scholes. The profit schedule for this call is given in column C on the strategy spreadsheet. Columns D through G contain profit positions corresponding to various spot prices (given in column A) for two more calls and two puts ranging over three strikes (K_1, K_2, K_3). These five basic options strategies can be used to generate the profit schedules for the more sophisticated strategies given in columns I through O. Let's examine these now.

An investor may wish to bet on share prices falling. One strategy that places such a bet is to take a short position in the call by selling call options. By doing so, the investor is exposed to unlimited risk should prices rise sufficiently. Short positions, in general, have exposure to unlimited losses and somewhat appropriately carry the moniker *naked shorts*. To hedge this risk, investors cover their short calls by holding a share of stock. Thus, we have the covered call payout, which is the net profit to selling a call and simultaneously buying a share. As we can see from the profit schedule given

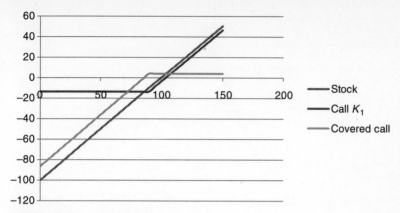

FIGURE 16.12   Covered Call

in Figure 16.12, this payout is maximized at $3.44 because at some point the call will be exercised (at $K_1 = \$90$ in this case).

Thus, the long position in the stock hedges the risk of having to buy a share at some future point in time at a price greater than $90 if the call is exercised, but at a cost, which in this case limits any profit to $3.44. This is a rather extreme case. In reality, the investor will not hedge the entire short position. Doing so would completely offset his belief that prices are more likely to fall than rise. The concept, however, is constructive in that it illustrates the natural hedging characteristics of covered short positions.

Similarly, a long put position hedges downside risk. A protective put (column J) allows the investor to also participate in the upside by holding a share. As shown in Figure 16.13, the profit schedule for this strategy indeed

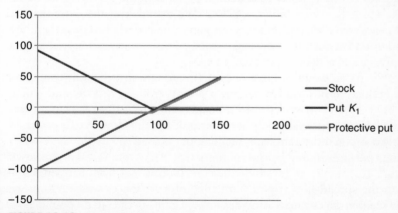

FIGURE 16.13   Protective Put

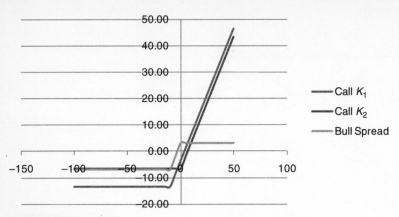

FIGURE 16.14   Bull Spread

limits the downside loss while allowing the investor to participate in the gains should share prices rise instead. In the early years of options trading, there were no puts. Investors created synthetic puts instead by holding a portfolio consisting of a short position in the stock and a long position in a call.

Spread strategies limit profits to a targeted range of spot prices while capping losses and gains. These are profitable strategies if the investor's spot price forecast is fulfilled. If, for example, the spot price is currently below $90 and we believe that over the life of the option that prices will stay in the range of $90 to $100, then we could buy a call with strike $90 and sell a call with strike $100. If prices rise above $90, we exercise the call and should they continue to rise, we book a profit until the price reaches $100, at which time the short call is exercised. We then deliver the share that we bought earlier at $90, which limits our gain. The profit schedule is therefore range-bound between the two strike prices. This strategy is referred to as a bull spread, and is depicted in Figure 16.14.

As the name would suggest, a bear spread is a strategy that counts on prices falling but not too far. Buying a put at strike $K_2 = \$100$ and selling another at a lower strike $K_1 = \$90$, pockets the profit from the short position but limits the gain should prices continue to fall below $90. If prices do fall below K_1 then the gain from the long put is used to buy the share when the short put is exercised by the counterparty. The profit schedule is shown in Figure 16.15. (We will exclude the contributing legs from here on out—refer to the spreadsheet if you want this information as well.) Again, we clearly see that this strategy provides limited gains in the region bounded by the strike prices.

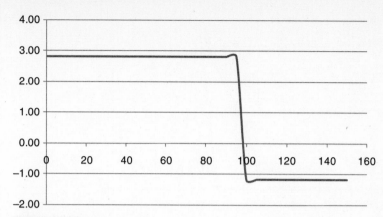

FIGURE 16.15 Bear Spread

Suppose an investor buys a share and a put with strike price $K_1 = \$90$ and sells a call option with strike price $K_2 = \$100$. This is identical to a long put and a covered call. What does this strategy achieve? First, the put provides downside protection. The long position in the stock allows the investor to participate in the upside movements in price as well but only if price does not exceed K_2. In that event, the long position in the stock covers the short call. This strategy therefore provides a capped profit should prices rise and limits losses should prices fall. It is called a collar and is illustrated in Figure 16.16.

A collar clearly limits participation in both the upside as well as the downside and therefore limits the effects of market volatility.

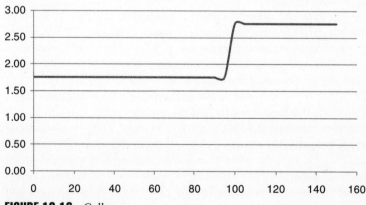

FIGURE 16.16 Collar

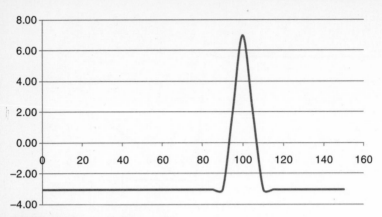

FIGURE 16.17 Butterfly Spread

A butterfly spread is a bet on stock prices being range-bound. In Figure 16.17, we see the profit on a long position in a share combined with a call at $K_3 = \$110$ and two short calls at $K_2 = \$100$. The two short calls offset the out-of-pocket costs of the investment in the share and the long call when price is low. As the share price rises toward $100, the profit from the short position is added to the price appreciation on the share until the short calls are exercised at K_2. If price continues to rise, the investor offsets the short call losses by exercising the long call at K_3.

The profit opportunity is potentially very large, depending on how we scale our positions. The long position in the share combined with the long call hedge the risk on the short calls. Thus, profits are range-bound and losses, though limited, are realized outside of the range of forecasted price. This is an aggressive strategy.

Suppose it is earnings season and we are anticipating a firm's earnings announcement. Earnings announcements, especially as they deviate from consensus expectations, result in earnings surprises and hence the possibility of rather large movements in share prices in either direction. If we anticipate a large movement in price but are unsure of the direction, we could purchase a put and a call with the same strike price and expiration date. This strategy is called a long straddle and its profit schedule is given in Figure 16.18. This particular straddle has a strike price of $100. Though these two options are priced at the money (ATM), they are not required to be.

A straddle is a volatility strategy that is direction-neutral with unlimited reward. Its payoff dependence on volatility should be obvious from the figure. If we allow for these two options to have different strike prices (but still impose the same expiration date), then the strategy is called a *strangle*.

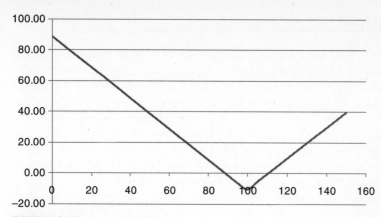

FIGURE 16.18   Long Straddle

Figure 16.19 illustrates the profit schedule for a strangle with a long put with strike price $K_1 = \$90$ and a long call with strike price $K_3 = \$110$. Both options are out of the money (OTM).

These examples provide a useful introduction to more sophisticated strategies. The spreadsheet can be used to simulate almost any combination of options strategies and to graph their profit schedules. The parameter settings can be changed on the option sheet to produce options prices for various volatility, strike prices, discount rates, and time horizons. These are automatically linked to the strategy sheet. Although the lattices are restricted to six nodes, it is straightforward to expand the number of nodes using the current spreadsheet as a template.

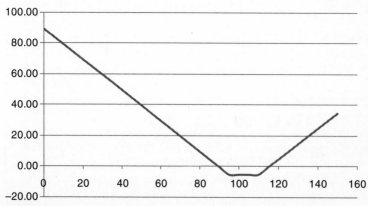

FIGURE 16.19   Long Strangle

REAL OPTIONS

Luenberger (1998) has a very nice running application throughout his book on the value of a lease to a gold mine. Conceptually, the decision to lease the mine depends on the perceived value of the lease relative to the asking price. Because the value of the lease depends on the price of gold, which is stochastic, then the lease itself is a derivative security. If gold's price dynamic is modeled using a lattice, then we can essentially determine the value of the lease, today, as the weighted present value of the complete set of state prices. This part of the problem is easy to solve because it follows directly from our earlier work on options. What makes the gold mine lease especially interesting is Luenberger's use of inherent optionality. In his example, the owner of the mine has the option at any time over the life of the lease of purchasing at fixed cost a production enhancement that improves the mine's output. Naturally, the likelihood of exercising this option will depend on the path that gold prices follow. The question we seek an answer to is how this option affects the value of the lease today.

EXAMPLE 16.2

🖳 Go to the companion website for more details.

Let's suppose it is December 30, 2001, and we are contemplating a 10-year lease on this mine. The price of gold on that date was $278 per ounce and the trailing annual volatility of gold prices from 1970 through 2001 was 20.5 percent. The yield on the 10-year Treasury was 5.07 percent. We shall assume that the extraction cost of gold is $200 per ounce and that 10,000 ounces are produced per year. Our parameters are therefore $u = e^{.205} = 1.23; d = e^{-.205} = 0.81$, with an annual discount rate equal to $1/1.0507$. In the absence of price volatility, the annual profit would be equal to $(\$278 - \$200)/1.0507^t$ for $t = 1, \dots, 10$. In this case, the value of the lease is $6 million (see the spreadsheet for details). But, in this case, gold would be a risk-free asset, which it is not. The price dynamic, therefore, over the 10-year period consistent with these parameters is given in the top half of Figure 16.20; the lease computations follow in the bottom half of the figure. The defining assumptions here are that the price of gold is the price that holds at the beginning of each year and that all cash flows occur at the end of the year. Thus, because the gold mine has to be returned to the owner at the end of year 10, then the mine has no lease value in the final year.

0.0	1.0	2.0	3.0	4.0	5.0	6.0	7.0	8.0	9.0	10.0
278.00	341.25	418.90	514.20	631.20	774.81	951.10	1167.50	1433.14	1759.21	2159.48
	226.47	278.00	341.25	418.90	514.20	631.20	774.81	951.10	1167.50	1433.14
		184.49	226.47	278.00	341.25	418.90	514.20	631.20	774.81	951.10
			150.30	184.49	226.47	278.00	341.25	418.90	514.20	631.20
				122.44	150.30	184.49	226.47	278.00	341.25	418.90
					99.75	122.44	150.30	184.49	226.47	278.00
						81.26	99.75	122.44	150.30	184.49
							66.20	81.26	99.75	122.44
								53.93	66.20	81.26
									43.93	53.93
										35.79

u	d	$R = 1 + r$	q
1.23	0.81	1.05	0.57

0.0	1.0	2.0	3.0	4.0	5.0	6.0	7.0	8.0	9.0	10.0
11.29	15.14	19.02	22.72	25.92	28.23	29.13	27.90	23.56	14.84	0.00
	5.68	8.44	11.24	13.80	15.83	16.95	16.68	14.39	9.21	0.00
		2.03	3.90	5.85	7.61	8.87	9.24	8.30	5.47	0.00
			0.15	1.14	2.36	3.54	4.30	4.26	2.99	0.00
				0.00	0.00	0.46	1.11	1.58	1.34	0.00
					0.00	0.00	0.00	0.00	0.25	0.00
						0.00	0.00	0.00	0.00	0.00
							0.00	0.00	0.00	0.00
								0.00	0.00	0.00
									0.00	0.00
										0.00

FIGURE 16.20 Mine Lease

It is worth noting that in June of 2011, the true price of gold exceeded $1,500 per ounce and that this price is captured in the range specified on our spreadsheet. The *valuations* at the beginning of year nine (bottom half) are tied directly to the year nine prices of gold (see the spreadsheet for details on the formulas). Letting (i,j) index the row and column in the lattice, we therefore have:

$$V_{i,j} = 10000(p_{i,j} - 200)/1.0507$$

The lease values for years 1 through 8 at each node are a function of the risk-neutral values of the two subsequent years plus the value of the gold mine in the current year, all discounted using the annual Treasury yield of 5.07 percent. That is:

$$V_{i,j} = \frac{10000\left(p_{i,j} - 200\right)}{1.0507} + \frac{qp_{i,j+1} + (1 - q)p_{i+1,j+1}}{1.0507}$$

Clearly, gold prices below the cost of extraction ($200 per ounce) will result in zero valuations. Working backward through the lattice, we find that the lease would have had expected value equal to $11.29 million at the close of 2001. The realized value over the subsequent 10 years would have depended on the actual path that gold prices took.

Now suppose that, in addition to this information, you are told that a one-time $1 million expenditure will purchase an enhancement to the production process, increasing productivity to 12,500 ounces per year (a 25 percent enhancement), which is partly offset by raising per unit costs from $200 per ounce to $240 per ounce. You have the option to purchase this enhancement at any time. As we shall see, the value of this option depends entirely on the path that gold prices take.

Figure 16.21 shows the value of the lease with this enhancement in place. The valuation functions are now given by:

$$V_{i,j} = 12500(p_{i,j} - 240)/1.0507$$

$$V_{i,j} = \frac{12500\left(p_{i,j} - 240\right)}{1.0507} + \frac{qp_{i,j+1} + (1 - q)p_{i+1,j+1}}{1.0507}$$

0.0	1.0	2.0	3.0	4.0	5.0	6.0	7.0	8.0	9.0	10.0
10.23	15.55	20.62	25.52	29.86	33.13	34.64	33.51	28.53	18.07	0.00
9.23	4.33	7.67	11.29	14.75	17.63	19.42	19.49	17.06	11.03	0.00
↑		0.77	2.63	5.06	7.43	9.32	10.19	9.45	6.36	0.00
			0.00	0.09	1.38	2.83	4.05	4.39	3.26	0.00
NET VALUE				0.00	0.00	0.00	0.44	1.11	1.20	0.00
					0.00	0.00	0.00	0.00	0.00	0.00
						0.00	0.00	0.00	0.00	0.00
							0.00	0.00	0.00	0.00
								0.00	0.00	0.00
									0.00	0.00
										0.00

FIGURE 16.21 Enhanced Mine

The value of the lease with the new technology is now $10.23 million, and after netting out the fixed cost of the technology, $9.23 million. Clearly, it does not pay to adopt the technology in the first year of the lease. The question remains as to whether it is ever optimal to adopt the new technology, and the answer is that it depends on how high the price of gold goes. In Figure 16.22, therefore, we compare the periodic value of the enhanced mine to the original lease, denoting in each year the cases in which the net cost of the enhanced mine exceeds the original lease values. That is, the enhancements are attractive as long as $p_{i,j}^{enhanced} - \$1 > p_{i,j}$. These cases are highlighted in the third lattice, given in Figure 16.22. Beginning with year nine and substituting these enhancements back into the original lattice and working backward, continuing to substitute as long as the highlighted values exceed those in the original lattice, we find that only when gold prices reach $514.20 by year three (and continues to rise) will it pay to exercise the option during that year. In any case, it neither pays to enhance the mine nor to wait to exercise the option on the lease. The decision hinges on the cost of the enhancement, the increased variable costs of extraction and the price of gold. In this case, the price of gold was not sufficiently high to make the option viable.

The exercise of the option in this case is not optimal until year three, and that is because of the possibility that gold prices had reached a level sufficient to sustain the viability of the expense of the new technology. That decision was not so obvious in year one, when prices were only $278. It is important to understand the intuition here. The basic valuation logic is still intact—in general, the lease value is the discounted present value of the future payoffs modeled by the lattice. The option itself has value that is a function of the profitability of the lease, which, in turn, depends on the underlying movement in gold prices. The factors affecting the value of the option are the underlying price volatility, the discount rate, and the duration of the lease. It would be an interesting exercise to find out how sensitive this exercise would be to changes in each of these factors.

0.0	1.0	2.0	3.0	4.0	5.0	6.0	7.0	8.0	9.0	10.0
9.13	*15.79*	20.11	*24.52*	*28.86*	*32.13*	*33.64*	*32.51*	*27.53*	*17.07*	0.00
	5.75	8.58	11.49	14.25	16.64	*18.42*	*18.49*	*16.06*	*10.03*	0.00
		2.04	3.90	5.86	7.63	8.91	9.32	*8.45*	5.47	0.00
			0.15	1.14	2.36	3.54	4.30	4.26	2.99	0.00
				0.00	0.00	0.46	1.11	1.58	1.34	0.00
					0.00	0.00	0.00	0.00	0.25	0.00
						0.00	0.00	0.00	0.00	0.00
							0.00	0.00	0.00	0.00
								0.00	0.00	0.00
									0.00	0.00
										0.00

FIGURE 16.22 Real Option

SUMMARY

There are several excellent texts on option theory. This chapter serves as an introduction to that theory as it pertains to our understanding of portfolio management and risk, but not as a substitute. My intention here was to provide an introduction to this important class of securities as investments in their own right but primarily as instruments to hedge risk. In Chapter 17, I cover mathematical models of stock price dynamics, which will lay the groundwork for conducting Monte Carlo simulations that serve to model the dynamics in asset prices and also to price various options. Chapter 18 will then return to the concept of hedging with options.

Real options are too important to leave out of an introductory course in options theory. The gold mine example used here is from Luenberger's *Investment Science* text but gold prices and discount rates are actual. Real options open up a treasure trove of thinking and conceptualization about the world around us; indeed, we find that options in many forms have always been an integral part of our everyday lives.

REFERENCES

Hull, John. 2008. *Options, futures, and other derivatives,* 7th ed. Upper Saddle River, NJ: Prentice-Hall, 501.

Luenberger, David. 1998. *Investment science.* New York: Oxford University Press.

CHAPTER 17

Models of Stock Price Dynamics

What is now proved was once only imagin'd.

—William Blake

STOCK PRICE DYNAMICS

In this chapter, we learn how to construct and model stock price dynamics and then analyze the characteristics of options pricing models like Black-Scholes, whose behavior is derived from these models. Let's begin with a familiar discrete time model of single periodic growth in the asset's price S_t, using continuous compounding:

$$S_t = S_0 e^{\mu t}$$

We established previously that μ is the growth rate in prices, or the return to the asset (see footnote 2 in Chapter 15). We will continue to adopt the convention that μ is the *annualized* return. This is a *deterministic growth model* having no stochastic element. Setting $t = 1$ and taking logarithms on both sides solves for the single period return, $\ln(S_1) - \ln(S_0) = \mu$. More generally, we express this relationship as follows:

$$S_{t+\Delta t} = S_t e^{\mu \Delta t}$$

This form allows us to model price dynamics over subintervals of the year equal to Δt. Now let's consider the possibility that in addition to the deterministic component, price changes also have a *stochastic* component in the form of a random shock ε over the interval Δt, that is:

$$S_{t+\Delta t} = S_t e^{\mu \Delta t + \varepsilon \sqrt{\Delta t}}$$

The shock ε acts like a volatility parameter and that is why it is accompanied by the square root of Δt, which makes its variance $\sigma^2 \Delta t$. With no loss of generality, assume zero growth ($\mu = 0$) for now and concentrate on the stochastic innovation to prices. Taking logarithms,

$$\ln(S_{t+\Delta}) - \ln(S_t) = \varepsilon\sqrt{\Delta t} = \Delta z$$

If, for example, $\Delta t = 1$, then log prices change by a random shock equal to ε. If we assume that ε is a draw from a standard normal distribution, $N(0,1)$, then Δz is a discrete time *Wiener process*. This says that price changes are purely random. We have, by definition, the properties:

$$E\left(\varepsilon\sqrt{\Delta t}\right) = \sqrt{\Delta t} * E(\varepsilon) = 0$$

$$\text{var}\left(\varepsilon\sqrt{\Delta t}\right) = \sigma^2 \Delta t = \Delta t \text{ since } \sigma^2 = 1$$

In the limit, as $\Delta t \to 0$, Δt becomes the continuous time derivative dt, and likewise $\Delta z \to dz$, which is a continuous time Wiener process.

In discrete time, setting $\Delta t = 1$ results in a *random walk* process. What is a random walk? For $\Delta z = \varepsilon\sqrt{\Delta t}$, setting $\Delta t = 1$ results in $\Delta z = \varepsilon$, which is a *white noise* process. Now, by definition, $\Delta z = z_t - z_{t-1}$. Therefore, $z_t = z_{t-1} + \varepsilon$. This is a random walk in *discrete time*. What it means is that changes in z are independent, normally distributed, mean zero, random variables with unit variance. Therefore, log changes in stock prices—and therefore, stock returns—are unpredictable in this model of stock price dynamics. If μ is nonzero, then returns have an expectation, or mean component, but movements around this mean are unpredictable.

Figure 17.1 shows one such discrete representation for a hypothetical daily price change in which values for ε are drawn from a standard normal

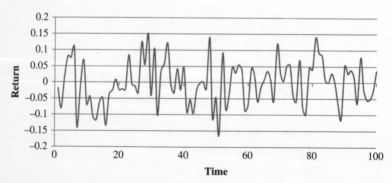

FIGURE 17.1 Wiener Process

distribution. This particular example is also a white noise process since $\mu =$ 0 and $\sigma = 1$. See the chapter examples spreadsheet for details.

We can generalize the Wiener process to include the mean return μ, which we refer to as a drift component (it's now a random walk with drift). If, for example, ΔS is a discrete time Wiener process with drift, we would model this as follows (where α and β are parameters to the process):

$$S_{t+\Delta t} = S_t e^{\alpha \Delta t + \beta \varepsilon \sqrt{\Delta t}}$$

Taking logs and letting $\Delta t \to 0$ means that $\ln(S_{t+\Delta t}) - \ln(S_t) \to d\ln(St) = dS/S$ and therefore:

$$dS/S = \alpha dt + \beta dz = \alpha dt + \beta \varepsilon \sqrt{dt}$$

Specifically, setting $\alpha = \mu$ and $\beta = \sigma$ results in a model of stock price dynamics. Figure 17.2 is a discrete time model of this process for a daily stock price with drift $\mu = 0.12$ per year, and that starts at $S_0 = \$15$ with annual volatility (σ) equal to 20 percent. Note that β is a parameter in this process, denoting volatility and not the CAPM β, which is a covariance with the market return divided by the variance of the market return. Note that we set $\Delta t = 1/250$ in this example to simulate daily movements. The simulations behind these examples are provided in the chapter spreadsheet under the Wiener and Generalized tabs.

By definition, we can extend this concept to model continuous returns expressed as dS/S. It is intuitively appealing to model *relative* changes in price; thus we could examine the generalized Wiener process:

$$\frac{dS}{S} = \mu dt + \sigma dz$$

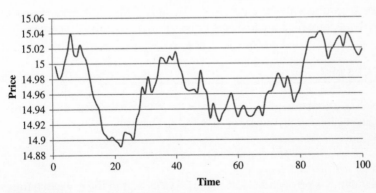

FIGURE 17.2　Stock Price Dynamic

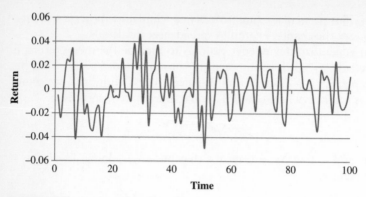

FIGURE 17.3   Brownian Motion

Equivalently,

$$dS = \mu S\, dt + \sigma S\, dz$$

This is geometric *Brownian motion*. To digress a bit, consider the nonstochastic part of the process $\frac{dS}{S} = \mu dt$. Integrating this over time dt yields:

$$\int_{S_0}^{S_t} \frac{dS}{S} = \ln S; \int_0^t \mu\, dt = \mu t$$

We establish, therefore, this chapter's first model, $S_t = S_0 e^{\mu t}$, which describes the deterministic growth in the stock price over time. The addition of the stochastic component $\sigma\, dz$ describes how shocks, in the form of ε, contribute to the growth process through time.

Figure 17.3 illustrates the case for 100 daily Brownian motion stock returns with an annual drift equal to 15 percent and volatility 20 percent.

ITO PROCESSES

Ito processes are generalized Wiener processes in which the drift and volatility parameters can also be functions of S and t. That is:

$$dS = \mu(S, t)dt + \sigma(S, t)dz$$

Ito's lemma is a powerful result that allows us to find the price dynamic for a derivative of S. The intuition is that for any security, say, G, that we know to be a derivative of S, then Ito's lemma can be used to solve for the Brownian motion process of G. Ito's lemma says that G must satisfy the following relationship (A proof is given in Appendix 17.1):

$$dG = \left(\frac{\partial G}{\partial S}\mu S + \frac{\partial G}{\partial t} + \frac{1}{2}\frac{\partial^2 G}{\partial S^2}\sigma^2 S^2\right)dt + \frac{\partial G}{\partial S}\sigma S dz$$

EXAMPLE 17.1

To illustrate, consider the following problem. Suppose a stock price follows a geometric Brownian motion, which is an Ito process $dS = \mu S dt + \sigma S dz$. We want to find an expression describing the dynamics in the *forward price* F on a nondividend-paying stock, S with $(T - t)$ time to delivery. That is, we want an expression for the security F given by the relationship $F = S\,e^{r(T-t)}$ if S follows an Ito process.

First, we recognize that the discount rate $d(0,T) = e^{-rT}$. We then compute the following partial derivatives according to Ito's lemma:

$$\frac{\partial F}{\partial S} = e^{r(T-t)}; \frac{\partial^2 F}{\partial S^2} = 0; \frac{\partial F}{\partial t} = -rSe^{r(T-t)}$$

Making the necessary substitutions, we arrive at:

$$dF = \left(e^{r(T-t)}\mu S - rSe^{r(T-t)}\right)dt + e^{r(T-t)}\sigma S\,dz$$

$$dF = (\mu - r)Se^{r(T-t)}dt + e^{r(T-t)}\sigma S dz$$

Finally,

$$dF = (\mu - r)F\,dt + \sigma F\,dz$$

This says that dF is also a geometric Brownian motion process with drift equal to the stock's risk premium.

EXAMPLE 17.2   Proof of Lognormal Prices

Suppose $dS = \mu S dt + \sigma S dz$ governs the movements in the stock price S. What is the process governing movements in $F = \ln S(t)$? To solve this, we use Ito's lemma. The process governing F is given by:

$$dF = \left(\frac{\partial F}{\partial S} \mu S + \frac{\partial F}{\partial t} + \frac{1}{2} \frac{\partial^2 F}{\partial S^2} \sigma^2 S^2 \right) dt + \frac{\partial F}{\partial S} \sigma S dz$$

We next compute the partial derivatives:

$$\frac{\partial F}{\partial S} = \frac{1}{S}; \frac{\partial^2 F}{\partial S^2} = -\frac{1}{S^2}; \frac{\partial F}{\partial t} = 0$$

Substituting these values into dF results in:

$$dF = d \ln S = \left(\mu - \frac{1}{2} \sigma^2 \right) dt + \sigma dz$$

Figure 17.3 is one example of this returns process and its derivation is given in the chapter spreadsheet under the Generalized tab. Figure 17.4 shows the corresponding price dynamics for the forward contract from Example 17.1 and this stock. The example normalizes prices to start at 100 and assumes that the risk-free rate is 5 percent while the annualized return and volatility on the stock is 15 percent and 30 percent, respectively.

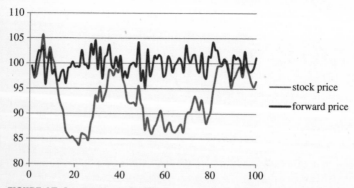

FIGURE 17.4   Application of Ito's Lemma

As Example 17.2 proves, there is less drift in the forward price. We can use this example to discuss confidence intervals and probability statements as well. Since the log price is normally distributed, we have in general:

$$\ln(S_T) \sim N\left[\ln(S_0) + \left(\mu - \frac{1}{2}\sigma^2\right)T, \sigma^2 T\right]$$

Thus, if T corresponds to one year, say, and the stock return has mean μ equal to 7 percent with volatility-squared equal to $0.15^2 = 0.0225$, then a 95 percent confidence band for simulated stock *return* will be contained in the range:

$$-z\sigma < \mu - \frac{\sigma^2}{2} < z\sigma$$

where $-z =$ Normsinv(.025), $z =$ Normsinv(.0975). Thus, the mean return is contained in the interval $(-0.294, +0.294)$.

LOGNORMAL STOCK PRICES

It would be useful at this point to stop for a moment and collect a few important results. We established the process of geometric Brownian motion whereby stock returns follow the process:

$$\frac{dS}{S} = \mu dt + \sigma dz;$$

We then used Ito's lemma to prove that for $dS = \mu S dt + \sigma S dz$, it must be that the logarithm of prices, $\ln(S_t)$, has the following form:

$$d\ln S = \left(\mu - \frac{1}{2}\sigma^2\right)dt + \sigma dz$$

These are both models of stock return dynamics, but they are clearly not the same. The difference is subtle with the log form having a small correction factor. In fact, as the variance of the returns gets arbitrarily small, the two are equivalent. Recall from Chapter 1 that the difference between the arithmetic mean and the geometric mean goes to zero with the variance of the random return. That logic is applicable to explaining the difference here as well and as we shall see, the assumption that the mean of geometric Brownian motion is equal to μ overstates the mean and the correction factor $\frac{1}{2}\sigma^2$

is required. Let's try to sketch out an explanation as to why this is the case. I will do this in two steps.

The first step will derive the mean of a lognormally distributed return. To do this, let me begin with a very general model that governs stock price movements over time, starting with the stock price S_t at time t and letting v_t represent a random shock at time t. Again, we assume that shocks are independent over time (independence means that the covariance of shocks is zero, for example, $\text{cov}(v\_t, v\_(t+s)) = 0$.) and we postulate that the difference between the current price and last period's price is due to the shock (which is caused by some event, anticipated or otherwise). As such, we model the basic price dynamic as:

$$S_t = S_{t-1} * v_t$$

This is not the deterministic growth model from the first equation. It is, however, related to the stochastic model $S_{t+\Delta t} = S_t e^{\mu \Delta t + \varepsilon \sqrt{\Delta t}}$, which reduces to $S_{t+1} = S_t e^{\varepsilon}$ if we restrict growth to zero. Implicitly, we assume that $v\_t = e^{\wedge}(\mu \Delta t + \varepsilon \sqrt{\Delta t})$. The two, therefore, are equivalent models of stochastic movement in stock prices. If we substitute for the lagged stock price, we get the following:

$$S_t = (S_{t-2} * v_{t-1}) * v_t$$

Successive substitution therefore generates the multiplicative model of stock prices as the product of the shocks:

$$S_t = S_0 * v_0 * v_1 * \cdots * v_{t-1} * v_t$$

This says that the price we currently see is the accumulated effect of the shocks, that is, the observed price is really the product of geometrically linking the individual shocks over time. It is important to note, if it is not already obvious, that for prices to remain positive, the shocks must also be positive. As we shall see further on, this property has implications concerning the probability distribution governing the shocks, v. If we take natural logarithms on both sides, we can represent this as an additive model, to wit:

$$\ln(S_t) = \ln(S_0) + \sum_{i=0}^{t} \ln(v_i)$$

Thus, the discrete time return (which is defined as the difference in the log prices—see Chapter 1) is a sum of random shocks

$$\ln(S_t) - \ln(S_0) = \sum_{i=0}^{t} \ln(v_i)$$

With continuous compounding, $P\_1 = P\_0\ e^{\wedge}rt$. Taking natural logs and noting that $t = 1$ for this example gives us the following: $\ln[(P\_1) = \ln[(P\_0) + r]]$. Equivalently, $\ln[(P\_1/P\_0) = r]$.

Let us denote the innovations to this returns process by $w_i = \ln(v_i)$. Equivalently, $v_i = e^{w_i}$. It follows therefore that the *logarithms* of the shocks given by $\ln(v_i)$ are normally distributed, which is consistent with the assumption that *returns* be normally distributed. The shocks must be strictly non-negative, since we are transforming them into logarithms and the log of a negative number is undefined (recall, $\ln(1) = 0$, while the log of numbers larger than 1 are positive and the log of a fraction is a negative number, which approaches negative infinity as the fraction approaches zero). Denote the mean and variance of the logarithms of these shocks, respectively, by w, σ^2. For example, w might be the annual expected return on a stock (for example, 15 percent in the examples in the previous section). It follows then that the shocks themselves (the v_i) are *lognormally* distributed.

As lognormal random variables, the shocks do not have a mean described by $E(e^w)$; rather, as lognormally distributed random variables, $E(v) = e^{w + \frac{1}{2}\sigma^2}$ and variance $\text{var}(v) = e^{2w + 2\sigma^2} - e^{2w + \sigma^2}$. An example of a lognormal distribution is given in Figure 17.5 based on the assumption that $w = 0.15$ and $\sigma = 0.3$. Prices are normalized to 100.

Notice that the lognormal distribution is skewed right (because prices must be positive). That is why the mean $E(v)$ contains the additive correction factor $\frac{1}{2}\sigma^2$ and this factor gives this distribution *fatter tails* than the normal distribution.

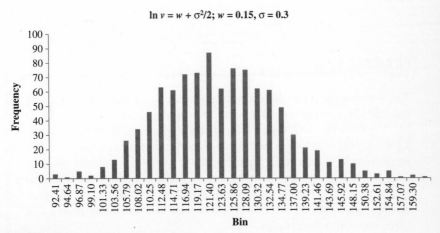

FIGURE 17.5 Lognormal Distribution

The second step involves showing that the mean in geometric Brownian motion is overstated and therefore requires the correction factor we see in Example 17.2. Again, let's begin with the same model of continuously compounded returns:

$$S_t = S_0 e^{wt}$$

The expected value of the stock price in period t is therefore:

$$E(S_t) = S_0 e^{wt}$$

Taking logarithms, we solve for the mean return w:

$$\ln[E(S_t)] - \ln(S_0) = wt$$

If $\ln[E(S_t)] = E[\ln(S_t)]$ then we would conclude that $E\left[\ln\left(S_t/S_0\right)\right] = E(w) * t = w * t$. But, this is not the case. In fact, $\ln[E(S_t)] > E[\ln(S_t)]$, indicating that the mean is overstated. As we showed in step 1, the mean is $w + \frac{1}{2}\sigma^2$ for the lognormal distribution and therefore, we must subtract the correction factor to establish the required equivalence, that is:

$$\ln[E(S_t)] - \ln(S_0) = \left(w - \frac{1}{2}\sigma^2\right) * t$$

This result is in accordance with the result in Example 17.3.

EXAMPLE 17.3

Assume that the monthly return has mean $\mu = 1$ percent and monthly volatility $\sigma = 4$ percent. Then the expected annual return would be $(0.01 + 0.0008) \times 12$ which is close to 12 percent with annual volatility $4\%(\sqrt{12}) = 13.86\%$ under the assumption that returns are independent and lognormally distributed. Price dynamics over discrete time intervals given by Δt—for example, Δt could represent fractions of a year, say, $\frac{1}{12}, \frac{1}{52}, \frac{1}{250}$ for monthly, weekly, and daily frequencies— would suggest mean returns equal to $\mu \Delta t$ and variances $\sigma^2 \Delta t$ for a given interval defined on Δt.

DERIVING THE PARAMETERS OF THE BINOMIAL LATTICE

This is a good point to stop and fit what we've learned into a one-period option model and finally answer the question about the origin of the parameters u and d. We have, from before, a model of log price changes (that is, returns):

$$\ln(S_1) - \ln(S_0) \sim N\left[\left(\mu - \frac{1}{2}\sigma^2\right), \sigma^2\right]$$

This shows the one-period movement in the stock price attributable to a single shock with volatility σ. In our lattice, this shock takes the form up (u) or down (d); that is, it is a binomial outcome. *Assuming that S_0 is 1*, then for this single-period model, we'd have the expected price equal to the probability weighted average of the two possible outcomes (that is, u or d)

$$E\ln(S_1) = p * \ln(u) + (1 - p) * \ln(d)$$

The variance of the expected stock price is therefore (we make use of the result in statistics that $\text{Var}(X) = E(X^2) - [E(X)]^2$):

$$\text{var}(\ln S_1) = p * (\ln(u))^2 + (1 - p) * (\ln(d))^2 - (p * \ln(u) + (1 - p) * \ln(d))^2$$

This expression factors to the following result:

$$\text{var}(\ln S_1) = p * (1 - p) * (\ln u - \ln d)^2$$

In sum, we have the mean and variance of stock prices in our lattice given by the two relations:

$$\mu \Delta t = p * \ln(u) + (1 - p) * \ln(d)$$

$$\sigma^2 \Delta t = p * (1 - p) * (\ln u - \ln d)^2$$

Note that we set $d = 1/u$ in our work from before. Doing that now simplifies these relationships as follows:

$$\mu \Delta t = \ln(u)(2p - 1)$$

$$\sigma^2 \Delta t = 4p(1 - p)(\ln u)^2$$

Therefore, we have two equations in two unknowns, p and $\ln u$. Start by solving for the probability p. Squaring the first equation (to get a term in $(\ln u)^2$) and adding this to the second equation gets us $(\ln u)^2 = \sigma^2 \Delta t + (\mu \Delta t)^2$. If we substitute this back into the first equation, we can solve directly for p as:

$$ p = \frac{1}{2} + \frac{\dfrac{1}{2}}{\sqrt{\dfrac{\sigma^2}{\mu^2 \Delta t} + 1}} $$

And, substituting this term back in to either equation allows us to solve for $\ln u$ as follows:

$$ \ln u = \sqrt{\sigma^2 \Delta t + (\mu \Delta t)^2} $$

which, in turn, implies that:

$$ \ln d = -\sqrt{\sigma^2 \Delta t + (\mu \Delta t)^2} $$

As $\Delta t \to 0$, the squared term goes to zero, indicating that $\ln u = \sigma \sqrt{\Delta t}$. Therefore, $u = e^{\sigma \sqrt{\Delta t}}$. Finally, we see that $d = 1/u = e^{-\sigma \sqrt{\Delta t}}$. The conclusion is that the magnitude of the up and down movements in the stock price in our lattice depends on the underlying volatility of the stock return scaled by the time interval Δt. In the call and put option lattices depicted earlier, we assumed $u = 1.06$ and that $\Delta t = 1/12$. Now, we know that this would be consistent with an annual returns volatility of 20 percent.

Go to the companion website for more details.

In general, as the asset's volatility rises, so does the value of the option. To see this, just change the value of sigma in the Chapter 16 spreadsheet from its current value of 0.20 to, say, 0.30. You will readily see that the binomial lattice values have expanded, indicating a much wider range of possible spot prices in the future and, with these, higher likelihoods that the options will be in the money. It is also the case that option values fall as the discount rate rises. The one-month discount rate was based on a 10 percent annual rate—this is the assumed risk-free rate with a flat term structure. In reality, we would replace the one-month rate with the one-month *short rates* and discount accordingly.

BLACK-SCHOLES-MERTON MODEL

As $\Delta t \to 0$, the number of nodes in our binomial lattice goes to infinity and we are essentially moving to a continuous time option model. The Black-Scholes model (independently derived by Robert Merton) is a closed form continuous time option pricing model. Its derivation is mathematically rigorous, but I think we can sketch its derivation using the tools we've derived thus far. The model is based on the assumptions that the underlying stock price is a geometric Brownian motion process and that the stock price S has a lognormal distribution. The intuition is this: there are three assets—a bond, a stock, and a derivative. These assets' dynamics can be described by the following respective models, which we've already derived:

$$dB = rBdt$$

$$dS = \mu Sdt + \sigma Sdz$$

$$dF = \left(\frac{\partial F}{\partial S}\mu S + \frac{\partial F}{\partial t} + \frac{1}{2}\frac{\partial^2 F}{\partial S^2}\sigma^2 S^2 \right)dt + \frac{\partial F}{\partial S}\sigma Sdz$$

We recognize, first, the deterministic return on a riskless bond followed by geometric Brownian motion describing the stock price movement and, finally, Ito's lemma, which describes the dynamics underlying the derivative on the stock. The insight behind Black-Scholes is that we could form a riskless portfolio consisting of the stock and the derivative, thus equating the return on this portfolio to the return on the riskless bond. This is the notion of constructing a replicating portfolio. Suppose we do this, selecting X units of the stock and Y units of the derivative. Then, at time t, we have the following portfolio:

$$P_t = X_t S_t + Y_t F_t$$

To replicate the payout of a bond, we choose X and Y so that this portfolio is riskless. Since it is riskless, this implies that it earns the same return as the bond, which means that $dP = rPdt$. This condition must be satisfied, otherwise there would be an arbitrage opportunity suggesting that one could short the security with the lower return and go long the other, earning a riskless premium. We need an expression for dP. To get this, we use the simple definition:

$$dP_t = P_{t+\Delta t} - P_t = X_t S_{t+\Delta t} + Y_t F_t - (X_t S_t + Y_t F_t)$$

$$dP_t = X_t dS_t + Y_t dF_t$$

As long as no money is added or taken from this portfolio, it will be self-financing and therefore have the following dynamic:

$$dP = XdS + YdF$$

We can substitute for dS and dF to get:

$$dP = X(\mu Sdt + \sigma Sdz) + Y\left(\frac{\partial F}{\partial S}\mu S + \frac{\partial F}{\partial t} + \frac{1}{2}\frac{\partial^2 F}{\partial S^2}\sigma^2 S^2\right)dt + Y\frac{\partial F}{\partial S}\sigma Sdz$$

Collecting terms:

$$dP = \left[X\mu S + Y\left(\frac{\partial F}{\partial S}\mu S + \frac{\partial F}{\partial t} + \frac{1}{2}\frac{\partial^2 F}{\partial S^2}\sigma^2 S^2\right)\right]dt + \left(Y\frac{\partial F}{\partial S}\sigma S + X\sigma S\right)dz$$

This simplifies. The reason is that we need this portfolio to be riskless. For that to happen, we must first eliminate dz as follows:

$$\left(Y\frac{\partial F}{\partial S}\sigma S + X\sigma S\right)dz = 0$$

This implies that $\left(Y\frac{\partial F}{\partial S}\sigma S = -X\sigma S\right)$, implying that $\left(-Y\frac{\partial F}{\partial S} = X\right)$. This will allow us to eliminate X as well. Making these substitutions, we get:

$$dP = \left[-Y\frac{\partial F}{\partial S}\mu S + Y\left(\frac{\partial F}{\partial S}\mu S + \frac{\partial F}{\partial t} + \frac{1}{2}\frac{\partial^2 F}{\partial S^2}\sigma^2 S^2\right)\right]dt$$

$$dP = Y\left(\frac{\partial F}{\partial t} + \frac{1}{2}\frac{\partial^2 F}{\partial S^2}\sigma^2 S^2\right)dt = rPdt$$

But,

$$P = XS + YF = -Y\frac{\partial F}{\partial S}S + YF = Y\left(F - \frac{\partial F}{\partial S}\right)$$

Therefore,

$$dP = Y\left(\frac{\partial F}{\partial t} + \frac{1}{2}\frac{\partial^2 F}{\partial S^2}\sigma^2 S^2\right)dt = rY\left(F - \frac{\partial F}{\partial S}\right)dt$$

Finally, eliminating Y and dt solves for the *Black-Scholes equation:*

$$rF = \frac{\partial F}{\partial t} + \frac{1}{2}\frac{\partial^2 F}{\partial S^2}\sigma^2 S^2 + \frac{\partial F}{\partial S}rS$$

This is a partial differential equation. Its solution depends on the option and the option's boundary condition. For European call options, we impose the boundary condition that $c(0,t) = 0$ (where c is the call option) and we want the value of the call to maximize the (risk neutral) expected value of the future stock price over the strike price, for example,

$$c = E[\max(S_T - K), 0]$$

The solution to the partial differential for this boundary condition is:

$$c = e^{-rT}[S_0 e^{rt} N(d_1) - KN(d_2)]$$

with d_1 and d_2 given by:

$$d_1 = \frac{\ln\left(\frac{S_0}{K}\right) + \left(r + \frac{\sigma^2}{2}\right)T}{\sigma\sqrt{T}}; \quad d_2 = \frac{\ln\left(\frac{S_0}{K}\right) + \left(r - \frac{\sigma^2}{2}\right)T}{\sigma\sqrt{T}} = d_1 - \sigma\sqrt{T}$$

$N(d_1)$ and $N(d_2)$ are cumulative standard normal densities (NORMSDIST in Excel). Admittedly, this looks intimidating. If you look at the call option value, the term in brackets consists of the difference between the expected growth in the stock price $S_0 e^{rt}$ over the strike price K. The normal densities essentially are derived from the expected value of a lognormally distributed random variable (the stock price). This difference is discounted using the risk-free rate over the period of the option. Simplifying, we get:

$$c = \left[S_0 N(d_1) - e^{-rT} KN(d_2)\right]$$

Again, we see that the value of the call is the difference between today's stock price and the discounted exercise price, both scaled by a constant evaluated under the cumulative standard normal distribution. The parameters of d_1 and d_2 clearly reflect the properties of the lognormal density, for example, $(r + \frac{\sigma^2}{2})$, $\sigma\sqrt{T}$.

THE GREEK LETTERS

Let's now take a closer look at this model. First, let us define the cumulative standard normal distribution function because we are going to need this to evaluate Black-Scholes:

$$N(x) = \frac{1}{\sqrt{2\pi}} \int_{-\infty}^{x} e^{-y^2/2} dy$$

$N(x)$ is bounded between zero and one since it is a probability. Thus, $N(d_1)$ for example, substitutes d_1 for x in this expression and is increasing in the value of d_1 which, itself, is a positive function of the difference between the current spot price S_0 and the strike price K as well as the risk-free return but is negatively related to the underlying volatility. From the definitions given earlier, it follows that d_2 is also declining in volatility. It is easy to demonstrate using a spreadsheet that both $N(d_1)$ and $N(d_2)$ are declining in volatility but that their spread is increasing in volatility and this proves that the value of the call option will rise with volatility. The intuition here is that as volatility rises, so does the likelihood that the option will be in the money. This, actually, is the notion of the option's *vega*—its sensitivity to underlying volatility.

These initial observations give rise to a host of questions regarding the sensitivity of the call option value to changes in the underlying parameters. These questions involve solving for the so-called *Greek letters*, a topic to which we now turn our attention. I will demonstrate these for the call option. Extension to put options is straightforward.

The first question of interest asks how sensitive the call option's value is to movements in the underlying spot price. This is called the option's *delta*, specifically, $\frac{\partial c}{\partial S_0} = N(d_1)$. The delta is therefore bounded like a probability—it is the cumulative standard normal density evaluated at d_1. From the discussion just had, it is going to be higher (lower) the lower (higher) is the volatility on the underlying security's return. Low volatility stocks, for example, are going to have a relatively higher delta because movements in price of any size are expected to be less likely than for higher volatility stocks. Thus, call value on lower volatility stocks is more sensitive to changes in spot prices. At the same time, delta responds to the relationship between spot and strike prices, moving higher as the option displays more *moneyness* ($S > K$) and vice versa. This result is also intuitive; option value is not going to be very sensitive to changes in price if the option is out of the money (OTM).

The option's delta can be thought of as a measure of risk with respect to movements in the underlying share price, itself a function of volatility. A delta of one means that if the stock price goes up a dollar, the call option value also goes up a dollar. So, if I had a portfolio that consisted of a long position in the stock (one share) and a short call, then that portfolio would be hedged against changes in the stock price. It would be *delta neutral*. If, on the other hand, delta were 0.5, then a one-dollar decline in the stock would decrease the value of the call by $0.50 and therefore, a portfolio of one-half share and one short call is delta neutral.

Knowing an option's delta is not only useful in evaluating the sensitivity of option value, it is useful as a tool to hedge portfolio risk.

EXAMPLE 17.4

A five-month call on a $1 stock with a strike price of $0.90. Let's apply this to our binomial lattice provided on the Chapter 16 spreadsheet examples for which $\Delta t = \frac{1}{12}; R = \left(1 + \frac{0.10}{12}\right) = 1.0083;$ $\sigma = 0.20; T = \frac{5}{12}$. The binomial lattice value is $0.145.

Solving Black-Scholes, we first get $d_1 = 1.20; d_2 = 1.07$ and a call value equal to $0.144. We establish the option's delta as $N(1.2) = 0.886$. This means that a *delta neutral* portfolio would consist of 0.866 shares long and one short call.

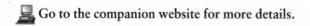 Go to the companion website for more details.

There's a hitch here—the option's delta is not constant. Therefore, a delta-neutral portfolio at spot price S_0 is not going to be delta neutral at S_1. There are some chapter exercises that illustrate the range of delta and the other Greeks further on, but for now, let's develop Example 17.4 a little bit more. As stated, the delta on this call option is 0.886 when the spot price is equal to $1. When the spot price is at $0.90, however, the delta is 0.65, indicating that the delta-neutral portfolio would consist of 0.65 shares and not 0.866 shares as solved earlier. Thus, the delta neutral portfolio is not constant. Since delta is a first derivative, its nonconstancy suggests we need a second derivative—the conceptual equivalent of bond convexity. For options, this convexity is captured in gamma.

The call option's *gamma* tells us how sensitive delta is itself to the underlying price. It is therefore the derivative of delta with respect to price and is given by the chain rule of calculus:

$$\Gamma = \frac{\partial^2 c}{\partial S_0^2} = N'(d_1)\frac{\partial d_1}{\partial S_o}.$$

The cumulative standard normal density has a first derivative given by:

$$N'(d_1) = \frac{1}{\sqrt{2\pi}}e^{-d_1^2/2}$$

and where this term needs to be followed by $\frac{\partial d_1}{\partial S} = \frac{1}{S_0 \sigma \sqrt{T}}$. Putting these two terms together, we get gamma given by:

$$\Gamma = \frac{N'(d_1)}{S_0 \sigma \sqrt{T}}$$

Therefore, while delta on the call option in Example 17.4 is 0.886, its gamma is equal to 0.106 (see the chapter spreadsheet labeled *Greeks* for more examples). This means that when the spot price on the stock changes by ΔS, the delta of the option changes by $0.106\Delta S$. If gamma is small, then delta changes slowly and the need to rebalance the portfolio to keep it delta neutral comes less frequently than if gamma were large. In our example, if the stock price changes by one dollar, the delta will change from 0.886 to $0.886 + 0.106 = 0.992$, and the hedge should be adjusted accordingly to keep the portfolio delta neutral.

We discussed the concept of vega already. I will leave it as an exercise to derive the following formula to solve for the sensitivity of the option with respect to changes in the volatility of the underlying stock:

$$v = \frac{\partial c}{\partial \sigma} = S\sqrt{T}N'(d_1)$$

The vega for the call option in our example is therefore equal to 0.53; thus, a 1 percent increase in the volatility (from 20 percent to 21 percent in this case) will move the option's value by the amount $0.53*0.01 = \$0.0053$.

I leave it to the reader to prove that the call option's sensitivity to time, called its *theta*, is given by:

$$\Theta = -\frac{N'(d_1)S_0\sigma}{2\sqrt{T}} - rKe^{-rT}N(d_2)$$

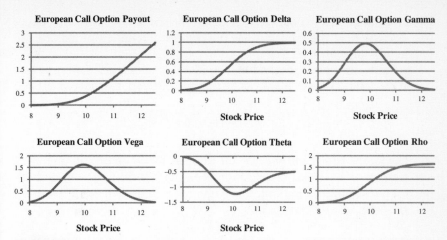

FIGURE 17.6 European Call Option Greeks ($S = 10, K = 10, T = 0.2, r = 0.05,$ $\sigma = 0.20$)

Figure 17.6 is taken from an example given in the chapter spreadsheet for a call option on a stock with current spot price equal to $10, with strike price $10 and a two-month expiry. Its purpose is to show the relationships between the various Greeks as the spot price deviates from the strike price of $10.

We can see, for example, that delta has an inflection point at $10 and that small movements around $10 result in the largest changes in delta as depicted by gamma. The delta on OTM calls rises at an increasing rate up to ATM and then at a decreasing rate. This should be clear from the sigmoid shape of delta and that is what gamma depicts, that is, that, while the option price is increasingly sensitive to the stock price up to $10, that sensitivity is somewhat muted once the option is in the money. Likewise, ATM option values have maximum sensitivity to changes in volatility (vega) but that sensitivity is muted somewhat away from $10. That is because as the spot price nears the strike, changes in volatility have bigger implications regarding whether the option will be in the money or not. Theta tells a similar, but inverted story; option value is most highly sensitive to the length of the contract (time to expiry) when the option is most out of the money. At the money, time sensitivity is lowest, and as an option moves further into the money, this sensitivity rises, but not as fast as it does as the option moves more and more out of the money. Like delta, rho rises monotonically with spot price, but at an increasing rate as the option approaches the strike price from below and at a decreasing rate as it moves further into the money. The intuition here is that small changes in the discount rate are more meaningful as the option approaches the strike price from any direction because near the money it has the greatest likelihood of making the option profitable (or not).

For puts, the boundary condition on Black-Scholes is $c(S,T) = c(\infty, t) = 0$, and the solution to the Black-Scholes partial differential equation is:

$$p = Ke^{-rT}N(-d_2) - S_0N(-d_1)$$

The Greek letters for puts are the same as for those on call options. I also leave as an exercise the derivation of the option's rho; its sensitivity to interest rate changes. For a call, rho is equal to $KTe^{\wedge}(-rT)\ N(d\_2)$ and for a put, rho is $-KTe^{\wedge}(-rT)\ N(-d\_2)$.

EXAMPLE 17.5

A five-month put on a $1 stock with a strike price of $0.95. Using the same parameters from the previous example generates a put value of $0.026 using Black-Scholes compared to $0.018 using the lattice. The delta for the put is equal to –0.256, implying that a *delta-neutral* hedge would require a short position of 0.256 shares against the short put.

 Go to the companion website for more details.

We can observe spot and exercise prices, discount rates, and time to maturity. But, as I argued in Chapter 11 on risk, we cannot observe volatility. This is the one input into option pricing models that must be estimated, either from historical data, or through revealed trades. Estimating volatility using observed option contracts is referred to as *implied volatility*. The VIX index is calculated as a weighted average of implied volatilities of various options on the S&P 500. We'll use the VIX in our risk hedging work in Chapter 18, on hedging risk. I set up an example in the Chapter 17 spreadsheet labeled *Greeks* using Excel's Solver and Black-Scholes that estimates volatility *implied* by an observed call option contract. This is a straightforward iterative exercise—given the market price of the option and conditional on the observed values for the discount rate, time to maturity, spot price, and strike price, we can back into the volatility implied by the observed price.

EXAMPLE 17.6

Implied volatility on a call option. A five-month in-the-money call option with strike $35 and current spot price $36 currently sells for $3.25. The yield on T-bills is 10 percent. What is the implied volatility? Referring to the Chapter 17 spreadsheet exercises *Greeks,* we see that Solver applied to the Black-Scholes model finds $\sigma = 20$ percent as the volatility implied by this contract.

 Go to the companion website for more details (see Greeks under Chapter 17 examples).

Options traders often prefer to quote implied volatilities instead of prices. Consider, for example, the call option in Example 17.6 that trades at time t_0 for $3.25 at spot price $36. The implied volatility is 20 percent. Suppose at time t_1, the same five-month call is trading at $3.71, with the underlying price at $37. The implied volatility is now 15 percent. So, while the price of the call has increased, it has actually become cheaper in terms of volatility. What do we mean by cheaper in this context? The intuition has to do with the cost of hedging. Recall that for a delta hedge, we are long the stock and short the call and the stock hedges the risk that the call will be exercised. As the price of the stock rises, the cost of the hedge falls. Thus, in terms of implied volatility, this option is cheaper because it is cheaper to hedge.

MONTE CARLO METHODS

 Go to the companion website for more details.

The Chapter 16 spreadsheet contains an example using the Black-Scholes-Merton model for a European call option on a nondividend-paying stock with spot price $S = 100$, strike $K = 105$, risk-free rate 3 percent, with volatility 14.4 percent, and one year to exercise. This option has value $4.90. Let's try to replicate the BSM result using Monte Carlo. We have the following representation from Example 17.2:

$$\ln S(T) - \ln S(0) = \left(\mu - \frac{1}{2}\sigma^2\right)T + \sigma\varepsilon\sqrt{T}$$

We can exponentiate this for easier simulation as follows:

$$S(T) = S(0)\exp\left[\left(\mu - \frac{1}{2}\sigma^2\right)T + \sigma\varepsilon\sqrt{T}\right]$$

In Excel, we substitute for $\varepsilon = \text{norminv(rand())}$,

$$S(T) = 100\exp\left[0.0196\,T + 0.144\,normsinv(rand()) * \sqrt{T}\right]$$

Taking $T =$ one year, Column A under the Monte Carlo tab contains 1,000 simulated prices for this stock S. Pressing F9 refreshes this spreadsheet calculation. As you can see, these solutions are distributed closely to the BSM solution of $4.90. Changing the parameter values on the spreadsheet will generate various problems that you can use to check against the analytic solution provided by the BSM formula.

Let's now take a look at *correlated Brownian motion*. Suppose we have two stocks, each following a lognormal process but which have correlation ρ. I will provide an application further on, but for now, let's concentrate on the task of simulating two lognormal stock prices that are also correlated. The sheet labeled *Corr BM* provides the details. Here is the intuition: the first step is to generate the Wiener processes. Columns A and B do this, generating 1,000 observations on $\varepsilon\sqrt{T}$, where T is one year in this case. If we wanted, say, monthly frequency, then we would use the command in Excel: Normsinv(rand())/12. We then construct a vector containing the drift components $(\mu - \frac{\sigma_i^2}{2})$, where μ is the risk-neutral rate (the risk-free rate in Black-Scholes).

The second step constructs the covariance matrix. In this example, I assume that the first stock has annual volatility equal to 14.4 percent while the second stock has annual volatility equal to 17 percent and that the correlation between their returns is 50 percent. The covariance matrix V is therefore the product:

$$V = S * C * S$$

Here, S is a diagonal matrix of volatilities and C is the correlation matrix. Making substitutions:

$$\begin{bmatrix} 0.0207 & 0.0122 \\ 0.0122 & 0.0289 \end{bmatrix} = \begin{bmatrix} 0.144 & 0 \\ 0 & 0.17 \end{bmatrix}\begin{bmatrix} 1 & 0.5 \\ 0.5 & 1 \end{bmatrix}\begin{bmatrix} 0.144 & 0 \\ 0 & 0.17 \end{bmatrix}$$

Thus, we have

$$V = \begin{bmatrix} 0.0207 & 0.0122 \\ 0.0122 & 0.0289 \end{bmatrix}$$

We need the Cholesky decomposition of V:

$$V_{chol} = \begin{bmatrix} 0.144 & 0.085 \\ 0 & 0.1472 \end{bmatrix}$$

Recall that $V = V'_{chol} V_{chol}$. Therefore, when we construct the correlated Brownian motion in columns C and D, we multiply the 1,000 × 2 matrix formed by columns A and B by the 2 × 2 Cholesky matrix, adding $\left(r - \frac{\sigma_1^2}{2}\right), \left(r - \frac{\sigma_2^2}{2}\right)$ as we go along. Columns C and D give this result.

In the last step, given in columns E and F, we exponentiate and multiply by the starting values for the stocks, in this case, $100. We can check our work if desired by estimating the covariance and variances of the simulated stock prices and compare these to V. Columns G and H are call options on each stock. The average of these calls should be close to the values calculated using BSM.

So far, this has been primarily an exercise in constructing correlated Brownian motions. Let's now explore the implications of the correlation property. Suppose we want to hold a call option on each stock. Does the value of the portfolio of call options depend on the correlation between the underlying returns?

On an intuitive level, the prices of the individual options should not depend in any way on the correlation between the returns on the underlying stocks. However, the value of the portfolio of calls could be sensitive to the correlation. To understand why, take the case in which the correlation $\rho = -1$ so that the returns are perfectly negatively correlated. This would suggest that the two stock prices move in opposite directions. Thus, when one option has high value, the other is likely to have low value. In this case, the portfolio of options will tend to have a mix of high and low value options at any given time, indicating that lower correlations lead to more diversification. On the other hand, when the correlation is close to 1, then the two options will also tend to track very closely in value at any given time period. It would make sense, therefore, to observe very low volatility across option value in the portfolio of options when correlations are high (and vice versa).

I constructed a Monte Carlo experiment that generates correlated Brownian motions, ranging the correlation from $-0.95 \le \rho \le 0.95$. For each value of ρ, I simulated 1,000 values for the two stocks reconstructing

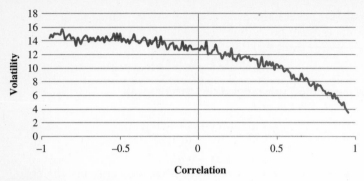

FIGURE 17.7 Call Portfolio Volatility

V to reflect the new value for ρ. At each of these 1,000 points, the difference between the two call values is computed and the standard deviation of this difference across the 1,000 calls is saved. The experiment therefore generates a volatility estimate for the call differences across the values of ρ. The plot is given in Figure 17.7.

As we can see, low values for ρ correspond to bigger differences in the two call option valuations and that the variability in their difference declines as ρ approaches 1. While this result was intended to illustrate how to generate correlated Brownian motion, it also illustrates that a portfolio of options will take on properties related to those on the underlying portfolio of stocks.

SUMMARY

This chapter had three objectives. The first was to tie together our work on the binomial lattice to the unifying underlying mathematics. That required us to develop a simple, yet appealing, model of stock price dynamics based on a stochastic extension of the basic model of continuous compounding. We introduced Wiener processes and generalized these with Ito's lemma to produce the basic lognormal property of stock prices and Brownian motion. The second objective tied the lattice parameters to the properties of stock price dynamics, in particular, their volatility and units of time Δt. From that discussion, we could develop the intuition of Black-Scholes-Merton and use this result to price options analytically. We learned that the BSM solution is the limit as $\Delta t \to 0$ in the lattice (that is, as the number of nodes in the lattice goes to infinity). Finally, we extended the Brownian motion model to accommodate correlated stock prices and used this basic model in a Monte

Carlo framework to check the accuracy of BSM as well as to offer a few thoughts on the properties of option portfolios as they relate to the correlation of the underlying stock price returns.

APPENDIX 17.1: DERIVATION OF ITO'S LEMMA

Let X be a generalized Wiener process whose law of motion is described by:

$$dX = \mu dt + \sigma\, dz$$

Now, define $f(x)$ as a real valued function of X—for example, $f(x)$ is a derivative of X whose law of motion we wish to determine. Expand $f(x)$ using a Taylor series:

$$f(X + \Delta) = f(X) + \Delta f_x(X) + \frac{1}{2}\Delta^2 f_{xx}(X) + \ldots$$

Then, in the limit, as $\Delta \to dt$ we get:

$$f(X + \Delta) - f(X) = df(X) = f_x(X)d(X)$$

We are recognizing here that this result holds because the higher order terms go to zero faster as Δ approaches zero. This is the fundamental theorem of calculus. But in stochastic calculus, the second order term $f_{xx} = dX^2$ does not vanish because X is normally distributed with positive variance, which converges in probability to dt. This can be conceptualized from the Wiener process itself, where the term $dX = \mu\, dt + \sigma\, dz$ has variance $\text{Var}(dX) = \text{Var}(dz) = \sigma^2 dt$, since $z \sim N(0, 1)$.

So, while the fundamental theorem of calculus is:

$$df(X) = f_x(X)dX + \frac{1}{2}f_{xx}dX^2$$

we must extend this to include functions of time (where $dt^2 \to 0$) so that for $f = f(X, t)$, we get:

$$df = f_x dX + f_t dt + \frac{1}{2}\left(f_{xx}dX^2 + 2f_{xt}dXdt + f_{tt}dt^2\right)$$

Equivalently,

$$df = f_x dX + f_t dt + \frac{1}{2}f_{xx}dX^2$$

because $f_{xt}dXdt = 0$, since t is deterministic and $f_{tt}dt^2$ vanishes.

This is the simplest form of Ito's lemma. If we have a model for the law of motion for X, then we can derive a model of the law of motion for a derivative of X.

Therefore, taking our generalized Wiener process from before and permitting the parameters μ and σ each to also be functions of X and t, then it follows by definition that:

$$dX^2 = (\mu dt)^2 + (\sigma dz)^2 + 2\mu\sigma dt\, dz = \sigma^2 dt$$

And, substituting for dX^2 *and then* dX, dX^2 and then dX,

$$df = f_x dX + f_t dt + \frac{1}{2} f_{xx}(\sigma^2)$$

$$df = f_x(\mu dt + \sigma dz) + f_t dt + \frac{1}{2} f_{xx}\sigma^2 dt$$

Rearranging, we solve for the law of motion for the derivative:

$$df = \left(\mu f_x + f_t + \frac{1}{2} f_{xx}\sigma^2\right) dt + \sigma f_x dz$$

CHAPTER 18

Hedging Portfolio Risk

Better to light a candle than to curse the darkness.
—Chinese proverb

We studied two examples of hedging in Chapter 2. These dealt with basic interest rate risk, specifically, the risk posed by having assets whose durations do not necessarily match the durations of liabilities. The first immunized the duration risk on a bond portfolio intended to defease a 10-year liability while the second example solved a more complicated problem that searched for a portfolio of bonds whose cash flows matched the cash flows on a set of pension liabilities. In general, hedges are strategies that insulate portfolios from adverse market movements. Hedges, properly constructed, perform the functions that firewalls do for computer operating systems—they act as barriers that block the impact of exposures to specified risks. The material in this chapter is not intended to serve as a comprehensive treatment of hedging instruments and strategies. Nevertheless, because hedging is so critical to understanding risk management, it is important that we develop this topic on both an intuitive and applied level. I therefore introduce to you in this chapter a few hedging applications that are useful in managing portfolio risk.

SIMPLE HEDGING STRATEGIES

Hedging can be traced to 350 BC to Greek merchants who initiated the first futures markets for olive harvests. Commodity futures are conceptually intuitive and it makes sense to use these markets to introduce the idea of hedging risk. Ranchers and farmers through antiquity have grappled with the uncertainty of future prices for livestock and produce when brought to market. Their risk lies in the possibility that market prices may fall between the present and some future date when they need to find buyers for their output. With futures markets, they could eliminate that risk by locking in prices today by selling their output forward, using futures. A livestock rancher, for example, may need to drive 1,000 head of cattle to a distant stock yard six months from now. He would like to hedge the risk that beef prices may fall in the interim by finding a counterparty (for example, a meatpacking company) that will agree today to buy those cattle at an agreed-upon price and take delivery in six months. Futures markets make this possible—the rancher, who has a long position in cattle today hedges price risk by selling cattle short in the futures market, that is, by selling (writing) a futures contract for future sale. The counterparty takes the other end of that contract; he is currently short cattle and therefore goes long by buying a futures contract agreeing to pay a fixed price when the contract expires and thereby locking in a buying price. It is possible as well that the counterparty is a speculator (and not a hedger) who bets that beef prices on the spot market will be higher than the futures prices. If they are, then the speculator's gain is the difference between the future market price of beef and the futures price. Hedgers, on the other hand, gain by eliminating price volatility.

Portfolio managers would like to hedge downside risk. The introduction, in 1983, of futures contracts on the S&P 500 made this possible when managers for the first time could sell S&P 500 futures (shorting the contract). If returns were to fall, then the gain from the short futures position would offset the loss on the portfolio. Intuitively, it works like this: suppose you own one share of stock and want to hedge the risk that its value falls by shorting a share of that same stock. The short sale creates a positive cash flow at the current market price. If the value does indeed fall, then so does the price of the shorted stock, which you now buy at the lower market price to cover the short position. The gain on the short position just offsets the loss on the long position. S&P 500 futures made hedging simple for portfolio managers by offering a hedge instrument with comparatively little basis risk in a highly liquid futures market. Without the S&P 500 futures contract, managers would face the task of cobbling together short positions in many different stocks to adequately match the exposure of their portfolios. The mismatch between the hedge portfolio and the portfolio under management is called *basis risk*.

Basic hedging strategies also use put and call options. Puts formed the basis of the original portfolio insurance products devised by Hayne Leland and Mark Rubinstein in the mid-1980s. Puts give us the option, but not the obligation, of selling all or part of our portfolio at some agreed-upon price (the strike price) at some future date (strike date). Thus, if the value of my portfolio is $100 today and I were to buy a put option that allows me to sell my portfolio for $90 one month from now, then this option hedges the downside risk to no more than $10 in losses. Thus, the put acts like an insurance policy. In this example, the deductible is the $10 in losses after which the insurance contract kicks in, eliminating any further losses. If prices don't fall, I let the option expire.

As we well know, volatility brings with it the risk of losses. A call option on the VIX (the implied volatility on S&P 500 index options) pays off as the VIX rises relative to a strike price, in this case, a preset level of volatility. In general, as volatility increases, then so does our exposure to both gains *and* losses. Buying a VIX call hedges that risk because the value of the call increases with volatility. We now look at these examples in more detail.

S&P 500 INDEX PUTS

On August 3, 2010, the S&P 500 index cost $1,121.45. The prices of various puts on this index are listed in Table 18.1. These puts are for strikes listed in the table's first column for expiration at the end of the month and centered on $1,000. The intent here is to show a ±20 percent range of puts prices around the current spot price for the index. To fix ideas, any strike below the current spot price ($1,121.45) is said to be *out of the money* (OTM) while any strike above spot is *in the money*. The OTM prices are of interest to us since we want to hedge downside risk.

Take, for example, the center strike of $1,000, which provides the option to sell the index on the strike date for $1,000. A decline in the index to this level would constitute a 10.83 percent drop in the value of the index (see the column labeled *Implied Move*). The asking price of the index on August 3 for this contract was $1.30 per share and the bid price was $1.20. (Note that we pay the ask price if we want the contract.) The contract, itself, is for 100 shares of the S&P 500 (each share currently worth $1,121.45).

The portfolio we want to insure is a large pension fund that has current market value equal to $49 billion and the public equity allocation in that fund is $22.8 billion. Suppose we wanted to hedge 50 percent of the public equity exposure to downside risk. In that case, the notional value of the hedge would be half the value of the equity exposure, or $11.4 billion. Since the share price of the index is currently $1,121.45, then dividing this amount into the $11.4 billion hedge target would suggest we need to purchase puts on about 10,165,411 shares, which, with 100 shares per contract, requires 101,654 contracts needed to construct the hedge.

TABLE 18.1 August 3, 2010, S&P 500 Puts

Underlying:	S&P 500
Current Px:	1,121.45
Option:	Put
Expiration:	August
Center Strike:	1000
Range +/-:	20%

		Strike	Implied Move	Bid	Ask	Last	Hedge Cost ($)	Hedge Cost (% TF, bp)
Total Fund Market Value($B)	49.0	800	−28.66%	0.05	0.10	0.05	1,016,541	0.21
		825	−26.43%	0.05	0.15	0.10	1,524,812	0.31
Public Equity Market Value($B)	22.8	850	−24.21%	0.15	0.20	0.15	2,033,082	0.41
		875	−21.98%	0.15	0.30	0.20	3,049,623	0.62
% of Program to Hedge	50%	900	−19.75%	0.30	0.35	0.35	3,557,894	0.73
		925	−17.52%	0.45	0.50	0.45	5,082,705	1.04
Notional of Hedge($B)	11.4	950	−15.29%	0.55	0.65	0.60	6,607,517	1.35
		975	−13.06%	0.75	0.85	0.85	8,640,599	1.76
Equivalent # of Shares	10,165,411	1000	−10.83%	1.20	1.30	1.25	13,215,034	2.70
Shares per Contract	100	1025	−8.60%	1.75	2.35	1.90	23,888,716	4.88
		1050	−6.37%	2.90	3.40	3.20	34,562,397	7.05
Contracts in Hedge	101,654	1075	−4.14%	5.20	5.90	5.70	59,975,924	12.24
		1100	−1.91%	10.00	11.20	10.50	113,852,602	23.24
		1125	0.32%	18.80	20.50	19.80	208,390,922	42.53
		1150	2.55%	33.30	35.20	34.88	357,822,462	73.02
		1175	4.78%	54.00	56.90	59.00	578,411,877	118.04
		1200	7.00%	77.80	81.00	76.00	823,398,279	168.04

Thus, at the strike price of $1,000, with an ask of $1.30 per share we'd have to pay $13,215,034 (equivalent shares times ask) in order to hedge 50 percent of our exposure. The last column gives us a relative sense of this cost as a proportion to fund value; for the $1,000 strike price, we'd therefore pay out 2.7 basis points of the fund to hedge a 10.83 percent decline in value. The 2.7 basis points is the insurance premium.

As the strike price declines, the cost of insurance falls with it as the market prices in the lower likelihood of the index falling to these levels. On the other hand, notice that in-the-money puts cost much more and, upon reflection, this makes sense; we are going to have to pay a premium for the right to sell our portfolio at a price higher than the current spot price. Individuals seeking the option to sell the S&P 500 for $1,200 at the end of August will pay a premium of 1.68 percent. More specifically, it will cost about $823.4 million to hedge the $11.4 billion exposure. That's for one month! This suggests that the market believes that the likelihood of the index being at this level by the end of August 2010 is quite likely and you will have to pay a premium to lock in a higher price.

Extending the analysis to tail risk, suppose we define the lower tail of the return distribution to be any return below the first percentile. Keeping things simple, if the annual expected return is 7 percent with annual volatility 15 percent, then an approximate normal density first percentile monthly return is −9.0 percent. Geometrically, 7 percent annual is 0.56 percent monthly and 15 percent annual volatility is 4.33 percent monthly volatility. The z score corresponding to the first percentile under the standard normal density is 2.31. Therefore, our tail region is any return below 1.0056 − 2.31*4.33. The table indicates that a tail hedge would cost between 2.7 and 4.88 basis points for the month.

The takeaway from this analysis is that we can incorporate this analysis into our portfolio management and use it to manage our exposure to market risks. Therefore, if we are managing an equity portfolio and want to hedge downside (or tail) risk, we simply need to scale the amount of insurance desired and enter it into put option contracts to execute this strategy. The cost of the strategy can be assessed relative to our expectations that these losses will actually materialize as well as the cost of alternative strategies.

SELLING VOLATILITY

During turbulent times, market participants face increased uncertainty and as investor sentiment crumbles, the demand for insurance rises. One gauge of the degree of perceived risk is the interest in the term structure of implied volatility as revealed in VIX futures. The intuition is that investors bid up prices of options as they compete to buy insurance that, in turn, drives up option-implied volatility embedded in the VIX. The VIX futures is the option market's forecast of volatility one month forward. If their fears are deep enough, then futures on the VIX will tend to appear to be overpriced. In that case, it may pay to sell volatility in the form of VIX swaps. That is, we would receive the spread between the VIX contract, which has a specified strike volatility and the actual volatility. For example, suppose the current volatility is 15 percent and we buy a one-month futures contract on the VIX at a 20 percent strike. If the observed volatility rises above 20 percent, then we earn the difference on a notional amount agreed upon with our counterparty. Since these are called *variance swaps,* the payoff to a long position is:

$$\text{Payoff} = \left[(\text{Future realized volatility})^2 - (\text{Strike volatility})^2\right] * \text{Notional}$$

Thus, unless realized volatility exceeds the strike level, the long position in the contract does not pay. A short position in this contract would be the equivalent of selling volatility back to the market. This is admittedly a simple case. In reality, we could look at more complicated forward variance contracts and their characteristics but the intuition is what's important at this point.

VIX CALLS

A related hedging product is a call option on the VIX itself. Table 18.2 is the VIX counterpart to Table 18.1's S&P 500 put. Here, we see that on August 3, 2010, the current VIX was at 22.14. We choose to center our strikes at 50 and use the same market value of the fund ($49 billion) with public equity component equal to $22.8 billion, of which we wish to hedge 50 percent, or $11.4 billion, which becomes the notional amount for the hedge.

Let's take the VIX one-month contract with strike 50. If the VIX exceeds 50, the call option would be exercised and the payoff would be the difference between the spot VIX and the strike value times the notional. This is a 125.84 percent increase in volatility from the August 3 level. For convenience, column three includes the implied S&P 500 move. For example, a 18 percent decline in the S&P 500 index is consistent with the 125.84 percent increase in implied volatility. Notice that strikes above 50 have no

TABLE 18.2 August 3, 2010, VIX Calls

Underlying:	VIX
Current Px:	22.14
Current SPX Px:	1121.5
Option:	Call
Expiration:	August
Center Strike:	50
Range +/-	100%

		Strike	Implied VIX Move	Implied S&P Move	Bid	Ask	Last	Hedge Cost ($)	Hedge Cost (% TF, bp)
Total Fund Market Value($B)	49.0	10	-54.83%	7.82%	13.90	14.20	16.23	1,012,694,337	206.67
		15	-32.25%	4.60%	8.90	9.20	9.00	656,111,824	133.90
Public Equity Market Value($B)	22.8	20	-9.67%	1.38%	4.10	4.30	4.20	306,660,961	62.58
		25	12.92%	-1.84%	1.25	1.35	1.35	96,277,279	19.65
% of Program to Hedge	50%	30	35.50%	-5.06%	0.45	0.55	0.50	39,224,076	8.00
		35	58.08%	-8.28%	0.20	0.30	0.30	21,394,951	4.37
Notional of Hedge ($B)	11.4	40	80.67%	-11.50%	0.10	0.15	0.15	10,697,475	2.18
		45	103.25%	-14.72%	0.05	0.10	0.10	7,131,650	1.46
ΔS&P-to-ΔVIX Beta (Hedge Ratio)	-7.22	50	125.84%	-17.94%	0.05	0.10	0.05	7,131,650	1.46
		55	148.42%	-21.16%	#N/A	N/A	0.05	3,565,825	0.73

(continued)

TABLE 18.2 (Continued)

Underlying:	VIX							
Current Px:	22.14							
Current SPX Px:	1121.5							
Option:	Call							
Expiration:	August							
Center Strike:	50							
Range +/–	100%							

		Strike	Implied VIX Move	Implied S&P Move	Bid	Ask	Last	Hedge Cost ($)	Hedge Cost (% TF, bp)
Equivalent # of Shares	71,316,503	60	171.00%	–24.37%	#N/A N/A	0.05	0.05	3,565,825	0.73
		65	193.59%	–27.59%	#N/A N/A	0.05	0.05	3,565,825	0.73
Shares per Contract	1000	70	216.17%	–30.81%	#N/A N/A	0.05	0.05	3,565,825	0.73
Contracts in Hedge	71,317	75	238.75%	–34.03%	#N/A N/A	0.05	0.05	3,565,825	0.73
		80	261.34%	–37.25%	#N/A N/A	0.05	0.02	3,565,825	0.73
		85	283.92%	–40.47%	#N/A N/A	0.05	0.05	3,565,825	0.73
		90	306.50%	–43.69%	#N/A N/A	0.05	0.05	3,565,825	0.73

bids, suggesting that the market places no significant likelihood on volatility risk to these levels (notice that the implied S&P move is about where we'd be in our tail risk hedge example). The asking price, however, is very, very cheap at these elevated VIX levels. As we move into lower volatility options, the cost of hedging rises exponentially, which makes sense intuitively, since these options are already in the money.

There is a term structure of sorts regarding implied volatility that is worth understanding. It suggests that implied volatility is conditional on both the *moneyness* of the option as well as the time to expiration of the contract. Longer-dated contracts will, in general, have lower implied volatility, due to mean reversion. Other things constant, moneyness—a measure of how much the option is in the money—will tend to drive up implied volatility, too, especially for shorter times to maturity. Figure 18.1 illustrates this relationship.

Understanding this relationship is critical to formulating strategies using various dated contracts as well as forming beliefs on whether existing contracts are over- or underpriced.

These three examples are designed to give you an idea of the types of strategies available to help manage portfolio risk. They are certainly not exhaustive and it is not hard to find textbooks entirely devoted to the subject. Nevertheless, these are valuable applications that illustrate both the intuition and application of practical hedging strategies.

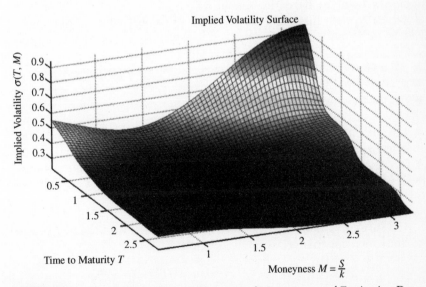

FIGURE 18.1 Implied Volatility as a Function of Moneyness and Expiration Date

LIABILITY-DRIVEN INVESTMENT

Let's switch gears a bit and think about hedging the risk of not being able to meet our liabilities. This risk arguably poses the greatest challenge to pension plans. In a recent paper, Robert Novy-Marx and Joshua Rauh (2010) estimate that liabilities exceed assets across the pension plans of the 50 states in the United States by approximately $1.27 trillion using Muni rate discounting and $3.26 trillion using Treasury discounting. Either way, there is a serious underfunding of these liabilities. Pension boards are grasping for investment strategies that hedge the risk of not meeting their liabilities, hence, the concept of liability-driven investment (LDI). As we shall see further on, LDI strategies change the objective function from one of solving for the mean variance efficient portfolio of assets to finding the mean variance efficient portfolio that maximizes the surplus return. The surplus return is the weighted return on assets over the growth rate of liabilities. Thus, the problem is set up with a slightly different optimization objective but is otherwise solved as before. Let's develop this problem in detail, solve it, and then examine the properties of the solution as a hedging strategy.

The mathematics of this particular problem can get complicated and I defer treatment of the problem to Michael Bazdarich's paper (2006). I present instead an applied version of the problem that we'll study as a spreadsheet exercise. But first, let's set the problem up and examine its first order conditions. I will use Bazdarich's notation.

Basically, we want to find the portfolio w that maximizes surplus return given by $(w'x - \rho/F)$, in which:

- x is a vector of asset returns with expectation μ and variance Σ.
- w is a vector of portfolio weights.
- F is the funding ratio (ratio of pension asset value to discounted liability value).
- L is the holding period rate of change on a dollar of pension liabilities (a growth rate).
- $L \sim (\rho, \eta^2, \chi^2)$, respectively, the mean, variance, and covariance with x.
- $A - L/F = w'x - L/F$ is the holding period change in surplus per dollar of assets.

The surplus variance (the variance of $w'x$ plus the variance of L/F plus two times their covariance) is:

$$\text{var}\left(w'x - L/F\right) = \left(w'\sum w + \eta^2/F^2 - 2w'\chi/F\right).$$

We want to solve for the portfolio that minimizes this variance subject to the usual constraints. That is,

$$min_w w' \sum w + \frac{\eta^2}{F^2} - \frac{2w'\chi}{F}$$

$$s.t. \quad w'\mu = M; \quad w'i = 1$$

M is the targeted return on the portfolio and i is a vector of ones to satisfy the fully invested constraint.

We can set this problem up as the Lagrangian:

$$L = w' \sum w + \frac{\eta^2}{F^2} - \frac{2w'\chi}{F} + 2\lambda(M - w'\mu) + 2\varphi(1 - w'i)$$

Taking derivatives with respect to the N weights plus the Lagrange multipliers, λ and φ, setting these $N + 2$ first order conditions equal to zero and solving yields the minimum variance portfolio.

Let's take the case of a two-asset portfolio like stocks (w_1) and bonds (w_2). In this case, we will have the following four first-order conditions to solve:

$$\frac{\partial L}{\partial w_1} = \left(2w_1\sigma_1^2 + 2w_2\sigma_{12}\right) - 2^\chi/_F - 2\lambda\mu_1 - 2\varphi = 0$$

$$\frac{\partial L}{\partial w_2} = \left(2w_2\sigma_2^2 + 2w_1\sigma_{12}\right) - 2^\chi/_F - 2\lambda\mu_2 - 2\varphi = 0$$

$$\frac{\partial L}{\partial \lambda} = 2(M - w_1\mu_1 - w_2\mu_2) = 0$$

$$\frac{\partial L}{\partial \varphi} = 2(1 - w_1 - w_2) = 0$$

We can rewrite this system in matrix form as follows to facilitate the solution in Excel after substituting values.

$$\begin{bmatrix} \sigma_1^2 & \sigma_{12} & -\mu_1 & -1 \\ \sigma_{21} & \sigma_2^2 & -\mu_2 & -1 \\ \mu_1 & \mu_2 & 0 & 0 \\ 1 & 1 & 0 & 0 \end{bmatrix} \begin{bmatrix} w_1 \\ w_2 \\ \lambda \\ \varphi \end{bmatrix} = \begin{bmatrix} \chi_1/_F \\ \chi_2/_F \\ M \\ 1 \end{bmatrix}$$

If we label this system $Vx = b$, then the solution is $V^{-1}b = x$. The spreadsheet for this chapter substitutes some hypothetical values for V and b using a three-asset portfolio and solves for the optimal portfolio that is presented further on.

This first case has zero covariances between liability growth and the assets' returns. Therefore, it is the standard asset-optimal portfolio.

225	40	10	−8	−1	w_1		0
40	144	30	−6	−1	w_2		0
10	30	16	−4	−1	w_3		0
8	6	4	0	0	λ		7
1	1	1	0	0	φ		1
	V					x	b

w_1	0.56
w_2	0.39
w_3	0.06
λ	30.80
φ	−105.11

OPTIMAL PORT

Assume that the three assets are U.S. equity, non-U.S. equity, and Treasury bonds, respectively. The targeted return of 7 percent pretty much freezes Treasuries out of the portfolio in order to meet the return target.

Now, look what happens if we make the third asset return correlated with growth in liabilities.

225	40	10	−8	−1	w_1		0
40	144	30	−6	−1	w_2		0
10	30	16	−4	−1	w_3		100
8	6	4	0	0	λ		7
1	1	1	0	0	φ		1
	V					x	b

w_1	0.74
w_2	0.03
w_3	0.24
λ	64.28
φ	−345.15

OPTIMAL PORT

Because Treasury returns are correlated with liabilities, the optimal portfolio is required to invest in them at the expense of non-U.S. equity and consequently requires a heavier allocation to U.S. equity. LDI in this case sees the correlation between Treasuries and the liabilities and, to hedge liability risk, holds a greater proportion of the Treasuries.

One of the concerns about LDI strategies is that they will force increased allocations to the lower-returning assets, which are correlated more with liabilities. In most cases, this is true—LDI does increase bond allocations because these assets' returns are more correlated with the growth in liabilities. But in some cases, like the one discussed earlier, it also requires an increased exposure to the risky asset.

SUMMARY

Pension plans are interested in liability driven investment strategies to hedge the risk that their assets may be insufficient to fulfill their future obligations to pay benefits. In this sense, the LDI strategy is very similar to the immunization strategy we studied in Chapter 2. Traditional portfolio management looks to maximize risk-adjusted returns on the asset side of the balance sheet. Pension management, on the other hand, looks at both sides of the balance sheet, treating liabilities as short positions in conjunction with the plan's long position in assets. Looked at this way, all pensions optimize some type of LDI strategy and, in most cases, it is not an immunization strategy (that is, LDI doesn't necessarily have to hedge all the liabilities and in fact it may not be optimal to do so).

We began this chapter with a discussion of tail risk hedges in the form of put options. These are straightforward hedging strategies that are practical, if priced right, and easy to apply. We also studied variance swaps as an alternative hedge strategy although here we are looking to hedge volatility risk. We would be selling volatility if we thought it was too overpriced. We rounded the discussion out with an introduction to VIX calls. These provided a reasonable introduction on how we might think about hedging portfolio risk and what methods or products may be available. They are not exhaustive and in fact there are new hedging instruments continually invested in markets. I ended with LDI because I wanted to impress upon you that too often investment managers act as agents maximizing asset returns when their principals (for example, trustees) face the objective of managing the short position (liabilities) as well. The point here is that the two objectives are not necessarily the same. For example, maximizing returns on assets may not lead to the liquidity a pension needs, for example, to fund future benefits. The liability side of the balance sheet in this case needs to be formally incorporated into the optimization problem which, we see, is not difficult and indeed gives the problem more flavor.

REFERENCES

Bazdarich, Michael J. 2006. Separability and pension optimization. *Journal of Fixed Income* (Winter).

Novy-Marx, Robert, and Joshua D. Rauh. 2010. *Public pension promises: How big are they and what are they worth?* Chicago: University of Chicago, Working Paper. Available at http://ssrn.com/abstract=1352608.

CHAPTER 19

Private Equity

Ask for much but take what is offered.

—Russian proverb

Rising allocations by institutional investors to alternative asset classes such as private equity have sharpened interest in how returns and risks are measured relative to public equity benchmarks. This is especially true for public pension plans since private equity generates a clear opportunity cost as dollars are allocated away from public equity. Thus, whether private equity is a viable alternative to public equity will depend upon how private equity returns are measured, benchmarked, and adjusted for risk.

In this chapter, I evaluate various measures of return and risk for private equity investments, including public market equivalents (PME), PME alphas (unadjusted for risk), internal rates of return (IRRs), and the Long and Nickels alpha (which is an excess IRR measure). This is referred to officially as the *index comparison method* (ICM) at www.alignmentcapital .com. We also discuss generalized method of moments (GMM) alpha and beta estimates, using both a capital assets pricing model (CAPM) and the Fama-French three-factor model with bootstrapped standard errors as outlined in Driessen, Lin, and Phalippou (2008). I highlight two important findings: First, the various performance measures often tell wildly different stories about performance. In particular, users should be aware of the sensitivity of IRR estimates to the timing of cash flows and, in general, should adopt several performance measures as robustness checks. Second, risk-adjusted performance statistics are sobering; risk-adjusted GMM estimates reject any claims that private equity outperforms the public benchmark. This is interesting because it is completely at odds with virtually all the IRR- and PME-based measures. Moreover, I argue that selective use of nonrisk-adjusted performance measures may have influenced increased allocations to private equity in the past and that private equity partners significantly underestimated the risks on their investments relative to their benchmarks.

On balance, the academic literature has been critical of claims of private equity outperformance. Moskowitz and Vissing-Jorgensen (2002), for example, study data from the Survey of Consumer Finances, the Flow of Funds Accounts, and the National Income and Product Accounts and find that risk-adjusted returns are low relative to public equity. Still, private equity continues to attract capital and this persistence may suggest that investors overestimate survival probabilities and therefore expected returns, or have a preference for skewness in the distribution of returns. These reasons notwithstanding, published academic literature finds little supporting evidence of outperformance of private equity in general relative to a public equity index such as the S&P 500 (Phalippou 2007). Kaplan and Schoar (2005) report results from a study of 746 funds and conclude that returns to limited partners (LPs) are essentially equal to that of the S&P 500 (their public market equivalent is 1.01). Phalippou and Gottschalg (2009) are even more critical, arguing that after adjusting for survivorship bias in the data (Thomson Venture Economics), and so-called living deads (residual values that do not get written off), then private equity underperforms by as much as 3 percent per year. Specific subclasses such as buyout and venture fare no better; Hwang, Quigley, and Woodward (2005) report slightly positive gross-of-fees relative performance for venture (implying low net-of-fee performance) while both Swensen (2000) and Phalippou and Gottschalg present evidence from analyses of private equity manager–supplied prospectuses that show gross-of-fees underperformance relative to a similarly leverage-adjusted S&P 500.

Risk-adjusted performance paints a bleaker picture. Estimated betas for venture lie close to two (Driessen, Lin, and Phalippou 2004; Woodward 2004; and Cochrane 2004). Buyout betas are lower. For example, Woodward reports a beta less than one while Driessen, Lin, and Phalippou calculate a beta close to zero. Estimates of beta on publicly traded firms that are recipients of private equity investment are around 1.3 (Phalippou and Gottschalg 2009).

Most of these studies measure returns using IRR and risk-using CAPM-type regressions. Kaplan and Schoar report PME estimates as well but do not extract excess IRR (see the discussion further on). Ick (2005), on the other hand, reports PME in excess of one, which, as we illustrate further on, indicates private equity outperformance (unadjusted for risk, however). Other studies, such as Ljungqvist and Richardson (2003) examine private equity cash flows and NAVs for a single large pension fund, and report annual excess returns in the 5 to 8 percent range (again, unadjusted for risk). If there is a consensus, it is that private equity risks are underestimated and that even for cases in which private equity outperforms the public market, risk-adjusted excess returns usually do not justify the investment. In these cases, we are reminded again by Moskowitz and Vissing-Jorgensen that there may be behavioral explanations that explain ever increasing capital flows to this asset class. Recent research suggests that some LPs are more experienced and, having learned how and whom to invest with, earn alpha while less experienced LPs do not (Lerner, Schoar, and Wongsunwai 2007). Fund-picking skills aside, there is evidence that limited partnerships (LPs) misprice deals, as they routinely underestimate fees (Swensen) and rely too heavily on IRR measures of performance (Phalippou).

THE PRIVATE EQUITY MODEL

As the name suggests, private equity assets are not exchange-traded shares. The fact that there are no closing prices, trading volume, bids or asks, or any other publicly available information poses several challenges to investors, foremost of which is pricing and risk assessment. With no trading, there are no observed closing prices, and therefore no frequency of observable returns and therefore no volatility. The tasks related to return and risk attribution are quite different for this asset class, as we shall see further on.

There are several subclasses of private equity investments, including, for example, the two main ones—venture and leveraged buyout, along with distressed, growth, subordinated debt, and energy. According to Phalippou, private equity managers had over $1 trillion under management in 2006, roughly two-thirds of which was in leveraged buyout funds. Funds are organized as limited partnerships with the LPs as primary investors generally drawn from the ranks of large institutional investors like pension funds. Limited partners commit funds to general partners (GPs) who manage the funds and whose compensation is determined by an agreed-upon fee structure. Funds are typically organized with a specific strategy (venture or buyout), target for committed capital, and life (typically 10 years). For example, the GPs might announce the formation of a new fund with targeted committed capital to be, say, $1 billion and then solicit LPs (investors) to commit capital to the fund until the target investment level is attained. GPs draw on committed capital, investing in projects (ventures or firms), until all capital is invested. GPs then determine when and how assets are sold and distributed to LPs as dividends on their invested capital. As the fund matures, distributions are made until the fund is closed and any remaining assets liquidated and paid to LPs.

The compensation structure for GPs has typically been the "2 and 20" model—GPs fees comprise a 2 percent fee on invested (sometime committed) capital and a 20 percent share of the return over a stated benchmark. Thus, if the fund earns 8 percent on $100 invested and the benchmark (or hurdle rate) is 6 percent, then the LP pays $2 in management fees off the top and then earns 6 percent plus 0.80 times the 2 percent (in excess of the hurdle) for a total payoff of $7.60 – $2 = $5.60, or 5.6 percent, on assets under management. All other things constant, this is less than had the $100 been invested in the passive benchmark. Given the likelihood that the GPs leveraged the investment to begin with, then this return is smaller than the benchmark but with more risk.

Typically, GPs and LPs report internal rates of return on investments as the following example illustrates:

Year	1	2	3	4	5	6	7	8	9	10	IRR
Cash Flow	−100	−150	−150	0	0	50	100	100	200	50	4%

Here, the LP commits $400, which is drawn in the first three years. Distributions begin in year six and the fund is closed at the end of the tenth year. The IRR is 4 percent *gross of fees*.

Unfortunately, IRR measures cannot be compared to returns on publicly traded assets. This problem arises because IRR is what is referred to as a *dollar-weighted* return while publicly traded assets report a *time-weighted* return. The yield to maturity on a bond, for example, is an IRR but this is not the same as the return on the bond, and in any case, a bond's yield to maturity that is, say, 5 percent per year, is not the same thing as a 5 percent annual return on a stock. Regardless of the confusing semantics surrounding the meaning of dollar versus time weighting, the distinction between the fundamental differences between IRR and the notion of the percentage change in the market value of an asset should be clear: IRRs are not based on market prices, but are instead cash-flow dependent. To compare, then, the performance of private equity (or private real estate assets, for that matter) to publicly traded assets, analysts sometimes compute the *modified Dietz* return to private assets, which is basically a time-weighted return that takes the percentage change in the market value of the private assets between two points in time (which is exactly how we've been doing returns all along in this book) but adjusts the computation for intraperiod cash flows. GPs mark their assets to market quarterly (under FASB 157 guidelines) that reflect the value of comparable assets that have transacted, and although these marked-to-market values are considered proxies to true market value, it should be emphasized that they are not the assets' market values since no transactions have actually occurred. Letting EMV and BMV stand for ending and beginning market value and CF as intervening cash flows in the form of either drawdowns or distributions (the latter being negative, since it is paid out), then the modified Dietz return for any given quarter is:

$$r_{mdietz} = \frac{EMV - BMV - \sum_{i=1}^{n} CF_i}{BMV + \sum_{i=1}^{n} w_i CF_i}$$

If there are no intraperiod cash flows, then the formula reduces to the standard time-weighted return. Here is an example:

Date	Transaction	Type	EMV	BMV	Σ CF	Σ w$_i$CF$_i$	Return
3/31/2008	30,274,282	Valuation					
5/28/2008	−51,246	Distribution					
6/30/2008	30,816,945	Valuation	30,816,945	30,274,282	−51,246	−18,584	1.96%
7/29/2008	−414,635	Distribution					
8/31/2008	−43,640	Distribution					
9/30/2008	30,968,250	Valuation	30,968,250	30,816,945	−458,275	−298,165	2.00%
12/31/2008	32,002,004	Valuation	32,002,004	30,968,250	0	0	3.34%

This fund began with an EMV of $30.27 million at the end of the first quarter 2008. It then had a distribution in the amount of $51.2 thousand on May 28 and another quarterly valuation on June 30. As such, the return numerator is the change in market value adjusted for the cash flow distribution. The denominator is the starting value, which is the beginning market value and the time-weighted cash flows, in which the weights are the proportion of time left in the current quarter, that is, the remaining time in the quarter that the cash flow is at work, so to speak.

Modified Dietz returns are intuitively appealing as well as practical counterparts to IRRs in the case in which assets and portfolios are marked to market with stable frequency. Private equity portfolios' performance can be compared in this fashion to that on publicly traded portfolios like the S&P 500. The weakness in this methodology lies in the marking to market; these are not actual transactions. In the preceding example, for example, the valuation reported at the end of 2008 is not an actual market value of $32 million; it is, rather, an *assessment* of value based on assets of similar duration and composition residing in similar sectors. The end of month closing price on the S&P 500, on the other hand, is a transacted value with no pricing error. Therefore, it should not be surprising to see pricing error on private portfolios when their assets are liquidated. Despite the incentive for GPs to overstate value (carrying assets at cost, for example), the science of valuing classes of assets like private equity is limited—private evaluation will always tend to lag market values and be based on small samples of carefully selected assets exposed to pricing error. That is why the more promising performance methodologies focus entirely on cash flows and not reported market values. We turn to these alternative pricing and performance methodologies now.

RETURN AND RISK METHODOLOGY

Measurement issues arise for nonpublicly traded assets for a host of reasons, for example, relative illiquidity, stale pricing, and irregularly timed cash flows, which confound attempts to compute standard time-weighted returns typical of publicly traded assets. Dollar-weighted measures, such as IRR, are most frequently reported but are not without their problems. For example, cash flows are not necessarily reinvested over the life of the fund at the measured internal rate of return as implicitly assumed. Neither can IRR be compared with time-weighted return, nor does IRR measure the opportunity cost of capital. We follow up on these criticisms in the discussion further on.

Public market equivalents are directed at measuring the opportunity cost of capital. These are mimicking portfolios that invest private equity cash flows in a publicly traded benchmark (for example, the S&P 500). Total dollars that would have accumulated in the benchmark are then compared to the dollars earned in the private equity investment. Indexing dollar distributions at time t by D_i and drawdowns, or dollar capital calls, by C_j and assuming the fund lives T periods, then with continuous compounding, PME is the ratio of the value of the private equity investment (distributions are reinvested in the benchmark) to the opportunity cost of funds:

$$PME = \sum_{i=0}^{T} D_i e^{r_i(T-i)} / \sum_{j=0}^{T} C_j e^{r_j(T-j)}$$

Private equity's excess return over the benchmark—its alpha gross of risk—is the scalar adjustment to the benchmark return in the denominator of PME necessary to equilibrate the future values of capital calls to distributions, that is, to make PME equal to 1. (This is why it is referred to in the literature as *excess IRR*.) That is, α solves the following but is still unadjusted for risk:

$$1 = \sum_{i=0}^{T} D_i e^{r_i(T-i)} / \sum_{j=0}^{T} C_j e^{(r_j+\alpha)(T-j)}$$

The Long and Nickels methodology combines IRR with a public market equivalent and compares the IRRs on two competing cash flows—those from the private equity investment and a matching set of cash flows in the public benchmark. For example, suppose an equivalent amount of capital invested with the general partner (GP) was invested in the public benchmark. When the GP makes a distribution, that dollar amount is also harvested from the public benchmark, that is, it shows up as a cash flow distribution for that period in the IRR calculation for the public benchmark. The remaining funds in the benchmark continue to grow at the market rate of return. In effect, the benchmark portfolio's cash flow size and timing is determined by the GP. When the GP liquidates the fund, the IRRs are computed for both the private equity and the benchmark investments. The difference between the two IRRs is the private equity alpha. This alpha is also gross of risk.

Timing can be everything. To see why, consider an illustrative example given in Table 19.1, in which we make a single investment of $100, which pays $200 at some point in the 10-year life of the fund. (All cash flows occur at the end of the year.) With no loss of generality, we assume a zero residual value at year 10. Assume the benchmark return is 7.2 percent so that it also returns $200 on the 10-year $100 investment. In this deterministic setting, a fund manager knows therefore that his multiple (distributions divided by capital calls) is equal to two no matter which year he distributes the $200, and his opportunity cost is the constant 7.2 percent benchmark return.

Let's begin with the last column in which the distribution occurred in year 10. The IRR and the benchmark return are identical at 7.2 percent per year, thereby generating a Long and Nickels alpha of zero. The PME is unity, since the future value of the distribution is equal to the future value of the capital call and this, in turn, implies that the PME alpha is zero as well.

Keeping the fund's life constant at 10 years, let's now incrementally shorten the duration of the $200 distribution. Note that the multiple and the benchmark return stay constant at 2 and 7.2 percent, respectively. The PME grows from 1.0 to 1.87 and the PME alpha (not adjusted for risk) grows to 6.9 percent. The IRR, on the other hand, grows exponentially to 100 percent and the Long and Nickels alpha grows likewise to 92.8 percent. Keep in mind that these are annualized figures and that even though the investment returned 100 percent in the first year, it returned zero in the last nine years. Yet, the annualized IRR does not change. Note the impact of time—when the $200 distribution moved from *year two* to *year one*, alpha tripled but the PME rose only from 1.74 to 1.87, meaning that, instead of $1.74, we would have had to invest $1.87 in the benchmark to generate a return equal to a $1 investment in the private equity fund. Thus, while the Long and Nickels alpha tripled from 34.2 percent to an annualized

TABLE 19.1 IRR, ICM-α, and IRR Example

Year	A	B	C	D	E	F	G	H	I	J
0	-100	-100	-100	-100	-100	-100	-100	-100	-100	-100
1	200	0	0	0	0	0	0	0	0	0
2	0	200	0	0	0	0	0	0	0	0
3	0	0	200	0	0	0	0	0	0	0
4	0	0	0	200	0	0	0	0	0	0
5	0	0	0	0	200	0	0	0	0	0
6	0	0	0	0	0	200	0	0	0	0
7	0	0	0	0	0	0	200	0	0	0
8	0	0	0	0	0	0	0	200	0	0
9	0	0	0	0	0	0	0	0	200	0
10	0	0	0	0	0	0	0	0	0	200
IRR	100.0%	41.4%	26.0%	18.9%	14.9%	12.2%	10.4%	9.1%	8.0%	7.2%
ICM-α	92.8%	34.2%	18.8%	11.7%	7.7%	5.1%	3.2%	1.9%	0.8%	0.0%
PME	1.87	1.74	1.62	1.52	1.41	1.32	1.23	1.15	1.07	1.00
PME-α	6.9%	6.1%	5.3%	4.6%	3.8%	3.0%	2.3%	1.5%	0.7%	0.0%

92.8 percent, the PME alpha rose by only 79 cents. Clearly, IRR-based performance measures tell a much different story in this example.

This exercise illustrates the huge range of these performance measures. Private equity managers often refer to their multiples but should know that multiples are essentially meaningless, since any given multiple is consistent with an unbounded range of IRRs as well as Long and Nickels alphas. PME is much less sensitive due in large part to it being a function of the benchmark return, which, in general, is much lower than computed IRRs.

Again, none of the preceding measures are adjusted for risk. To get at risk, Driessen et al. estimate the fund's beta in a CAPM context (along with alpha) using the generalized method of moments (GMM). They also extend the single-factor CAPM to the three-factor Fama-French model to identify funds' style factors.

The basic GMM model draws on the PME setup. Since a detailed discussion can be found in Driessen, Lin, and Phalippou, I stick to a high-level presentation here. The objective is to define moment conditions that will provide estimates of alpha and beta in the CAPM setting. To do that, recall that each fund i invests $C_{i,tj}$ *at time* tj and distributes $D_{i,tk}$ *at time* tk. The first step is to future-value each cash flow to the liquidation date (l_i) of the fund and then average these over n_i, the number of investments (capital calls) for each fund:

$$\frac{1}{n_i} \sum^{n_i} \left[D_{itk} \prod_{s=tk+1}^{l_i} (1 + r_{f,s} + \alpha + \beta r_{m,s}) \right]$$

$$\frac{1}{n_i} \sum^{n_i} \left[C_{itj} \prod_{t=tj+1}^{l_i} (1 + r_{f,t} + \alpha + \beta r_{m,t}) \right]$$

The second step collects these into portfolios with N_p funds per portfolio. A portfolio might consist of the funds within a subclass of private equity such as venture, or a portfolio might consist of all funds originating in a particular vintage year. Averaging again, this time across the N_p funds in the portfolio, generates the desired moment conditions:

$$V^D(\alpha, \beta) = \frac{1}{N_p} \sum_i \frac{1}{n_i} \sum^{n_i} \left[D_{itk} \prod_{s=tk+1}^{l_i} (1 + r_{f,s} + \alpha + \beta r_{m,s}) \right]$$

$$V^C(\alpha, \beta) = \frac{1}{N_p} \sum_i \frac{1}{n_i} \sum^{n_i} \left[C_{itj} \prod_{t=tj+1}^{l_i} (1 + r_{f,t} + \alpha + \beta r_{m,t}) \right]$$

Finally, iterate on (α, β) to minimize the quadratic loss function given by:

$$\min_{\alpha, \beta} \sum_p \left[\ln V^{D_p}(\alpha, \beta) - \ln V^{C_p}(\alpha, \beta) \right]^2$$

There are as many moment conditions for GMM estimates as funds. Aggregating cash flows by vintage year would generate as many moment conditions as vintage years. Cash flow aggregation by vintage year tends to reduce idiosyncratic risk, which, in turn, will improve the precision of GMM. However, there are cases in which vintage year aggregations can confound bootstrapping procedures when the distribution of funds across vintage years is either too thin or highly variable, as it is in our case. Bootstrapped standard errors are estimated by randomly drawing N funds with a replacement, where N is the total number of funds in the group, and using GMM to estimate the model parameters of the bootstrap sample. This sampling procedure is repeated N times. The z scores are computed using the standard deviations of the parameter estimates in the N bootstrap samples.

The Long and Nickels methodology is an interesting one; it forces the benchmark to match the private equity cash flows. In effect, it asks whether a given cash flow sequence that is determined by the GP would have earned more or less on an IRR basis in the public market. It does not ask whether the opportunity cost of the investments to private equity over, say, a 10-year horizon is too high. That is a different question and one that sometimes yields a different answer. Consider a $1 two-year investment for which private equity and the public benchmark earn 75 percent and 0 percent, respectively, in year one and 0 percent and 100 percent in year two. Assume the GP harvests dividends of $0.75 after year one and the public benchmark must match this policy. Then the GP has cash flows of –$1, $0.75, and $1.00 for an IRR of 44 percent while the public benchmark has –$1, $0.75, and $0.50 for an IRR of 18 percent. But left alone, the benchmark would have doubled its investment to $2 in two years versus $1.75 for the GP. This measures the true opportunity cost of fund, not the IRR.

If the limited partner (LP) wants to know whether a particular *sequence* of cash flows would have earned more in the public market, then the Long and Nickels alpha would seem to provide a useful solution methodology. If, on the other hand, the LP wants to know about opportunity cost, then PME is more direct. And extending PME to a CAPM structure and using GMM provides risk-adjusted performance. In any case, we tend to get conflicting results, depending on the method used.

To prove this point, let's set up a CAPM model with the Russell 3000 returns to simulate private equity returns as a test of Long and Nickels.

We have quarterly returns to the benchmark on 77 quarters, spanning June 1989 to June 2008. We simulated private equity return series using the CAPM, setting alpha and beta before the event. For example, if we set alpha equal to zero and beta equal to two, we created a return series with twice the risk of the benchmark. Returns were subsequently permitted to accumulate over time in both the benchmark and the simulated private equity series. We then select a set of random distribution dates with random distribution amounts (not to exceed available funds) from the simulated return series and match these distribution amounts in the benchmark portfolio as prescribed in the Long and Nickels methodology. The IRRs to the benchmark and the simulated series were then computed and differenced to estimate the Long and Nickels alpha.

As a baseline, we first simulated a series using $(\alpha,\beta) = (0,1)$ to generate two identical cash flows which, by definition, produce zero alpha. In a deterministic single-factor model like this one, the simulated return r_i is linear in the benchmark r_m according to:

$$r_{i,t} = \hat{\beta} r_{m,t}$$

The expected excess return is:

$$E(r_{i,t} - r_{m,t}) = E(r_{m,t})(\hat{\beta} - 1)$$

Now, the average annualized return to the Russell 3000 over this time was about 10.35 percent, which, for simplicity, we'll round to 10 percent. Thus, beta equal to 1.0 implies zero excess return, beta equal to 1.5 implies an excess return of 5 percent, beta of 2 implies 10 percent, and so forth. Note that alpha is zero by design—excess return is from risk and not skill. Then we estimated Long and Nickels alpha. It was zero in the first case as it should be, but as beta rose, the Long and Nickels alpha began to increase exponentially, for example, beta of 1.5 generated an average Long and Nickels alpha in 1,000 trials of 17.5 percent (standard deviation of 0.78 percent). The Long and Nickels alpha for beta equal to 2 was 34.6 percent (standard deviation of 1.75 percent)—almost three times as high as what the expected excess return would indicate. When beta is set to 3, the Long and Nickels alpha was a whopping 62 percent (with standard deviation of 2.2 percent).

It is possible that this exaggerated outperformance is due to cash flow matching. Private equity distributions will generally be larger in a high beta environment and the public benchmark must match the dividend policy of a much riskier investment. This is clearly favorable to the private equity manager if his performance is gauged relative to the less risky public benchmark.

In effect, cash flow matching alters the production function of the public benchmark to the extent that its capital has been depleted by a rule that acts as a constraint on its opportunity set. If, for example, the investment horizon were two years, the benchmark would have returned more than the private equity investment on an annualized basis. On the other hand, cash matching would have crushed the benchmark because the benchmark portfolio would have been required to harvest most of its first-year capital. Thus, it is possible that Long and Nickels, in addition to not adjusting for risk, may bias private equity performance in favor of the GP.

SUMMARY

Limited partners who invest in private equity should be aware of how these funds fit into the larger portfolio in regard to risk and return. Alpha should not necessarily be the sole objective for private equity programs; rather, it should be a mix of diversification (for example, buyout strategies or bear market hedges), sector tilts (for example, distressed firms, energy), and explicit beta bets (venture). Interest in GMM methods to measure risk-adjusted returns should be encouraged as prudent measures of risk management, if nothing else. If GMM estimates are not practical, as would likely be the case for small and new programs, then we could still try matching GP investments in firms with other publicly traded firms in relevant GIC sectors and estimating betas and risk-adjusted returns on those publicly traded proxies. Finally, it should be emphasized that without risk-adjusted returns and armed only with IRR estimates, we risk overallocating to investments whose risks are essentially unknown.

APPENDIX 19.1: CAPM

CAPM as a Basis for Deriving IRR, PME, and Risk-Adjusted Returns

I am going to derive all the performance measures from the basic CAPM relationship.

Basic CAPM:

$$r - r_f = \alpha + \beta r_m - r_f$$

Assume risk-free rate is zero for now and rewrite the asset's return as:

$$\frac{P_1 - P_0}{P_0} = \alpha + \beta r_m$$

Solve this for P_0 to get the pricing form of the CAPM:

$$P_0 = \frac{P_1}{(1 + \alpha + \beta r_m)}$$

This is a simple two-period discount model. Generalize the future price as a stream of cash flows (dividends) in discrete time.

$$P_{t-1} = \frac{D_t}{(1 + \alpha + \beta r_{m,t})} + \frac{D_{t+1}}{(1 + \alpha + \beta r_{m,t})(1 + \alpha + \beta r_{m,t+1})} + \ldots$$
$$+ \frac{D_T}{(1 + \alpha + \beta r_{m,t})(1 + \alpha + \beta r_{m,t+1}) \ldots (1 + \alpha + \beta r_{m,T})}$$

If we set $t = 1$ and assume the market rate is constant at r_m, then this looks like the simple textbook dividend discount model, but with a CAPM discount factor, that is a function of the asset's β with the market return, plus Jensen's index (α).

$$P_0 = \frac{D_1}{(1 + \alpha + \beta r_m)} + \frac{D_2}{(1 + \alpha + \beta r_m)^2} + \ldots + \frac{D_T}{(1 + \alpha + \beta r_m)^T}$$

The discount factor is the risk-adjusted market rate of return plus the alpha. Equivalently, we can express this as a future value by multiplying both sides by $(1 + \alpha + \beta r_m)^T$ to get:

$$P_0(1 + \alpha + \beta r_m)^T = D_1(1 + \alpha + \beta r_m)^{T-1} + D_2(1 + \alpha + \beta r_m)^{T-2} + \ldots + D_T$$

Finally, we can rewrite this in PME form as:

$$1 = \frac{D_1(1 + \alpha + \beta r_m)^{T-1} + D_2(1 + \alpha + \beta r_m)^{T-2} + \ldots + D_T}{P_0(1 + \alpha + \beta r_m)^T}$$

The terms in the parentheses are the discount factors that make the risk-adjusted value of the investment (P_0) just equal to the sum of the risk-adjusted value of the dividends.

GMM is an econometric method that estimates the values of the CAPM parameters α and β that, in conjunction with observed market returns (the opportunity cost of capital), equate the risk-adjusted present value of the investment to its return over time.

Other performance measures such as IRR, PME, and Long and Nickels alpha are all extensions of this basic relationship but with restrictions on the values of α and β. These performance measures must come at a cost and therefore, in principle, are inferior to the CAPM. The costs materialize because they impose specific restrictions on the level of risk (β) and abnormal return (α) that are not necessarily consistent with the underlying cash flows given the market returns for the investment period.

Let's now generalize the basic CAPM relationship:

$$m = \frac{D_1(1+\alpha+\beta r_m)^{T-1} + D_2(1+\alpha+\beta r_m)^{T-2} + \ldots + D_T}{P_0(1+\alpha+\beta r_m)^T}$$

We get the following set of relationships with their required restrictions:

Metric	Restrictions	Solved Parameters
Multiple	$a = \beta = 0$	m
PME	$\alpha = 0, \beta = 1$	m
IRR	$m = 1, \beta = 0$	$a = \text{IRR}$
GMM	$m = 1$	α, β

Case 1: Multiple ($\alpha = \beta = 0$)

$$m = \frac{D_1 + D_2 + \ldots + D_T}{P_0}$$

Case 2: PME ($\alpha = 0, \beta = 1$)

$$pme = m = \frac{D_1(1+r_m)^{T-1} + D_2(1+r_m)^{T-2} + \ldots + D_T}{P_0(1+r_m)^T}$$

Case 3: IRR ($m = 1, \beta = 0$, solve α)

$$P_0 = \frac{D_1}{(1+\alpha)} + \frac{D_2}{(1+\alpha)^2} + \ldots + \frac{D_T}{(1+\alpha)^T}$$

Case 4: GMM ($m = 1$, solve α, β)

$$1 = \frac{D_1(1+\alpha+\beta r_m)^{T-1} + D_2(1+\alpha+\beta r_m)^{T-2} + \ldots + D_T}{P_0(1+\alpha+\beta r_m)^T}$$

REFERENCES

Cochrane, John H. 2004. *The risk and return of venture capital.* Chicago: University of Chicago Graduate School of Business, Working Paper.

Driessen, Joost, Tse-Chun Lin, and Ludovic Phalippou. 2008. *A new method to estimate risk and return of non-traded assets from cash flows: The case of private equity funds.* Cambridge, MA: NBER Working Paper.

Hwang, Min, John M. Quigley, and Susan E. Woodward. 2005. An index for venture capital, 1987–2003. *Contributions to Economic Analysis & Policy* 4(1): 1–43.

Ick, Matthias. 2005. Performance measurement and appraisal of private equity investments relative to public equity markets. Working Paper.

Kaplan, Steve, and Antoinette Schoar. 2005. Private equity performance returns, persistence, and capital flows. *Journal of Finance* 60(4): 1791–1823.

Lerner, Josh, Antoinette Schoar, and Wan Wongsunwai. 2007. Smart institutions, foolish choices: The limited partner performance puzzle. *Journal of Finance* 62(2): 731–764.

Ljungqvist, Alexander, and Matthew P. Richardson. 2003. *The cash flow, return, and risk characteristics of private equity.* Cambridge, MA: NBER Working Paper W9454.

Moskowitz, Tobias J., and Annette Vissing-Jorgensen. 2002. The returns to entrepreneurial investment: A private equity premium puzzle? *American Economic Review* 92(4): 745–778.

Phalippou, Ludovic. 2007. Investing in private equity funds: A survey. *Research Foundation Literature Reviews* 2(2): 1–22.

Phalippou, Ludovic, and Oliver Gottschalg. 2009. The performance of private equity funds. *Review of Financial Studies* 22(4): 1747–1776.

Swensen, David F. 2000. *Pioneering portfolio management.* New York: Free Press.

Woodward, Susan E. 2004. Measuring risk and performance for private equity. Sand Hill Econometrics, Working Paper.

CHAPTER 20

Structured Credit

If something happens once, it will never happen again. But if something happens twice, it will surely happen a third time.
—Paulo Coelho, *The Alchemist*

The objective of securitization is to pool securities (debt instruments) to distribute risk and then issue new securities backed by the cash flows from the pool. In principle, all assets can be securitized as long as they have a cash flow; hence, the general reference for securities issued with these pools' backing as asset-backed securities (ABS). Collateralized debt obligations (CDOs), collateralized mortgage obligations (CMOs), and collateralized loan obligations (CLOs) are all products of securitization that differ mainly by the types of securities forming the pools (credit card debt, car loans, bank debt, mortgages, and so forth) and the manner in which they structure prioritized claims on the pool (called *tranches*).

Mortgage securitization, for example, involves taking an illiquid asset, mortgages, pooling them and issuing a security backed by the cash flows received on the pool. What distinguishes these from other securities is their inherent prepayment option. Thus, because a mortgage can be paid off at any time, all the cash flows may be received at once. This makes the duration of this asset (and, therefore, its cash flows) a function of factors that influence prepayment behavior. For example, when interest rates fall, prepayments rise as homeowners refinance their mortgages. Therefore, prepayment behavior will influence the duration of bonds issued against the pool and therefore their risk.

Figure 20.1 illustrates the basic elements of structured credit. When banks originate loans, they create new assets on their balance sheets. With these assets comes credit risk and banks shed that risk by removing these assets from their balance sheets by selling pooled loans to special purpose

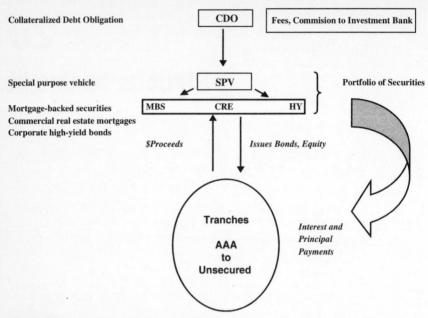

FIGURE 20.1   Structured Market Credit

vehicles. The SPV is a trust that is separate from the bank's balance sheet. It creates new securities (bonds), whose risks are prioritized in *tranches* and which are backed by the cash flows of the pool. Thus, the SPV effectively isolates the *credit risk* from the balance sheet of the originator of the CDO, shifting that risk to investors in these tranches. An investment in these tranches is the same as buying a bond with a prioritized claim to the pool's cash flows. The bank creates the SPV, which, in turn, designs the structured credit product (CDO, CMO, ABS, and so forth), which shifts the credit risk to investors while the bank continues to collect service fees and commissions.

SECURITIZATION

To understand the role of the SPV, think of a commercial bank in the business of originating residential mortgages. The bank lends its reserves to homeowners and holds these mortgages on its balance sheet as assets earning monthly cash flows in the form of mortgage payments. Without securitization, the bank's ability to originate mortgages is limited by the amount of its reserves. With securitization, the bank can pool these assets together and issue bonds against them—that is, the bank borrows more reserves by issuing bonds and the mortgage payments act as coupons on these bonds. These bonds become liabilities to the SPV, which inherits the credit risk on these bonds (bonds may default if the underlying mortgages default). The SPV therefore takes title to the loans and thereby removes the credit risk exposure from the bank's balance sheet.

In this manner, the bank can expand its mortgage origination function; hence, the rationale behind government sponsored entities (GSEs) such as GNMA, FNMA, FHLMC. The Federal National Mortgage Association (Fannie Mae) was established in 1938, the Federal Home Loan Mortgage Corporation (Freddie Mac) was established in 1970, and the Government National Mortgage Association (Ginnie Mae) was established in 1968. These government sponsored enterprises (GSEs) had different missions—Ginnie Mae to promote home ownership (it is a wholly owned subsidiary of HUD) which offers full government backing, Fannie Mae to promote mortgage lending, and Freddie Mac to expand the secondary market for mortgages. Fannie and Freddie mortgage securities enjoy the implicit guarantee of the federal government. Investment banks securitize these assets by buying mortgages from originators, pooling them and issuing bonds; mortgage originators such as commercial banks and savings and loan institutions retain the fees from servicing these mortgages through their amortization periods.

The credit risk is then shifted from the originator of the mortgages to the bondholders. Thus the structure of the SPV insulates the originator from credit risk. That way, the business of loan origination and securitization are separate. In sum, the bank originates a pool of loans, securitizes these as an SPV, issues bonds against the expected cash flows on the pool, and repeats this process as new pools originate. The credit risk is therefore isolated to the SPV structure and not the bank.

If the SPV issued claims that were not prioritized but were simply fractional claims to the payoff on the pool, then the structure would be known as a *pass-through* securitization, which is the operational model for the GSEs. Investors simply get a pro rata share of the pool's capital. Thus, if the pool consists of $100 million in mortgage loans and an investor buys 25 percent of the pass-through securities, he received one-quarter of the principal and interest cash flows until the mortgages in the pool are paid off. Since the expected loss is the mean expected loss on the underlying securities, the portfolio's credit rating would be given the average credit rating of the pool. In this case, there is no credit enhancement.

Pass-through securities are originated from pools of conforming loans and guaranteed by GNMA, an agency of the federal government, or implicitly by one of two government sponsored enterprises, Fannie Mae or

Freddie Mac. The guarantee requires that the loan pool conform to certain standards regarding loan to value and mortgage size; hence, the conforming nature of the underlying loan pool. GNMA is explicitly backed by the federal government, while the GSEs have implicit guarantees (this implicit guarantee comes at a cost—the bonds issued by the GSEs carry a higher yield).

CREDIT ENHANCEMENT

Structured finance produces a capital structure of *prioritized claims* known as *tranches* (see Figure 20.2) against the underlying pool of collateral. If constructed correctly, the CDO will provide credit enhancement for all tranches in the capital structure except for the first loss tranche (also called the *equity tranche*—the SPV generally retains ownership of these bonds). We now show how this works.

The tranches are prioritized in how they absorb losses from the underlying portfolio. Senior tranches absorb losses only after the junior claims have been exhausted, which allows senior tranches to achieve credit ratings that are higher than the average rating of the underlying pool. The degree of protection provided by junior tranches is known as *overcollateralization*, and it plays an important role in determining the credit rating of more senior tranches.

In its simplest form, the process of credit enhancement can best be understood by considering two securities (mortgages), each of which pays nothing upon default but one dollar otherwise (Coval et al. 2009). Both

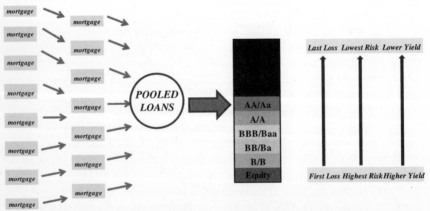

FIGURE 20.2 Structured Credit: Collateralized Mortgage Obligations

securities have the same probability of default. Suppose we combine these two securities into a $2 pool and issue two tranches against the pool. The junior tranche absorbs the first dollar loss and pays $1 in the event that neither mortgage defaults. The senior tranche pays $1 if at least one mortgage does not default. With the junior tranche absorbing the first loss, the senior tranche's credit rating is thereby enhanced, due to securitization. Assume that the default probability is equal to 10 percent on each mortgage but is uncorrelated across mortgages. The junior tranche defaults with probability equal to 19 percent while the senior tranche defaults with probability equal to 1 percent. The junior tranche defaults with probability $2 \times 0.1 - 0.12$. Thus, the senior tranche ends up with a credit rating that is higher than the average rating of the underlying pool. This is credit enhancement—the ability to create tranche(s) that are more secure than the underlying collateral.

Figure 20.3 shows how this probability is computed. Letting A and B represent the two mortgages, then from elementary probability theory and the knowledge that the junior tranche defaults if *either* bond defaults, the likelihood of the junior tranche defaulting is equal to the probability that mortgage A defaults *or* mortgage B defaults, minus their intersection (the joint likelihood), which translates into $\Pr(A) + \Pr(B) - \Pr(A \text{ and } B)$ equal to $0.10 + 0.10 - 0.01 = 0.19$, or 19 percent. Because the junior tranche absorbs the first loss, then the senior tranche defaults only in the event that both mortgages default together, which is $\Pr(A \text{ and } B) = 0.1^2 = 0.01$ or 1

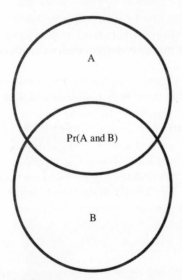

FIGURE 20.3 Venn Diagram of
Joint Default Likelihood

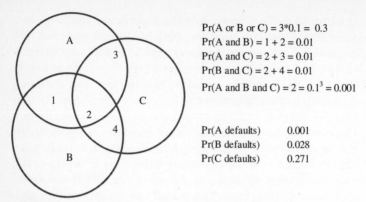

$$Pr(A \text{ or } B \text{ or } C) = 3*0.1 = 0.3$$
$$Pr(A \text{ and } B) = 1 + 2 = 0.01$$
$$Pr(A \text{ and } C) = 2 + 3 = 0.01$$
$$Pr(B \text{ and } C) = 2 + 4 = 0.01$$
$$Pr(A \text{ and } B \text{ and } C) = 2 = 0.1^3 = 0.001$$

Pr(A defaults)	0.001
Pr(B defaults)	0.028
Pr(C defaults)	0.271

FIGURE 20.4   Venn Diagram of Joint Default Likelihood

percent. Clearly, the credit enhancement offered to mortgage A bonds is due in part to the assumption that defaults across mortgages are uncorrelated.

As the number of securities in the pool increases, so do the prospects for credit enhancement under certain conditions. Figure 20.4 illustrates a three-tranche case. Tranche C, the most junior, defaults if any of the three bonds defaults. Tranche B defaults if two of the three bonds defaults and tranche A defaults only in the case that all three bonds default. Again, we assume that the probability of default is 10 percent and default is independent, that is, the likelihood of any bond defaulting does not depend on the likelihood of the other bonds defaulting. This is a key assumption as we shall see and, indeed, pooling bonds from diverse zip codes enhances the chances that this assumption will hold.

Tranche C is junior and it defaults if any bond defaults. This is therefore the probability that A or B or C defaults (0.3) minus the intersection, which is three times 0.01, and we then add back in region 2 to avoid double counting, giving us Pr(C defaults) = 0.3 − 0.03 + 0.001 = 0.271, or 27.1 percent. Tranche B defaults if any two bonds default. There are three ways this can happen: Pr(A and B), Pr(B and C), and Pr(A and C). This is 3 × .01 = 0.03. But this has triple-counted region 2 and we should only have counted it once. Therefore, the probability of tranche B defaulting is 0.03 − 3 × 0.1³ + 0.1³ = 0.028 = 2.8 percent. This represents credit enhancement. Finally, the probability of tranche A defaulting depends only on all three bonds defaulting together, which is 0.001, or 0.1 percent; again, credit enhancement.

Now consider applying these principles to the securities in just the junior tranches of separate CDOs. Suppose, for example, that we take two CDOs' junior tranches, each of which has a bond that defaults with probability equal to 10 percent and pool these into a new CDO (this is called a CDO^2). Again, form two tranches. Under the assumption that the default correlation is still zero across bonds, either bond defaults with probability equal to 19 percent. $Pr(A \text{ or } B) - Pr(A \text{ and } B) = 0.20 - 0.01 = 0.19$. The senior tranche therefore defaults with likelihood equal to $(0.19)^2 = 3.6$ percent. Again, there is credit enhancement.

This gives an idea on how CDOs attract investors with different risk preferences. Those wanting higher risk exposure and, consequently, higher yields, will hold bonds from the more junior tranches. More risk-averse investors will migrate to the top of the capital structure. On the other hand, if these securities were constructed as a pass-through, then all bonds would have default risk equal to 10 percent. Structured finance therefore appeals to the spectrum of risk appetites and in that sense distributes risk efficiently.

Consider now the possibility that default risks are not independent. This could happen because loan pools originate from the same zip codes or that some systemic risk event has developed that makes default dependency nonzero. In such cases, default correlations are no longer zero and the senior tranches are therefore less secure. In the extreme case in which default correlations are 1, then both tranches default with probability 10 percent and there is no credit enhancement. More to the point, intermediate default correlations can reduce credit enhancement significantly, thereby increasing the risk to investors holding these securities.

It is interesting that rating agencies like Standard and Poor's, Fitch, and Moody's used credit rating models that were basically identical to those used for other liabilities, like corporate bonds. Why would the standard credit rating model not be applicable in the case of CDOs? First, corporate credit risk is probably more heavily influenced by fundamentals within the firm and not management decisions made at other firms. Second, loans that were pooled to form CDOs (and other forms of collateralized obligations) began to gain exposure to the same sources of risk. This was especially true for regional pools of loans that originated from California, Florida, Arizona, and Nevada mortgage originations, or home equity, car, and credit card debt that were all exposed to the same macro risk factors like unemployment. As the credit crisis unfolded in 2007, SPVs were holding pools of highly correlated risks that were not being priced into the underlying tranches of the CDOs.

Historically, mortgage loans were of much shorter duration. Thus, during the depression of the 1930s, banks that found themselves with much lower reserves (due in part to their huge capital losses when equity markets imploded) could not roll over mortgage debt. As a result, homeowners who did not have the cash on hand to pay off their mortgages, found their homes foreclosed upon. The government's response was Fannie Mae and the long-term mortgage. This model worked reasonably well until the 1970s, when the explosion of money market funds sparked disintermediation of deposits from savings and loan institutions and the subsequent banking crisis, whose solution was to impose stricter capital requirements on banks. Ironically, these capital requirements are to some degree responsible for the credit crisis begun after housing prices peaked in July of 2006. Banks were required to hold more capital against their holdings of mortgage loans and CDOs than bonds issued by the GSEs. Therefore, banks accelerated the securitization of their loan originations and bought GSEs instead. GSEs, on the other hand, through tacit policies designed to promote home ownership, vastly increased their securitization of mortgage debt. Many of these pools began to show increasing signs of default stress brought on by subprime lending practices (including Alt-A and low documentation loans, high LTVs, and nonamortizing debt). Thus, the relatively low capital requirements on GSEs induced investment banks to hold large quantities of these bonds that they purchased with the proceeds of their own securitization efforts. Investment banks, for example, would create a special off-balance-sheet investment vehicle called a SIV, which would have a line of credit at a commercial bank. The SIV would sell commercial paper and use the proceeds to invest in CDOs. As long as the yield on the CDOs exceeded the yield on commercial paper, banks could safely manage huge portfolios off their balance sheet. But, as defaults began to rise and the value of the CDOs began to fall, the commercial paper market began to dry up. The SIVs then began to fail and eventually this contagion spread to the balance sheet of the investment banks themselves. Thus, SPCs and SIVs in the so-called shadow banking system

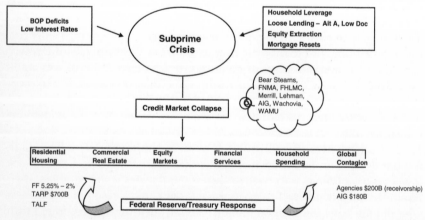

FIGURE 20.5   Credit Market Collapse

(investment banks like Bear Stearns and Lehman) were getting crushed, which eventually led to huge on-balance-sheet losses as assets began to wither while liabilities remained unchanged—all because default correlations increased on the underlying collateral of CDOs.

BASICS OF PRICING INTEREST RATE DERIVATIVES

An investment in any collateralized obligation is the purchase of an asset whose value, like any bond, is determined by discounting its expected cash flows. Because cash flows in the form of principal and interest are received over time, the discount rates used will generally be tied to the term structure. Intuitively, the investor prices the bond today as the weighted average of the present values of the bond's cash flows using various paths that discount rates may take over time, depending on their inherent volatility.

Drawing from our term structure work in Chapter 3 and options work in Chapter 16, we can construct a lattice that models short-rate volatility over time. Examples can be found in the spreadsheet accompanying this chapter. For starters, let's assume that annual volatility in short rates can be modeled using parameter choices $u = 1.3$ and $d = 0.9$. We develop this model in more detail further on but, for now, we are interested in the underlying intuition. Assuming the one-year short rate is equal to 2 percent, we present a lattice covering a 10-year period in the top half of Figure 20.6 consistent with these parameter choices. Now, consider a one-dollar par bond. The elementary price of this bond is $1 at time zero. The forward values of this bond are given in the lower lattice and are consistent with the term structure embedded in the short rates. You can examine in detail how this lattice was constructed by referring to the chapter spreadsheet.

We compute the elementary price in state s at time t, $p_{s,t}$, as the equal-weighted discounted average of the two previous elementary prices using the following rule at each node and where $d_{s,t}$ is the reciprocal of the short rate in the top lattice.

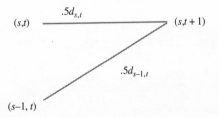

Short rates

Node	1	2	3	4	5	6	7	8	9	10
1	0.0200	0.0260	0.0338	0.0439	0.0571	0.0743	0.0965	0.1255	0.1631	0.2121
2		0.0180	0.0234	0.0304	0.0395	0.0514	0.0668	0.0869	0.1129	0.1468
3			0.0162	0.0211	0.0274	0.0356	0.0463	0.0601	0.0782	0.1017
4				0.0146	0.0190	0.0246	0.0320	0.0416	0.0541	0.0704
5					0.0131	0.0171	0.0222	0.0288	0.0375	0.0487
6						0.0118	0.0154	0.0200	0.0259	0.0337
7							0.0106	0.0138	0.0180	0.0234
8								0.0096	0.0124	0.0162
9									0.0086	0.0112
10										0.0077

(The short rates 0.0439 and 0.0304 in column 4, and 0.1155 and 0.3499 in column 3, and 0.1344 in column 5, are circled.)

$$0.2251 = .5(0.1155/1.0439 + 0.3499/(1.0304))$$

Elementary prices

Node	1	2	3	4	5	6	7	8	9	10
1	0.4902	0.2389	0.1155	0.0553	0.0262	0.0122	0.0056	0.0025	0.0011	0.0004
2	0.4902	0.4797	0.3499	0.2251	0.1344	0.0761	0.0412	0.0214	0.0107	0.0051
3		0.2408	0.3528	0.3425	0.2750	0.1967	0.1297	0.0801	0.0468	0.0259
4			0.1185	0.2311	0.2801	0.2695	0.2246	0.1689	0.1173	0.0760
5				0.0584	0.1422	0.2066	0.2316	0.2204	0.1863	0.1436
6					0.0288	0.0842	0.1425	0.1824	0.1951	0.1832
7						0.0142	0.0485	0.0938	0.1350	0.1603
8							0.0070	0.0274	0.0596	0.0953
9								0.0035	0.0153	0.0369
10									0.0017	0.0084
11										0.0009

1.0000

	1	2	3	4	5	6	7	8	9	10
Bond price	0.9804	0.9593	0.9367	0.9125	0.8868	0.8595	0.8307	0.8004	0.7688	0.7360
Spot rate	0.0200	0.0210	0.0220	0.0232	0.0243	0.0256	0.0269	0.0282	0.0296	0.0311

FIGURE 20.6 A 10-Year Short-Rate Lattice

The bond prices given in the second-to-last row are the sums of the elementary prices. It is easy to prove algebraically that these prices are the discounted sum of the previous period's elementary prices. For example, the bond price two years from now is equal to the discounted sum of the possible bond prices one year from now:

$$0.9593 = \frac{0.4902}{(1.026)} + \frac{0.4902}{(1.018)}$$

These bond prices are therefore consistent with the term structure represented by the short-rate structure in our lattice. They are therefore *zero coupon fixed income securities*.

The spot rates given in the last row are estimated directly from the bond prices and are therefore consistent with the short-rate lattice. The problem, however, is that they may not be consistent with the observed term structure, and this is the problem we turn to now.

INTEREST RATE DYNAMICS

The goal is to derive a model that is consistent with the observed interest rate dynamics and matches the term structure. We will look at the Ho-Lee and the Black-Derman-Toy (BDT) models. Ho and Lee was one of the early models that matched the term structure. I illustrate how this is accomplished in the chapter spreadsheet, using Excel's Solver.

Ho and Lee propose a linear short-rate model $r_{t,s} = a_t + bs$, where b is a constant volatility parameter, specifically $b = 2\sigma$, where σ is the annual volatility of the short rate. The annual drift rate is given by a_t which, following Luenberger (Chapter 14) is treated as a variable to be solved in such a way that the short-rate lattice constructed is matched to the current term structure. The continuous time counterpart to the Ho and Lee model is given by $dr = \alpha_t dt + \sigma dz$, where dz is a standard Wiener process. Therefore, the parameter a_t is a drift component, while $(b \times s)$ is the volatility factor. In our lattice, s is the state variable that measures the number of up-movements in rates (similar to the binomial lattice). It therefore represents the volatility given by the standard extrapolation measure used in the options lattice of Chapters 16 and 17, that is, $\sigma\sqrt{T}$. The results for the August 1, 2008, term structure are given in Figure 20.7.

This lattice is tied to the term structure by solving for the parameters a_t so that the differences between the observed spot rates and those computed off the estimated bond prices are minimized (see Solver on

Short rate

Year	1	2	3	4	5	6	7	8	9	10
	0.0218	0.0316	0.0427	0.0510	0.0605	0.0664	0.0748	0.0818	0.0899	0.0979
		0.0216	0.0327	0.0410	0.0505	0.0564	0.0648	0.0718	0.0799	0.0879
			0.0227	0.0310	0.0405	0.0464	0.0548	0.0618	0.0699	0.0779
				0.0210	0.0305	0.0364	0.0448	0.0518	0.0599	0.0679
					0.0205	0.0264	0.0348	0.0418	0.0499	0.0579
						0.0164	0.0248	0.0318	0.0399	0.0479
							0.0148	0.0218	0.0299	0.0379
								0.0118	0.0199	0.0279
									0.0099	0.0179
										0.0079

Elementary prices

Year	1	2	3	4	5	6	7	8	9	10
	0.4893	0.2372	0.1137	0.0541	0.0255	0.0120	0.0056	0.0026	0.0012	0.0005
	0.4893	0.4767	0.3445	0.2196	0.1300	0.0735	0.0401	0.0213	0.0110	0.0056
		0.2395	0.3479	0.3342	0.2651	0.1882	0.1237	0.0770	0.0458	0.0263
			0.1171	0.2260	0.2703	0.2571	0.2122	0.1592	0.1111	0.0732
				0.0573	0.1378	0.1975	0.2185	0.2057	0.1731	0.1338
					0.0281	0.0809	0.1349	0.1702	0.1798	0.1676
						0.0138	0.0463	0.0880	0.1246	0.1458
							0.0068	0.0260	0.0555	0.0870
								0.0034	0.0144	0.0341
									0.0017	0.0079
										0.0008

	1	2	3	4	5	6	7	8	9	10
1.0000										
Bond price	0.9787	0.9533	0.9232	0.8913	0.8568	0.8230	0.7881	0.7534	0.7182	0.6828
Spot rate	0.0218	0.0242	0.0270	0.0292	0.0314	0.0330	0.0346	0.0360	0.0375	0.0389

FIGURE 20.7 Ho-Lee Model

the spreadsheet for details). One problem with Ho and Lee, however, is that negative short rates are not ruled out. The BDT model resolves this problem using the form $r_{t,s} = a_t e^{bs}$. Again, we assume that the volatility parameter is constant across the term structure. The continuous time version of BDT is:

$$dr = \left(\alpha_t + \frac{1}{2}\sigma^2\right)rdt + \sigma rdz$$

where, again, dz is a Wiener process. This is a lognormal model similar to the one derived in Chapter 17. Note that the drift component is lognormal and proportional to the short rate. The BDT lattice is given in the chapter spreadsheet for comparison purposes. Notice that the bond prices are identical to those from the Ho-Lee model.

CMO VALUATION

Consider an allocation to the investment grade AAA tranche of a CMO. This tranche (call it tranche A) is entitled to 25 percent of the principal and interest on a pool of mortgages consisting of prime and subprime loans that have been structured so as to enhance the credit ratings within the pool, using methods discussed at the beginning of the chapter. To keep things simple, let's refer to tranche A as a single bond and assume that this bond is priced in the market at 103. Is this a fair price?

To price this bond, we first need some facts. First, let's assume that it is August 1, 2008, and that the term structure is a presented in the Ho-Lee and BDT models. Furthermore, assume that 2 percent of the loan pool is prepaid annually except when short rates fall, in which case the prepayment rate rises to 5 percent. The average mortgage rate on the pool is 4 percent. Using the template from Chapter 2, we estimate that the conventional 30-year annual mortgage payment is $5.78 per hundred dollars and that annual interest on this tranche is $25\% \times 0.04 = \$1$. Let's assume that tranche B is entitled to 50 percent of the principal and interest in the CMO, and a third tranche C is entitled to 25 percent. Tranche C is subordinated to the first two tranches and receives no payments until tranches A and B are retired. Tranche A received principal and interest first, while tranche B is paid interest only until tranche A is retired. Tranche C accrues interest until the first two tranches are retired. Thus, tranche C carries the highest risk in the event there are defaults. It also carries the highest interest rate risk in the event that prepayment rates exceed expectations.

Year	1	2	3	4	
				0.0605	
			0.0510	0.0505	Short
		0.0427	0.0410	0.0405	rates
	0.0316	0.0327	0.0310	0.0305	
0.0218	0.0216	0.0227	0.0210	0.0205	
				0.9224	
			0.9412	0.8941	Pool
		0.9604	0.9124	0.8668	size
	0.9800	0.9604	0.9124	0.8668	
1	0.9500	0.9310	0.8845	0.8402	

FIGURE 20.8   CMO Valuation Using Ho-Lee

To minimize labor while maximizing intuition, we will price the tranche A bond going out three years. Figure 20.8 therefore borrows the first four nodes from Ho and Lee and appends a matrix indicating the remaining pool size consistent with our earlier assumptions concerning prepayments. (See the chapter spreadsheet for all computational details.)

The pool size reflects the remaining principal conditional on the movements in the short rates in the top half of the table. Our first task is to keep track of the principal due to tranche A, which begins with 25 percent at time zero but is diminished as principal and interest are paid from the pool. The computations are given in the chapter spreadsheet, but here is the intuition: the remaining principal is equal to the previous principal, which grows at 4 percent per year (the mortgage rate) but is decremented by the impact of the reduction in the size of the pool each year. The declining pool size affects both the current year principal as well as the remaining principal in the other tranches. Thus, while the discount factors in the short-rate lattice have no direct impact on the remaining principal, they do have an indirect impact through prepayment behavior. Thus, assumptions about prepayments will drive part of the CMO pricing.

Our second task is to discount the cash flows associated with each principal amount at each node, and working backward, arrive at the present value of the bond. Again, refer to the spreadsheet for computational details. Values for the terminal nodes reflect the discounted value of the principal associated with that node, itself conditioned on the matched short rates and pool size. Values for interior nodes reflect the average discounted values of the two subsequent nodes based on the principal amount that node is entitled to. Figure 20.9 shows the principal and value for this tranche.

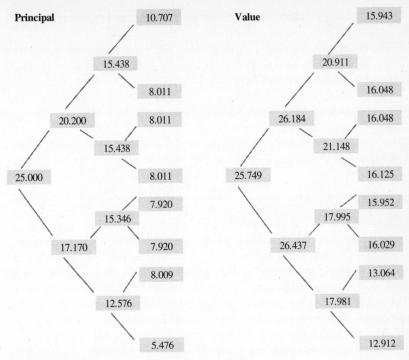

FIGURE 20.9 Principal and Value for Tranche A

The value of the bond is therefore $25.75. A final computation indicates that this bond would sell at 25.75/25 = 103, relative to par. Thus, the bond is fairly priced, according to our model.

THE CRASH OF THE HOUSING BUBBLE

Explosion of Residential Mortgage Debt

According to the Case-Shiller housing index, residential housing prices peaked in July of 2006. Housing prices were still in decline at the time this chapter was written (summer of 2011). Credit for the bubble can be attributable to policy objectives as well as easy credit. Policy during both the Clinton and Bush administrations was clearly focused on increasing home ownership. This motive was not new; GSEs were established to expand the secondary market in mortgages by purchasing and securitizing conforming loans and creating mortgage-backed securities (MBS), transferring ownership (and risk) of cash flows to investors. MBSs were essentially plain vanilla pass-through securities with no credit enhancement and stable credit risk.

GSEs essentially enjoyed a carry trade in MBS due to their low borrowing costs; they were backed by the government and therefore had the highest credit quality. Some pertinent facts:

- Twenty percent of the mortgage debt was funded by MBS in 2003 (up from 5 percent in 1992).
- Forty-seven percent of all mortgage debt was held by GSEs in the form of MBS and whole loans by 2003.

Government's Role

As mentioned earlier, there has been a clear policy mandate aimed at increasing home ownership in the United States, for financial reasons (home equity was considered a form of savings) as well as for less tangible purposes. For example, home ownership is part of the American dream. HUD specified in 1996 that 42 percent of GSE purchases be mortgages to borrowers below median income and 12 percent below 60 percent of the median. These shares rose to 50 percent (20 percent) in 2000 and 52 percent (22 percent) in 2005.

GSEs reached these targets by lowering credit standards and raising LTVs. Home ownership rose significantly but many of these loans were either subprime (risky, high LTV, lower credit scores), Alt-A (good credit rating but low or no documentation), or nonamortizing (option ARM recasts, which pay less than monthly accrued interest for the trial period). In 2003, 60 percent of all mortgages were conforming, 10 percent were junk, and the rest were jumbos. In 2005 and 2006, one-third of all originations were conforming and one-third were junk. Credit expansion had clearly laid the groundwork for an unstable bubble in housing prices.

Household Leverage and the Housing Meltdown

Rising housing values and expectations that the trend would continue incentivized homeowners to take on second mortgages and tax-deductible home equity lines of credit (2 percent of mortgages in 2002 involved a second lien while 30 percent did so by 2006).

The tax deductibility of mortgage interest also provides more incentives for renters to transition to home ownership. Moreover, home owners greatly underestimated the risk of losing their homes to default.

By 2001, 45 percent of the $215 billion of subprime and Alt-A mortgages were placed into private label ABS. By 2005 and 2006, this had risen to 80 percent of $2 trillion. Because private label securitization fell outside the mandates of GSEs (these were nonconforming loans), their contribution to the credit risk of securitized pools of mortgages went undetected. Originators used SPVs (for example, Bank of America, Countrywide, WAMU, GMAC Mortgage LLC), which held title to these pools off their balance sheets and out of sight of regulators.

What contributed to the explosion in below-investment-grade tranches was in some part due to the carry trade—BASEL accords established capital requirements of zero on government bonds, 8 percent on commercial loans, 4 percent on residential mortgages and 1.6 percent on GSE pass-throughs. Since SPVs could attain a AAA rating on over 80 percent of an ABS issue, then banks accelerated their holdings of MBS.

Hedge funds and special investment vehicles like Citigroup, Lehman, and Bear Stearns levered up, increasing their debt-to-equity ratios to 30:1 and held the below-investment-grade tranches because they felt there was no downside risk since housing prices were thought to have only upside volatility. These investments went from $500 billion in 2000 to about $2 trillion in 2008. At the same time, SIVs started issuing commercial paper to buy junk. They also had lines of credit with commercial banks in case holders of commercial paper would not roll their debt. Thus, the commercial banks were exposed to all of the risk on the SIV investments.

The acceleration in housing value, which tripled over the 10 years from 1998 to 2007, sparked a construction boom. The supply of housing eventually overwhelmed demand by July 2006, and housing values thereafter began to decline. As they did, defaults on subprime and Alt-As spiked and the credit quality of the CDOs and MBS fell.

As market prices on these securities declined, spreads over Treasuries blew out, erasing balance sheets on SIVs and SPVs (recall that they retained the junior tranches for themselves) and eventually the GSEs themselves. The market for commercial paper virtually went away (picked up by the Fed) and credit markets collapsed. Without access to cash, funds could not meet their margin requirements, assets were liquidated at a fraction of their booked values and what ensued was a string of investment bank and thrift failures.

SUMMARY

The failure of regulators to recognize changes in credit risk on structured products contributed to and exacerbated the economic impact of the housing bubble meltdown, beginning in the third quarter of 2006. I began this chapter with some background on how securitization works in general and the role that the federal government has historically had in this process. Securitization originally pooled mortgages whose cash flows were used to back pass-through securities issued by the GSEs. Private label issuance led to the pooling of cash flows from credit card debt, student loans, car loans, and personal loans, as well as mortgages that were structured to provide credit enhancement. The concept of credit enhancement worked as long as credit defaults were truly independent and identically distributed. This turned out not to be the case. Rating agencies grossly underestimated risk on these securities, which by 2008 had grown in such proportion to the size of the economy that defaults effectively cascaded, destroying bank balance sheets and drying up the credit channel, which, in turn, choked off growth throwing the global economy into a recession not experienced since the Great Depression.

This chapter develops models that show how the securitization process works, how credit enhancement led to unanticipated risks and how the securities created in the form of collateralized obligations are priced. In the process, we developed the theory underlying interest rate derivatives and use it to derive our pricing models. Abundant examples can be generated from the chapter spreadsheet.

REFERENCE

Coval, Joshua D., Jakub Jurek, and Erik Staford. 2009. The economics of structured finance. *Journal of Economic Perspectives* 23(1): 3–25.

CHAPTER 21

Optimal Rebalancing

*Intuition is nothing but the outcome of earlier
intellectual experience.*

—Albert Einstein

Fluctuations in the prices of risky assets affect overall portfolio value as well as the relative allocation of assets within the portfolio. Periodic rebalancing policies are therefore designed to preserve targeted allocations of risky and safe assets relative to their respective weights in a benchmark portfolio. Targeted allocations (for example, a 60/30/10 mix of stocks, bonds, and cash) are ultimately a statement of the portfolio's exposure to risk and, therefore, weight adjustments are necessary to prevent drift in risk due to underlying price volatility. Rebalancing also serves to minimize movements in the durations of portfolios of fixed income securities due to yield volatility, indicating that even portfolios of safe assets (for example, Treasury issues) are not immune to risk.

The objective is to rebalance to add value but minimize the risk of not meeting liabilities. Clearly, a do-nothing, buy-and-hold strategy will not control for risk. Calendar rebalancing may add value and minimize risk at the time rebalancing occurs, but the temporal nature of this rule-based policy means it cannot serve to optimally control risk and add value over time because of its arbitrary timing. Dynamic policies (constant mix and various forms of portfolio insurance) provide upside or downside protection, depending on the time series properties of asset prices (for example, rising, falling, mean reverting, or volatile periods), but the inherent randomness in asset prices prevent any one dominant policy. Hence, these policies are essentially regimes that work best in a compatible market. Without the ability to forecast asset prices, they are essentially reactionary policies.

Transactions costs complicate the problem—rebalancing must now trade off the benefits (adding value, reducing risk) against the costs of doing so—but they also serve to recast the problem as one in which the decision is the outcome of an optimization problem whose objective it is to maximize the net benefits of rebalancing. At the simplest level, the setup provides some insight into solving for trigger solutions, that is, the optimal time at which the decision is made to rebalance. For example, when the benefits of rebalancing (reduced risk, say) are quadratic in the drift from the target weight(s) and costs are linear, then the trigger point (expressed as a function of the magnitude in the drift of the current portfolio weight from the target) is easily solved (it is the maximal amount of drift allowed that signal a rebalancing). How much rebalancing is an appropriate response, when triggered to do so? In a quadratic setup, it is always half the trigger point. For example, if rebalancing is triggered at 6 percent drift (the difference between the portfolio weight and the target), then rebalancing will proceed back to 3 percent drift and not all the way back to benchmark. Why? Because the costs of rebalancing produce a drag on the benefits, both explicitly and implicitly.

TRIGGER STRATEGIES AND NO-TRADE REGIONS

Trigger strategies are attractive because they are outcomes to an optimization problem, meaning that they minimize the possibly unnecessary (and redundant) costs of rebalancing on a purely calendar basis. But they are also static, meaning that they assume costs and benefits are constant through time. To understand this better, consider a setup for which costs are constant but benefits are measured as a Value-at-Risk (VaR) dollar amount portfolio risk exposure. VaR is a function of the correlations in the portfolio returns, the returns themselves, and the value of the portfolio, at each point in time. Clearly, this quantity is not constant, and in fact, may be highly volatile. In such a setting, the optimal solution to the problem of choosing a time to rebalance, as well as the degree of rebalancing, is one that maximizes the net benefits of doing so over *all* points in time. It is a *dynamic strategy*. As such, it is not so much a problem of knowing *when* to rebalance; technically, maximizing the net benefits occurs at each point, so rebalancing is really a continuous process—it is a random variable. Rather, it is knowing how much to rebalance in each period. In this type of problem—an *optimal control* problem—the objective is to maximize the function (say, net benefits) over time, that is, to solve for the optimal rebalancing path that maximizes the objective function continuously. What is attractive about this approach is that it combines the aspects of a calendar strategy (defining each point in time, for example, quarterly, monthly, daily) within an optimization problem (at each point in time, how much rebalancing is indeed optimal).

Two points need to be made. With respect to a trigger strategy, the time to rebalancing is a random variable, but the amount is not. On the other hand, the optimal control problem chooses the amount as a random variable but the timing is continuous (or practically speaking, it is periodic, say, monthly). The timing choice in a sense becomes one of the control variables—should rebalancing occur monthly, quarterly, or annually? The answer lies in the VaR. An optimal path (continuous, that is, defined in terms of dt) for rebalancing can be solved explicitly. Choosing to exercise rebalancing periodically is acceptable and does not change the nature of the problem or its solution. The classic control problem involves extracting fish from a lake. The fish reproduce at a rate and fishing depletes this renewable resource. The objective is to choose the optimal rate of fishing (analogous to our rebalancing argument) that keep the fish population within acceptable levels while maximizing the market value of the fish sold. Fishing is technically continuous, but practically speaking, periodic, for example, daily or weekly. But, choosing to wait too long within the dt interval increases risk, perhaps to unacceptable levels. Thus, the timing decision should be a function of the volatility in VaR. More volatile environments require more frequent rebalancing.

Leland (1999) suggests that the optimal policy involves a no-trade region around the target weights. Asset volatility and trading costs produce a region, or interval, around the targeted weights for which no rebalancing is optimal. Choosing not to rebalance will, in turn, reduce turnover. The no-trade region takes the form of a convex region, which, in the n-asset case, lies in R^n. When actual portfolio weights lie to the right (left) of this region, then rebalancing occurs back to the boundary points, but not to the original target levels. This is a trigger strategy, but it is a continuously updated procedure for determining that strategy because the no-trade region continuously changes as a function of the movements in the underlying asset prices. Basically, the objective is to maximize, again, net benefits. Drift from the target produces utility losses, which are reduced through rebalancing. Drift, itself, is a function of the underlying asset dynamics (Wiener process), and since portfolio weights are functions of the asset price movements, then Ito's lemma produces a functional whose arguments include the weights (to be rebalanced) and the costs. The solution is a partial differential equation(s) that maximizes the discounted present value of the optimal path for net benefits. Underlying volatility in asset prices is the source of the no-trade region. Thus, we have a trader who wishes to hold risky assets in target proportions but for whom divergence between actual and target levels create expected losses (tracking error). Losses can be reduced by trading more frequently, but that leads to higher transaction costs. The optimal strategy minimizes the sum of the tracking error and transaction costs.

Application of this principle is costly because of the difficulty in locating the no-trade region—it is the outcome to the solution of a set of partial differential equations (assuming a solution exists—in general, it does not and quasi-optimal solutions need be identified). At present, this strategy is not readily implementable, certainly not without significant costs.

AN OPTIMAL CONTROL PROBLEM

Some light can be shed on the nature of this problem, however, and its solution. What follows is an approach that provides some middle ground. It is a dynamic optimal control problem that carries less baggage relative to Leland, that is, the asset dynamics are less involved and so are the differentials to be solved for, but it has a well-defined objective function whose solution (the level of rebalancing) provides a significant amount of insight into the rebalancing problem. It is also implementable, as will be illustrated empirically at the end of this chapter.

First, let's begin with a statement of the problem. Once again, assume that a trader wishes to hold risky assets in target proportions but for whom divergence between target levels and actual (market) levels create increases in portfolio risk (as measured using VaR). For expositional simplicity, assume a single risky asset (the analysis will generalize to the multiple asset case). Define the following:

- Divergence from target weights: $\left(w(t) - w^T\right)^2 = w^2$
- Portfolio value at time t: $M(t)$
- Portfolio risk at time t: $\sigma(t)$
- Rebalancing amount: $w_u(t)$

In what follows, we ignore explicit time subscripting. Value at risk (VaR) changes as market weights diverge from target levels. Define VaR then as:

$$VaR = z_\alpha M\left(w(t) - w^T\right)^2 \sigma = z_\alpha M w^2 \sigma$$

and where z_α is the critical value corresponding to a α percent left-tail loss under the standard normal distribution (for example, 2.5 percent of the time, z is less than -1.96). Thus, VaR at time t is the product of the period t estimated portfolio risk σ, dollar exposure $M(t)$, and tracking error w^2.

We consequently define VaR as the risk function, that is, it is the minimization of this risk due to tracking error that is to be minimized (portfolio risk à la Markowitz has already been addressed at portfolio inception). This risk is reduced due to rebalancing at cost:

$$C = c(w_u)^2$$

We wish to minimize the net loss:

$$L = -\left(z_\alpha M w^2 \sigma - c(w_u)^2\right)$$

with control variable w_u. More specifically, we wish to choose a time path for the control (rebalancing) that minimizes the loss function along its entire path between periods t_0 and t_1. The periods t_0 and t_1 are arbitrary. Since this occurs for a specific interval of time $(t_1 - t_0)$, we then minimize discounted losses. This can be represented by:

$$\min \int_{t_0}^{t_1} e^{-rt} - \left(z_\alpha M w^2 \sigma - c(w_u)^2\right) dt$$

subject to:
$w' = w_u + (\mu + dz); \quad dz = \varepsilon\sqrt{dt}$, which is a Wiener process.

Here, $w' = \frac{dw}{dt}$ is a differential that describes the evolution of the weights; part is due to rebalancing and part to market-induced stochastic movements in asset prices (the Wiener process). The final step in the setup is to set the end point (transversality) conditions. We require that the weights at t_0 equal $w(0) = w_0$, and at t_1, weights be $w(1) = w_1$. If $w_0 = w_1$, then the target does not change.

The solution technique involves first setting up the current period Hamiltonian:

$$H = -e^{-rt}\left(z_\alpha M w^2 \sigma - c w_u^2\right) + \lambda(w_u + (\mu + dz))$$

Differentiating with respect to the state variable (w) and the control variable (w_u) produces two first-order conditions:

$$\frac{\partial H}{\partial w_u} = 2c e^{-rt} w_u + \lambda = 0$$

$$\frac{\partial H}{\partial w} = -2 e^{-rt}\left(z_\alpha M w \sigma\right) = 0$$

It is straightforward to show that the second-order conditions (with respect to w_u) satisfy a minimum. The first equation can be solved to show that:

$$w_u = -\frac{\lambda}{(2ce^{-rt})}$$

while from the second first-order condition, it is the case that:

$$\frac{\partial H}{\partial w} = \lambda' = -2e^{-rt}(z_\alpha Mw\sigma)$$

Solving:

$$\lambda^* = \int \lambda' dt = \int -2e^{-rt}(z_\alpha Vw\sigma)dt = -\left(\left(\frac{2z_\alpha Mw\sigma}{r}\right)e^{-rt}\right) + c_1$$

where c_1 is the constant of integration. Substituting this solution into w_u from before and solving yields:

$$w_u = -\frac{\lambda}{(ce^{-rt})} = \frac{z_\alpha Mw\sigma}{cr} - \frac{c_1}{2ce^{-rt}}$$

Recalling that $w' = w_u + (\mu + dz^{-1})$, then substituting it for optimal w_u solves the optimal path for the actual weights as:

$$w = \int w' dt = \left(\frac{z_\alpha Mw\sigma}{cr}\right)t - \left(\frac{c_1}{2cr}\right)e^{rt} + (\mu + dz)t + c_2$$

The last step is to impose the endpoint restrictions that solve for the constants of integration c_1 and c_2. (We do this by solving $w(t = 0)$ and $w(t = 1)$ individually for c_1 and c_2.) Doing this and substituting the values for these constants back into w and w_u yield the optimal paths:

$$w_u^* = \frac{z_\alpha Mw\sigma}{cr}\left(1 + \frac{r}{1 - e^r}e^{rt}\right) - r\left[\frac{(w_1 - w_0) - (\mu + dz)}{1 - e^r}\right]e^{rt}$$

$$w^* = \left(\frac{z_\alpha Mw\sigma}{cr} + (\mu + dz)\right)\left[t - \frac{1 - e^{rt}}{1 - e^r}\right] + \left[\frac{(w_1 - w_0)}{1 - e^r}\right](1 - e^{rt}) + w_0$$

It is then easy to check that w^* is correct, since $w(t = 1) = w_1$ and $w(t = 0) = w_0$, that is, the state variable satisfies the transversality conditions. The control variable w_u^* is of particular interest since it is the value of this variable in each period that is set to minimize the net cost of additional risk induced by divergence of w from w^T (w^*, on the other hand, is the optimal path for the state variable).

IMPLICATIONS

Clearly, the magnitude of rebalancing is greater, the higher the portfolio risk ($z_\alpha M w \sigma$) or any of its components, where, again, each of these variables are period specific, for example, $M = M(t)$. It is lower, on the other hand, the higher the marginal costs of rebalancing or the higher the discount rate. Moreover, the rebalancing rate is lower for assets with more inherent volatility (captured by the Wiener process) but higher for portfolios with greater allowable drift ($w_1 - w_0$) between t_0 and t_1. Since w_u^* can be either positive or negative, then optimal rebalancing can move in either direction (as in the Leland case). There is a no-trade region as well, where $w_u^* = 0$ and is defined by setting w_u^* to zero and solving to get:

$$|w| \le \left| \left(\frac{(w_1 - w_0) - (\mu + dz)}{z_\alpha V \sigma} \right) (cr) \left(\frac{A}{1 + A} \right) \right|$$

$$A = \frac{re^{rt}}{1 - e^r}$$

As an example, let $r = 0.05$ and assume $t = \frac{1}{12}$ for monthly monitoring. Moreover, let $z = 2.3$ and assume that c is proportional to the value of the portfolio so that $c = \alpha V$. Finally, keep the target weights constants so that $w_1 = w_0$. Then the allowable portfolio drift is contained in:

$$|w| \le \left| \frac{\alpha(\mu + dz)}{\sigma} \right|$$

Thus, the no-trade zone is proportional to the Wiener process. As long as portfolio drift does not exceed the amount on the right hand side, then no rebalancing is required.

Theoretically, any portfolio with drift—and hence, tracking error—will need rebalancing. The question is when. In the context of this optimal control problem, when is not as important as how much. Sometimes, the amount will be zero. Other times, not. Nevertheless, the problem itself is analyzed continuously. Rebalancing, however, is undertaken periodically. We focused in our analysis on the interval $t_1 - t_0$ and implicitly set this interval to length one (that is, one year, or $t_1 - t_0 = 1$). We then solved for the optimal rebalancing rule that minimizes the net risk in terms of value at risk over that interval. Since choosing to rebalance in any period affects the value and therefore the risk position of the portfolio from that point forward (just as fishing affects the stock of fish and its value from that point forward), then we face what is essentially a control problem through time (hence, the optimal control framework).

Nevertheless, the interval could easily be subdivided. For example, $t_1 - t_0 = 1$ year can be divided into 4 or 12 intervals. Rebalancing is then performed at each of these subintervals in time as indicated by w_u^*. In the limit, rebalancing could be continuous. Theoretically, it is continuous rebalancing that is optimal. If we choose to rebalance, say, quarterly, then all of the adjustment is performed four times per period. This obviously entails higher absolute costs (and benefits), as these have accumulated through the intervening periods. Waiting too long may increase risk to unacceptable levels. The empirical simulations in the next section are designed to test this implication.

OPTIMAL REBALANCING IN A STATIC OPTIMIZATION MODEL

We desire to minimize the two-part loss quadratic as a function of portfolio drift subject to the standard adding-up constraint with portfolio return equal to the weighted sum of individual asset returns:

$$\min(w - w^T)V(w - w^T)' - (w - w^T)k \quad s.t.\, w_i = 1, w_r = R$$

Here, $V = $ variance-covariance matrix of returns, w is row vector of weights on a three-asset mix (stocks, bonds, cash), T indexes the target weight, and k is a column vector of transactions costs. Drift increases losses quadratically (the first term) but drift also avoids trading costs (second term). The net cost is convex in drift, which, in principle, possesses a minimum. The constraints require that weights sum to unity and that the target portfolio return is R.

Imposing the constraints, differentiating with respect to the weight vector and collecting terms generate (in the three-asset case) the following matrix of first-order conditions:

$$\begin{bmatrix} \sigma_1^2 & \sigma_{12} & \sigma_{13} & -1 & -r_1 \\ \sigma_{21} & \sigma_2^2 & \sigma_{23} & -1 & -r_2 \\ \sigma_{31} & \sigma_{32} & \sigma_3^3 & -1 & -r_3 \\ 1 & 1 & 1 & 0 & 0 \\ r_1 & r_2 & r_3 & 0 & 0 \end{bmatrix} \begin{bmatrix} w_1 \\ w_2 \\ w_3 \\ \lambda_1 \\ \lambda_2 \end{bmatrix} = \begin{bmatrix} \phi_1 \\ \phi_2 \\ \phi_3 \\ 1 \\ R \end{bmatrix}$$

$$\phi_i = \sum w_i^T \sigma_{ij} + k_i; \quad j = 1, 2, 3$$

The square matrix has determinant:

$$\Delta = \sigma_{13}(r_2 - r_1)(r_3 - r_2) - \sigma_{23}(r_3 - r_1)(r_2 - r_1) + \sigma_3^2(r_2 - r_1)^2$$
$$+\sigma_{12}(r_3 - r_2)(r_1 - r_2) + \sigma_2^2(r_1 - r_3)^2 + \sigma_{32}(r_2 - r_1)(r_1 - r_3)$$
$$+\sigma_1^2(r_3 - r_2)^2 - \sigma_{21}(r_3 - r_1)(r_3 - r_2)$$
$$+\sigma_{31}(r_2 - r_1)(r_3 - r_2)$$

In the case of zero covariances, this reduces to:

$$\Delta = \sigma_3^2(r_2 - r_1)^2 + \sigma_2^2(r_1 - r_3)^2 + \sigma_1^2(r_3 - r_2)^2$$

In general, Cramer's rule generates solutions:

$$w_i = \frac{\Delta_i}{\Delta}$$

Specifically,

$$\Delta_1 = R\big[(r_3 - r_2)(\sigma_{12} - \sigma_{13}) - (r_3 - r_1)(\sigma_2^2 - \sigma_{23}) + (r_2 - r_1)(\sigma_{32} - \sigma_3^2)\big]$$
$$-r_2\big[(r_3 - r_2)(\phi_1 - \sigma_{13}) - (r_3 - r_1)(\phi_2 - \sigma_{23}) + (r_2 - r_1)(\phi_3 - \sigma_3^2)\big]$$
$$+r_3\big[(r_3 - r_2)(\phi_1 - \sigma_{12}) - (r_3 - r_1)(\phi_2 - \sigma_2^2) + (r_2 - r_1)(\phi_3 - \sigma_3^2)\big]$$

Solutions to Δ_2 and Δ_3 can be derived by similar means. Each of the computed weights is a rather complicated linear combination of variances, covariances, target weights, and relative returns. It can be shown that the comparative statics $\left(\frac{\partial w_i}{\partial k_j}\right)$ do not depend upon the covariances. Since this simplifies the comparative static computations, the remainder of the analysis assumes zero covariances, which generate, in addition to the zero-covariance value for Δ already given earlier:

$$\Delta_1 = R\big[(r_1 - r_2)\sigma_3^2 + (r_1 - r_3)\sigma_2^2\big]$$
$$-r_2\big[(r_3 - r_2)\phi_1 - (r_3 - r_1)\phi_2 + (r_2 - r_1)(\phi_3 - \sigma_3^2)\big]$$
$$+r_3\big[(r_3 - r_2)\phi_1 - (r_3 - r_1)(\phi_2 - \sigma_2^2) + (r_2 - r_1)\phi_3\big]$$

$$\Delta_2 = r_1\big[(r_3 - r_2)\phi_1 - (r_3 - r_1)\phi_2 + (r_2 - r_1)(\phi_3 - \sigma_3^2)\big]$$
$$+R\big[(r_2 - r_3)\sigma_1^2 + (r_1 - r_2)\sigma_3^2\big]$$
$$+r_3\big[(r_3 - r_2)(\sigma_1^2 - \phi_1) + (r_3 - r_1)\phi_2 + (r_1 - r_2)\phi_3\big]$$

$$\Delta_3 = r_1\big[(r_2 - r_3)\phi_1 - (r_3 - r_1)\phi_2 + (r_1 - r_2)(\phi_3 - \sigma_3^2)\big]$$
$$+R\big[(r_3 - r_2)\sigma_1^2 + (r_3 - r_2)\sigma_2^2\big]$$
$$-r_2\big[(r_3 - r_2)(\sigma_1^2 - \phi_1) + (r_3 - r_1)\phi_2 + (r_1 - r_2)\phi_3\big]$$

THE COMPARATIVE STATICS OF TRANSACTION COSTS

Treating the determinant Δ as a constant, then $\frac{\partial w_i}{\partial k_j}$ can be derived solely from Δ_1, Δ_2, and Δ_3 by differentiating each with respect to k,j for $j = 1, 2, 3$. (Recall, that transaction costs are captured by the aggregate term ϕ_i, and so differentiation is with respect to this term.) For the three-asset case, these comparative statics are:

$$\frac{\partial w_i}{k_i} = \frac{\left(r_j - r_k\right)^2}{\Delta} > 0$$

$$\frac{\partial w_i}{k_j} = \frac{\left(r_k - r_j\right)\left(r_i - r_k\right)}{\Delta}$$

where k, j, and i index the assets. The first result says that an increase in the own t-cost will increase the drift. The second result examines the cross-asset weight sensitivity, whose sign depends on the relative return spreads. More specifically, the asset i weight change generated by a change in the asset j transactions cost depends on a comparison of the returns to these assets relative to the return on the third asset. In general, if they both exceed (both are less than) the return to the remaining asset k, the sign is negative. To make sense from this, consider a specific case using Δ_1 and differentiate this determinant with respect to ϕ_2 (representing asset two's transactions cost). When k_2 rises, w_2 rises unequivocally. But the effect on w_1 depends on $(r_1 - r_3)$ and on $(r_2 - r_3)$. If $r_1 > r_3$, then w_1 wants to rise. But, if $r_2 > r_3$, then the net effect on w_1 is negative. Why? Two reasons. The first is that the sum of the new weights must satisfy the adding-up constraint. So, if w_2 rises, then the sum $(w_1 + w_3)$ must decrease by an equal amount. Since $r_1, r_2 > r_3$, to keep risk minimized, then w_1 must fall and w_3 will rise. If, on the other hand, $r_1 > r_3$, but $r_2 < r_3$, then the following adjustment takes place: An increase in k_2 raises w_2, and as before, $r_1 > r_3$ puts positive pressure on w_1. However, now, since $r_2 < r_3$, then this upward pressure is reinforced and w_1 rises (and w_3 falls to satisfy the adding-up constraint). The following tables summarize all the possibilities (each cell is the sign of the partial derivative with respect to k_j).

	k_1	k_2	k_3	
w_1	+	−	+	
w_2	−	+	−	$r_1 > r_2 > r_3$ and $(r_3 > r_2 > r_1)$
w_3	+	−	+	

$$
\begin{array}{llll}
w_1 & + & + & - \\
w_2 & + & + & - \qquad r_2 > r_3 > r_1 \text{ and } (r_1 > r_3 > r_2) \\
w_3 & - & - & +
\end{array}
$$

$$
\begin{array}{llll}
w_1 & + & + & - \\
w_2 & + & + & - \qquad r_1 > r_3 > r_2 \text{ and } (r_2 > r_3 > r_1) \\
w_3 & - & - & +
\end{array}
$$

$$
\begin{array}{llll}
w_1 & + & - & - \\
w_2 & - & + & - \qquad r_2 > r_1 > r_3 \text{ and } (r_3 > r_1 > r_2) \\
w_3 & + & + & +
\end{array}
$$

Optimization Formulas

Optimization routine for targeted tracking error

$$
\begin{aligned}
\text{Objective}: \quad & \min_{w_t}(w_t' V w_t)^{1/2} + |w_t - w_{t-1}|' \cdot k \\
\text{Subject to:} \quad & w_{it} \geq -1 \\
& w_{it} \leq 1 \\
& (w_t' V w_t)^{1/2} \cdot t^{1/2} = te \\
& \sum w_{it} = 0
\end{aligned}
$$

Optimization routine for rebalancing to a percentage boundary

$$
\begin{aligned}
\text{Objective}: \quad & \min_{w_t}(w_t' V w_t)^{1/2} + |w_t - w_{t-1}|' \cdot k \\
\text{Subject to:} \quad & w_{it} = w\text{min}1_i && \text{iff } w_{it-1} \leq w\text{min}_i \\
& w_{it} = w\text{max}1_i && \text{iff } w_{it-1} \geq w\text{max}_i \\
& \left.\begin{array}{l} w_{it} \geq w\text{min} \\ w_{it} \leq w\text{max} \end{array}\right\} \text{ iff } w\text{min}_i \leq w_{it-1} \leq w\text{max}_i \\
& \sum w_{it} = 0
\end{aligned}
$$

Example and Definitions

$$
\mathbf{w}_t =
\begin{array}{c} Portfolio \\ Weight \\ \begin{bmatrix} .24 \\ .59 \\ .17 \end{bmatrix} \end{array}
-
\begin{array}{c} Strategic \\ Weight \\ \begin{bmatrix} .25 \\ .60 \\ .15 \end{bmatrix} \end{array}
=
\begin{array}{c} Active \\ Weight \\ \begin{bmatrix} -.01 \\ -.01 \\ +.02 \end{bmatrix} \end{array}
$$

$\mathbf{w}_t = N \times 1$ vector containing the optimized active portfolio weights (where $_t$ represents new weights and $_{t-1}$ represents weights before optimization).

$V = N \times N$ matrix containing the VRS AA covariance matrix conditioned to the subperiod.

$k = N \times 1$ vector containing the expected t-costs for each asset in percentage terms.

te = scalar representing the targeted expected tracking error.

t = scalar representing the number of subperiods in each year.

wmin $= N \times 1$ vector of minimum underweights for each asset.

wmin1 $= N \times 1$ vector of underweights that will be targeted if a lower boundary is violated.

wmax $= N \times 1$ vector of maximum overweights for each asset.

wmax1 $= N \times 1$ vector of overweights that will be targeted if a upper boundary is violated.

REFERENCE

Leland, Hayne E. 1999. Optimal portfolio management with transactions costs and capital gains taxes. Berkeley, CA: University of California, Haas School of Business, Working Paper.

CHAPTER 22

Data Problems*

There are two possible outcomes: if the result confirms the hypothesis, then you've made a measurement. If the result is contrary to the hypothesis, then you've made a discovery.

—Enrico Fermi

When historical returns series vary in length, covariances are typically estimated using a shorter common subset of returns, thereby discarding some information contained in the longer series. Problems associated with returns truncation are particularly troublesome for allocations across broad asset classes; there are typically only a small number of classes, and because many of these are relatively new (for example, TIPS), they contribute little information to covariance estimates. Covariance precision will necessarily suffer for more severely truncated returns, and the information loss from truncation will generally produce inefficient and, in some cases, biased covariance estimates (Stambaugh 1997). Perhaps more important are the obvious adverse implications for plan-wide risk management—at a minimum, it is likely that exposures will be miscalculated as will the investor's overall exposure to risk. I present Monte Carlo evidence further on that supports this assertion.

It is also well known that the reported returns to some asset classes (for example, real estate, private equity) are smoothed estimates of the underlying true returns. Smoothing will cause these returns to have artificially lower volatilities and covariations with the remaining asset classes, which, if uncorrected, will bias allocations toward the smoothed asset classes. Smoothing is a data problem whose origins lie in the way the returns are

---

* Much of this chapter appeared in Peterson and Grier 2006. Asset allocation in the presence of covariance misspecification. *Financial Analysts Journal* 62(4): 76–85.

computed and reported, for example, as moving averages of previously observed prices (real estate appraisals) or as a timing issue in which returns are reported at irregular intervals (private equity valuations). In any case, smoothing alters the time series relationships that, when combined with truncation, may produce seriously misleading covariance estimates and exacerbate exposure to unwanted risk.

In this chapter, I draw primarily from Stambaugh (1997) and Fisher and Geltner (2000) to resolve problems associated with returns truncation and smoothing, using return streams from seven asset classes commonly analyzed by institutional investors. I also present results from a Monte Carlo experiment that generates mean-variance optimal portfolios for both cases, that is, when returns are smoothed and truncated against mean returns and covariances drawn from identical series with the effects of smoothing and truncation removed. The following section develops the covariance model as a response to the aforementioned considerations. A discussion of the data I use for my analysis follows in the third section followed by general findings and results from the Monte Carlo experiment and some concluding remarks.

COVARIANCE ESTIMATION

The covariance estimator for returns series of differing lengths was first introduced by Stambaugh (1997), and the methodology was extended in Pastor and Stambaugh (2002). We summarize and discuss Stambaugh's derivations in Appendix 22.1 at the end of this chapter and the reader is referred there for details. The intuition, however, is based on an application of the multivariate normal distribution for which the conditional moments of the distribution of returns to shorter history assets depend on moments for the longer-lived assets.

Consider, for example, a bivariate case consisting of two assets, J and K, but with J having a longer history. The truncated maximum likelihood estimator (MLE) uses the assets' separate histories to estimate unconditional means and variances but uses the history truncated at K to estimate the covariance. As such, asset K's moment estimates are not only inefficient, as is the covariance estimator, but there is no guarantee that the covariance matrix will be a positive definite. Stambaugh shows that these estimates can be improved by appealing to the properties of the bivariate normal, that is, the conditional distribution of asset K (conditional on information contained in asset J returns) has mean and variance that are linear functions of the information contained in the longer return history. If the return histories are independent, there is no informational gain generated by using the MLE for the conditional distribution of returns. In this case, the conditional distribution yields the truncated estimator.

Although the conditional distribution provides exact solutions for estimators of first and second moments, these estimators implicitly assume that the linear relationships among asset returns are constant over time. For example, the conditional mean for asset K in the preceding example is a linear combination of its unconditional mean and the product of its beta with asset J and asset J's mean return in the period preceding asset K's return history—see equation (22.6). All equation references refer to Appendix 22.1. Thus, the unconditional mean is augmented with the information contained in the longer series return history not observed for asset K with the magnitude of this extra information determined by its time-invariant beta. Time invariance holds for conditional second moments as well—see equation (22.7). In effect, MLE averages the impact of structural changes in the linear relationships among returns series.

There are really two issues here. One is the implied time-invariance, which, if overly restrictive, suggests some degree of estimation error that contributes to poor out-of-sample performance. Sample moment estimators, in general, often produce extreme portfolio positions that are inconsistent with equilibrium market capitalization weights (Black and Litterman 1992). The other issue relates to sample size itself; for very short histories (like TIPS), conditional moment estimates fall victim to a degrees-of-freedom problem in the unconditional distribution that could translate into less precise estimates of the conditional moments. In these cases, the conditional moments may not be representative of the characteristics of the shorter series. This might be especially relevant in the event that shocks are peculiar to a single series, say, or institutional changes alter the structural relationships among series. Contagion, for example, diffuses across markets, and depending on the rate of diffusion, will alter the structural relationships between various series, but its impact will continue to be averaged with older data. The point is that perceived gains in efficiency depend on being able to extract stable and meaningful linear relationships between series. We note that time-varying estimation schemes are available using Bayesian dynamic linear methods in which both means and covariances are recursively updated as new information on returns becomes available. See, for example, Kling and Novemestky (1999).

Estimation risk, which complicates this process, arises when sample estimates of parameters of return distributions are implicitly assumed to be the true parameters. Consequent portfolios may be, quite plausibly, inadmissible once estimation risk is explicitly incorporated into the analysis (Klein and Bawa 1976). More recently, Jorion (1986) and Frost and Savarino (1986) introduce Bayesian estimates of multivariate unconditional returns based on informative priors. Stambaugh shows that the Bayesian predictions (with a diffuse prior), relative to MLE, do not alter estimates of mean returns but scale up MLE covariance estimates due to estimation error. Because the difference between the MLE and Bayesian covariance estimates is shown to be small for portfolios consisting of relatively few assets, I report and discuss MLE only.

In a multivariate world, asset K's moments are functions of its betas with all other assets of equal or longer returns duration and the conditional maximum likelihood estimators, though still assumed to be time-invariant, use information contained in all the longer return histories. The exact multivariate estimation procedure is described further on in the results section. I do not address data problems pertaining to missing observations or gaps in returns series but note that these issues are adequately addressed using data-augmentation methods such as the EM algorithm (an iterative MLE method that effectively treats missing data as parameters to be estimated) and Gibbs sampling (to bootstrap the Bayesian PDF).

Returns smoothing only complicates attempts to resolve the truncation problem. Both are information problems; truncation throws information away, while smoothing filters it. In general, affected series must be unsmoothed beforehand. Working (1960) first commented on the impact that aggregation has on smoothing, noting that a random walk, when averaged, induces serial correlation but with an upper bound ($\rho = 0.25$). One would expect returns averaging to induce some degree of serial correlation in an otherwise efficient market. Nevertheless, observed levels of correlation, especially for real estate and private equity returns, appear too high to be explained by simple aggregation. The effects of smoothing are especially well documented in the real estate literature (Geltner [1991, 1993a, 1993b], Quan and Quigley [1991], and Ross and Zisler [1991]) but correlation may also be the consequence of nonsynchronous trading (see Campbell, Lo, and MacKinlay [1997] and the references therein), or nonperiodic marking to market. The smoothing of real estate returns is tied largely to the appraisal process, in which estimated property values are linear combinations of past subjective appraisals. Similarly for private equity, returns are based on subjective valuations of nonpublicly traded firms. In both cases, market returns are not observed, that is, valuations are not tied to a unique market-determined price for a single publicly traded security.

In Appendix 22.1, I summarize and discuss a method, proposed by Fisher and Geltner, to unsmooth real estate returns in which observed returns are assumed to be an infinite order moving average of past market returns (based on property appraisals). If the moving average process is stationary and invertible, then the unsmoothed returns series can be recovered from the observed lagged, but smoothed, series of returns (see Appendix 22.1

for details). We will use this method to unsmooth both real estate and private equity returns in our seven-asset study. The unsmoothing parameters (α) for real estate and private equity in equation (22.10) are estimated to be 0.728 (t-stat $= 10.5$) and 0.436 (t-stat $= 4.39$), respectively.

Other approaches to unsmooth return series can be found in Shilling (1993) and Wang (2001). These are multivariate approaches; Shilling implies the degree to which the variance in observed returns has been smoothed by exploiting the properties of a biased ordinary least squares (OLS) estimator (true returns are not directly observed, thus creating an errors-in-variables problem that biases OLS estimates) and its consistent instrumental variables counterpart. Wang, on the other hand, exploits certain co-integrating relationships to get at the degree to which returns variability has been smoothed.

AN EXAMPLE

The basic building blocks for estimating the covariance matrix are return series for each of the underlying assets. In practice, analysts have several important decisions to make regarding the selection of these basic building blocks. Notably, they will want to choose historical data that are representative of the asset classes that they would consider including in their portfolios. For illustrative purposes, I have chosen common benchmarks for seven asset classes that are frequently considered by institutional investors. The qualitative results of this analysis were robust to the choice of alternative benchmarks for each of these asset classes, the inclusion of additional asset classes, using mixed frequency data, and return series with longer histories. Table 22.1 lists the return series that were chosen for each asset class and a risk-free rate, series inception date, and number of quarterly observations. Because the real estate and private equity return series are provided only quarterly, we geometrically linked the higher frequency returns to generate quarterly returns. All analysis in this paper was performed using quarterly excess returns, which were calculated by subtracting the risk-free rate from the aforementioned returns. Likewise, all results are presented in quarterly excess return format.

While all seven return series end in December 2004, their inception dates range from February 1997 for TIPS to December 1975 for fixed income. The differing inception dates normally force the truncation of longer time series in order to estimate covariances. A set of estimated correlations, standard deviations, and mean excess returns for the seven asset classes are presented in Table 22.2. Correlations are normalized covariances by dividing the latter through by the product of the two asset classes' returns

TABLE 22.1 Return Series Descriptions (All Data Ends December 2004)

Asset Class	Inception Date	Return Series Description	Observations
TIPS	Feb-97	Lehman TIPS All Maturities	31
Non-U.S. Equity	Jun-89	Citigroup Global BMI ex-U.S.	62
High Yield	Aug-86	Merrill Lynch High Yield Master II	73
Private Equity	Dec-83	Venture Economics All Private Equity*	84
U.S. Equity	Dec-78	Frank Russell 3000	104
Real Estate	Dec-77	NCREIF NPI	108
Fixed Income	Dec-75	Lehman Aggregate	116
Risk-Free	Dec-25	Ibbotson U.S. 30-day T-Bill	n.a.

*Returns prior to March 1984 were censored due to lack of representation.

standard deviations. This means that variances (covariances between assets J and K where J = K) normalize to unity (diagonal elements in Table 22.2) while off-diagonal (J ≠ K) covariances normalize to correlations ρ, such that $-1 \leq \rho \leq 1$. These are the unconditional covariances based upon the truncated series. We will refer to these as the set of naïve estimates. Again, individual variances are estimated from each series' history, while covariances are truncated to each common historical pairing.

In the Monte Carlo study reported further on, we take the investment period to begin in the first quarter of 2005 and assume that all managers are mean-variance optimizers who estimate mean returns and covariances

TABLE 22.2 Naïve Correlation Matrix, Standard Deviations, and Mean Returns (Quarterly)

Asset Class	TIPS	Non-U.S. Equity	High Yield	Private Equity	U.S. Equity	Real Estate	Fixed Income
TIPS	1	−0.42	−0.15	−0.55	−0.64	−0.13	0.36
Non-U.S. Equity	−0.42	1	0.46	0.55	0.78	0.13	−0.02
High Yield	−0.15	0.46	1	0.24	0.56	−0.10	0.13
Private Equity	−0.55	0.55	0.24	1	0.60	0.18	−0.17
U.S. Equity	−0.64	0.78	0.56	0.60	1	0.00	0.21
Real Estate	−0.13	0.13	−0.10	0.18	0.00	1	−0.29
Fixed Income	0.36	−0.02	0.13	−0.17	0.21	−0.29	1
Standard Deviations (%)	2.27	9.10	3.89	5.87	8.33	1.66	3.51
Mean Returns (%)	1.15	0.85	1.16	1.77	2.06	0.60	0.72

using information through 2004, solve the minimum variance portfolio, and hold that portfolio thereafter. We are especially interested in portfolio composition (that is, possible extreme positions), expected returns and risk.

EMPIRICAL RESULTS

The naïve covariance estimates, which are equivalent to unconditional MLE for individual returns series but use the truncated series to estimate covariances are presented in Table 22.2. The set of corrected MLE returns, presented in Table 22.3, are the product of a two-step procedure in which we first remove the effects of smoothing from Private Equity and Real Estate returns by applying the Fisher-Geltner transformation outlined in Appendix 22.1. The covariance matrix was then estimated with a recursive application of Stambaugh's methodology in the following way:

Return series were organized in descending order of length. The longest—fixed income, which dates to 1975—was used to estimate its own mean and variance. The next-longest series, real estate (unsmoothed), was then regressed against fixed income and the results were then used to update the conditional mean for real estate and its covariance with fixed income as given by equations (22.6) and (22.7). The returns to fixed income and real estate then constitute a matrix of instruments on which successively shorter returns series are regressed recursively, with covariances being revised according to equations (22.6) and (22.7). At the end of each recursion, the matrix of instruments is expanded once again. The new matrix of instruments is always truncated to a length equal to the series forming the

TABLE 22.3 Corrected Correlation Matrix, Standard Deviations, and Mean Returns (Quarterly)

Asset Class	TIPS	Non-U.S. Equity	High Yield	Private Equity	U.S. Equity	Real Estate	Fixed Income
TIPS	1	0.19	0.44	−0.25	0.06	−0.23	0.89
Non-U.S. Equity	0.19	1	0.48	0.52	0.82	0.09	0.22
High Yield	0.44	0.48	1	0.21	0.61	0.03	0.51
Private Equity	−0.25	0.52	0.21	1	0.64	0.13	−0.22
U.S. Equity	0.06	0.82	0.61	0.64	1	0.03	0.19
Real Estate	−0.23	0.09	0.03	0.13	0.03	1	−0.25
Fixed Income	0.89	0.22	0.51	−0.22	0.19	−0.25	1
Standard Deviations (%)	3.38	9.46	4.45	9.13	8.32	4.36	3.51
Mean Returns (%)	0.92	0.83	1.12	2.07	2.05	0.61	0.72

next-longest series, the regression is estimated, and revisions made. That last regression involved TIPS, with a starting date of February 1997, and the matrix of instruments included the remaining six (unsmoothed) return series truncated to this date.

A comparison of Tables 22.2 and 22.3 indicate several sign reversals, most notably TIPS (the shortest series), and a scattered few for the remaining series. The results in Table 22.3 further suggest that TIPS is no longer so strongly and negatively correlated with U.S. equity, which highlights the informational differential between truncated and longer series. For example, variances and covariances based on short histories of truncated relationships will be overestimated if truncated series correspond to high volatility states. If short and long series are positively (negatively) correlated, then the *conditional* covariance MLE for the short series will be adjusted downward (upward) as indicated by equation (22.7). Its *conditional* mean, given by equation (22.6), will also be adjusted but the direction is uncertain; it will be adjusted downward when the truncated mean on the longer series exceeds its long-run average. This is an especially powerful result that shows how vulnerable covariance estimates are to shorter return series effects in the presence of truncation.

As discussed earlier, returns smoothing decreases volatility. The standard deviations increase significantly from Table 22.2 to Table 22.3 for private equity (5.87 percent to 9.13 percent) and real estate (1.66 percent to 4.36 percent). The naïve return volatility for TIPS, based on the truncated sample, is likewise revised upward from 2.27 percent to 3.38 percent. Other things constant, the naïve portfolio would have overallocated to these three asset classes and the magnitude of this misallocation rises with volatility underestimation.

Figure 22.1 maps the efficient frontiers implied by each covariance matrix, using the naïve historical mean excess return for each asset class. These indicate quite clearly that the naïve covariance matrix underestimates risk and overestimates returns relative to the more efficient revised covariance matrix, a result consistent with Stambaugh's (1997) findings. The difference in the locations of the two frontiers is largely due to the underestimated standard deviations of the smoothed return series.

A Monte Carlo Experiment

This section reports the results from a Monte Carlo study designed to answer the following question: Are both capital misallocation and portfolio performance significantly affected in the presence of substandard covariance estimates? Though we find that misallocation is indeed significant, and that portfolio performance suffers as a result, the magnitude and cost of

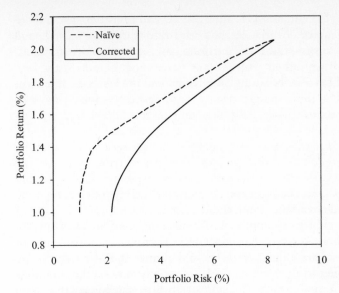

FIGURE 22.1 Efficient Frontier

misallocation will, in general, depend on the severity of truncation and smoothing and the number of affected assets. We present a simple case with two of seven assets having truncated returns and a third with smoothed returns.

The optimal portfolio corresponds to the vector of asset weights that solves the mean-variance optimization problem using as arguments a vector of mean returns and a covariance matrix. For the following experiment, we use as arguments the corrected parameter estimates given in Table 22.3, which consist of the unsmoothed Stambaugh-corrected covariance matrix and corresponding corrected mean returns. From these, we generate repeated samples of returns of length equal to 100 (25 years of quarterly returns) for each of the seven asset classes.

Specifically, if the estimated covariance matrix V is a positive definite, then it will have a Cholesky decomposition—a lower triangular square matrix A such that $V = AA'$. Then, for any vector of mean returns μ, a single realization of a (7×1) vector of simulated returns, with covariance structure given by V, can be generated from $\mu + A\varepsilon$, where ε is a (7×1) vector of standard normal random variables. Repeating this process over $t = 1, \ldots, 100$ generates a (7×100) sample of returns with mean $E(\mu + A\varepsilon) = \mu$ and covariance $E(A\varepsilon\varepsilon'A') = V$, since $E(\varepsilon\varepsilon')$ is the identity matrix. For each generated sample, we truncate the simulated series for TIPS and non-U.S. equity to 25 and 50 periods, respectively, (these match the historical series lengths for TIPS and non-U.S. equity relative to fixed income), smooth real estate, and estimate covariances, and returns for three cases: (1) the full set of simulated returns—this is the portfolio based on full information, (2) the truncated and smoothed returns—our naïve model, and (3) the corrected means and covariances using Stambaugh and the Fisher-Geltner corrections. Separately, these sample mean-variance estimates were then used to solve the minimum variance, long-only, fully invested portfolio,

$$\min\left(\frac{1}{2}w'Vw\right) \qquad \text{s.t} \sum_{i=1}^{9} w_i = 1, \qquad w_i \geq 0$$

where V is case specific, that is, it corresponds to either the full information, naïve, or corrected covariance matrix.

Note that the choice of smoothing parameter, α, is 0.5 and was selected to generate a smoothed series that understates volatility by about one-half (empirically, we estimate this parameter in the range $0.4 - 0$. Returns are smoothed according to $r_{s,t} = \alpha r_{s,t-1} + (1 - \alpha)r_t$, where $r_{s,t}$ is the smoothed return and r_t the actual return. The simulation program is available upon request.

The misallocation question was approached by measuring the sum of the *absolute* differences between the full-information weight vector in case (1) and the weight vectors in cases (2) and (3). This means we are interested in the distributions of the statistic:

$$z_{n,j} = \sum_{i=1}^{7} w^* - w_{i,j} \qquad \text{for } n = 1, \ldots, N, \quad j = 1, 2$$

where w^* denotes the full-information optimal portfolio, w_j the optimal portfolio associated with either the naïve or corrected moments estimates, and N the number of replications in the experiment. We generate N matrices of returns each of size (100X7). Each matrix is then used to estimate expected returns and covariances for each of the three cases defined earlier, and these moment estimates solve three mean-variance efficient portfolios. Therefore, z_n measures the absolute amount of misweighting between the full-information portfolio and each of the portfolios based on the naïve and corrected covariance estimates, respectively.

The weights in the preceding summation are matched pairs, by asset class, and their sum measures the aggregate deviation from the optimal portfolio weighting. The long-only constraint and absolute differences place an upper bound on the maximum misallocation equal to 2. Consider, for example, a two-asset problem. Maximum misallocation occurs when the two weight vectors are orthogonal, that is, $w_1 = (0,1)$ and $w_2 = (1,0)$ whose sum of absolute differences is equal to 2. Thus, the statistic z_n, when divided by 2, measures the amount of misallocation, in percent, relative to the maximum allocation loss. Of primary interest is testing for relative misallocation, that is, whether z_n is higher for the naïve model relative to the corrected covariance model. To this end, we drew $N = 10,000$ samples of returns using the Monte Carlo method just described. A simple test of the null hypothesis that this statistic has zero mean is a parametric t-test on the coefficient in a regression of the difference in the paired returns on a constant. These t-statistics are supplemented with the nonparametric Wilcoxon test for matched pairs. Since z_n is a sum of absolute differences, its distribution is not necessarily normal; indeed, it is positive and skewed right. The nonparametric tests are distribution free and are reported as a check on the robustness of our results. Relevant statistics and test results are presented in Table 22.4. The Wilcoxon test is applied to the same three sets of matched pairs—the differences between the full-information portfolio and each suboptimal portfolio (that is, the naïve and corrected portfolios) and a third, measuring the difference between the naïve and corrected portfolios. Wilcoxon is a test of medians; specifically, that the median of the differenced distribution (the paired differences) is zero, that is, the two returns distributions share a common central tendency.

Panel A of Table 22.4 shows that the average misallocation for the naïve portfolio is 28.66 percent and the test of Wilcoxon easily rejects the null that they share a common median. Using the Stambaugh and Fisher-Geltner corrections reduces misallocation to 20.52 percent, which is about 8.14 percent less, but interestingly, the test of Wilcoxon cannot reject the null that the corrected and full-information weight distributions share the same median. Clearly, though, the mean misallocation difference between the naïve and corrected covariance portfolios is significant and, in this case, about 8.14 percent on average in each quarter.

Portfolio performance measures are straightforward computations using expected returns, which are the product of the mean-variance optimal weights and mean returns specific to each case $(w'r)$, and portfolio risk $(w'Vw)^{\frac{1}{2}}$, where again, w is the case specific mean-variance optimal weight vector and V is the case-specific estimated covariance matrix. Results, which are presented in Panel B of Table 22.4 show that misallocation results in more extreme positions as evidenced by lower portfolio returns and higher portfolio risk. Indeed, the median quarterly return under the naïve approach (0.787 percent) underperforms both the optimal return (0.873 percent) by 0.086 percent per quarter and the corrected covariance case (0.896 percent) by a little over 0.081 percent per quarter. The naïve portfolio's tendency to take extreme positions can be seen in the volatility of its returns; 2.51 percent per quarter relative to 2.16 percent and 2.22 percent for the full information and corrected cases, respectively, as well as the lowest Sharpe ratio (measured over the 10,000 replications).

TABLE 22.4 Monte Carlo Simulation Results

Panel A—Misallocation[a]	Mean (%)	T-statistic	Wilcoxon[c]	Wilcoxon P-value
Naïve	28.66	391.87	−31.57	(p = 0.000)
Corrected	20.52	203.28	−0.41	(p = 0.680)
Naïve—Corrected[b]	8.14	64.51	−29.31	(p = 0.000)

Panel B — Performance[d]	Returns		Risk (%)	Sharpe
	Mean (%)	Median (%)	Risk (%)	Sharpe
Full-information optimal	0.873	0.873	2.169	0.404
Naïve	0.787	0.759	2.510	0.313
Corrected	0.868	0.848	2.221	0.391
Return Differential	Mean (%)	T-statistic		
Full-information—Naïve	0.086	44.365		
Full-information—Corrected	0.005	4.052		
Corrected—Naïve	0.081	43.153		

Panel C—Extreme Positions[e]	Long-only zero wts	Shorting allowed	
		min weight	max weight
Full-information optimal	0.00	−10	40
Naïve	13.00	−108,450	91,950
Corrected	5.00	−130	160

[a] Mean absolute weight differential relative to full-information portfolio
[b] Naïve-corrected mean absolute weight differential
[c] Ho: optimal minus stated weight vector has zero median
[d] Quarterly performance in percent
[e] Percent over full-information

The long-only constraint places bounds on extreme positions. Nevertheless, Panel C reports that naïve portfolios contain approximately 13 percent more extreme positions v(zero positions on an asset class) while portfolios generated from the corrected moment estimates produce roughly 5 percent more zero positions relative to the optimal portfolio. When the long-only constraint is removed, extreme positions are accentuated but only for the naïve case. Here, the range of weights for the naïve case is huge (−108,450 percent to 91,950 percent) while those for the corrected covariance case (−130 percent to 160 percent) and the optimal full-information case (−10 percent to 40 percent) remain reasonably narrow. The weight range for the naïve case is not due to outliers; indeed, the interquartile range is about 300.

The naïve model's rather significant tendency to bias portfolio weight-ings generates increased risk primarily because it misallocates capital to the wrong asset classes. Bias, itself, tends to favor the smoothed series and, to the extent that a truncated series is currently experiencing a period of low volatility, bias overweights those assets as well. As a result, the naïve model will produce understated value-at-risk estimates, which may lead managers to take on bets that are not otherwise supported by the data. The magnitude of the weighting bias is a function of both the proportion of assets with lim-ited histories and their relative series lengths—shorter histories will exacer-bate the bias, as will the magnitude of smoothing.

OVERLAPPING OBSERVATIONS

A final topic concerns the analysis of returns series constructed on mov-ing windows of historical returns. It is common, for example, to smooth the noise in observed returns by constructing moving averages. An example is Shiller's 10-year moving average of trailing earnings on the S&P 500 that he uses to filter noise in earnings. This smoothed earnings number is used to estimate the p/e ratio. Three-year or five-year moving averages of monthly returns or volatilities, for example, are often found in presentations of portfolio performance. A three-year moving average will typically construct the current month smoothed return, using a sam-ple of 36 months of trailing returns. A time series of three-year moving averages means that adjacent months have 35 observations in common. Observations on the moving average that are two months removed have 34 observations in common and so on. Since the moving averages over-lap in this fashion, they constitute a serially correlated time series, and this property has implications concerning the information content of the newly constructed series as well as its statistical properties.

Let's think about the information content first. The reason the assump-tion of independence of returns is so attractive is that each return can be thought of as a truly novel byte of information. Independence implies that there are N distinct bytes of information in a sample of size N. So, for exam-ple, if returns were independently distributed across time, then a three-year trailing sample of monthly returns contains 36 independent sources of in-formation. Serially correlated observations, by construction, remove that property. Two adjacent moving averages constructed off of 36-month trail-ing returns hardly constitute independent sources of information simply be-cause they contain so much in common. Moreover, the dependence of the moving averages is embedded for some time to come. For example, we re-quire the passage of 36 months to remove this dependence. Figure 22.2

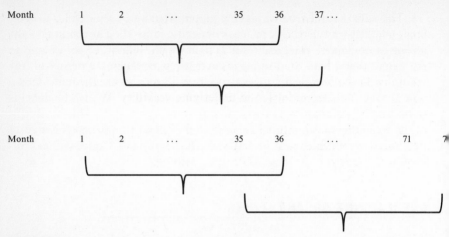

FIGURE 22.2 Serial Dependence of Moving Averages of 36-Month Trailing Returns

illustrates this property. The top panel shows the obvious dependence of overlapping returns at the one-month interval while the bottom panel shows how slow this dependence deteriorates.

This dependence structure seriously limits the information content of time series constructed on moving averages. A three-year time series of 36-month moving averages, for example, has only a single truly independent observation because technically all of the observations in this sample are correlated. This behavior poses certain challenges to how we approach the measurement of various statistics, the most important one being volatility estimates. You may recall from basis statistics that the standard deviation of a sample of returns is based on the assumption that the returns are independently distributed. If they are serially correlated instead, then one has to make corrections to adjust for that property. The case most students are familiar with addresses correcting for serial correlation in the estimator of the residual variance from a linear regression. A model of first order serial correlation, for example, can be written as follows:

$$\varepsilon_t = \rho\varepsilon_{t-1} + u_t$$

Here, $-1 < \rho < 1$ is the correlation coefficient and $u_t \sim IID$ (identically and independently distributed random variables) and the ε_t are the residuals. If we compute the variance of ε, we get:

$$\sigma_\varepsilon^2 = \rho^2\sigma_\varepsilon^2 + \sigma_u^2$$

$$\sigma_\varepsilon^2 = \frac{\sigma_u^2}{1 - \rho^2}$$

This says that the true variance is understated by a factor of $1/(1 - \rho^2)$. So, if $\rho = .9$, then the true variance is understated by 10. The parameter ρ is telling us how much information is common (and therefore not unique) to adjacent observations. Smoothing (as in moving averages) creates serial correlation and the observed variance of moving averages created by overlapping data will therefore filter the underlying volatility. We adjust for this smoothing by dividing by $(1 - \rho^2)$.

Let's make an attempt to generalize this concept. Suppose we have a time series of N demeaned returns on K stocks, each denoted by X_{ij} as follows:

$$
R = \begin{bmatrix}
X_{11} & \ldots & X_{k1} \\
X_{12} & \ldots & X_{k2} \\
X_{13} & \ldots & X_{k3} \\
. & \ldots & . \\
. & \ldots & . \\
. & \ldots & . \\
X_{1N} & \ldots & X_{kN}
\end{bmatrix}
$$

The covariance matrix we studied in previous chapters was estimated by (assuming returns are demeaned already), $V = R'R/N$. That estimator assumed that returns were independent and identically distributed (IID). Let us now allow for serial correlation of order m; for example, each of these returns could be an mth-order moving average. An estimator for V that is a positive definite (V has full rank and is invertible) is given by Newey-West (1987) and can be written for our case here as follows:

$$
V = V_0 + \sum_{j=-m}^{m} \left(1 - \frac{|j|}{m+1}\right) * \left(X_{it}'X_{i,t+j}\right)/(N - |j|)
$$

This is a sum of (positive semi-definite) covariance matrices. V_0 is the covariance estimated from the smoothed data with no adjustment for serial correlation. The adjustment factors are covariance matrices that estimate the serially correlated covariances. Assuming $X = R$ is a matrix of demeaned returns, then $\left(X_{it}'X_{i,t+j}\right)/(N - |j|)$ is a covariance estimate for X and its jth lag. For example, let's consider the case in which X_{ij} could be a three-month moving average of returns so that $m = 2$. The March moving average is the average of January, February, and March. The April moving average is the average of February, March, and April. Hence, they have $m = 2$ months overlap. Then X_{1t} is correlated with X_{1t-2} as well as X_{1t+2} and this is why $-m \leq j \leq m$. The chapter spreadsheet labeled *Overlapping* has a sample of demeaned monthly returns for Citigroup and Cisco spanning April 1992 to December 2006. Columns B and C contain the demeaned returns and columns D and E contain three-month moving averages of these returns. The unadjusted covariance matrix is given at the top of the sheet:

$$V_0 = \begin{bmatrix} 0.002 & 0.0014 \\ 0.0014 & 0.0058 \end{bmatrix}$$

The Newey-West adjusted covariance is given at the top of columns R and S as:

$$V = \begin{bmatrix} 0.0042 & 0.0031 \\ 0.0031 & 0.0130 \end{bmatrix}$$

Clearly, no adjusting for serial correlation would have led to a significant *underestimate* in the risk matrix. Fortunately, Newey-West estimators are available in most software packages so one can avoid having to construct these adjustments individually.

CONCLUSIONS

The fundamental premise of modern portfolio theory is that risk can be measured, targeted, minimized, and otherwise managed. Most challenging in this premise is measurement. The covariance matrices presented in this chapter are outcomes of considerable empirical effort. We have adjusted what would otherwise be considered standard methods for measuring covariances for the smoothing of returns (real estate and private equity), and short return histories, as well as overlapping observations. These adjustments remove potential biases and improve efficiency by maximizing the information content of our estimates. Finally, we explicitly address the shortcomings associated with covariance estimation using smoothed and truncated series. Specifically, we examine the risk and allocative consequences from a Monte Carlo experiment and conclude that the naïve covariance estimates generate significant weight bias, undesirable allocative tilts, and higher portfolio risk.

Further research might be directed at improved unsmoothing algorithms, especially for non–real estate classes such as private equity and hedge funds (hedge funds are not examined in this paper). Moreover, that research should examine more closely competing theories of smoothing. Attention, too, to the time-invariance property may also be productive. For example, covariance relationships among short and long series may be more efficiently estimated using recursive methods that update each period (for example, Kalman filtering). Nevertheless, the applications presented in this chapter clearly improve allocative efficiency while illuminating some of the deficiencies associated with conventional covariance estimates.

APPENDIX 22.1: COVARIANCE MATRIX ESTIMATION

Consider the simplest case with two return series $r_{1,t}$ for $t = 1, \ldots, T$ and $r_{2,t}$ for $t = 1, \ldots S$ where $S < T$. Truncation to S would imply that means be equal to their maximum likelihood estimates:

$$E \begin{bmatrix} r_{1,t} \\ r_{2,t} \end{bmatrix} = \begin{bmatrix} \mu_1 \\ \mu_2 \end{bmatrix} \tag{22.1}$$

Here, μ_1 and μ_2 are the sample MLE for the truncated sample of size S. Similarly, the MLE covariance matrix based upon S is equal to:

$$V = \begin{bmatrix} V_{11} & V_{12} \\ V_{21} & V_{22} \end{bmatrix} \tag{22.2}$$

where V_{ij} are scalars. The parameters μ_1 and V_{11} are typically replaced with their MLE counterparts based on the full sample of size T.

Consider now the likelihood function for these series, which can be written as a combination of the information unique to $r_{1,t}$ (that is, the observations in r_1 not common to r_2) and the information common to both series, for example, the joint likelihood given by:

$$P(r_{1,t}r_{2,s}|E, V) = \prod_{t=s+1}^{T} \left[(2\pi)^{-\frac{1}{2}} |V_{11}|^{-\frac{1}{2}} \exp\left\{ -\frac{1}{2}(r_{1,t} - \mu_1)'V_{11}^{-1}(r_{1,t} - \mu_1) \right\} \right] \tag{22.3}$$

$$x \prod_{t=1}^{s} \left[(2\pi)^{-1} |V|^{-\frac{1}{2}} \exp\left\{ -\frac{1}{2}(r - E)'V^{-1}(r - E) \right\} \right]$$

The second part of the likelihood is the distribution of *joint* information while the first part describes the contribution to the likelihood function from the information *unique* to $r_{1,t}$. The truncated estimator ignores the first half of the likelihood function. Ordinarily, one would maximize this likelihood with respect to E and V, but unfortunately these two sets of parameters do not appear in both halves of the likelihood. Stambaugh uses a result from Anderson (1957) that rewrites the joint likelihood as the product of a marginal $P(r_{1,t})$ and a conditional density $P(r_{2,s}|r_{1,t})$. Assuming returns to be multivariate normal, we get the familiar result that the conditional mean of $r_{2,s}$ (conditional on $r_{1,s}$) is equal to:

$$\mu_2 - V_{22}^{-1}V_{21}(r_{1,t} - \mu_1) \tag{22.4}$$

where $V_{22}^{-1}V_{21} = \beta$, is the regression coefficient of $r_{2,s}$ on $r_{1,s}$. If $r_{2,s}$ and $r_{1,t}$ are positively correlated ($\beta > 0$) and a return $r_{1,t}$ is observed to be above its mean μ_1, then μ_2 is adjusted downward from its unconditional value. (This is what statisticians mean by "regression toward the mean.") Furthermore, the conditional covariance given by the multivariate normal is:

$$V_{22} - V_{21}V_{11}^{-1}V_{12} \tag{22.5}$$

In the more general multivariate case, r_{1t} is a vector of returns on N_1 assets all with $T > S$ observations and $r_{2,t}$ is an N_2 vector of returns on the shorter time series. In that case, μ_1 and μ_2 are mean return vectors of size N_1 and N_2, respectively, so that E is an $N = N_1 + N_2$ vector, V_{11} is: $(N_1 x N_1)$, V_{22} is $(N_2 x N_2)$, V_{12} is $(N_1 x N_2)$ and $V_{21} = V'_{12}$. Furthermore, $V_{21}V_{11}^{-1} = \beta$ is now a $(N_2 x N_1)$ matrix of regression coefficients.

The objective is to derive estimates for these covariance matrices. To estimate the maximum likelihood estimators for the moments of the conditional density, regress $r_{2,t}$ on $r_{1,t}$ using S observations, saving the covariance matrix of the residuals as $\hat{\Sigma}$. Likewise, estimate mean returns for μ_1 and μ_2 using T and S observations, respectively. Then, applying the results in (22.3) and (22.4), adjust the truncated mean for $r_{2,t}$ given in (22.1) by conditioning on the information in $r_{1,t}$:

$$\hat{\mu}_2 = \hat{\mu}_{2,s} + \hat{\beta}(\hat{\mu}_{1,T} - \hat{\mu}_{1,S}) \tag{22.6}$$

Therefore, if the two returns series are positively correlated and the mean of the longer series exceeds its truncated mean, the mean for the shorter series is adjusted upward. That is, the truncated mean is most likely biased downward. Likewise, the truncated covariance matrices are adjusted according to (see Stambaugh):

$$\hat{V}_{22} = \hat{\Sigma} + \hat{\beta}\hat{V}_{11}\hat{\beta}'; \; \hat{\Sigma} = \left(\hat{V}_{22,s} - \hat{\beta}\hat{V}_{11,s}\hat{\beta}\right), \; \hat{\beta} = \hat{V}_{21,s}V_{11,s}^{-1}$$

thus

$$\hat{V}_{22} = \hat{V}_{22,s} - \hat{\beta}\left(\hat{V}_{11,s} - \hat{V}_{11}\right)\hat{\beta} \qquad (7)$$

$$\hat{V}_{21} = \hat{\beta}\hat{V}_{11}$$

$$\hat{V}_{21} = \hat{V}_{21,s} - \hat{\beta}\left(\hat{V}_{11,s} - \hat{V}_{11}\right)$$

It is easy to show that $\hat{\beta}\hat{V}_{11}\hat{\beta}'$ is identical to $V_{21}V_{11}^{-1}V_{12}$ in equation (22.5). In equation (22.7), it is also true that the covariance between $r_{1,t}$ and $r_{2,t}$ is a linear rescaling of the covariation in $r_{1,t}$ with the magnitude depending on the strength of their covariation. Moreover, revisions to $\hat{V}_{22}, \hat{V}_{21}$ depend on the how much the covariation in the longer series changes over the time interval $T - S$.

Removing the Effects of Smoothing

Consider, for example, the appraised value P, which is a moving average of current and past comps P_{t-i}^*:

$$P_t = w_0 P_t^* + w_1 P_{t-1}^* + w_2 P_{t-2}^* + \cdots$$

$$\sum_{i=0}^{\infty} w_i = 1 \qquad (22.8)$$

Rewrite the weights to be geometrically declining such that $w_i = (1 - w_0)^i w_0$ for some scalar value of $w_0 < 1$. Let $a = 1 - w_0$. Note as well that $a = \frac{w_1}{w_0}$. Substituting into (8) yields:

$$P_t = w_0 P_t^* + a w_0 P_{t-1}^* + a^2 w_0 P_{t-2}^* + \cdots$$

Now, replace P with its natural logarithm, lag one period, and subtract the resulting expression from (22.8), yielding a moving average of returns:

$$r_t = w_0 r_t^* + a w_0 r_{t-1}^* + a^2 w_0 r_{t-2}^* + \cdots \qquad (22.9)$$

where $r_t = \ln(P_t) - \ln(P_{t-1})$. Obviously, returns are a weighted average of past market rates of return and this is the source of the smoothing. Solving (22.9) for r_t gives us:

$$r_t = w_0 r_t^* + a_1 r_{t-1}$$

$$r_t = w_0 r_t^* + \frac{w_0}{w_0 r_{t-1}} \qquad (22.10)$$

$$r_t = w_0 r_t^* + \frac{w_1}{w_0} r_{t-1} \qquad (22.10)$$

We seek the unsmoothed component r_t^*, which is:

$$r_t^* = \frac{r_t - \left(\frac{w_1}{w_0}\right) r}{w_0} \qquad (22.11)$$

Thus, we use the observed smoothed returns to recover the market return. An estimator for $\frac{w_1}{w_0}$ can be obtained from an OLS regression of observed r_t on its lagged value. This is a special case of an ARMA model for which the moving average component, under certain stationarity conditions, is invertible. An invertible infinite order moving average is equivalent to a first-order autoregressive (AR) model whose parameter is estimated using ordinary least squares. The series can then be unsmoothed and covariances estimated thereafter.

REFERENCES

Anderson, Theodore W. 1957. Maximum likelihood estimates for a multivariate normal distribution when some observations are missing. *Journal of the American Statistical Association* 52(278): 200–203.

Black, Fisher, and Robert Litterman. 1992. Global portfolio optimization. *Financial Analysts Journal* 48(5): 28–43.

Campbell, John Y., Andrew W. Lo, and Craig A. MacKinlay. 1997. *The econometrics of financial markets*. Princeton, NJ: Princeton University Press.

Fisher, Jeffrey, and David Geltner. 2000. Quarterly unsmoothing of the NCREIF indexes without assuming an efficient market: A transactions-based version of the NCREIF index. Bloomington, IN: Indiana University, Graduate School of Business, Working Paper.

Frost, Peter A., and James E. Savarino. 1986. An empirical Bayes approach to efficient portfolio selection. *Journal of Financial and Quantitative Analysis* 21(3): 293–305.

Geltner, David M. 1991. Smoothing in appraisal-based returns. *Journal of Real Estate Finance and Economics* 4(3): 327–345.

Geltner, David M. 1993a. Temporal aggregation in real estate return indices. *Journal of the American Real Estate and Urban Economics Association* 21(2): 141–166.

Geltner, David M. 1993b. Estimating market values from appraised values without assuming an efficient market. *Journal of Real Estate Research* 8(3): 325–345.

Jorion, Philippe. 1986. Bayes-Stein estimation for portfolio analysis. *Journal of Financial and Quantitative Analysis* 21(3): 279–292.

Klein, Roger W., and Vijay S. Bawa. 1976. The effect of estimation risk on optimal portfolio choice. *Journal of Financial Economics* 3(3): 215–231.

Kling, John, and Frederic Novemestky. 1999. *Portfolio analysis with Bayesian dynamic linear models and conditioning information.* Pullman, WA: Washington State University, Working Paper.

Newey, Whitney K., and Kenneth D. West. 1987. A simple, positive semi-definite, heteroskedasticity and autocorrelation consistent covariance matrix. *Econometrica* 55(3): 703–708.

Pastor, Lubos, and Robert Stambaugh. 2002. Mutual fund performance and seemingly unrelated assets. *Journal of Financial Economics* 63(3): 315–349.

Peterson, Steven, and John Grier. 2006. Asset allocation in the presence of covariance misspecification. *Financial Analysts Journal* 62(4): 76–85.

Quan, Daniel C., and John M. Quigley. 1991. Price formation and the appraisal function in real estate markets. *Journal of Real Estate Finance and Economics* 4(2): 127–146.

Ross, Stephen A., and Randall C. Zisler. 1991. Risk and return in real estate. *Journal of Real Estate Finance and Economics* 4(2): 175–190.

Shilling, James D. 1993. Measurement error in FRC/NCREIF returns on real estate. *Southern Economic Journal* 60(1): 210–219.

Stambaugh, Robert. 1997. Analyzing investments whose histories differ in length. *Journal of Financial Economics* 45(3): 285–331.

Wang, Peijie. 2001. *Econometric analysis of the real estate market and investment.* New York: Routledge.

Working. H. 1960. Note on the correlation of first differences of averages in a random chain. *Econometrica* 28(4): 916–918.

About the Author

STEVEN PETERSON received his PhD in economics from Indiana University with concentrations in econometrics, macroeconomics, and finance. He has taught at Virginia Commonwealth University for the past 23 years and has worked as a consultant during that time to state government as well as the banking and financial services sectors. He is currently the director of research and senior risk officer for the investment team of the Virginia Retirement System. Dr. Peterson continues to pursue an active research program, publishing peer-reviewed papers in over a dozen academic journals, including the *Review of Economics and Statistics,* the *Journal of Portfolio Management,* the *Journal of Real Estate Research,* and the *Financial Analysts Journal.* He is an active journal referee and has served on 20 graduate thesis committees. He lives with his wife and daughter in the tidewater region of Virginia.

Index